# The Endless Tide

# The Endless Tide

◆

## Iain R. Thomson

*Illustrations by the author*

BIRLINN

This edition first published in 2008 by
Birlinn Limited
West Newington House
10 Newington Road
Edinburgh
EH9 1QS

*www.birlinn.co.uk*

ISBN13: 978 1 84158 706 6
ISBN10: 1 84158 706 0

British Library Cataloguing-in-Publication Data
A catalogue record for this book is available from the British Library

Typeset by Iolaire Typesetting, Newtonmore
Printed and bound by CPI Cox & Wyman, Reading, RG1 8EX

To Mingulay

# Contents

# Acknowledgements

Appreciation is due to many for information and stories, to others for much tolerance. To the latter, I apologise.

To Lady Thatcher, ex-PM; D. Scott Johnston, past Director General of the National Farmers Union of Scotland (SNFU); John Cameron, Balbuthie, SNFU; past President John MacGillivary (Gigs) for depicting him as a serious chap; to a couple of namesakes for hinting that they might enjoy a 'wee toot' from time to time, i.e. Iain Thomson, ex-Director of MacDonald Fraser, Livestock Auctioneers, Perth, and Iain Thomson of Badachro; to Kenny MacLennan (Kenny, the Manager), for any suggestion of eccentricity; Archie and Martha Crawford for instigating their Highland adventure; and many more to whom I say, in these litigious times, please don't.

To those who have provided me with factual material and photos, plus opportunities for the fun and games which have involved numerous amusing escapades, a special thanks:

Oliver Griffin, friend and ex-business partner, many friends in Barra, in particular the late Lach MacLean, and his wife, Bell, their sons, Archie and Sandy, at Craigston; the late Neil Sinclair and his wife, Morag, at Ledaig; Neil's brother Donald P. Sinclair; John Macleod and his son Donald Beag; John Allan MacNeil, ex-Lifeboat coxswain;, Rhuaidh MacNeil, ex-Lifeboat engineer, George Macleod; The Castlebay Hotel; John, the Bar; Father Calum, Eriskay; and a host of others, often at my elbow in the aforementioned establishment. To Gigs MacGillivary for introducing me to sailing and our many good trips together; and, last but by no means least, Rob Adam, Badachro, and Anne Pilcher-Gough, Balindalloch, Duffton, the shipmates who saw me safely back across the Atlantic.

Without the advice and encouragement from Jan Rutherford, PR

Consultant, Roseburn, Edinburgh, and the professional editing and layout skills of Julia and Scott Russell, Deanie Lodge, Glen Strathfarrar, you would not be reading these words. I raise a glass in thanks to all.

Iain R. Thomson
Strathglass, Inverness-shire

# Preface 2008

Many of the issues which I raised in writing this book some four years ago are in sharper focus. The Jewish invasion of Palestine in 1947 may yet prove globally critical. US, the main ally of Israel, is engaged in a proxy war with Iran who, supported by Russia and China, is the arch enemy of Israel. Concern for the role of all religions and their impact on society, politics and world events has prompted a European Commission grant of £2 million to a grouping of nine European Universities, led by Oxford, for the study of religion in all its many aspects. The project is code-named Explaining Religion. It will examine the historic evolution of theology from the ancient multi-faceted gods of the natural world to our comparative newcomer on the stage, monotheism. All this as ex PM Blair – not a noted pacifist – becomes a newly enrolled member of the Roman Catholic Church, and sets up an International Faith Foundation. Concentration on the ethics of humanism might be a more appropriate activity. Enough blood is shed on clapped-out theologies. Time for an intelligent assessment?

Researchers are currently probing the electro-chemical basis for such mental activity. Neuroscientists are examining the role played by neurotransmitters in affecting the degree of religiosity or otherwise in the human thought processes. Early work suggests that levels within the brain of the amusingly termed neurotransmitter 'dopamine' have some bearing on belief. Cultural influences apart, may some of us be more genetically likely to become an archbishop rather than an atheist? We seem to be saddled with brain areas which are responsive to aesthetic inputs, be it a funeral mass or sunsets over the Atlantic.

Before spiritual adherence declines to a tourist ritual, symbolic of an eclipse of power similar to Trooping the Colour, those in the religious business should freely acknowledge the historic role of myth, pomp and idolatry and admit they are no better able to provide an answer to the hereafter than is science or the man in the street. Far from throwing in the towel they should concentrate on the morality of sympathy for life in all its forms, avoid intolerance, and until, or if, some more plausible form of enlightenment turns up, offer the simple comfort of hope.

More pressing from a secular standpoint is the future of our present mode of civilisation and the ability to feed our species in the face of rapid environmental change. As I wrote four years ago, 'within the kernel of climate change lies the seeds of anarchy and mass destruction'. Rate of change is accelerating, not least that of the wealth gap. The first food riots have taken place, for the moment, within hot spots of shortage in developing countries. Half the world's population, advanced or otherwise, exists in great conurbations; they are the most vulnerable. The world's major cities, as a general rule, possess less than a week's supply of food. Starvation on any widespread scale is not presently obvious. If it appears, charity food handouts and the poor and elderly of inner cities will take the first hit.

In theUK, the early footsteps of an exodus from city environs is taking place, the wealthy galloping to the fore. Farmland prices are climbing steeply. A 30 per cent rise in the second half of last year, 75 per cent in some areas to figures of around £6,000 per acre. Corporate money is chasing a commodity of declining availability. City traders and investors are the predominant buyers – the commuting 'lifestyle farmer'. The more speculative buy cheaper acres in Eastern Europe. Nor is the US falling behind in this latter-day exodus. Against their monumental fall in house prices, land has risen by 13 per cent last year and is climbing again this year. An unprecedented influx of new settlers to the Highlands are seeking crofts and remoteness living.

This should surprise nobody. Cultivatable land is under threat from a range of factors – ice melt, drought, soil degradation, etc. Our two staple crops, wheat and rice, have problems. World buffer grain stocks have plummeted to less than forty days. The wheat price has more than doubled, and with minor fluctuations is set to continue rising. The crop itself is presently under threat from an east to west spread of brown rust, a fungal infection. Drought in major areas of production is a serious factor in reducing world tonnage. Coupled to temperature trends are the ecological changes inflicted by the chemical usage of industry and agriculture. The widespread pollution impacts are unpredictable, often hitting features of our food chain, crop pollination, toxic bloom, etc. Our ability to find techniques that tackle these effects without further destabilisation is critical.

Escalating world fertiliser usage is outstripping manufacture. The oil hike is hitting food production costs in a spectacular way. Fertiliser and pesticide used in current systems of production have tripled, offsetting any gains achieved by rising farm gate prices. Other grains are following this upward spiral, squeezing some intensive beef, pig and poultry producers out of business. Export bans of staple products have been introduced by India, China and others, in an effort to stem shortfalls. Shifting food round the world is becoming expensive. Shopping baskets have only just begun to feel the pain, a first step in curtailing lifestyles for all but the affluent.

Agriculture is guilty of approximately 30 per cent of global $CO_2$ emissions; not easy to avoid if you regard food as more important than your 4x4. Topping up you tank with ethanol is more to do with pump prices than reducing atmospheric carbon levels; it's cutting into rain forests, edible crops and hand-outs to the starving. Last year, in the interests of energy security, the Bush administration dealt out a package of incentives to biofuel producers. The Brazilian biofuel industry is making heroic strides into their rain forests and savannah grasslands. Sugar cane plantations, soya cultivation and consequent pollution on a massive scale for areas the size of Scotland that are now under mono-cultural production. Diverse ecosystems are passing through a filling station nozzle. The US government has pumped billions into putting corn through the petrol tank, a process which releases more $CO_2$ per gallon than using straight fuel. 'Shucks, it keeps folks a drivin'.'

Common sense should tell us that the more complex any system becomes, the more it is prone to breakdown. Do not imagine that global climate change will be a nicely predictable linear graph which levels out if we control atmospheric $CO_2$ at 485 parts/ million. The positive feedbacks involve multifaceted, interdependent aspects, each with its tipping point. Given that headway on controlling $CO_2$ output is making such lamentable progress, breakdown will be an accumulating effect, bearing in mind the ethos etc. The ethos which drives the banking sector, leaving the world's financial in-

stitutions to operate Carbon Trading agreements, should fill nobody
with confidence. Moreover, $CO_2$ emissions are only one of many
factors in excessive consumption. The totally unforeseen, it is a
feature of any system coming under increasing stress.

All organic life-forms are on the bandwagon of change at varying
rates, mutating, adapting, spreading or becoming extinct. Some
shifts are beneficial, some pathogenic and pandemic. We are up
against the greatest pitfall of this mode of civilisation, its interdependent complexity. Given that the approaching planetary de-
terioration is within certain limits, those with space about them in
remoter areas who adapt their lifestyles to subsistence level are best
placed to hang on until the human population falls sufficiently to a
sustainable number. We are probably generations away from facing
this prospect, and perhaps it could be avoided if forward thinking
takes root now. Gauging what conditions may evolve even a
hundred years hence involves much guesswork. Meantime, the
general public would be wise to get out of the oil trap, not easy
for those who haven't the means, and what is the alternative?

Adaptive action must be directed by practical people, not the
pathetic government agencies set up by politicians. The snag is, those
in control are far removed from understanding the fundamentals of
land use. Prising power out of the hands of these ineffectual organisations may only come about as and when the food supply turns critical.

Scotland could take the lead and divert considerable funding into
the expansion of our research institutions. New GM crop and tree
varieties to face a range of conditions must be in the pipeline; very
difficult when growing conditions and disease spread are becoming
unpredictable. Enhancement of the photosynthetic process and the
ability of some plant-root system to utilise atmospheric nitrogen
must be a priority.

Meantime, there's still capacity to feed the nation, and, better
still, for the health of humans and the environment, turn it over to the
sanity of organic production and re-jig forms of land utilization. The
anti-meat-livestock, farting cows lobby should be stamped on. Soil
fertility is best ensured by dung and lime. Should a future situation
require intervention, have a framework of working farmer-controlled
bodies in mind with executive powers to direct food production. These
units would be similar in style to those which operated successfully

during the 1939–45 war. Keep the pen-pushing 'experts' at bay.

Land adjacent to population centres could be earmarked for allotments, not car parks. There are lengthy waiting lists for a plot of ground. Farmers on town fringes might consider setting up and renting out allotment areas, with water, power and paths laid on. The school curriculum should include hands-on teaching of the skills involved in growing food by experienced agricultural instructors. Corners of what's now left of school playing fields after sales for building sites should be made over to vegetable gardens and children given the experience of eating what they have grown. Perhaps at home, fancy lawns and rose beds will become tattie plots. This is not scaremongering, just common sense.

Anarchy is still a faint dream for you and me; not in the minds of those running the country. A range of public suppressants is taking shape. Tasers are just the first toys to be handed out; robotic weaponry is round the corner. Taxpayer cash is finding methods of quelling any hullabaloo in the cities. No point in watering the window box, drawing the blinds and studying 'getaway holiday' flights. Only by sensible retrenching, a curbing of exotic planetary lifestyle, will there be a chance of passing our rapidly evolving species along the line. At the end of the day we are at the mercy of the antics of the good old sun, its spots, eruptions and all. Just now there's every reason to lift our foot off the accelerator.

Food supplies and planetary stability to one side, the greatest of all political follies is about to unfold, i.e. the expansion of nuclear energy. Plans for ten new nuclear plants are to be launched in the UK, and another thirty in the US. Progressively enriching uranium fuel boosts its output, a figure known to reactor operators as gigawatt-days per tonne of uranium and called the 'burn-up' rate. Improvements to this ratio have been achieved in current pressurised water reactors, doubling the 'burn up' ratio to 40 gigawatt-days per tonne in the past thirty years. New designs to be built are expected to lift this figure by another 25 per cent. However, at these conversion ratios dangers to the reactor cladding are increased; any loss of cooling water would trigger rapid oxidation and the possible leakage of plutonium into the building. The radioactive half-life of any spillage outwith the confines of the plant would be into an environment already under pressure.

Equally pressing is the storage problem of radioactive waste. Enriched uranium with a high 'burn-up' efficiency can create a waste that is up to 50 per cent more radioactive than fuel which has the lower rates of this factor. An underground storage facility is proposed. However, much higher temperatures are generated in the radioactive waste produced by enhanced 'burn-up'. This poses potential danger to waste containers and subsequent leakage into surrounding rock strata.

As a result of these higher rates of radiation and the heating factor involved, much greater storage space will be required. In crude terms, this stuff doesn't pack like sardines. By the year 2080, if these ten new reactors get the green light, the radioactivity levels of their combined waste output will peak at twice the levels of all the waste existing from the nuclear plants currently operating. So right on, boys, this white hot hope of ameliorating the effects of climate change by attempting to hold down $CO_2$ levels by the expansion of a 'clean' form of energy output may not impress future generations battling on many fronts.

Are we hoping to divert one major problem by creating another? The ultimate tragedy would be the destruction of a civilisation which is capable of probing space, both physically and mentally. This year's switching on of the Hadron Fast Particle Collider in Geneva will see science delving amongst questions relating to the origins of matter and energy, the ethereal mystery of particle entanglement and perhaps even the nature of gravity. There is much to lose if we fail to behave responsibly towards our current base.

Four critical strands are entwining. Climate change and food supply, religious fervour and plutonium. Have we the intelligence to avoid their stranglehold? The good old sun's face must be as glum as the flashing sign which tells drivers they're doing more than thirty. Harness the sun, on your roof, in the poly-tunnel, photosynthesise the fields, concentrate his heat into power; he's generous, has all the power we'll ever need. Only stupidity exceeds the speed limit. The ancients had it right: worship the sun.

Iain R. Thomson
June 2008

# Born of the Waves

Wild heaving shoulders, ocean's strength,
Drawn by moonpath's way,
Reaching arms, a turquoise bay,
A pristine torpid land.

Surging waves the seed of life,
A soul, horizon's heart,
And mane proud crests in potent foam,
Still fall upon the sand.

Oh lucky wave, oh lucky strand,
For through each pounding thrust,
Is born a child of beauty.

## Prologue

# Enchantress of the Hebrides

The stern of my boat carried the island's name, the Norseman's name, *Mingulay*. A name unchanged in twelve hundred years, spoken by the voice of the Viking. Hear in the lilt of its saying the daring of ocean rovers, feel in the roll of its sound the crash of breaking waves and know of a courage that faced the surging Atlantic storm. Know of men with the soul of the sea in their hearts.

Mingulay, the music in its saying speaks of men who lived, loved and steered by the stars, who read the weather by the moods of the moon, revelled in the wisdom of Odin's raven, called their boats by its name, loosed the knowing bird from a swinging cage to seek new lands, followed its flight, revered its croak of doom. Men who spread terror by the Dragon bow, cast death to the longship's wake, merciless pagans, heedless killers, antichrists who preyed upon a civilisation in spiritual subjection.

Possessed ocean wanderers, superstitious in their fascination for the unknown, drawn by space, solitude, by an endless search, by an aching of their minds for that knowledge which exists beyond the bounds of this world's experience. And closest to the truth, in the rhythm of the tide, the beauty of its endless flow, they beheld the mirror of an immortality open to all creation through the adventure of thought and imagination.

The wind that blew from the north brought these ferocious venturers to the Hebrides. To islands of settled fields and humble society, of stone circle, ghost and legend, to a people learning the worship of Christian hermits who followed the mission of Saint Columba. Brave men of a new God who faced Onund Wooden-Leg, the first Viking plunderer to ravage the southern Hebrides in the year AD 871. A sailor and navigator by Norse Saga, fearing neither wind nor wave, he and the crews of his galleys swarmed ashore, winged helmets, leather tunics, targe and sword, to savage helpless islands. Wild conquerors, streaming the Raven banner from their mastheads, ruling the Sea of the Hebrides by the crunch of keel on sand and the slash of their brutal swords.

Men from the fjords, the ice and gale of the high latitudes, men who lived to fight, to die in a certain belief that the souls of their valiant would be borne heroic from battle, sweet in the arms of the Valkyrie maidens to an existence above the towering clouds. There they would rest, honoured amidst the Heroes of Asgard in the halls of Valhalla.

There, sure as the endless tide, they were brought to the joys of feasting at the hand of Odin their warrior god. His grasp, the lightning strike, the storm on his brow, yet tender to Freya, his wife of faithful love. Proudest both of Thor their son of strength, beating a heavenly anvil with thunderous hammer blows, defending all humanity against the Demon. To the Norsemen's elemental affinity this great pantheon of gods bequeathed flights of fancy and their abiding love of freedom.

And they found Mingulay. An island crowned by ocean splendour, remoteness mantled by circle cliff, white sand bays and beauty's child, born to the swirl of The Minch's tide. Soaring wing of Atlantic storm, your wildness matched the roving men. Sun and moon bestrode their paths that crossed your shore. Island home, you fed your race, island found, made minds of space, made the way of island life.

Sunrise, birth, and sea-ringed sky.
Setting, death, and west by sail, lost to watching eye.
Circles and cycles a woman's day, fieldwork and bend,
    and aching creel.

Birdcliff harvest, mackerel sea, seal oil and peat to a
　　winter hearth.
Snug fire gable, yet danger, pain, and childbed suckle,
Eyes that pled. Sea, oh sea, bring him safely home to me.

Then laughter played long climbing days,
Childhood swam the turquoise bays,
And honey-filled the wild bee's hide,
Till flowered hill, full birdsong mellow, rested its turret
　　cloud.
Then huddled thatch in driving rain talked of thunder seas,
And knee-sat stories in winter's dark,
Took young fed hearts to wait the tide, and boats to set
　　them free.
Free to the surge of longship bow, the crash of following sea.
Courage, romance and spirit strong.
Mingulay, Island of the Viking.

For some of today, an island desolate and aloof, contemptuous of
the weak, cruel in gale-lashed days, melancholy in silence, a menace
in its threat of self-reliance, a dread in its severance from speaking.
Lost from assurance, the touch of a hand. Yet a dreamer's sail to an
isle of dream, an existence shed of human sound, security cast that
will conform to the pawl on society's wheel. A journey to the
enchantress of the Hebrides.

Alluring she lay that November day, wrapped in the folds
　　of the sea.
Gentle the fullness of her fields, smooth the flesh of curved
　　white sand,
Where lovers played on the lap of her turquoise strand.
Temptress of a sailor lost, your wind-fresh scent, your
　　lip-wet spray.
Lust will flow in ocean's sway, and woman's warmth drive
　　human heart,
In a space of endless sea.
Mingulay home, home to reality.

Steer by the main, cried the wind's refrain.
Near, then far, came the seabird's wail.
A cry forlorn, a voice in whispered sorrow,
To fade and choke by the hiss of a tumbled sea.
A mercy prayer in shipwreck storm,
A soul amidst a wanton waste,
A sob in last torment, in drowning plea,
It whispered to a sailor,
Alone upon the sea.

Yet stronger still, above the seabirds' mew,
The chaos in the wave top light,
A piping wind in templed sky, came calling, singing,
Clarion clear, to fill the mind, swell a bursting heart,
For that November day I caught, of countless memory,
A Song upon the Sea,
And pounding on the beach of Mingulay,
It beat the pulse of freedom.

# 1

# 'Will you Go to Sea?'

Genealogy, ancestry or, for those who fancy their printout runs to a 'pedigree', then the word lineage may be preferred. So be it, discovering one's roots is all the rage. Most Highland families, and doubtless those from elsewhere, can rattle bones back in the 1700s, direct ex-pats to a moss-covered stone and dig out great-grandfather's death certificate from that trunk with the broken lock. Some families, by no means all, admit to certain procreative indiscretions, but think of the fun before the black sheep put a branch on the family tree and became a skeleton in the cupboard.

As for nostalgic roots, if you fantasise about your ancestors leaping off a Viking longship, no need to break a leg proving it or testing your imbibing stamina at Up-Helly-Aa, a pinprick will suffice. For a suitable fee, your mother's mitochondrial DNA or dad's Y chromosome can be checked against computer models of gene distribution down the centuries. Were your forbears sancti-monious stay-at-homes or leg-over rakes? Did your supposed Viking progenitor have his wife aboard or wave her goodbye and spread his charm around the Saxon belles?

There are gene patterns common to stable indigenous popula-tions or those which indicate your ancestors knocked about a bit.

Your ethnic origins laid bare amongst Europe's earliest settlers, or elsewhere on the globe for that matter. Forty thousand years ago, far enough for the moment? Curious?

Try it, unless of course you suspect your curly black hair and a flat nose don't quite tally with the Aryan image of flaxen locks and blue eyes. In which case perhaps great-grandfather was a bit of a lad and you're more of a mongrel than you thought. Good for the old dodger. As any cattle breeder will tell you, a touch of cross-breeding provides that invaluable edge, 'hybrid vigour', a factor the Viking possessed in full measure. Perhaps the longship lads weren't pure bred after all. Who is?

Be that as it may, a mere flip of forty generations separates us from a Pictish leader with fortified domain over a fish-rich seaway, flat and fertile coastlands and a vital fording of the River Ness. In all the Scottish Highlands, no two ancient hill forts are more commanding of aspect than those which claimed mastery over the six-knot narrows of the Inner Moray Firth. Tidal currents and churning fresh water divided these strongholds. Across on the Black Isle, a rumble of stone on the shoulder of the Ord Hill is the northerly fortress. On the southerly prominence stood the fort of Craig Phadraig, stronghold of Brude, King of the Highland Picts. For certain, between these two vantage points no sail filled nor oars pulled but they fell under watching eyes.

West of the two forts, beyond the shallows of the inner firth, its herring shoal and salmon run, on the dry raised beaches above the wildfowl marshes, were the homes of his tribesmen. Hut settlements and duns, stone-cleared fields and signal towers. A history swirling in the mists of stone circle and chambered tomb lay beneath a skyline of watershed peaks and the remote lands of wolf and beaver.

In settled times this chieftain looked down from Craig Phadraig to cultivated fields, grazing cattle and harvest on the alluvial outpourings of the Great Glen. This clefted fault in the Earth's crust cuts the Highlands east and west by deep loch and scaling hillside. Glenmore Alban, its rightful name, though seldom called such today, a defence line of native tribes, barrier to the southern invaders who drove before them early peoples and their ancient name, the Albans. Roman array forced 'Britannia' to the Border boundary wall, Irish Celts brought us 'Scotus-land', but instinct tells us still, old Alba's space lies north of nature's bold divide.

Today's single span, twin pillars and concrete, banished ferries to west-coast duties and put the crossing on wheels. A line of lights populates the Black Isle shore and Inverness sprawls with undignified progress towards the one-time site of a large Pictish symbol stone. It stood by the road to Errogie and on short-trousered Sunday walks I ran my fingers round the carved outline of a wild boar, grooves of humped shoulders and a staring eye. Discreet family ambles, Father with walking stick, Mother with handbag, were allowable for a town which drew seemly blinds on the Sabbath and kept the radio turned down. One Sunday indulgence we explored Craig Phadraig and I skipped at my father's heel as he expanded upon Highland histories in deep measured tones.

Montrose's well bubbled near the foot of our climb and I learned that, after his defeat at Carbisdale, betrayed by Macleod of Assynt for the princely sum of twenty-five thousand Scots pounds, the Duke was offered a drink as he rode a prisoner to Edinburgh to be hung and disembowelled without trial. 'Yes, boy, proud Montrose passed here.' Dripping moss and fern, dark and sour under sunless trees, a heron flapped from the pines. I scurried ahead and the town below unfolded. Early Scottish kings and their dealings with Inverness emerged as we paused for breath. King David made the strategic crossing of the Ness a Royal Burgh and built its first stone castle; King Alexander founded the Dominican Priory which became the Inverness Royal Academy, and presently we walked among the grassy humps on the Craig's summit, the Pictish ruler's fort.

'This was the seat of King Brude, the last Pict,' Father announced, before pointing across the firth to the Ormonde Hill which overlooks Munlochy Bay and proudly continuing, 'The remains of a twelfth-century castle lie on that hill – your grandfather took me to it when I was a boy. Its chieftain, the Thane of Ross, a man Andrew Murray, fought and died beside William Wallace at the great victory over the English at Stirling Brig,' and then in ringing tones, 'those were the days, in the fight to free our nation, when leaders wielded a claymore in the thick of the fray, ready to die for their cause, not skulking at the back, ready to run.' There was no doubting Father's opinions on leadership or his enthusiasm for Scotland's freedom.

His walking stick picked out Redcastle over on the wooded Black Isle shore, the home of Fraser cousins and boyhood jaunts, 'Built by William the Lion about 1150, one of the oldest inhabited houses in Scotland.' The stick wandered to a ridge opposite us, 'Drumderfit, the Shoulder of Tears – they say there was a fierce clan battle in the 1300s, the cairns are there yet.' A final sweep caught the cottage-dotted slopes below the Ord Hill where stood the whitewashed home of the Paterson family. He told of their generations as pilot masters to the harbour of Inverness, 'They knew the sailing days, rival pilots raced their cutters to be first alongside an incoming ship,' and his eye looked out to sea, 'more exciting than the motor boat with its white painted "P".'

My father knew the Patersons well and one clear spring Sunday we crossed the Kessock Ferry aboard the *Eilean Dhub*. A gull eyed me from her rail. Childhood concentration stared back. Parents are for pestering. 'Why has that bird a red spot on its bill?' One squawk, yellow paddling legs and it joined a flock of wings which rose and slipped over the creamy wave tops that speckled the firth. I watched its undulations twist away to a ragged thread as the screaming grew faint. Gradually it trailed, white on blue, towards distant nesting hills, hills that through time were to become my shepherding home.

A handful of houses and a hotel made the Black Isle village of North Kessock. We climbed to the pilot's cottage. Four, no more, I trotted to keep up. Inverness, out across the narrows, a village whose house and street left sweeps of the Ness to search out woodland and hillside. Castle ramparts, sandstone pink, cathedral towers, square and jutting, and a riverbank of tapered spires. Only black and glum on sun-yellow fields sat Tomnahurich's tree-rounded mound, 'Hill of the Yew Trees', of fairies and graves, for, beyond the turreted castle-bridge and leafy islands, loch and hill followed Glen Mor into history and myth. The curious silver gasometer at the back of Granny's house alone stood incongruous. 'Not view enhancing,' laughed Mother.

In a rack on the wall of the Paterson's porch stretched several long brass telescopes, open and shiny, ready for a spy on incoming ships. At the open door one was held to my eye. 'It's all black,' I complained. Laughing, Father adjusted the focus, down the firth Fort George sprang into view. Telescopes would become part of a later life.

◆

Coast Lines, a Liverpool shipping company, owned a busy fleet of cargo ships. Black and white, smart from stem to stern, with the Company 'V' on their funnel and 'Coast' in all their names, they supplied Inverness for many years. The old *Moray Coast* had wheel and controls amidships but her replacement, the *Northern Coast*, was a fine ship, aft bridge and fo'ard holds. They sailed in general cargo from Liverpool to ports all around Britain, and between the two world wars my father left deep sea and sailed the company's weekly north run. Liverpool's Liver Birds and Monday's tide down the Mersey; Belfast and the North Channel of fast and heavy tides between Rathlin Isle and the Mull of Kintyre; up The Minch to Stornoway, east to Cape Wrath, through the Pentland Firth and follow the coast to Inverness. Time to say hello at Granny's Inverness flat on Innes Street then east to Aberdeen, Dundee and Leith. Back the following week, weather or no.

Into port on a tide, out on the next and a taste of salt in the Pentland race or off Cape Wrath. The bridge of the old *Moray Coast*, barring a canvas screen, was open to the teeth of the weather. She loaded perhaps five hundred tons and was a good sea boat, but on one trip Dad turned the ship at the Cape and ran for shelter in Loch Eriboll. 'You could lean on the wind.' The ship was reported overdue. Without ship-to-shore telephone, Mother waited, as many wives of seafaring men have done. Dad would remark after a rough winter rounding, 'The men who fish those waters, bare hands in a gale of sleet, pulling nets on a heaving deck, they're the hardiest of the hard.' As a young first mate, he sailed under a Captain Quirk. Shifting deck cargo, heavy seas – Quirk left the bridge to help. He was washed overboard and lost, off Cape Wrath.

Inverness harbour had two attractions for a five-year-old left to run wild – the berthing of the *Northern Coast* and a chuffing saddle-tank steam-engine, double of Thomas the Tank Engine. Safety inspectors weren't invented. Into the engine-cab I'd climb as it shunted wagons about the pier, all smack of buffers, roaring firebox, steam-gauge needles and the smell of hot oil and smoke. A swig of tea from the fireman's lemonade bottle and I felt part of the crew. No engine about and I'd be climbing the stacks of cattle-feed bags in Coast Line's shed, their dockside depot run with patience by Dan MacGillivary and his huge ginger cat.

The downstairs of Granny's Innes Street flat berthed a Captain Paterson, his last port of call after a lifetime's sailing of 'wind-jammers' round the world. A small brass plate on his sea chest read plain 'Hugh Paterson'. Highland modesty, no mention of rank, no need, its dignity showed in his face. Two neighbouring spinsters, the Miss MacDonalds, cared for the old man who was well into his nineties. Their kindness put his supper on a tray each evening and often I was chased out, '*Mach a seo, a' bhalaich,*' they had plenty Gaelic.

The Captain's house seemed always dark, its velvet curtains, bottle-green and golden fringe, always musky with the smell of gas. An evening fire in the tiny iron grate shone on a black-leaded surround and above a pitch pine mantelpiece, from two brackets of ornamental brass came the soft hiss of gaslight. His box bed, fashioned from mahogany, ruddy and polished, resembled the cabin bunk of a master mariner out from Shanghai River and the aroma of the first tea of the season racing to London. Faded drapes at either end were tied back until night. Against its pillows the old skipper sat upright, his lined features fresh with yesteryear's vigour. Striped flannel nightshirt, stocking cap and tassel, but the firm mouth and lantern-jaw were that of a man who had laid a steady hand on the helm of adventure. The gas mantle from its frost-patterned bowl cast points of light in eyes that lived again, sailing the oceans of youth. I listened from the curved lid of a sea chest.

His stories took me aboard wool clippers bowling down the Tasman Sea, the Cape became Cape of Good Hope. Rounding the Horn, I heard of sea-smothered decks, sails torn out, men lost when the yards dipped. Names rolled like an ocean swell, Valparaiso, Fremantle, the Straits of Malacca. His voice held the thrum of the 'trades', he would call deck orders in a harsh tone, raise a bent arm, 'Square the yards, Mister Mate,' or 'Get aloft there, break out the royals, we'll put the Azores hull down before the moon catches us.'

Slanting decks came alive, the crack of filling canvas, a bowsprit circling the stars, he gave it all the zest a young mind could take filled to overflowing with excitement and imagination.

Sometimes he spoke as a dream, his eyes on a beckoning horizon. 'I took a gap in the reef on the starboard tack, where the sea was darker, we came in between rollers breaking on coral, just main and jib. The leadsman took up sand at nine fathom.' The old skipper's voice gathered authority, 'Strike sail, Mister Mate. Bare up the helm.' and quietly to me, 'We lost way.' Then, cupping a hand, 'Anchor away, Bosun.' He said nothing more for a little and then slowly, 'Well, it was the bonniest lagoon, the huts were up a little from the shore, under the palms, I still catch their scent, the wind was off the island, sweet as syrup. The canoes were alongside in moments and the girls singing – oh the girls, the girls, the bonnie girls, brown and laughing. We lay a week, loading copra. Paradise, boy, close as you'll get on this side of life, sand and sun, green in the shade, and the sea, the lovely sea, turquoise as a peacock's feather.'

Childhood memories mould later life. They remain crystal clear when yesterday's happenings are beyond recall. That evening I felt sadness behind his words. After a long silence with only the hiss of gaslight in the room, he abruptly spoke of my father, 'You're Hector's boy,' and turning quite sharp, 'Will you go to sea?' The spell of his dreams were on me, 'Yes,' I said in a small voice. 'Well, boy, I took this from Suva in the Fiji Islands,' his eyes looked away, 'forty, yes maybe fifty years ago.' His voice fell, 'I should never have left them,' he paused, 'or her,' he whispered and he gave me a beautifully carved South Sea catamaran.

◆

Sir Thomas Lipton, from Glasgow Irish errand boy to millionaire grocer and philanthropist, raced his classic yacht *Shamrock* in the Admiral's Cup before the First World War. An uncle home from the Faeroe Islands spotted a scale model of her in Fraser's Furniture Auction and bought it for three pounds. Two sets of sails, light canvas and heavy weather, flying jib and topsail, the tip of her mast reached above my head. My father carried her to the Caledonian Canal and we sailed her on the Muirton Basin.

She was a thoroughbred, gunnel under when pressed, then up into the wind, ease off, and away again, the mind's eye had me at the helm.

Homewards from the canal meant tea at Tom MacKenzie's on Fairfield Road, 'Your uncle the chemist,' I was told in a tone hinting of a touch of grandness. Looking at our yacht MacKenzie remarked laughingly, 'This boy'll make a pirate someday,' and gave me a copy of *The Sea Hawk*. I could only just read *Swallows and Amazons*, but cap-firing 'sixguns' were out, a plank in a tree, rope and grappling irons were for me.

In those days two distilleries and their drifting steam on the banks of Telford's Canal gave the environs of Muirton a fine smell of 'draff'. Walking home after one yacht-sailing 'adventure' we encountered Captain Paterson steering a purposeful course with a stick. Pleasantries passed as he studied my 'ship'. I told him her name and how she sailed. 'Well, I'll tell you this, boy, *Shamrock* was born to the sea.'

Out of earshot, Mother remarked, 'He'll make the hundred yet.' Forever to a boy of five. I looked back to the old man. 'How will he?' Nodding at the distillery she said without censure, 'He walks everyday to the Glen Alban for a drop of medicine.' Whether or not he made the century I can't remember but his recipe impressed me, as did the name Glen Alban.

◆

Liverpool for a young boy. Black men, white-edged eyes, huge and rolling, loose-limbed down Dale Street to the docks. A pigtail hanging down the back of a carriage seat. Scurrying Chinese boarding the *Dingel*, a rickety overhead railway which took you the length of a maze of dockland warehouses and wharfs and thick oily water. Tate and Lyle Sugar in letters you could read a mile, a lattice of cranes with nodding heads and giant grabs spilling grain, and the ships, the funnels. A skyline, smoking, moving, smelling. Spice in gusts from the river, curry from shanty cafés and every-where horse sweat and dung and the clank of iron rims on the cobbles. Sometimes a steam lorry with red cinders in its belly and a honking rubber horn if squeezed. Ships' sirens drifting from the Mersey, one low and long, a Cunarder, perhaps the *Queen Mary* filling the Princess Landing Stage and casting off for the New World.

A sister of Granny, Highland girl, fourteen and shy, more Gaelic than English and down from Ross-shire into service. Taking in neighbours' washing grew to laundries and eventually a family chain of sixty dry-cleaning shops. The turning point had come by securing the linen contract for the Canadian Pacific Liners. Hand-carts of washing pushed from the floating Princess Landing Stage below the Liver Buildings. The Stage's covered ramps were hinged, sloped uphill or downhill, according to the twenty-foot tide and the great yellow funnelled *Empress of Canada* towering alongside, dwarf-ing the Birkenhead and Wallasey ferries. Tubby little ships, the *Royal Iris*, the *Royal Daffodil*, stately names but slightly grubby, plying the river all day with flat-capped crowds and much hooting. And they did their bit, sailing to the evacuation of our troops from the beaches of Dunkirk.

All that business success long before Great-aunt Maggie's son, Uncle Norman to me, was to witness the recovery of the bodies of the submariners lost in HMS *Thetis*. Prior to the Second World War, *Thetis*, newly launched in Barrow-on-Furness and Britain's latest submarine, underwent trials in Liverpool Bay. She failed to surface after a dive. A week passed, knocking signals on the hull, 'We are still alive.' Finally they ceased. She was eventually raised and towed to the Princess Landing Stage. Bodies which had fought for air were removed. I listened, war was closing. Grown-up voices were serious. A few years later I felt the thud of bombs and saw the night clouds red from a blazing dockland.

◆

The First Mate was moving the *Northern Coast* to 'bunker'. A father and his three-year-old son passed the policeman's courtesy salute with a nod, children were not allowed on the docks. The ship swung close to the corner of a wharf. Father caught a shirt neck and seat of the pants, a crewman stood at the ship's rail. Dark green filthy water churning below, I see it yet. 'Catch the boy,' he shouted to the man. I flew, Father jumped, moments later I clambered with him on to the bridge. The seaman at the wheel paid no attention, the ship edged through a lock gate. Men below in jerseys were moving cargo in the hold. 'Keep an eye on the boy,' they were told. Round the ship, over ropes, down grated ladders to watch thumping engines, struggling over a high step into the saloon, to one seaman's relief soon I was playing with the ship's cat.

◆

Captain Park, the Marine Superintendent of Coast Lines shipping company, sat behind Burmese mahogany, brass handles and a large crystal inkstand. Immaculate model ships, to scale in every detail, filled the rows of polished glass cases which surrounded his office. Pride of the company, the *Antrim Princess* carried their flag on the crack Liverpool–Belfast ferry service and lay berthed across from the Super's office in the Princess Dock awaiting her overnight passage. She also lay in the largest showcase on a pedestal behind impressive gold braid and clear sharp eyes. On frosted windows at the Captain's back, Coast Lines Ltd. in gold letters, read backwards. Through upper panes a worldwide symbol of maritime supremacy looked in, the Liver Birds.

'You're sixteen in November and have a more than adequate leaving certificate. Yes, we will be happy to put you to sea as an apprentice deck officer.' He went on to speak of the war. Father had died four years previously. Company schedules had been halted and twelve of their skippers called in to flank his coffin as a mark of honour and respect.

'I'm concerned about eyesight, sir.' He penned a note, 'Take this across to the Liver Buildings, they'll see you.' I entered the sanctum of a world's shipping trade. Cunard, Canadian Pacific, Blue Funnel, gleaming brass plates, four rings of gold braid on sleeves, high ceilings and marble columns. The note ushered me past seated uniforms and beards. Straight in. Flashing lights and letter board, one eye exceptional, the other useless. Failed.

Captain Park sat back, disappointment in look and voice, 'I'm sorry, we can gladly take you in any other capacity you wish, but not for a deck command, I'm afraid.' 'Thank you, sir. I appreciate your offer but I'd set my mind on being a ship's captain.' 'I thought you might have,' he smiled and, with a firm handshake, 'Good luck, young man, whatever you choose.'

A train took me back to the north. 'Will you go to sea?' The smell of gaslight, a fire's flickering, old eyes shining with youth's venture. I looked away. Carriage window filled with hill and lochan. Sixteen! The spindle of the world turns at your feet, sweetly.

# 2

# Uncle Sam, Ahoy!

Hyperborea – a name given by Latin scholars of the Classical Age to some mist-ridden ice world which they fancied lay beyond their known horizons. A land beyond the North Wind. They knew it full well as the source of fabled natural wealth, the home to hunter-traders. Curved tusks of walrus ivory and the valuable spiralled teeth of narwhal dolphins, ivory again, were prized and paid for by Mediterranean affluence and its love of elaborate carving. Hunter-traders indeed. Trappers of the gyrfalcon, a pair said to be worth a king's ransom. Purveyors of Irish gold, tin, the pelts of 'white water bear' and blue fox. Meat from the flightless great auk, seal oil, skins and the gorgeously translucent amber resin in shades of red and yellow. This fossilised oozing of unending coniferous forests which covered northern latitudes a hundred million years ago was crafted into lucky amulets and love charms with which to supplement the romantic ardour of civilisation's Golden Age.

Hyperborea, but where beyond the North Wind? Who were the Hyperboreans? Brittany, now called, was known to the Greeks and Carthaginians of antiquity as Armorica and its people, the Armoricans. Traders, seafarers and prosperous, their powerful seventy-foot merchant ships controlled a two-way trade between north-west Europe and the Mediterranean. By coasting the Bay of

Biscay or journeying French rivers, Armorican 'middlemen' brought the primary produce of the Hyperboreans south to Massilia, a wealthy Phocaean city at the mouth of the Rhône and today's Marseilles. Returning north, Armorican galleys shipped pottery, fine cloth, bronze weapons and amphorae full of Mediterranean wines. Hunters or no, the illusive Hyperboreans were clearly a people who kept a good cellar.

According to sixth-century Carthaginian sailing directions, the Armoricans made their trading rendezvous with the Hyperboreans in the Oestrimnides, a group of islands off the south-west tip of Alba. Almost certainly this was the Scilly Isles, Alba being the name by which today's Britain became known to both the classical Greeks and Romans. The Albans by description could be taken as cousins of the Armoricans. Medium-sized, round-headed, black-haired, dark-eyed and sharp-featured, they would share common ancestry with tribes throughout the western seaboards of France and Iberia. From Wales to the Western Isles, many today would fit this identikit. It suggests origins that are more probable than the romantic notion of rampant Spanish sailors shipwrecked from the Armada swimming ashore to the Isle of Lewis and siring dark-eyed belles.

The culture inherited by these supposedly primitive Alban hunters is magnificently enduring. Numerous stone circles, henges and dolmens range from Carnac in Brittany to Callanish in Lewis, Stonehenge to the Ring of Brogar, from the tumuli of Galicia to the massive corbelled burial chamber of Maeshowe in Orkney. Immense physical toil, bare hands and levers, levitation, myth or otherwise, but sweat and swear, the labour of a people driven or inspired. Did these stone-masons believe in supernatural powers, perceive some divine agency? Did they connect life and death with the planets, the revolving heavens? Believe the moon's cycle governed their fertility, the sun their creation? Were they attuned to instincts left to us as echoes in odd feats of extrasensory perception or déjà vu? What made them tick?

Is your portentous Sunday horoscope just an amusing leftover, a self-fulfilling diversion which many readers half-believe? Astrology was big business for the ancient Babylonians, became standard science for the Greeks and Romans, albeit the Greek designers of the zodiac knew of only five planets. The Middle Ages of Europe were still awash with astrologers – no fairground read-your-palm-for-a-pound but serious historically influencing stuff, much frowned upon by those in the religious trade. None the less, anyone of consequence, from a king downwards, had their private occultist – a practice yet to be discarded, as President Reagan has proved.

Square on the hypotenuse, Pythagoras, the Greek maths teacher and philosopher of 500 BC, went one better than run-of-the-mill astrologers. The mystical properties he attributed to space and numbers included immortality and transmigration of souls – a natty theory which the philosopher worked up to be a politically influential faith. But, unlike his triangles, it did for only a thousand years. By AD 500, his southern Italian brotherhood ran into competition with the simpler theories of less numerate Christians and lost the count.

More mundanely, about 320 BC, another Greek was to twig a nautical use for triangles. Citizen of the trading centre of Massilia and eminent mathematician, Pytheas became the first scholar to show that ocean tides were controlled by the moon and the man's abilities with geometry led him to another first – the devising of a reasonably accurate method of calculating relative latitudes. Lacking anything more accurate than a sandglass, the calculation of longitude for east–west passage remained in the realms of successful guesswork, or fallible intuition, until the eighteenth century, and John Harrison's inspired timepiece put Greenwich Meantime aboard ship. At least knowing north and south positions prompted the drawing of the earliest charts.

Pytheas had a brain. Not so the victorious Admiral Shovell who, in 1707, when returning from Gibraltar, ran three of the British fleet on to rocks off Brittany. Only hours before the shipwrecks, a common sailor, with some notion of calculations, warned the admiral of the danger. 'Subversive navigation,' screamed the great man. 'Mutiny!' The sailor was hanged instantly. Two thousand men drowned and the admiral, washed ashore alive, had barely opportunity for due reflection on the pitfalls of pomposity before being murdered by a local woman for his fancy rings.

In the days of Pytheas, the 'holkas' was a Greek trading ship. These were broad-beamed vessels of Lebanese pine on oak, often seventy feet overall and canvassed under a single loose-footed square sail. Slow but seaworthy, they were ideal for exploration. Unfortunately for a man itching to try his latitude trick, up-and-coming Barbary pirates operating from Carthage controlled the western Mediterranean sea routes. This Tyrrhenian outpost on the North African coast, now reduced to fleecing tourists, had been founded a thousand years previously by the Phoenician Princess Dido who, thwarted in love, committed suicide rather than marry a local prince. True or a good story, her trader sailors ventured regularly to the 'Tin Islands', which may well have been Cornwall, a fact to which Pytheas would have been privy.

About 330 BC, the Carthaginians lifted their blockade of the Pillars of Hercules and Pytheas, checking his navigational notebook, slipped a sturdy 'holka' from Massilia between the Pillars and turned north. The search for the Hyperboreans was on – an expedition combining curiosity, intelligence and daring. Fragments of his book remain – the first written eyewitness account available to the 'civilised' world of the existence of Alba. Travel writing and armchair adventurers have not parted since.

Sun-angle shots taken by Pytheas to ascertain his latitude were remarkably accurate. The Armorican island of Uxisma, today's Ushant, is out by a mere thirty miles. Sailing up the Irish Sea and keeping Alba to starboard, his observations next place him near the Isle of Man. Its locals justify the term 'autochthonous', Greek for aboriginal and a shade unflattering. Loch Broom, at today's Ullapool, is recorded accurately and surely he visited the Summer Isles. Cruising The Minch, his assessment of the natives mellows. The Ebudae and their islands, the Ebud Isles, are possibly his attempt to write the name by which the locals knew themselves. So it's to this tough Greek navigator we owe the lyrical name which has travelled the world, put a lift in the step of many's the homecoming and a yearning in the heart of every exile – the Hebrides.

Cape Wrath rounded, a boisterous Pentland crossing and Pytheas named the twin archipelagos of Orkney and Shetland the Orcadies – Islands of the Orcas, orcas being the sea monsters which the navigator related to the walrus bulls. They were huge creatures – fourteen feet long, a large rowing boat with flippers, tusks, hide and a ton of meat. Cash or barter? Lydians of the seventh century BC in Anatolia, under their King Croesus – he of the Midas touch and shades of the fabulous Golden Fleece – scored a first in the Western world by minting stamped coinage using electrum, a local mix of gold and silver. Pytheas would probably have cash about him but did he catch sight of the sea monsters and sniff out the source of the ivory trade? Perhaps not – after correctly recording the latitude of Muckle Flugga as 60 52'N, he put the Orcas Isles hull down and pressed north.

Six days' sail into unknown waters. Ice and fire. Volcanoes? He sighted 'Thule', the northernmost land – a chunk of the globe, up until then, only invented by chairbound pundits of natural phenomena and philosophy, writing the science fiction of the time. At last the Land beyond the North Wind existed. Hyperborea, proven by a voyage of heroic stature. Was it Iceland? Were Alban walrus hunters the fabled Hyperboreans?

◆

Northern seas ten thousand years ago teemed with wildlife, the harvest ground of sailor hunters. Walrus numbers alone ran to many millions and their herds ranged from Biscay and the British shores up to Iceland, Greenland and down the eastern seaboard of Canada. Their faces, baggy eyes, whiskers and jowls compare not unfavourably with a blimpish colonel on the booze but, for Alban hunters, the ivory from these giant walrus 'tuskers', weight for weight, had the equivalent value of gold.

From the Phoenician colonies of North Africa to the Tartar Steppes of Siberia and any civilised stop in between, walrus ivory was a luxury item. The material lent itself superbly to all forms of ornamental carving. Resulting works were much sought after for weaponry handles, jewellery, the ostentation of wealthy households and by religious cults specialising in phallic symbolism. Should we be shocked? Apparently the latter organisations found its size and shape of erotic appeal and, though rubber and plastic now replace ivory, the ancient worshippers of such artefacts would be happily at home browsing any of today's Soho sex shops.

A less tempting utility was the hide of the walrus. Shields of its leather, an inch thick, could turn a sword blow and, in later days, a musket ball. For warriors it was top of their defence budget. Cut a hide spirally and it turned into two hundred feet of rope, the common rigging and cordage on most ships right up to the reign of the 'Virgin' Queen and her 'Sea Dogs'. Rendered carcass fat became a glutinous, salt-resistant water-proofing – the dubbin of its day. Split a skin into thinner layers and you had highly durable sheathing for a wooden boat's hull. Hungry skinners? The dark powerful meat sustained handling a ton and more of carcass and no rubber gloves. A useful animal indeed, walrus were heading for a hard time.

Mass slaughter of these trusting, approachable mammals was brutal in the extreme. Whole herds were driven away from the sea. They lumbered up the beaches until exhausted. Axes split their skulls. By the days of Pytheas, Biscay and the British waters had already been cleared to extinction. The Alban hunters, in their swift, skin-sheathed vessels, chased the receding stocks of walrus northwards. Scarcity improved the price. Hunters sought the creatures in more distant sanctuaries. It took a thousand years and a lack of raw material for the destruction process to reach the point of non-viability, for extraction to become extermination.

Gung-ho employees of the English-financed Muscovy Company during the seventeenth century reached Bear Island in the Arctic and successfully killed thousands of walrus a year. Lead shot in the eye became the preferred method of immobilising the animal, before dispatching them with a slashing pole. As many as twenty-five thousand a year were taken from the Gulf of St Lawrence during the eighteenth century. A British Naval Officer reported in 1798, 'The sea cow fishery is totally annihilated.' Ten years on and my great-grandfather was born. Time shuts like a telescope– do we still hold it to a blind eye? The current extinction of planetary species, from simple life forms to higher mammals, is at its highest rate since the dinosaurs called it a day and, for a variety of reasons, 'homo zap' is the villain.

Certainly from the Newfoundland Banks to the North Sea shelf, 'fished out' is no new phenomenon and, incidentally, on land, during the same 'bye-bye sea cow' era, the Hudson Bay Company performed an equally splendid job of wildlife reduction, principally to massage the ego of ladies of social aplomb with pretensions, oblivious to the connotation of 'ladies – all fur coat and no knickers'.

How far did the Albans follow this dwindling resource? Certainly to Iceland and probably Greenland. The warming epoch, which began six thousand years ago following a mini ice age, slowly reduced the extent of the Arctic ice cap. Climatic amelioration along the Arctic Circle by AD 500 allowed for cultivation. The latitude of hunters needing a handy base from which to pursue the retreating raw material of their ivory enterprise?

The sixth-century voyage of Irish priest Saint Brendon, in a cowhide, wicker-framed curragh, is no myth. He and his crew sailed from Ireland to discover a 'land of saints' far to the west and north. Perhaps the Faeroes or even Iceland? Alban craft were similar in design – hulls of walrus hide that flexed with the waves, strong and fast. Did Brendon meet Christianised Albans? Thanks be to the Romans, Christianity was spreading fast – the outbreak of another religious plague. By AD 850, pagan Vikings were pushing west into Greenland. The Albans would be displaced, house sites utilised and their cultivations annexed. Whither now Albans, Scotland's distant cousins? Well, had boats, could travel. There may be a convincing case for these seafaring walrus hunters settling in Newfoundland. Canadian archaeologists are puzzled by substantially built stone pillars, overlooking certain inlets and channels on the Labrador coastline, which appear to be navigational marks to aid the inshore pilotage of a relatively featureless coastline. Foundations roughly the shape and dimensions of a Viking longship are considered by these experts to be the conclusive evidence of Norse settlement. However, as the Alban skin boats preceded Viking galleys and were similar in length and shape, they could well have provided a template for the wooden longship builders. These hunters would be practical lads who could turn to whatever nature provided to make themselves secure in rough conditions. They knew about survival.

Perhaps latter-day 'specialists' are unaware of a practice once common from Barra to Unst. No old boat rotted. Dependent on its size, when turned upside down on a stonewall base and roped securely it served as anything from a hen shed to a house. I saw inverted fishing boats in Shetland, housing the native several-coloured 'morrit' sheep – a watertight, frugal and common-sense shelter. The Vikings took to the sea hundreds of years later than the Albans but one day of driving rain would teach them the trick.

Creating a bridgehead on defensible promontories was the Norse-men's first tactic in take-over bids. Such incursion might involve a forced wintering away from fjord homelands. Simple, 'take out' a few Albans and turn over your longship.

Uncle Sam, ahoy! Three known factors stand out. Climatic conditions during that period were favourable for a northerly human migration. Alban walrus hunters, prior to Norse expansion, pursued a declining asset and latterly, both in Iceland and Green-land, they felt the 'move-along' prod of a Viking sword. Belated revenge? How sweet, if the Europeans to dislodge the Vikings as the first discoverers of the land of Mickey Mouse and chewing gum should turn out to be the fabled Hyperboreans of Pytheas, the Albans of dear old Alba. Aw, shucks.

# 3

# The Marvel of Jacob's Pillow

Invaders of the Highlands, Vikings apart, always arrived from the south. Walrus shortage or not, the Albans of Britain, in the few centuries before Christ, were obliged to withdraw north and west-wards before a southerly wave of determined farmer-settlers. As of today's European Union, so in the pre-Brussels bureaucracy of 500 BC, the Celtic peoples were domineering Indo-European tribes whose power centre revolved around their Hallstatt iron-smelting culture in south Germany.

Celtic influence, one way of describing their brutal approach to negotiating a deal, stretched from the Danube to the Atlantic. With expansion in mind, come the second century BC one tribal offshoot, the Belgae, settled comfortably in the fertile lands of north-west France. Twenty miles of water, a fair wind and they soon accom-modated themselves in southern Alba. These pushy Goidelic Celts, fair-haired, pale-skinned, blue-eyed Aryans towered over the slim Mediterranean tribes. Their womenfolk, tall and strong-shouldered, dwarfed the nimble Latin men. To thoughtful Greeks, these people were the 'Keltoi' and, with a sound appreciation of their wartime tactics, much feared.

In short, the Celts were headhunters. The severed trophies of those they slew in battle dangled about their horses' necks until carried home and nailed up at the front door. A special hairdo emphasised a height advantage on the battlefield. Any wishing to try their method should rub lime well into the hair, wet it and comb upright before drying. More alarming, some evidence suggests that Celtic warriors fought in the nude, holding the belief, if nothing else, that nakedness afforded the protection of supernatural powers.

Daunting as weapon-wielding nudity and white hair on end may have been, from stone slings to 'nukes', it's superior killing power that counts. These farmers-cum-ironmasters specialised in metal swords, war chariots and the expeditious but unnerving solution to any prisoner problem of on-the-spot slaughter. Iron slave chains excavated at Celtic sites across Britain do prove some leftovers, though classical sources indicate their low value. A slave could be bartered for a jar of wine or as little as a drink – a rate which might suggest a plentiful supply in human merchandise or a profound fondness for alcohol.

When not dispatching their opponents, Celts on the home front were a cultured, artistic society, albeit a tad introspective. Not being literate seemed little drawback – they concentrated on the powers of memory and regarded eloquence as superior to brute strength. Attention to personal cleanliness and appearance gave rise to the invention of soap, complexion creams and perfumes for the ladies. A flair for bright colours, tidiness and a neatness in the dress of even the poorest marked out a certain pride of race, if not an arrogant superiority.

Day-to-day, the Celts subscribed to a world of the supernatural and an intense superstition. It permeated much they did and thought. Their complex religious belief centred upon the head as the repository of man's mortal soul and the road to immortality. Attention to this point of view was stimulated by ghoulish human and animal sacrifices performed deep within sacred oaken groves. An elite Druid priesthood had society by the scruff of the neck.

At the ceremonial climax, fresh blood must flow. Golden sickles reflected the menstrual moon. A priest cut and ritually blessed the seminal mistletoe from a sacred oak. Winter branches shivered patterns, black claws on a moonlit circle. Gliding footsteps. Leaves rustled. Faceless forms bent, hooded, robed, shrieking incantations. Sickles glinted. Screams choked in gurgling sobs. White blobs squeezed from the mistletoe mingled with spurting blood. Holy semen and menstrual flow. Fertility rites, the mystery of carnal creation combined with a vivid demonstration of the certainty of death. This biannual ceremony is now, fortunately for most, modified to a kiss under the mistletoe.

Preternaturalistic priests standing over the spectacle of a fresh corpse did, however, add a dimension of spiritual comfort for the trembling laity. Druidic knowledge of astronomy laced the bitter pill of death with the promise of immortality, even a prospect of reincarnation. Evil and death's terrors could only be assuaged by the hope, kindly provided by the priesthood, of some form of glorious eternity. Hope and a touch of healthy fear – the psychological impact of an enterprising theology. Esoteric learning and elite power, it put the screws on mass ignorance and a dread of the unknown – arm-twisting as required – the handy tool kit of most religious persuaders in times past.

Thankfully the mother goddesses of the Celts were more kindly inclined. Being associated with water, they gave their names to many European rivers, including our own Clyde and Dee. Reverence for river systems and the fertility of alluvial soils was highly meaningful to our earliest farmer pioneers. Mesopotamia, cradle of man's civilisation, may yet erupt over water wars as much as Western oil requirements. Ancient Persians believed that, from the waters of the Fertile Crescent, a Goddess of Virgin-birth arose to intercede between Mankind and his Cosmic Creator. A theme later modified and assimilated by Christianity.

Worship, in a pagan world, had four main aims: to fend off plague and starvation; to promote reproduction; to plead for an 'afterlife'; and to obtain supernatural assistance in doing your enemy one in the eye. It took the importunate Christians, espousing Greek philosophy, to deal in forgiveness, penance and turning the other cheek – the latter ideal, demanding a face-about in human nature, being slow to catch on.

Amidst the historic blending of myth and modern religious rite, baptism by water is one of our oldest relics of paganism – long predating Christianity. Sun worship, equally old, survives, unnoticed by many, in the halo surrounding most Holy heads. The Celtic cross itself, the arms of a crucifix set within the circle of a sun disc, is a brilliant piece of cross-belief crafting, 'spin' in modern parlance. This astuteness is attributed to Saint Patrick, the Welsh-born Roman who cast snakes out of Ireland and replaced them with prelates. Three thousand years and echoes from Persian beliefs live on in the Hebrides via Celtic mythology. Today's commemoration of Saint Brigid of Kildare, patroness of childbirth and the honoured midwife to the Virgin Mary, traces through the Celtic myths of millennia ago. Brigid, for them, was the daughter of a father-god who straddled a river to mate with the war-raven goddess, Morrigan.

Religions grew, triumphed and died and will still evolve on the heels of fresh insight. Scientific inspiration may open the next window into mysterious unknowns. The realms of science fiction provide a seedbed for fresh ideas as fertile as the banks of the Euphrates were for the gifted Babylonians, as they worshiped the spirits of their river. Belief is a projection of understanding.

Only a few pedestrian thinkers now claim the world is flat or doubt the broad theories of evolution. Erasmus Darwin, physician, poet and gifted freethinker, took cover from the Canon of Lichfield after writing, 'All life we see today has a common microscopic ancestor, a single living filament' – remarks which church authority viewed as seditious. Keeping his head down, he wrote *The Temple of Nature*. A truly monumental work published in 1803, it presages today's human genome project and, when read by his grandson Charles, on the *Beagle* voyage, helped shape, along with the ideas of Alfred Wallace, *On the Origin of Species*, a quantum leap for understanding – an epoch-creating work, as important to natural theology and humanity as the New Testament is to Christianity.

In the first quarter of the eighteenth century, the Rev. Edmund Massey trumpeted an attack from his pulpit on the evil smallpox vaccination which he described as 'an attempt to escape God's punishment'. A disease which killed or maimed one in ten of the world's population he saw as applied by his God to punish sinners and keep the rest on a path of righteousness, as defined by Mr Massey. Many might now call his views insular and few subscribe to such thundering, but the gentleman held to a conviction he saw as virtuous, in keeping with the whims of his Almighty. Is religious belief an unshakeable faith in a delusion? Not for Reverend Massey.

Is bigotry strength; the questioning mind a weakness; corpus knowledge an exchange of subjective intuition? Whatever may be, the battlefield of interpretation is littered with the casualties of intolerance.

The Celts, bright, intelligent, their beliefs but a reflection of theories current for the age, were also a highly superstitious bunch and, by way of frightening themselves, dabbled freely in the occult. More weirdly than a chat with a long-cold grandpa, they toyed with an 'other world' of heightened consciousness – where humans and divinities could easily interchange in form and shape. The crossbred result often appeared, unsurprisingly, as erotic hybrids. Stag gods, wild boar or divine bulls, there was a choice – the latter, perhaps harking back to the myth of the Cretan Minotaur, a lascivious ogre with a penchant for seven young maidens per annum, a half bull, half man, well endowed, priapic and virile, clearly an appetite enhancer and the precursor of today's musclemen in porno magazines or hunky icons poncing about on underpants adverts.

Wild nights and exotic entertainment are one thing but fierce Celtic charioteers and their barbaric methods of war quite another. The Albans took the high road. This diffusion of Celtic/Aryan blood had barely settled into ploughing the Scottish Lowlands when it too began to feel pressure from the south. In 54 BC Julius Caesar dropped off five Roman legions on a Kent beach and not in swimming kit. Yet it took another ninety years before the Romans thought of taking on the Brythonic Celts, a breed of Celt from Gaul who, by then, farmed much of southern Alba. Emperor Claudius, firing dispatches back to Rome lauding his conquest, coined the name Britannia from the Bryttas, a tribe of these ex-Breton Celts. Considering the natives' wellbeing, Claudius, prior to being poisoned by Agrippina, his fourth wife (he executed his third), decided on forced subjection as the most charitable means of providing the benefits of Pax Romana – a familiar attitude still advanced by powers attempting to disguise self-interest as welfare but not a view widely shared by the Celts at the time. Witness an uprising in AD 60 by Warner Bros' model, Queen Boudicca. True Celt, she was a massive woman, her strident voice and flaming eyes set off by a mass of bright red hair which fell about her knees. She led her tribe into battle, a beautifully twisted golden torc crowning her hair, a tunic of many colours under a flying mantle held at her throat by a brooch of gilded silver. A forearm thick and muscled as a man's leg carried a spear that would pierce a heart at three paces. Her Norfolk Iceni tribe had been violently annexed by Rome, she herself stripped and scourged and forced to watch her daughters raped – all in the pursuit of Pax Romana.

Boudicca rallied her followers. London burned, likewise St Albans and Colchester. She had a good day, dispatching some seventy thousand Romans. Came revenge, a crushing defeat and the annihilation of her 'Britons' near Chester. Boudicca took poison rather than Roman mercy – a warrior queen, a leader from the front, unlike the squirming, television-promoted political champions of today's conflicts. The Legions slogged north. For them, the name Alba now applied to a wilderness up ahead. By AD 83, Highland Albans faced disciplined Roman troops and defeat at the crucial battle of Mons Graupius; their last bloody stand, probably at the Back of Bennachie in rural Aberdeenshire – a locale not unfamiliar with fights even down to my 'orraloon' nights at the local dances.

Lipstick, rouge and dyed hair are generally adopted as beauty-enhancing techniques. From the Queen of Sheba to Marilyn Monroe, it's no new ploy, however; on some faces the effect can prove frightening. Aware of this aspect, the Albans of Northern Britain were addicted to daubing their faces and bodies with the blue dye of a local plant when planning a fight. Impressed Roman chroniclers christened their 'made-up' Mons Graupius opponents Picti, 'the painted ones'. Although soundly beating the Picti with supposed losses of ten thousand, the Romans voted these painted attackers lacking in glamour. The Antonine Wall – a simple turf dyke stretching from the Clyde to the Forth, constructed about AD 150 – aimed at confining bands of 'blue-rinse' warriors to their wolf-ridden homeland.

European domination by Rome lasted a remarkable eight hundred years. Land hunger creates aggression. Emerging from East Germany in AD 410, the Visigoths crossed the Tiber and sacked the Citadel. Decadent and defeated, history's most influential Empire collapsed. The Legions pulled out of Britain a hundred years prior to this showdown and Highland Picts were enjoying a breather when, around AD 400, the Celtic Scoti of Ireland arrived, uninvited. 'Scotia', a thousand years ago, simply referred to an area of Celtic Ireland. Here were more infernal Celts – extending their northern Irish Kingdom of Dalriada to include part of Pictdom. An inferiority complex was setting in for the woad-wearers.

Christianity and the roots of Scottish education arrived with the sweet-smelling Irish Celts. Their invading nobility promptly had themselves crowned as Kings of Dalriada at the Pictish hill fort of Dunadd, near present-day Oban. Worse, by AD 600, Brude, nervously watching events from his Inverness fort, received a foot-in-the-door visit from a certain Donegal-born leader of royal Irish lineage. Enter, stage left, Columba. Although this revered aristocrat's name means 'Dove' his warring appetite for monastic possessions in Ulster brought about banishment – an inauspicious exit which saw him paddling a curragh for the island of Iona, along with twelve of his pals. Evangelism headed north. Brude barred the door. Insistent knocking with a Holy Cross gained Columba admission. The Highlands' last Pictish king saw the wisdom, not to say advantage, of toeing the latest line in religion.

By the eighth century, the Christian crowning of these Irish Celtic interlopers took place perched on the 'Stone of Destiny', otherwise a plain chunk of rock incised with a cross. This holy relic added a dutiful solemnity to the occasion by being the very pillow which cushioned the head of biblical Jacob during his dream of angels playing up and down a ladder which vanished into Heaven. Far from a feather bolster, at three hundredweight, two and a half thousand years of trapped fingers and reverential grunting were required to transport its bulk through Egypt, Spain and Ireland, finally to arrive in the kingdom of Dalriada. Despite this appreciable delay in delivery, its heavenly connection found instant royal approval. Jacob's Pillow has solemnly chilled regal bottoms at crowning ceremonies ever since. The originator of this witty notion is unknown. Writer of *Whisky Galore!*, Compton MacKenzie, recogniser of a good yarn when he met one, cast doubt on the belief by averring, perhaps through pique, that the holy sandstone block was quarried just outside Oban. Well, crown me, Royal snakes, Holy ladders and cold bottoms.

So be it, four hundred years and a number of coolish seats later, by AD 843, Celtic Kenneth MacAlpine, preening himself as King of Alba, thirty-sixth King of Dalriada and King of the Picts to cover anywhere he'd missed, was packing Jacob's Pillow and hastening eastward to a new capital at Scone, in the security of Perthshire. MacAlpine's Irish 'incomers' also transported their identity, 'Scoti'. World over, names are written by victors. The name Scotia spread. By the eleventh century, it applied it to all land north of the Firth of Clyde divide. By the early fourteenth century, only the district names of Galloway and Lothian remained to be swallowed. The title Scotland embraced all. Alba no more.

And the problem which had prompted the Scoti's easterly flitting? Matching the panic of MacAlpine's withdrawal came a prayer to the lips of every monk and priest, Picti and 'white-settler' Celt in their newly christened land of Scotia: 'From the fury of the Northmen and sudden death, good Lord deliver us.' Viking sails, driven by the north wind, swept from a horizon of fear – 'Odin's Wolves, the sons of death'. The shores of old Alba trembled.

Not so the helming hand of Old Captain Paterson as it reached for another tot and taught me the well-nigh forgotten name, Glen Alban.

# 4

# 'Bank Humour Won't Swallow G. and T.'

One of Scotland's great prides is the worldwide prominence of Aberdeen Angus cattle. A twelve-year-old boy doodling at a school desk outside war-torn Liverpool fell for colourful brochures amplifying such propaganda. They arrived, from the Perth offices of the Aberdeen Angus Society, depicting glossy black beauties, all heart-melting eyes, proud heads and prize tickets – smooth, deep-bodied money-makers standing in yellow straw, apparently without legs. A fatal study for a youth whose prospects of following cousins into Cambridge academia were already undermined by an unaccountable interest in cattle and memories of childhood fresh air in the Highlands.

'Now, Thomson, what's all this nonsense?' I stood stiffly before Major Dickson, the headmaster. 'Do you realise how much your education has cost your parents? Aberdeenshire "orraloon"? What on earth is that? Are you proposing some outlandish occupation in a foreign country?' Goodbye, school. 'Look here, Thomson . . .' I stood before Mr Joe Blossom, Agricultural College Principal and name to fit the job. 'we had the highest expectations of you but your behaviour cannot be tolerated any longer.' Bye-bye college. Ten years on, the luck to step on the farming ladder with a tenancy at Cluanie, a hill farm above the Beauly River, a little west of

Kilmorack Braes. I'd nipped back over the border into the good old 'foreign country', just in time.

No longer the exodus of Highlanders, with the backside out of their breeks, there came a turn in the human tide. At first this barely wet the remaining native feet – just a ripple – but then a wave, an invasion from the south which, in twenty years, swelled to convoys of furniture vans breaching Hadrian's Wall. Hunger for a croft in the hills gnawed at the sentiments of traffic-jam specialists and tube-train jockeys.

Anglo-Saxons, Cockneys, Geordies, Welsh Celts and Chinese restaurateurs, all were sweeping north of the Grampians, equipped with cash from a southern house sale and an invite from the Highlands and Islands Development Board. A tsunami of settlers set to swamp the Highlands and effect the most significant economic and cultural change since the Jacobite Rebellion prompted General Wade's roads, southern sheep hastened the Clearances, shooting lodges required railways and the North Sea needed rigs.

Loud 'behind-the-hand' lamentations by many whose ancestors played the same trick in times past and, it need be said, generally arrived uninvited with a robust display of vigour. Today the take-over is more subtle but ethnic origins stand out, manners and accents differ and resentment smoulders amongst the entrenched brigade. Days when Norman Frasers forced themselves on Beauly, when Chisholms battered the last Caithness Celts are long for-gotten. Like it or not, new blood has a life – the old dog lost. Integration and the twang of bedsprings herald a change – the MacHeinz tartan is in the making.

◆

Five-foot snowdrifts flattened The Cornfield, bogged The Haywain. Three men, one woman and a baby advanced on the Highlands from the oaks and spires of Suffolk's Constable Country. They were to winter amidst the wastes of Glenstrathfarrar, semi-marooned in the remote shooting lodge of Deanie on the wide Lovat Estates.

In the late sixties, this vanguard of the nineties' settler boom comprised a brewer, a financier and a salesman– an amalgam of talent. With malt in mind for the whisky stills, the conspirators, hatching their strategy, naturally gravitated to the Struy Inn, a

secluded drinking den at the foot of Strathfarrar in the heart of
Strathglass. The boldest and most successful enterprise to hit
Highland agriculture in a hundred years was about to unfold.
Farming within visiting distance of their conspiratorial lair, I
chanced to fall amongst their scheming elbows.

For the plotters, three ingredients had to gel: Golden Promise, a
genetically modified, prophetically named variety of grain which
produced a malting sample of appeal to the distilling trade; Ham-
bros Bank, which sported young Master of Lovat's eye for a likely
speculation; and, by no means last, ideas and energy, supplied in a
bushel measure by Oliver T. Griffin, Esq.

By now the tremors of post-war modernisation had shaken
Britain – bomb sites were no longer gaping holes. Remodel the
old, scrap the rest. Without the slightest encouragement from the
Luftwaffe, merely myopic councillors and planning vandals on the
spree, Inverness demolished its uniquely attractive Castle Bridge,
the historic Queen Mary's House and much else besides. In a
tasteless rampage, which continues unabated, girder and concrete
gifted the town the obscenity of the Highlands and Islands Development Board building and a view of the town's Castle fronted by a
nondescript café. A town of dignity and charm was reduced to the
ubiquitous façades of sprawling supermarkets and an unending
display of second-hand cars.

The margin of the Moray Firth around Inverness, fertile and
farmed, as viewed by King Bude, was a boyhood route for
scrubbed-up Sunday strolls. Plover flight paths still operated across
a little windsock airfield, wading birds journeyed from shoreline to
fields and through an open carriage window of the London express
on a clear dawn, to an excited schoolboy, came the freshness of the
smell of the sea. A greeting set to falter. The march from the bucolic
to the banausic reached the capital of the Highlands. The Long-
man, as these spacious river flats were known, succumbed to an
industrial estate and a gull-probed rubbish tip. Factories sprouted
and, most prominently, the 'spritting' barley and steam of the
conspirators, Moray Firth Maltings.

From Elgin to Caithness, the north's cereal farmers rushed to
grow Golden Promise. Contractors raced to build silos and, come
harvest, queues of lorries tipped shining corn. Passing nostrils on

brightly veined noses twitched with delight at the deep brown aroma. Malt was in the making. The three lads as shareholding directors also began harvesting. The first year's malt had been forward-sold before farmers clamoured for cheques. Cash in the bank. Golden Promise was no misnomer.

I took the fashion of calling by the 'Maltings' after hours to do a 'quality check', so to speak. Oliver and I might then adjourn our 'deliberations' to the Tarradale Hotel in Muir of Ord, a quiet pub owned by Iain MacLean, brother of Alastair, the popular author. Iain served a cool pint and we fell to doing mathematical calculations on his bar counter. An index finger in a little spilt Guinness served as a computer. A scheme grew and, furthermore, the wipe of a sleeve guaranteed its secrecy.

'You'd better be chairman, Thomson – fifty-fifty, OK? We'll call it the T. and G. Cattle Company – bank humour won't swallow G. and T.' By now, the 'Maltings' were producing large quantities of a residue suitable for cattle feed. Bar-counter calculations indicated a method of processing this windfall material into beef. As a distinct aid to progress, Oliver became a popular addition to Highland society: a Holmsian Inverness cape swept into parties to reveal his buttonless waistcoat – most intriguing for the ladies; his gruff voice dispensed erudite conversation – most flummoxing for the men; and a burst of outrageous charm defrosted any formal hostess quicker than a blow lamp up a frozen drainpipe.

Two roistering parties with bank manager George Murray in his flat above 'the money dispensary' put us in an advanced position. I adopted a business demeanour and Oliver, already in possession of same, added a gold-locked leather briefcase full of bar-top calculations. Without a whinge about collateral or repayment, Inverness Bank of Scotland provided 'T. and G. Cattle' with a two hundred and seventy-five thousand pound facility. It was not a moment to draw attention to the obliging nature of Clydesdale Bank which was also providing an ex-shepherd, already running a twenty thousand pound overdraft, with an additional seventy thousand for the purchase of his Breakachy farms. In a word, nodding for cattle around auction rings in the name of 'T. and G.' was on. To consolidate our position we wheeled into the Station Hotel. 'Thank you, Robbie, a brace of G and Ts please.'

Cash facility, embossed paper, a rolled copy of *The Financial Times* and T. and G. Cattle Company hired a toytown plane to fly its newly appointed Chairman and Finance Director, myself and Oliver, from Inverness to Benbecula for an on-site assessment of the potential for outsourcing our merchandise, otherwise known as weaned calves from the Outer Hebrides. I was getting the jargon, it felt important.

We sat behind the pilot in a flying hencoop. It undulated into the air. I expected the novelty of flapping wings but no – the contraption banked around bulbous clouds which the pilot considered impenetrable with only a flick of its tail. Boy Scout training is invaluable and, over his shoulder I watched the compass as it hovered around a big W – inspiring confidence in our direction. Lances of sunshine stabbed the Highland landscape. I leant out. The Breakachy washing waved up – a fine drouthy day. The pilot looked down. 'D'you know that hill up ahead by any chance?' He pointed. 'Very well,' not mentioning the bank, 'it's mine,' I shouted over a whirr akin to the unwinding of an elastic band. 'What height is it?' 'Probably short of three thousand.' The altimeter read twelve thousand, he twiddled a knob, set the needle at two thousand and seemed satisfied. I read OS on the trig point as we skimmed the top.

An updraft bumped us over the east–west watershed, its nobbled spine dividing ninety inches of rain a year down capillary gullies. I peered over the pilot's shoulder. Spy rocks beckoned, familiar; I'd leant, dog and rifle in times of sheep and ghillie. Hinds and calves dotted Kintail hills. They bunched, heads high, ears forward. An eagle shadow flitted through their private corries.

Ahead and Skye, scree and bare-boned Cuillin. Narrow peaks of rope and piton, rock that grips the climber's sole, they appeared harsh and grey, unlike the Trotternish pastures beneath us, sheep-cropped and green with sweetness. We turned a little south above the strewn stones and solitary tower of Duntulm Castle, once a Norsemen's fortress guarding the north end of the island. Its ruins hung on the edge of a gull-nesting promontory and tiny birds, wheeling and twisting dots below, made foraging flights out to The Minch, whose waters were ruffled here and there with the cat's paws of summer warmth.

Faint amongst the powder blue, a trace, a tip, pencilled on a sheet of sky, then another and another. Shapes broke free, deft and slender, the darker blue of islands edged with a sea in slow, deliberate motion. Croft-scattered fields wandered on to slopes of crouching hills – a sea-girt land, proportioned in curving elegance by the ice of a tilting earth, its beaches swept into being by mooncircle and surf. Sea surf on jutted rock, black limbs amidst the white of cockle sand. From the profundity of ultramarine, fleck and ripple softened to the opulence of emerald, and then, only then, as though in some ploy of unending recall, it melted into turquoise – the turquoise waters of a paradise, transient as the blink of sun which sought it out, enduring as the memory that spread its crumbling surf on the sunburnt beaches of an old sea captain's eye.

A jolt. Touchdown. The hencoop's 'prop' burred to a stop, made way for the cries of curlew rising in scattered groups from strips of machair interspersed with concrete and tarmac. Summer colour in the unassuming good taste of a wildflower carpet unrolled below the steel windows of squat buildings, red brick and square. Serious-looking antennae swivelled beside a gantry of surveillance cups, neither likely to be attuned to the curlew mimicking starlings which flocked from wormy dung pats to evacuate on War Department property. To complement these tracking devices, the WD plonked an early warning bubble on a North Uist hillside with the attractiveness of a piece of discarded chewing gum. It leered seaward, off-white and ugly. Benbecula and its rockets, launch pads and warheads, toys for the mentally deficient. Military might – saviour or oppressor?

Strangely, the ingenious morons responsible for designing the latest in our destructive arsenal, be it the meanness of a booby trap, a foot-depriving landmine or the fabulous daisy-cutter bomb, seem blithely immune to blasting humans into shrapnel or the sight of a hobbling child with a leg blown off. I have yet to meet one of these depraved inventors or any perverted scientist who might claim credit for perfecting such as a cluster bomb. The slyness of cowards, selfishness without a shred of compassion, a lack of any human decency. Intelligence still wears nappies. War's ignorance will not solve world problems. The IQ and motives of its proponents must be suspect.

A hired car and a Development Board official provided us with a conducted tour. Two VIPs, we sped about, our chauffeur honking at cattle that dozed on the road, flicking flies and leaving pyramids for the car-wash conscious to drive around. On a hillside above the South Uist road, where each junction allowed a single track to head for a croft on the edge of the sea, perhaps by way of a counter-balance to the bulbous WD edifice in the north, stood a monument to matronly intercession. Vast and finger pointing, a statue of the Madonna gazed over the Atlantic.

In the shimmer of midday, we paused where the Uists ended, where razored machair grass bound sugar sand with knotted roots and purple shells lay strewn and red-legged gulls bent chocolate heads amongst the drying wrack. And Eriskay, green and homely across the sound, croft gabled to an islet sound, sand-blown isles, cast on water that put hand-shields to the eye, so thin and bright the glitter of its light. And the glory of the sea, dark below the Barra hills that washed translucent to our feet a fabled turquoise story, so envied by the sky.

And scent to fill the lungs and mind. Breath of sea, tang of tide, air of primal age, crystal cut and sharp. Ends of earth, Atlantis in its majesty. Horizons widen, diminish modern worth, unfetter sophis-tication's hold. I looked steadfastly as sea stretched into sky and thoughts dissolved to dreams.

And children of a Uist croft in ragged hand-me-downs ran to rock pools warm and blue. Played where ochre tangle hid the orange starfish or the scuttling crab and wagging collies snapped at lost reflections. And childhood shrieks joined cries of terns, forked tails spread to fish a sprat-filled bay. Little told these happy sounds apart, on the languorous breeze and its ripples barely stirred the rim of a listening sea.

Hand-holding, unspeaking, they came shyly from the beach to watch the strangers talking to their father. One little curly, red-haired girl with bright green eyes sucked the torn hem of a turquoise dress, her sturdy brown feet would not know shoes that summer.

Oliver seemed surprised. That night he talked with genuine concern of hardship and child poverty but, unspoken, I knew these children of the tide had a wealth, abounding as the grains of sand on the beaches of their childhood.

◆

That October, we bought three hundred head of cattle from the Outer Hebrides and put them to winter quarters with Bill Campbell at his swept and tidy Newton of Cromarty farm across in the Black Isle. Lucky beasts, with straw to their oxters, they soon forgot the days when rain arrived parallel to the machair and throve towards making a ring-filling auctioneering session in the Inverness mart for friend and Aberlour whisky specialist, Iain M. Thomson.

Each autumn at weaned calf sales from Perth to Thurso and cattle marts in between, I leant on auction rails, bidding away the bank's money. Steadings around the Beauly Firth and well beyond filled up. By the end of November, T. and G. owned a thousand head and more of smart beef calves all ready to munch the winter away on barley straw and malting nuts. Spring reversed the system. Calves graduated to store cattle and, ready for grazing, they circled back through auction rings to kick their heels in fresh air and fattening grass. Our cash flow impressed the bank. Auctioneers were thrilled, doffed their bonnets and took me for drams.

T. and G. was an enjoyable wheeze. Oliver and I ran it for a number of years, ne'er a cross word and many's the planning meeting. Budding ideas drew us both to different 'ploys'. The bankers, busy as always pressing their pinstripes and checking the takings, missed the fun but didn't complain; their money landed back in the vaults and some besides.

Cattle came and went, memory fails, but not of a world of space and the red-haired child of the turquoise dress that matched the turquoise tide.

◆

Oliver went on adding business ventures to Inverness. Tore Mill is now a large progressive cattle-feed factory. Alice Ales Brewery, named after his daughter, harked back to O. T. G.'s original skill as a brewer. It became Oliver's favourite enterprise, supplied a sharp distinctive pint and, although deliveries round the town were by Clydesdale and dray, it didn't elbow its way on to enough counters.

'Start a fresh business every five years' and, following his own advice, he put his son's name on a venture into marinated fish and Daniel's Sweet Herring became a huge success. A newly hatched business using 'layers mash' from his feed mill wasn't so lucky. It fell victim to wild allegations of mass salmonella infection in Britain's second-favourite morning habit, 'go to work on an egg', made by PM Major's bed-friend, Edwina Currie. A little informed pillow talk might have saved the poultry industry its decimation.

Ahead of the pace of thinking, Oliver's final brew was an organic beer, Lincoln Green. This venture staged his retirement from Scotland to the English shire of poaching fame. Something approaching a squire, he now farms rolling acres from an oak-beamed residence surrounded by his wife Christina's horses. A modest, amusing intellectually-minded man with enthusiasm for many facets of rural life from Lincoln Cathedral's silver to his beloved cattle and sheep, Oliver finds a morning inspection of his pampered Angus cattle, as he collects breakfast rolls from the baker, still requires a copy of *The Financial Times* tucked below his oxter.

Wide, lateral thinker, tough in business, kind and generous behind a gruff façade, the Highlands and many individuals have much for which to thank O. T. G. and, incidentally, some local parties now lack a certain – shall we say? – novel approach.

My first experiment with pedigree cattle settled on white-coated animals. The Whitebred or Cumberland Shorthorns are a hardy, now rarish breed which, when crossed with Galloway cows, produce the once highly sought-after Blue Grey female. These exceptionally motherly cows, generally sold with a pair of running shoes as a 'luck penny', if mated to an Angus bull, put beef on to dinner plates that has no equal for saliva-drooling flavour.

Oliver described these white cattle as a 'village breed', essentially for moleskin and cloth-capped farmers, as opposed to Angus cattle, which he saw as more tiara and stately home. Throughout the fifties and sixties, anybody with a title attached to tree-dotted 'policies', which rolled away from drawing room windows, and money, which rolled towards the bank, had to boast the most expensive Angus cattle Perth sales could provide to grace their chestnut shade. Smooth chubby hands would flutter bids at the auctioneer with an air of nonchalance at twenty or thirty thousand – and guineas not pounds. As in cattle, so in society, status reflected conceit plus cash.

Cloth cap in place, I journeyed to Carlisle, judged at the Whitebred Cattle Society's pedigree sale and bought a bull for eight hundred guineas. Travelling into the fell country of stone dyke and millstone grit, I bought a bunch of heifers for the basis of a herd. The folk of the dales, with their kindly manner, unhurried yet purposeful, were honed to match the harshness of life in a country-side of trout becks and bare open hills. I admired them.

My purchase, Aimshaugh Prince, turned out to be a bull with a boisterous approach to duty and, ignoring the hazards, in a burst of professional enthusiasm, snapped his penis. Not, however, before he had serviced his sister, whom I also bought. Result, a fine bull calf and, with Cleopatra's Needle in mind and an inkling that the Nile dynasties based their bloodlines on brother and sister unions, I hit on Pharaoh of Breakachy. As a rampant yearling, he went to Simon MacKenzie for use on his Ross-shire hill farm. The results were dramatic. Pharaoh filled his father's hoof-prints, siring champion calves and the most beauteous of females for both MacKenzie and the surrounding neighbourhood, without regard to fences or the safety of his conjugal appeal. Well, well, the insight of the ancient Egyptians, pyramid design eclipsed by the success of incest.

Schoolboy ambition and the seventies upswing in farming for-tunes set me building a herd of pedigree Aberdeen Angus at Breakachy. The earliest and most successful purchases were from the Easter Ross farm of Cullisse. Charles and Isabel MacKenzie owned perhaps the finest clay farms north of the Grampians and ran a classic herd of powerful cows. The old boy remembered some distant relations and a cousin did his farm books. These tenuous connections led me to a field of in-calf heifers and MacKenzie said generously, 'Take your pick.' I took the ten which appealed to the eye without knowing their pedigrees, at three hundred pounds a head.

My first-choice heifer calved a bull calf the night of a New Year party at Breakachy and I called him Jasper, after the unsteady rendering of a rugby song by the late Donnie Fraser. The calf turned into a yearling bull good enough for my first showing at the world-famous Perth bull sales. He took a third prize and pulled one thousand seven hundred and fifty guineas from a crowded ringside. A price eroded by the fun involved, but encouraging.

With the help of Simon MacDonald, a hardy young lad from North Uist, prize tickets and top prices followed at the Inverness bull sales. The *Scottish Farmer*'s 'photo snapper', John Fraser, sauntered along to record our sale champion for his paper. Simon led the bull to a stance outside the mart; Fraser, about to click, paused. The bull passed comment on the photographer's talents. I raced in to tidy up and was caught, full shovel, plus steam. John, proud of creating amusement in the *Farmer*'s office, dispatched a slightly blurred photo to me, cheekily entitled 'The Phantom Shit-Shoveler'.

Christmas approached – drinkies and office parties. I opened a Walkers shortbread tin, removed the biscuits, refilled it with a contribution from the bull pens and parcelled it off. Boasting his popularity, Fraser opened the tin in the midst of their Yuletide revels. The stench cleared the room and the party was something of a flop.

Aberdeen Angus worshippers of that era bowed towards New-house of Glamis and doyen of the breed, Robert M. Adam, with bulls notching up thirty thousand, had an expert eye for both cattle and clients. From a clerk at the Perth auction firm of Macdonald Fraser he progressed to master livestock breeder and the prosperous tenant of a glorious farm, complete with stately Georgian house, on the Bowes-Lyon estates of Queen Elizabeth, the Queen Mother – a lady with whom Bob, by his stories, seemed to have been on rather familiar terms.

I parked my Austin 35 van beside a Rolls Royce numbered RMA1. House and stairway were complementary. Bob, a man of some bulk, relaxed in the sitting room and talked back to the motorbike days of his early beginnings – how, on a trip to Orkney with John Buchanan, he threw a match on a trail of petrol which shot from a passing car. The flash came close to blowing up the Kirkwall Hotel.

John Buchanan, with an Angus herd near Aviemore, was both Bob's mentor and a relation by marriage. Bob arrived one June day, bike, no helmet, no goggles, to find old John leading a team of men hoeing turnip under a sweltering sun. The pair were about to set off on some bull-foraging trip when Bob pointed out, 'John, you left your jacket on the dyke.' 'Whisht, man,' whispered Buchanan, 'they'll think I'm coming back.'

Amusing episodes rambled on, to the accompaniment of a silent television which flicked across channels as though it had an ear to the yarns. During a pause in stories Bob noticed its antics. 'What the hell?' He rose grudgingly. The machine steadied at once – he'd been sitting on the buttons and laughed fit to bust. Photos of champions covered the walls of an immaculate office – no price without zeros. We viewed lordly cattle and, by no means least, his collection of Highland Cattle paintings by king of the genre, Louis B. Hurt. But the signature at the foot of Bob's letters, which curled across the page with ornate complexity, was, for me, the epitome of a man who combined an elaborate style with the common touch.

◆

Such was the elan of Angus breeders in the north that nothing would better suit our club's annual jaunt than a visit to the Castle of Mey, a gloom-laden fortress perched on the edge of the Pentland Firth and summer retreat of our patron, the Queen Mother. Led by a highly polished Edwin Gillanders, word-pruner of both the *Angus Review* and the farming pages of the Aberdeen *Press and Journal*, we parked an assortment of backfiring Land Rovers and jaded cars on her front gravel without so much as a helmet in sight, far less a frisking of some of the cavalcade's more dubious occupants.

Barely had we alighted and were sauntering towards the castle's rivet-studded front door, when Captain Ben Coutts, the esteemed secretary of our Society and a man not given to self-effacement, was spotted hustling away from the tradesman's entrance with his kilt on a coat hanger. He nodded, didn't linger and was gone before the Queen Mother stepped out to bid us a few head-inclining words of welcome.

Headscarf, tweed skirt and welly boots, she could have been anybody's dear old granny and seemed undaunted by the array of halter-holders on her doorstep. Together with a couple of ladies-in-waiting, she escorted us through the walled garden, past the rhubarb patch which seemed to be doing well and along to a steading full of her favourite Aberdeen Angus. Donald, the cattle-man, paraded their stock bull on the lawn beside a couple of cannon and passed some remark to her which, perhaps just as well, we didn't hear. She laughed and looked tiny.

No bowing and scraping from us boys, just cattle enthusiasts enjoying another breeder's mistakes. 'Have you come far?' she enquired, the twinkling eye indicated a joke would not go amiss. I refrained from replying, 'Far enough with this lot.' Yes, she knew Beauly, Campbell's famous tweed shop, such a lovely village square. How long had I been breeding Angus cattle? She moved casually amongst us, question and comment as though we were all old friends. 'Now, I'm sure you're ready for refreshments,' she smiled knowingly. Nobody dissented and, given the propensity of some of the party to stampede at even a hint of 'refreshments', it was with commendable restraint that we wandered back to the castle.

Two black pageboy statues stood either side of dividing stone stairs. To the right, the Queen Mother offered the ladies the powder room; to the left, we men followed the word 'refreshments'. We were not disappointed. A long oak table followed the wall. Bottles of Hundred Pipers Whisky stood in ranks. A lad dressed in some North-West Frontier army uniform with chain mail on his shoulders called them to attention. After several stops on the run north we were on parade again. 'Cattle breeders, preeee-sent elbows.' 'Stand easy, bottles.' By the time apprehensive wives returned from powdering their noses and a peek at the castle, party-mood was gathering momentum.

Not a moment too soon, sandwiches appeared. Our hostess circulated, offering platefuls of dainties. 'Plenty of sale for the drink but the sandwiches are slow,' I heard her to remark to one of the helpers. Noticing watercolour paintings on the wall above the bottles, I took an egg and cress and politely enquired, 'Who's the artist?' 'Oh, that's Philip – he's really keen.' Bob Adam was right – what a girl.

Jock Ross interrupted our chat about painting. Whisky glass in hand, a mouthful of dainties, he helped himself to another from the proffered plate and, blowing crumbs, began to question the royal cattle breeder about her stock bull. He got spirited replies – the little lady had learnt something from Bob. I sensed a deal. 'You'll have to speak to Donald,' she winked at me as Ross devoured another sandwich.

Jollification required a halter. Before songs could break out, Edwin, of the circumspect demeanour, knowing the calibre of the membership and their potential for outstaying a welcome, called a vote of thanks. No standing on dignity for farmer lads, to rousing cheers and a parting swig of the Hundred Pipers, our hostess led us to the door, shook hands all round and wished success to our cattle – a touching moment. Donnie MacGillivary, a dashing blade, overtaken by emotion, kissed the little lady goodbye. Still smiling she waved us away. It appeared regal; it might have been relief.

Spirits piping high, we headed south. The *Press and Journal* vehicle seemed to be trailing. I lost it in the mirror and drove back, expecting songs and a ditch full of car. No, just a breakdown. Three in the boot and sitting on knees, the lesser evil than a night in Caithness peat, I loaded the lot and we made for a Golspie hotel. Here, it was pointed out, due to the shortcomings of his car and our consequent discomfort, the Agricultural Editor's expense account should stand us supper.

A most fortunate choice of venue. Hardly had knife and fork hit steak and chips than the beat of a Scottish dance band lifted the tempo. Kilts, waltz – could we be eating the remains of a wedding breakfast? Say no more. The Famous Grouse took flight and, in moments, I became aware of dancing with a glamorous girl in a lacy white dress. Tap on the shoulder. 'Which side of the family are you?' A none-too-casual enquiry as we frisked away into a freestyle eightsome. The young man appeared a tad unhappy – it was his nuptial night but I didn't notice the bride complaining.

What a dance. We considered ourselves honoured guests. 'Dickie bows' and kilts seemed a mite wary but we soon slackened their traces. The only regret was that we hadn't invited our new friend, the Castle of Mey cattle breeder – a great girl. She'd have had no end of fun.

## 5

# 'Fifteen Thousand Guineas – Going, Going . . .'

The eyes of auctioneer Iain M. Thomson flickered over intent faces, studying the last pedigree heifer to be sold at the close of a Perth Angus sale in the old, wooden mart of MacDonald Fraser. They lighted on me – remarkably piercing, I thought, considering the extent of our previous night's 'deliberations'. His hammer hovered. 'Six hundred guineas, six hundred, it's against you now.' Eyes met, keen auctioneer and back bidder, the tiniest wink, the merest lift of an eyebrow and she might be mine. I waited a second too long. Thomson looked away. Crack! Too late, sold to some nod in the crowd. My first mistake.

That morning, I'd spotted a girl giving a pre-sale shampoo and set to a shapely young heifer. Both were Irish and charming. An obscure pedigree need be no bar to beauty – milkmaid or bovine – and Ruth, the animal's name, by the way, represented a first trip to Perth for Ulsterman Walter Shortt. My fancy had been tickled. Well, well, I'd lost her for a bid. Next night I phoned Ireland. 'Tell me, pretty maiden, are there any more at home like Ruth?' A man's voice answered. 'Ah, to be sure, dare are a few, just one or two – yous'll come on over.' Ah, der pull o' der brogue – a week later Oliver and I were at Walter's farm in rolling Tyrone.

A whiskey/Irish welcome and we fell for Florrie, his wife. Red hair, green eyes, soft Irish lilt – Walter hurried us to the byre. Three enormous backsides framed by a stall greeted us – a sort of row of bovine Botticellis, just what the butcher ordered – and the middle bull, for sure, a brother of the bonnie heifer. We were viewing something special. Casually, a not-really-interested voice, 'Five thousand pounds for the middle one?' A long pause. A surprising price. A mini-fortune in the currency of the mid seventies. 'Well, don't you see now Iain, Rockie's booked for the next Perth sale.' One up to Walter – wise man. Rockie of Woodview had to be mine.

We were the first Scots visitors to the Shortt's Woodview herd and I was to make many happy visits to their home near Omagh, show-judging and buying pedigree cattle. Arriving on one occasion outside the fated town of Omagh in the early hours of the morning, two dark figures stepped into the road and flagged me down. Rifles appeared at the car window. 'Well, boys, what's the problem tonight?' They withdrew silently. My accent? Murder – the hallmark of doctrinal division. Solving the Irish problem does not lie in partisan politics goaded by religious fervour.

Leaving Rockie the bull innocent of either worth or Perth, Oliver and I checked through an army command post, sped into southern Ireland, looked at a design of 'cloverleaf maltings' and drew up at a stylish pub outside Dublin, just as screeds of pinstripes quaffed 'home-time pints' before a counter full of Guinness pumps blessing the holy brew with a shamrock on the froth. Affluence and cigar smoke clogged the air. Out of the haze shuffled a floor-length ex-army greatcoat. No buttons, string round the waist, two winds of a muffler below an open-skipped bonnet and no sign of a face.

The coat stopped at the bar beside me. 'Evening.' No word. Shortly a barmaid thumped down a Guinness and plate of onion sandwiches. A hand from the sleeve reached under the muffler and, with an extraction swifter than a backstairs dentist, placed a grinning set of saliva-laden dentures on the counter beside my pint. Another hand appeared. A steady, two-handed munch processed the meal somewhere twixt muffler and skip. Splendid company – boiled shirt and stockbrokers and an off-duty scarecrow, a scene from Milligan's *Puckoon* on stage.

We drove out of Dublin before six on a Wednesday morning. A

man hurried along an elegant Georgian street carrying a large harp. To be sure, time and parties don't relate in the land of original charm.

◆

A 40 per cent fug hung over the legendary Perth bull sales. Cattle shampoo, steaming bull shit and fumes from show 'kist' bottles blended with the Market Bar and frequent trips across the road to the Waverley Hotel. The 'coothie' wooden mart overflowed. Straw, sawdust and bulls everywhere, heads over rails, bellowing, eating, sometimes kicking, often farting. Some waddling for a wash, some to the show ring. Some bulls standing on three feet of straw looking big. Big bulls on three feet of straw looking immense. Boilersuits carrying pails, water, secret mashes; brushing hair, blackening hooves; wiping bulls' bottoms – all to the din of screaming hair-dryers as touting owners pinned up prize tickets and pinned down victims. And that only half the melee.

Red-faced farmers, tight braces and goose-greased boots, Barbour jacketed factors, deerstalker 'gents' careful where they stepped and a posse of Stetsons with Texan drawls invariably accompanied, as we bull boys were wont to note, by the deadly glamour of lipsticked blondes. A polymorphous mob choking the pathways between pens bursting with pride and joy. Poking, prodding, studying heads, hair, legs and hips, all preparing for that thrilling wallet opener, that omnipotent gamble – selecting a stock bull.

Eleven sharp. Clang of the bell, an amphitheatre of faces. Some flushed with excitement, many by a morning's 'top-up', others, less prone to elation, studied catalogues, enemy bidders and the last of their fingernails. Into an equally crammed ring, white-coated cattlemen led bewildered bulls, cocky bulls, shy bulls and some who tramped on toes and towed their attendants round the arena backwards. Oh, the waft of wallets, hair-fixing lotion and Famous Grouse whisky, a critical equilibrium. On stage, was the mesmerising Roley Fraser, grandson of the mart's founder. Let contest commence – waving hands, sly winks, any subterfuge counted. Witty and debonair, the conjurer was quickly bouncing about his rostrum inducing attacks of bidding fever. Sometimes, sad to say, followed by inside-pocket fits of depression. But now . . .

Rockie of Woodview entered the ring. Ruth's brother. My bull. A red rosette on his halter, Walter justly proud, he'd bucked the politics of judging on a first outing. A second-prize bull had just netted me three thousand five hundred guineas. Morale? Rocket boosted. Time to reinvest? I consulted my equilibrium. Good thinking.

'A thousand guineas, come along now.' Florrie below the rostrum, red hair, green eyes, smile and blush. That did it. In I went. Slight nod, a lift of the eyebrow. 'Thank you, twelve hundred, fifteen, two thousand. Gentlemen, you're just beginning to see this bull,' To make it simple, Roley raced into the thousand guinea bids, a roller-bank ride. Rockie, boy, you're some bull.

The price spirals as fast as I raise an eyebrow. By eight thousand, a gasp from the crowd; nine thousand; at ten thousand guineas, not a catalogue flutters – it's serious money. Faces silent, straining. I'm against the MacClaren brothers, both in the ring beside me. Donald's finger lifts – eleven thousand. Roley to me – twelve thousand? I glance, he takes me. The crowd motionless. Roley waltzes to the MacClarens, 'Come on, you can't stop now.' Thirteen thousand, the brother glance round. Bid. 'Fourteen thousand, fourteen thousand, don't miss him, look at the length and quality.'

I hesitate, my overdraft, fever touches mania, just a flick of the eyes – I'm in at fourteen thousand. 'Fifteen thousand guineas, gentlemen?' The brothers crimson faced, excited, will they go? Damn, both bid. 'Are you together?' 'Yes.' 'Fifteen thousand, thank you. Now it's again you, Iain.' Roley's riding the box, next call, sixteen thousand? Maybe eighteen thousand?

I dropped my eyes, 'Fifteen thousand guineas – going, going . . .' Electric suspense. I looked at the bull I'd set my mind on – he was a topper. Would I look up? Smack. Gone. The highest price for many, many years. My second mistake.

With Roley now in dancing form, the sale romped on. Bitterly disappointed, I pushed round to the box. Auctioneer Thomson, keen-eyed, watching the bids, bent over. 'Iain,' I said, 'I went far enough, I think.' He gave me a sharp look, 'Not far enough, young man. I could have sold shares in him tonight and put you in profit.' Oh, to be a judge of men and bulls as well.

Later that sale I made do with Rockie's half brother, Roger.

Three thousand, six hundred guineas and less adrenaline. The spell had burst? Not quite. That night, at a dance in the Perth's historic Salutation Hotel, I met the Liverpool Moores. Once the band tired, I carried two pairs of shoes and helped Jane Moores and her friend back to the Queen's Hotel. Their songs and my accordion kept guests thumping the ceiling till four in the morning.

A year on, Bob Adam phoned. 'D'you remember a heifer called Ruth?' 'Very well, a sister to Rockie – I put their sire champion when I was judging at the Omagh Show.' The darling heifer I'd lost for a bid had vanished to an obscure herd. The master breeder's scanning eye had fallen on her first calf and, for a high figure – I heard ten thousand pounds – it became the stock bull at Newhouse of Glamis.

Rockie's first son, bred by the MacClarens at Clashlochie, swept the boards, took the Perth Sales Championship and made eighteen thousand guineas for John Moores, owner of both an Angus herd near Liverpool and Littlewoods Pools. He couldn't have gone to a finer chap.

Ruth, then 'Rockie'. Both lost in Perth, yet a strange connection. You see, Rockie's champion, eighteen thousand guinea son went to North Moss Farm at Formby, a farm to which, in days long before John Moore's ownership, I delivered newspapers and, as a schoolboy marooned in England, I'd first dreamed of breeding Aberdeen Angus cattle.

## 6

# 'The Ghost of Christmas – a Day Late'

A pair of weary legs stretched at sixty degrees towards a roaring stove. The railway signalman rested snugly enough in his cabin but glowered frequently at the shining brass tops of the brutish signal levers he'd just polished as he felt gingerly under his truss. Had last year's rupture popped out again? What a night outside – the blizzard had snowflakes cavorting like moths to a candle round the dim lights of Lentran Station. He sighed between yawns.

Ignored by an 'auto age' which hurtled along the adjacent North Road, this wayside stop, six miles west of Inverness, was once the pride of a stationmaster with ample time between the sporadic trains to cultivate prize roses and trailing herbaceous borders along its well-swept, but deserted, platform. Though a top hat no longer welcomed alighting gentry, it did retain something of a leisured, Victorian charm amidst the pealing paint and the faint strains of the hourly flush of its cascading Gents urinal – a sound, I assure you, which did nothing to detract from the station's magnificent stance amongst the grandeur of Highland hills and the gentle lap of the Beauly Firth upon its curving embankment. It was a stance, none the less, best appreciated under more clement conditions.

Lassitude inflicted by Christmas leftovers overtook the signal-man. Dyspepsia blended Boxing Night blues with concerns for his rupture. He scratched obscenely as is the way of those perceiving themselves unobserved. The silence of Lentran signal box was disturbed only by the crackling stove, his affliction and the lulling tick of an antique LMS timepiece above his drooping head. He stretched, scratched and yawned again. One eye opened. Roman numerals winnowed in convection warmth. The last train of the night was due in five minutes. The signals were pulled off – all clear. He leant reluctantly over the chair arm and wiped a steamed pane. Snow swirled down the platform – he might just see train lights.

'Eeee, ow!' Both eyes shot open, his hair stood on end – no mean achievement after forty years plastered down with paraffin cream – his feet hit the deck, his body stood rigid. He hovered between flight and a less fortunate lapse.

Two huge saucer eyes glared in at him, wide apart in a white face. A great flat nose pressed against the glass. Smoke – or was it steam? – belched from flaring nostrils. 'Mercy on us,' he blurted, 'the ghost of Christmas – a day late.'

◆

A blazing log fire at Breakachy added much to the comfort of two easy chairs on a snowy Boxing Night. Two pairs of feet risked roasted socks and chilblains. Three balloons, arranged on the wall in suggestive fashion, wafted gently in the rising heat. Guffaws also arose, occasioned by a particularly vulgar line in a Spike Milligan novel.

Bang. The centre balloon burst – a timing attributable only to a poltergeist with a sense of humour. It shook me. At that exact moment, the phone rang. Betty, my wife, put her head round the door. A second shock – 'It's the police.' 'Help, it wasn't that loud, was it?'

'This is the Inverness-shire Constabulary. Are you the owner of a considerable number of cattle at Lentran?' 'Er, I could be.' Never admit anything without careful thought, especially from the depth of an armchair during a blizzard. 'Well, sir, I suggest you come and find out – a large herd has brought the A9 traffic to a standstill.'

I prised John 'The Artist' from the opposite chair and issued him with a scarf.

Headlights blazed, snowflakes swarmed in yellow beams, steam billowed from chugging exhausts and, more particularly, from the nostrils of a herd of side-heaving cattle which milled amongst policemen and crawling traffic. Drivers in between parties hastily chewed peppermints. We viewed a Christmas canvas from the wings. Not a roistering Dickensian scene. No jolly holly, galloping stagecoach or trumpeting post-horns, rather more impressionistic, postmodern-ish, you might say – oscillating blue snow, weaving cars and bawling cattle. It captivated 'The Artist'.

Controlling the round-up with a commendable sense of balance for a Boxing Night was cattleman, terror of farm manager and factor alike, 'Fearless Fred'. Understandably the police stood back. The size of stick operated by Fred required space and nor was it a night for wetting notebooks.

Happily, the traffic seemed to be moving. Motorists slithered and slewed, revving tyres shot heavily stained slush on to following windscreens. Jingle bells, goodwill to all men? Yuletide spirit was on hold. Drivers vowing ill-will to all farmers and road-fouling cattle hurried off to more Christmas frolics – we to the crunch of snow under boots. Peace descended on the hush of snow on earth – a figment of imagination disrupted by the return of Fred.

'Ee, lads, theere's still abowt sixty 'ead amissing.'

'Fearless', with an ungrudging application of his cudgel and phrases not quoted from a nativity play, had the bulk of the herd back in the steading examining their remedial treatment.

Sixty missing, eh? I tugged my deerstalker. Three hunched figures examined the snow for spoor. A magnifying glass proved unnecessary. A mammoth trail of snow-churning hoof prints led towards Lentran Station with the turmoil of migrating buffalo joining the London rush hour.

'Have you seen any, er, any cattle about here tonight?' I enquired cautiously of an ashen-faced signalman. It seemed an innocuous question for ten o'clock on a snow-blasting Boxing Night. 'Cattle!' he screamed at me and sat down – a mite weakly, I thought. 'They went that way,' he flapped a hand and spoke a little jerkily, 'I couldn't caution the Wick train, I waved from the platform, the guard got out to drive them.' He groaned, 'It hasn't reached Dingwall yet.' I trusted the latter referred to the train and not the herd. The midnight streets of Dingwall enlivened yet further by cattle romping amongst the revellers would require both Fred and a degree of subtle explanation at the police station.

Moonlight filtered through twirls of snowflakes, stretching steel into twinkling perspective, drawing a stencil of fencepost and tree – most pleasing to the aesthetic mind. It encouraged 'The Artist' no end. We trudged west, collars up, following the tracks, hoof, rail and, I presumed to the artistic eye, a touch of blemish where cattle had soiled the snow.

Two miles proved enough for us, the guard and sixty non-paying rail users. There stood two groups of shapes and shadows, black impressions on moonlit snowfields. Most appealing to 'The Artist', most annoying for me – they had landed in separate fields, on either side of the track.

'Gather your men tomorrow, two o'clock on the minute,' I instructed 'Fearless', 'and tell farm manager Hunter – cattle back the way they came. OK, zero watches.' I conjured up Wild West prairies, a buffalo herd stampeding before the smoke-belching iron horse and added, for a touch of colour supplement, 'Code name, Operation Cow Catcher.'

Next afternoon, 'Cow Catcher' swung into action. At two o'clock, I raced into the signal box, suitably distraught and breathless. 'The cattle have broken back on to the track.' The signalman slumped against his polished levers. 'Oh my God, not again! The ten past two has just left Dingwall. I can't caution the driver now – he'll be at sixty passing Beauly.' I began to view the code name with misgivings. It could tempt the arrival of a train with a heifer, and possibly Fred, riding the buffers.

The signalman, anticipating a similar scenario, grabbed his emergency phone. 'Get me the Chief Accident Inspector.'

Oh dear.

Meantime, Farm Manager Hunter, at precisely fourteen hundred hours, was unloading a gang of local helpers beside the track. A varied selection, they would not have appeared miscast in a stick-'em-up movie hanging from the roof of an iron horse, intimidating the engine driver with Colt 45s. Enhancing the Wild West effect was the addition of the farm manager's glamorous, auburn-haired wife. Quite a belle, even minus buckskin, she added a sort of 'Annie get your gun' effect on ice.

Organised by Fred, a natural for gun-slinging and colourful 'whooping', the animals reassembled on the line and the troupe, blithesome as schoolkids snowballing the village bobby, were soon sleeper-hopping along British Rail tracks behind a string of sniffing cattle.

Not to be confused with a leader of men, Hunter retired to a commanding knoll. Nary a 'toot' of warning, with eye-popping alarm and heroic concern, he watched the sixty-mile-an-hour Dingwall–Inverness express tear round a bend and bear down upon the leisurely drove.

Fifty yards. He closed his eyes.

The day held a breathtaking tranquillity – the ugliness of mankind's impact on the face of nature smoothed by the innocence of snow. A sense of its utter beauty, not without a little difficulty, reached deep into the soul of 'Fearless'. He turned the better to admire such splendour. To a prospect of snow-drooping trees and sun-drenched hillsides was added the looming face of an engine under emergency brakes. Sparks shot from wheels, passengers from seats and the driver did a 'windscreener'.

'Leap for your lives, lads,' yelled Fred, already in mid-air. Men and beasts, plus our beautiful heroine, dived for side-drains, the next best facility to a dugout, given the time-span available.

Hunter shot into reverse, to the phone. 999. Gasp. 'Police, a train has just ploughed into a herd of men and cattle, not to mention my dear wife,' he ended with a sob.

Unknowing but nervous, back at operations centre, I felt for the reassurance of my hip flask. Loud ticking clock. Tense waiting was abruptly shattered by blue flashing lights. I put the flask away.

Breathless bobbies flung open the door, 'Where's the accident?' Accident, holy six-shooters, how the hell did they find out? I stood impassively at the signal box window. If ever there was a time for panic, this was not the occasion. I pointed up the track. 'The train's coming now.' A signalman, two policemen and I stood in silence, almost to attention. I prepared to doff my deerstalker – it could be a cortège.

The train chugged towards the station at a pace indicating something untoward. Perhaps its brakes were stuck or . . . I peered at the buffers. Blood, hair? Nothing. It pulled slowly past. The driver appeared to be wiping his window with a reddish hankie. He lifted his hand in none too friendly a manner.

Presently a trickle of cattle sauntered towards the signal box. The police eyed them suspiciously. A large car handbrake-turned in the yard. The Chief Accident Inspector ejected, all flurry and official forms, only to be surrounded by inquisitive cattle, Fred and his desperadoes.

'Do you own these animals?' the challenging face of officialdom barked. 'Well, yes, in a manner of speaking.' Mentioning T. and G. seemed a jot frivolous, given the colour of the Inspector's cheeks. Instead, applying the adage that attack beats defence, I continued, 'They would not have troubled you, Inspector, had the entrance to your premises boasted a cattle grid or possibly even a gate on its hinges.' For added menace, I introduced 'Fearless', something of a human missile held in reserve for the next volley. The Inspector omitted a handshake.

With admirable understanding the police lost interest. Courteous as ever, they held up the traffic. 'Fearless' marched his charges back to billets. The Inspector departed with 'You will hear more of this outrage' floating over his shoulder.

The signalman took early retirement and developed a nervous twitch. Fred? Maybe not the ScotRail Award for Gallantry but surely a worthy mention in the Inspector's report.

# 7

# 'Never Trust a Man who . . .'

A faded Union Jack, much in need of a swish of biological washing powder, drooped from a pole which stuck out at a suggestive angle from the balcony of number 17, Grosvenor Crescent. Georgian elegance, a flight of steps to the front door, a prominent brass doorknocker and, I may confide, one of the better addresses to be had in our proud City of Edinburgh. In short, a building of style and refinement, amply suiting the pre-eminence of our farming industry in Scottish affairs of state and providing Wellington space at the tradesmen's entrance.

A flag of Saint George and the Dragon might have fitted the occasion in question better. My suggestion was vetoed. None the less, below the Land of Hope and Glory banner, on the sandstone doorpost, our plaque had been freshly 'Brasso-ed' as a mark of respect. It proudly announced The Scottish National Farmers Union. A collective term which, perhaps it should be mentioned, brought frowns to those members who believed unions were best left to employees. The connotations of association they considered more in accord with the social dignity of our agricultural profession and certainly more safely in tune with the fanfare about to herald the nation's mighty 'Union Slayer'.

Up the banistered stairway, past the step-by-step, portrait-by-portrait display of presidential gravitas, climbed Falkland's heroine, symbol of Britain's finest hour, Prime Minister, the Right Honourable Margaret Hilda Thatcher and followers, chiefly Dennis. My advice had been dismissed out of hand. 'At the least a musical tribute to her entrance,' I pleaded. 'A note or two of Handel? *Judas Maccabeus*, 'See the Conquering Hero', 'Arrival of Queen of Sheba', *Water Music*?' Our Director was not in sunshine mode. 'Look, Thomson, this is no occasion for antics.' 'Dear boy, fear not, the day shall be larded with sycophancy.' 'Don't do anything,' he growled, adding, 'and keep away from the drinks.'

I fixed a smile, the polished boardroom smiled, we all smiled, top brass of one of our nation's guiding hands that we were, albeit on occasion guiding by elbow rather than by hand. And fittingly, for a gathering of countryside-lovers, to that memorable morn was added, heavy and fragrant from the glade across the road, the scent of chestnut blossom. Through the open sash window it wafted, gently dissipating any hint of intemperance which might linger upon those who perhaps the night before had felt a need to inflate their welcome.

In marched blue eyes, laser-stunning, arcing across the room, high-voltage blue, singeing a muster of Sunday suits. Blue as a farmer's language when he touches the electric fence by mistake. What an intensity! Sexy in a dangerous kind of way, even her blue outfit looked pale. Then that blonde sweep, piled and styled, a demeanour suited to Britannia spending too long on the penny. Wolf whistles? What a little honey! 'Pray silence, gentlemen. Please welcome our Prime Minister, The Right Honourable Margaret Hilda Thatcher, and Dennis.' We clapped, discretely, just one hand, admirably conservative.

A black handbag thumped on to the table, stentorian tones loosened ceiling plaster, the flag fluttered for the first time that morning. Oh lor', the little lady's in lecturing mode. Any lack of attention at the back? I stuffed an exercise book down my trousers and nodded approvingly, for safety. Any mention of the *Belgrano* sinking or a kindly enquiry for the health of her friend President Pinochet I discounted for the moment – one would not suspect a sense of humour lurked beneath the glare of this feminine version of the British Bulldog.

◆

One wheeze which enlivened the twenty years farming Tighnaleac of Breakachy was an involvement in farming politics. The Presidency of Inverness Farmers Union led to Council Delegate and jaunts to serious Edinburgh committee meetings. From thence descended a most grave responsibility – the Convenorship of the Union's Highland and Islands Committee and elevation to the plotting centre of farming politics, a top table seat amongst the Grosvenor Crescent cabal – the cynosure for any aspiring farmer of serious political intent and a splendid opportunity for me to bid at Victorian painting auctions en route to meetings. The whole uproarious outfit was run by Director General Scott Johnston, a debonair lad of lively mind and sunny disposition who wrote speeches for his presidents and handled all levels of politicians and bureaucrats with the skill of a circus ringmaster. Our previous careers missed connecting by a month or two when we each attended teacher-training courses at the Army Education Centre in stockbroker-belted Beaconsfield. Instant friends, Scott suspected the connections I'd forged with farming to be misguided and furthermore my approach to matters of national politics inclining towards the light-hearted, yet he bore many indiscretions with fatherly patience. I christened him 'Sunshine'.

As convenor by an unrigged election, I sat with John Lefley, the committee secretary, in his paper-strewn office, top floor, 17 'Gros Cres'. We sniffed the political wind – south-east and reeking of cash. EC Brussels bureaucrats had hit on doling out extra agricultural aid to far-flung regions disadvantaged by geography, pouring rain and lack of any infrastructure beyond rutted tracks. Could it reach the deprived Highlands? Perhaps. A money boat might arrive, a 'puffer', unloading sackfuls of cheques on to 'coup carts', prams or the bicycle crossbars of oppressed West Coast crofters. Thirty million could be siphoned. Sunshine reckoned a statue to me on Stornoway pier the very least tribute – hand on lapel, head high, arrogant and above dog-cocking level.

An Agricultural Development Programme for the Highlands and Islands of Scotland? Yes, that's the bait for Brussels. An ambitious title, the first disguise for masking a master plan wilfully concocted to distribute ecus faster than a 'one-armed bandit' on the blink. Subterfuge, the second ingredient, vital for throwing Westminster off the scent. After all, the British Government was dedicated to shutting down UK farming, not sponsoring its development. Mmm, now for tactics. A tiptoe along corridors of power and we surreptitiously squeezed our confidential document under the door of Ronnie Crammond, second-in-command of agricultural matters at the Scottish Office.

Tea, with biscuits left from the war effort, plus reassuring eye contact, about as far as any civil servant goes without checking the grease on the pole, and yes, tacit approval. Ronnie? Good lad, our first friend in high places. He murmured the name of an EC mandarin and, raising only one eyebrow over the clause I'd slipped in aiming at a touch of environmentally friendly farming, ushered us out by the back door. Cloak and dagger, 'The Highland Pimples' were ready to burst into Brussels.

Back at base the word 'environment' cropped up in a proposed farming programme for the first time. Progressive 'prairie' farmers looked it up in the dictionary and choked. The Union didn't like it. Any inkling that agriculture's unrestricted romp into high-pressure land use since Hitler's war could equal the farmers' attack on the balance of our countryside's ecology could sound sirens in 'do-gooder' minds. The role of ploughboys as best guardians of the countryside could be questioned. Worse, the Department of Agriculture had no wish to feed a fledgling Nature Conservancy Council opening its maw, at their expense, for a larger share of Treasury budget. Anyway this whole 'environmental thingy' might melt away if Prince Charles tired of listening to Laurens van der Post and talking to flowers.

Roll on our next trick, a high-profile bandwagon with access to somebody else's petty cash. Lunch with Iain Campbell of Sligachan in Skye, Chairman of Highland Regional Council, more lunches with the Highlands and Islands Development Board. We soon enjoyed enthusiastic backing. G&Ts tightened waistbands. On well-oiled wheels and our growing inclination towards VIP treatment, Lefley and I leapt on a BA flight to Brussels.

Guided by Stella Artois and *Sortie, Utgang* signs, we emerged from a subway before an array of waving flags and a parabolic building of vast, glass frontage. Twenty-five acres of window cleaning, its architect didn't train with a ladder and shammy leather. 'Some model of limo they sell here, John.' Wrong, almost. No salesmen, no car bays but the Berlaymont Building, HQ of the European Common Market and showroom of earnest pen-pushers, stacked in layers, ten to a box, each considering the minimum size of cage for a battery hen to give birth to an egg in comfort. We knocked.

Fronds of exotic greenery hung over a bottom-hugging couch. Lefley and I lounged, almost out of sight, drinking coffee and chatting affably. Another step towards the money mine, the hallowed apartment of the Chief Commissioner for European Agriculture.

He turned out a fine lad. Hailed from east Belgium, a Walloon – little dark eyes, quick but kindly. He'd been in Scotland during the war, liked the Highland folk and their feet-on-the-desk approach, lack of frills and ceremony. Commissioner Raymond Craps – we were on first-name terms immediately – seemed interested. 'Did I farm?' 'Och yes, but really I'm just a hill shepherd.' 'Just!' Raymond jumped with excitement, 'I always wanted to be one – you're the very first in this office,' he exclaimed, glancing at the carpet. We liked him and shook the hand of friendship. Help assured and a promise to come and see us in Edinburgh, top form, we slid down the banisters as Lefley remarked, 'Your shepherding blarney did the trick.'

True to his word Raymond appeared in 'Auld Reekie' and met various dry cough Department officials before we taxied him to a shirtsleeve welcome from John Cameron, our Union President. Steam locos puffed incongruously on the presidential office walls, rather to Raymond's surprise. When not gathering sheep on his fifty thousand acres John played trains for real. A creeper-covered steam engine abandoned in the Zambian jungle reappeared on his farm as the 'Union of South Africa'. Once polished up, Cameron drove it round Scotland, tooting at farm crossings and leaning out of the cab with a dirty face under an oily peaked cap. A style which shunted him into the Chairmanship of ScotRail.

Of more concern to our plot, Cameron was the progressive descendant of Inverness-shire's eighteenth-century Corriehoillie, the king of cattle drovers and neither a hill shepherd nor a down-trodden crofter but Europe's largest flockmaster – not the image we were peddling. However, a master of political subterfuge, John played the couthie card and entrusted Raymond to our care. 'These boys will see you safe home, Commissionaire.' Less confident was Director General Sunshine who issued a behind-the-hand warning along the lines – he is Mr EC Agriculture, a very, very VIP, so discretion, no drinking and NO 'low dives'. We escorted our friend that night to an exclusive Italian restaurant just off Princes Street.

Well, Raymond was a topper, loved our national bev, if just a tad rusty on uptake. Malt upon malt, the joint was packed, the meal fair fancy and, by the time we reached liqueurs, the boyo called for a biro, drew a map of Europe on the tablecloth and filled in budgets, past, present and future for the whole jing-bang Euro conglomeration. We were in there, top of the draw – what a friend. The waiter fitted our coats, put us on the street. Man, I had the accordion in the back of the car. 'The Dashing White Sergeant' takes three – Lefley and Raymond made it a twosome, up and down the cobbles. What a night! I hope Raymond remembers it. The best official I ever met, he would have made a hill shepherd right enough – a fact which I assured him of several times and also his taxi driver.

The security doorman at the European Parliament in Strasbourg had a good Scots tongue, treated us as lost brethren and allowed us to wander in and out at will. MEPs needed to get our message officially, outwith 'tearoom' sessions. Lecture theatres were booked, headphoned interpreters snoozed behind glass panels, politicians wandered in and the leader of each political group chaired our efforts. Councillor George Stevenson, victim of our previous evening on the expense account of the *Scottish Daily Express*, sobbed over the hardship of life in Orkney and held up hands full of hacks from clipping turnips. Florence Grains, 'Flarence' in Shetland vernacular, began her 'spiel' by bemoaning the rain and gales of her native islands. Interpreters were baffled, the chairman held up his hand, 'Quel language avez vous parlez, si vous plaise?' If only I had the Gaelic instead of the shepherding plus fours.

Jaunts continued. At nine o'clock one morning, we had an appointment with the Strasbourg Parliament's President, Sir Henry Plumb. Our very own President, mega-flockmaster Cameron, had been his pal on their way up the political pole. Director General Sunshine, Cameron and I wound around the parliament's circular corridors – all King Arthur layout, democratic and round tables.

We knocked on a door identical to the rest. 'Sir Henry won't be long,' his secretary assured us. 'Do sit down.' The room was spacious, except for what we took as a huge filing cabinet taking up a whole corner. The girl retired.

Silence. Nobody. Without prompting, John began his assessment of Sir Henry. 'Not the good old plain Henry I used to know . . .' Words such as pompous crept into the description. 'How the hell he got this job . . .' Cameron's sharp voice was cut short by the mighty flush of a lavatory. Out from the cabinet stepped Sir Henry, refreshed from his morning 'constitutional' and with an equal flush on his face. The meeting went off-key, stiff and formal. No coffee. The secretary pointedly showed us out. A crestfallen trio, we stood in the corridor. 'Well, boys,' I counselled them, 'you know the old saying – never trust a man who shits in his filing cabinet.'

All was not doom. To the rescue came Madame Écosse, alias Winnie Ewing, the Scottish Nationalist MEP. From the visitors' gallery, Sunshine and I had witnessed her sparkling performance – that was, of course, before we tired of politics and drifted off to a French hostelry where, after a bev or two, the local lad sportingly gave me a shot of his accordion. Anyway, we'd noted Winnie could sweep into the parliamentary amphitheatre, dress billowing, catch the President's eye, give a blast of Scotland's case and retire to the 'tearoom' – plus she got results. Style? We liked it. Our kind of girl.

By now Highland Region, in the person of Duncan MacPherson, had clambered aboard the bandwagon. Second-in-command of their Council, he farmed at Cromarty Mains on the Black Isle and was known privately to us as Ranting, after the fiddle tune 'Mac-Pherson's Rant' and an ability to talk. His inclusion on the crusade was a major boost, though not without peril.

The squeal of brakes reached me whilst sauntering down a hotel corridor, draped in but a towel, en route from my bedroom to the 'naughty' mixed sauna. Bobbie Faskin of the Highlands and Islands Development Board, who was lending weight to our proceedings, called me in for a 'freshener'. I glanced out of his window. 'A squashed frog?' Not a kind remark. Ambulance men loaded a prone figure. Sauna delights over we dressed or, should I say, put clothes on for dinner. No Duncan.

Duncan, ex-fighter pilot and our doughty leader, delayed in the call of duty to our cause? Drifting back to our 'digs' in the Holiday Inn after a late 'discussion' in the Strasbourg 'tearoom', Duncan encountered the bonnet of a carelessly driven Volkswagen Beetle. He did arrive, dressed for dinner with his arm in a sling but otherwise unfazed. Ah, man, wounded in the noble cause of steering an Agricultural Development Programme towards his needy constituents.

Persuading Europe's Parliament to vote 'yes' for our handouts to the Highlands programme became imperative before we dared tackle Westminster. It required more groundwork. I watched storks repairing nests in spring-blossomed trees beside Strasbourg's seat of power and I became a familiar in Brussels' Charlemagne Hotel – it was my first encounter with heated underfloor bathroom tiles and a bath requiring a life-jacket for non-swimmers.

John Lefley, fired by a testy Director-General for his untidy office, was replaced by Tom Brady, an efficient secretary, even if something between a wild colonial boy and a night prowler. Strolling Brussels' backstreets late one evening, he and I were overtaken by a noiseless hurrying figure in a dappled leotard. It flitted past – a narrow beaky face and straggling hair under the yellow street lamps. It didn't grin but fangs could protrude over cruel lips. 'Dracula?' muttered Brady. Beside this phantom padded a huge black panther, reassuringly secured by a collar and chain.

'Follow the cat,' I whispered. It led down a darkness-hugging vennel – or should I say venal? – to an unlit door and vanished. After some banging, followed by negotiations via the keyhole, a crack of light let us in. An enormous black bouncer relocked the door and growled, 'Dis way.' We followed the white of his teeth down a maze of unlit passages. Were we being lured towards providing the panther with supper? The big chap quietly unlocked another door. We stepped into a den.

Bow ties, blue-white shirts and the deepest cleavages leaned over cocktails, eyes catching. Music poured over us. Relax, man. Drift. Get syncopated, drink that slinky rhythm. Soft, cigar-smoky light draped even softer women, fleshed, not dressed, in the luxurious curves of the sweet incense of desire. We were prey to the intoxication of depravity after a hard day's politics. Leotard and panther were caged inside chrome bars on a small stage, both doing tricks to the crack of a whip.

Without warning, lights out, blackness. Police? *Scotsman* headlines. Union disgrace. Sunshine. Help. My wallet? No. Seconds later
a blinding flash lit the cage. Gone cat and prancing lcotard.
Replacement, behind the glitzy bars, a swaying nymph, straight
off a pre-Raphaelite canvas, minus any coyly placed hands. Never
had Venus graced such a shapely mount. A beauteous creation,
designed in every curve and dimple by Mother Nature giving
lessons in seduction.

She stepped out of custody. Scent and music got me. We danced
the night away, on stage. Brady said my tweed plus fours cut some
dash. I asked the lovely if they tickled. 'Delightfully,' she smiled,
easing off my jacket. Later, much, it could have been another night,
we repaired to dim quarters which nights just previous had seen a
British soldier shot dead. Brave lads, the danger we faced in the line
of duty.

◆

Charismatic Winnie did her trick at the European Parliament. A
swingeing speech carried the chamber. Victory in Strasbourg.
Bravo. Nothing less than a thank-you luncheon. We all flew in.
Cameron, Scott, Ranting, the lot. The meal, beautifully served in
the Parliament's dining room and aided by Château de Monteux
'63, was triumphant. Replete and cheerful, each leader of our joint
delegation rose from the trencher to commend in fulsome terms our
gracious MEP and her achievement. Applause rippled. Finally, up
stood our Union President – John of the fifteen thousand ewes and
mostly well-chosen words. Winnie basked, Cameron was masterly.
'And now, Mrs Ewing,' he finished, 'with gratitude from the hard-
pressed farmers and crofters of the Highlands, please accept this
token.' He groped below his chair. Hands and knees. Nothing. The
Caithness glass bowl, engraved words and all, memento of victory,
nicked by a passing waiter.

That night Ranting, alias Duncan, and I headed for 'Winnie's
party', a phrase and location with which the taxi driver seemed
surprisingly familiar. The electric 'shout-upstairs' lock let us in.
What a pack of merriment and lack of chairs! MEPs of every shade
were four to the couch, two to a chair, sitting on the floor, leaning
on the wall and the welcome – Highland at its best. Winnie in flying

form, John Hulme marching up and down singing Irish ballads, English poems from Bobbie Faskin, Gaelic laments. 'Come on, Iain!' Minus accordion I gave them 'The Road to the Isles', freehand. Wild applause, followed by the smell of burning soup. One chorus too long. Our hostess raced for the kitchen.

To admire the view of a city at night, Duncan and I stepped on to the balcony, steaming soup bowls in hand. One sip. 'This is hellish!' Ranting tipped the contents smartly over the rail. Voice from below, 'I say, old chap.' Moments later, let up by the vocal lock, in stormed a furious late-arrival MEP from the English shires, burnt head, shoulders and stripy suit splattered with Winnie's tomato soup. I nodded to Duncan, 'Parachute over the edge or the Road to the Door?' We thanked our hostess and dived for the safety of the bright lights of town.

Farewells and official photos next morning, we hung around our heroine in desultory fashion. Up raced the Rev. Ian Paisley who, for no obvious reason, joined in the snap. We spoke briefly. He conveyed a powerful impression of the vehemence of Almighty God on Judgement Day though I noted, at the same time, Our Lord's lieutenant in this life didn't appear shy of a mug shot.

Sometimes we cadged a lift home from Strasbourg on the special MEP charter plane. Dry flight but plenty duty-free passing 'Go'. Abandoning Sunshine after a few off the top, I sat with Barbara Castle and was stunned by her intellect as we talked and she read documents at the same time. 'You're a likely looking lad,' shrewd eyes and bouffant hair style surveyed me. 'About your project – you need some true-blue friends.'

# 8

# 'I'll Bet I Can Produce a Pair of your Knickers on TV'

Powerful allies had been secured in Europe but it was still pound for pound, EU and UK and the latter cash machine under the stiletto heel of the Little Blue Lady with the Electric Eyes. So be it. Now for our assault on Westminster and the Treasury. Full-frontal, guns blazing or gently from the heights? I'd gathered sheep from high corries – a good dog on the ridge, just showing his ears at the right time and place.

I sat with Tom Brady in the anteroom at London's Dover House reading the *Private Eye* magazine I'd picked off a table whilst awaiting the presence of Scottish Secretary, Lord Gray of Contin. To grace his title, doubtless for ancestral reasons, His Lordship had chosen Contin, a tiny Ross-shire village, which I knew rather better as the abode of a family of the Highland's finest poachers, the Bartletts, athletic lads who utilised the local Fairburn Estate and far beyond to the panting displeasure of police and landowner, Captain Roderick Stirling, Lord-lieutenant of Ross-shire – an amusing charade which I chose not to disclose to His Lordship on this occasion.

Ushered into a stately room, something approaching a regal audience chamber, I admired the massive, gilt-framed portraits of bygone personages. Strangely, they were stacked against the walls. Lacy cuffs, ruffs and smooth faces, aristocratic snouts that had guzzled enough from the trough to end as oil on canvas. We sank into cushions, real bottom-softeners. Shepherding took a back seat. Lord Hamish Gray, whom I knew more accurately as 'The Slater', by virtue of his roofing business up in Inverness, approached, with Ian Smith, Scotland's top agri-bureaucrat.

Friendly but formal. 'This Development Programme, Mr Thomson, expensive. What about £10 extra a head on the hill cow subsidy for the Highland area instead?' 'Excellent idea, Minister, thank you, meantime.' No small talk, just coffee and out. More friends though, we shook hands. To pot with flummeries. 'Well, Hamish,' I said to His Lordship at the door, nodding towards the leaning paintings, 'you had a hell of a party here last night.' 'Yes, Iain,' he grinned. 'Mercifully you were not present.'

Progress, albeit at pen-pusher pace. Radio and TV interviews, press statements and sundry articles kept up the pressure. Hamish 'The Slater', our Highland supporter, gave way to another political Lord in Scotland's top job. The person of Lord Mansfield surfaced, a major Perthshire landowner with a 'lang pedigree' but an all-round good chap nonetheless, whom we fondly called Willie Mansfield, out of his earshot. A television face-to-face with him on the subject of this Agri-Development Programme had been arranged unbeknown to a friend of singular attraction.

Giving scant thought to the pending weighty deliberation but perhaps more to the subject of 'scanties', I approached her delicately, 'Modest girl that I know you are, I'll bet I can produce a pair of your knickers on TV, should you care to watch Tuesday evening's Scottish news.' I took her white pair, ironed and flimsy, to the studio, tucked in the top pocket of my best plus four suit.

A wink to the boys on camera, 'Watch my right hand – don't miss it.' Thinking I intended to pull an armpit derringer on His Lordship, they nodded eagerly. An assassination hot on set – instant news. Wow! As 'Willie' and I talked, my hand reached slowly towards my top pocket until, with a flourish, I withdrew the knickers and blew my nose.

Those watching the plot wet themselves. Secretary of State for Scotland, Lord Mansfield, every inch a statesman as he considered the problem from the Treasury perspective, remained oblivious. Sunshine, on discovering the ploy, was apoplectic. 'The dignity of the Union stripped by a pair of the girlie knickers,' he screamed, striding his office, arms flailing, face screwed. 'Ah but, Scott boy,' I soothed, 'think of the sex appeal I've just put into this damned Agricultural Development Programme – we're bound to sell it now.'

Next, our most difficult trick – good timing. Vital. Any political acrobat will tell you so. Election looming, we circulated back stage amongst the harlequins jostling for a part in the Westminster pantomime. Our script? Word perfect. Any auditions? Dandeno, Baron Hardbrass, Widow Twanky?

Secretary Tom Brady and I approached Sir Hector Munro in his Houses of Parliament chamber. We sat waiting. I idly cleaned my fingernails with a six-inch flick knife which I used for cutting the string on hay bales. 'Oh, my sainted aunt,' Brady whispered hoarsely, really, most really, concerned. 'No joking, boy, we'll be arrested. Scott'll go crazy. How the mischief d'you get through the electronic hoop with that weapon? You could stab the PM.' I finished the left hand. 'Ach, no, I'm a Tory sometimes.' Sir Hector appeared, cutting short my manicure. We talked of rugby and some of the Border chaps whom I knew. Hunter Gordon, down from the north, Tom Elliot and his falling-out-of-window antics, with just a mention of our pet Development Programme in the passing. A friendly blether, another fine chap, might put in a 'wordie' with the Fairy Godmother. Who would know?

◆

Rapt attention and smiles of approbation gave way to frowns and a faint shuffling of disapproval. The atmosphere in the boardroom of 17 Grosvenor Crescent was cooling. The 'Iron Lady' blended hauteur with a stern message to farmers. 'Your industry must stand on its own feet, become more efficient' and, by implication, be the flunkeys serving our nation's table ever-cheaper food. Not a message willingly digested by 'clod-hoppers' forever whining, on platforms or in print, with such hackneyed rhetoric as 'give us a level playing field with Europe' and similar futile requests, which every government deliberately ignored once the wartime's submarine fright died down. To lads out at cattle, at six each morning, seven days a week, and coffee for inspecting Department pen-pushers at eleven, it rose hackles. The PM's final salvo sounded emphatic. Farmers were to challenge the future with their own cash, enough of these dole-outs from the taxpayer. Applause did not register on the Richter scale nor did I detect the merest whisper of 'Rejoice, rejoice.'

Rather unwisely, when John Cameron, our President, introduced me to the regal lady, I overestimated her interest in the science of ecology by immediately expounding my belief in an environmentally friendly approach to putting tatties on the table, non-chemical farming for the health of the nation, good old dung and a dash of lime. I even used the term, unheard of thirty-odd years ago, 'biodiversity'. A searing look from commanding blue eyes followed by three deliberate words, 'Not cost-effective.' Was I condemned to the Tower? Had I blown the ADP? The PM circulated towards saner conversation.

I fared better with Dennis. He looked towards me, twirling an empty glass. A wink at the lassie with the tray, a spread of fingers indicating two Gs, one tonic, and I eased away his empty for a refill. He beamed – we had a basis for 'discussion'. Noting my 'Campbells of Beauly' plus four tweeds, smart but keeperish, I was obviously a ghillie. Dennis launched into a theory for the demise of red grouse populations in Scotland. Long heather, sheep ticks, lack of shooting the old birds. I thought privately of one old bird in need of winging but followed his drift until the initials HRH cropped up. I frowned. 'You know Philip?' 'Ah, yes.' He seemed amused when I told of the fun we'd had with this gentleman's mother-in-law. We parted on such good terms he forgot his coat. I hoped I was not held responsible.

Shell-shocked after our mauling by the 'Iron Lady', a rousing fling seemed the only solution to lifting the ennui which now settled upon our fated cause. The clammy hand of bureaucracy must be rung again, nay but squeezed. And it so happened – the Brussels new Chief Commissioner, Paul Dalsayer, was booked to address our Union's Council Delegates in Edinburgh one morning. The message filtered through to Ranting and his back-room boys at Highland Region. A prank is required.

Give Paul a helicopter whiz around the barren hills and glens of the north, let him wave to the odd bog-bound crofter, maybe throw out a food parcel here and there, then flip him straight back to the prestigious Newton Hotel at Nairn, in time for a grand banquet. What better means of illustrating the wealth gap? Fittingly, the much-vaunted Nairn venue was once the regular stop-off of Charlie Chaplin. 'What about a screening of the little man in *The Gold Rush*?' Scott didn't raise even a smile. Misgivings? I saw he needed humouring.

A Paul speech, a snore, a swanky lunch and Sunshine and I headed north with his 'limo' handling the A9 like it was Silverstone. We lost Paul's helicopter about Perth. I suggested respectfully to the Director General a refuelling stop at the Bruar wayside howff. Brakes and smart right-hand down. That's my boy.

Humour restored, misgivings allayed, we frolicked over the Drumochter Pass, up the remaining A9 to Harry Nilsson and Scott in a heart-rending duet, 'Can't live, if living is without you, can't give, I can't give any more.' I wondered. The chopper, parked on the lawn, had won by an hour. Paul, in the grip of the press, was enlightening them on his airborne assessment of Highland problems. A splendid opportunity to draw breath and steady ourselves for the feast, I remarked to Sunshine as we strolled towards Nairn's version of a 'speak-easy'.

Seven sharp, boiled, white shirts spreading without a wrinkle, pressurised buttons that hid sporrans on pressed kilts, regulation height above the hairy stocking flashes, of the dignitaries of the north. The rumble of superior conversation hushed as each impressive guest had his name shouted by doormen flanking the entrance of a lofty banqueting hall and struggling with the lingo. A variety of European Commissioners, with an interest in agricultural production and, in particular, its arrival on a plate, had flown in to support their chief.

I enjoyed the honour of escorting our gracious lady guest, Madame Dalsayer, to her seat beside me. The waiter slid chairs beneath us and kindly spread our linen napkins. Silver and cutlery – I hadn't seen such an array outside a sack marked 'swag' in the *Beano*. I caught the dear lady's hand. How charmed I was to join her, at table, I added. Bonhomie? The very word was invented to convey my emotions, dampened, but just a jot, by Scott's hovering eye across the influential throng.

Mince and tatties? Not on the menu? 'Mon Dieu, menus are so boring.' I discovered my companion's French to be A level at least, in spite of her being Dutch. She smartly analysed the grub on offer. Courses appeared; the cutlery got less; I lost count. We compared countries. Had she been to Amsterdam? 'Je reste sur Suisse.' I liked her smile. She worried about Paul's heart condition, in convivial tones. Next down the trough from us, I could see her man lost no time shovelling 'twixt plate and lip'.

The blazing chandelier dimmed before blazing faces, 'Mon dear, try a . . .' I avoided the word snort. Snifter? 'Ah, mais non. Er, a little, une petite pour vous cheri? Er, waiter, comme sa monsuier? Avez vous une bottle de Glenfarclas. Malt? Cent sonte years, at least.' He bowed. The evening improved.

Then to coffee-dreary speeches, oiled with only a dab of liqueur. Totally lacking in 'joie de vivre' I thought – not the 'true spirit' of the Highlands. My right-hand diner, Gordon Elliot, he of the Highland's Development Board, was already clapping and shouting, 'Bring on the dancing girls.' The scope of the Board's remit rose in my estimations.

I stood. Lord Elgin, at an Aberdeen Angus bicentenary bash before the Queen Mother the previous year, had given me this toasting tip. One foot on my chair, I broke into speech, in English. 'The Auld Alliance has not died,' I cried, ignoring the German Commissioners and any Sassenach present. 'Shoulder to shoulder we march.' Two feet on chair, looking down on Mme D. I burst into song, 'Land o' the shining river, Land o' my heart forever, Scotland the Brave. *Slainte mhath.*' On to the table, swaying, kilt swinging, under, but not grabbing, the chandelier, I gave them, full volume, Rabbie Burns, 'A man's a man, for a' that', and glass upraised, 'Comrades, a toast.' The banquet rose, 'Unity and the common man, Europe forever.' Glenfarclas down in a oner. I burst into 'La Marseillaise' as Gordon, sound friend, lent a hand to assist me off the table.

Applause! The room erupted. Madame Dalsayer clapped ecstatically and waved her hankie. Had she been peeping, naughty girl? My efforts towards furthering international friendship brought the banquet to a close. Clutching our honoured guests and the remains of the Glenfarclas, I ushered Paul and, I forget her name, Mme D.

through to rest a little on a couch in the spacious drawing room and presented them with a copy of my new book, *Isolation Shepherd*. After all, I reasoned, the Commissioner and his Brussels chums spent enough on sheep subsidy. Paul was delighted. He signed another copy of my book as well and said he was thinking of writing a book. 'Really, Paul, I hope to be President of the NFU shortly.' 'Ah, mais oui, bravo, Ean.' Scott looked pained. 'How's about coming up the town, Paul? There's bound to be dance somewhere – join the local culture.' Paul appeared enthusiastic, Mme D. decided. Hubby, bed. 'He has to be careful, you know.' Goodnights were gushing and extended – both cheeks but no tweeks. The Dalsayers slowly ascended the grand staircase, turned and waved. Great folk really – for foreigners.

The room darkened. Was there a power cut, an eclipse? Sunshine loomed over me. 'Well, Thomson, this is it – you've done it this time. You made a right arse of everything tonight.' His teeth were grinding – I hoped they weren't dentures. 'You've made the Union a laughing stock in front of . . .' I leapt to my feet – or so it seemed. 'You're telling me, boy! Who the . . . ?' Whoosh, bang, wallop, at the foot of the stately stairs. Ranting to the rescue before too much damage showed. Scott was indeed a patient, indulgent friend who perhaps feared for his job.

Bright September sun bounced through the window. I arose and escorted our guests down the lawn to board their helicopter. Much hand-pumping, the French especially. 'Au revoir, Ean. Last night, your speech, la toast, c'est magnifique. We send pour vous at our next revolution.'

Such bursts of high spirits had greased a pole I was probably fortunate not to climb. Six years as Highland and Island's Convenor brought an end to my role in the long-running ADP campaign. Ultimate success in pulling off the thirty million honey pot for the Highlands and Islands went deservedly to Jimmy Forbes, the capable Nairnshire farmer who followed me into the Convenorship. Money rolled, yet surprisingly no statue appeared. So what? Think of the fun I gave Sunshine. Only the loitering dogs on Stornoway pier were disappointed.

# 9

# 'Youngish Chap, Cancer of the Throat . . .'

Dig for Victory spades rust away to immaculate lawns and ever-greens; roses arrive from the Garden Centre; Sunday suits and sermons on the evils of drink retreat before the whiz of an electric Flymo at 'chez nous' with a view, mostly, inwards. 'Darling, do you feel the velvet curtains really match our Chesterfield? Such a delightful home the Joneses have made, don't you think?' 'Yes, dear. Have you seen my gloves?' A house on the edge of the countryside, not too close, avoids the smell – nice for the dogs to wander. Church out, house in – it's the latest religion. Revelations by the Book of Barratt. Worship a new kitchen, step-down sauna. Mortgage and a yawn before the twenty-four-inch, wrap-around sound. Eat a product, artificially grown, at a falling price. 'Dig the garden? You're joking. Organic community allotment? What's that?'

'You see, Minister, we're a manufacturing or, should I say, service economy. We need cheap food, wherever it's grown. Helps our balance of payments, I told the Chancellor. Competition's tough, world market you know. Fact of life, dear boy.' Absolutely PM and, at this point in time, I have to say I'm quite relaxed about supplies, yes, absolutely relaxed. System seems robust, at this point in time. Nasty fall on Wall Street, Margaret. Oils are up though. How's your Burma shares?' 'Doing nicely, thank you. Food, yes, it's all right, useful stuff, but we really need oil to survive.'

Wise crofting neighbour of Breakachy farming days, Alec MacRae at Ardochy, of whom I wrote in *The Long Horizon*, was for many years a governor of the North of Scotland College of Agriculture in Aberdeen. This body of agri-boffins toiled with pipette and test tube under the astute chairmanship of the old Maitland Mackie. Milk and eggs supplied to the Granite City during the war helped build the foundations of an Aberdeenshire farming empire for the Mackie family. Eventually it turned up a knighthood and a noted brand of ice cream.

Old Maitland, the chairman, had a side to old 'Ardochy' and, on one occasion, took MacRae to visit the Mackie secret of power – a steading stacked to the roof with bags of nitrogen fertiliser. To a man steeped in traditional husbandry methods, who trod the soil with a reverence second only to his Free Church affiliations, 'Ardochy' viewed this pile of 'artificial' as a time bomb set in due course to blow farming apart though, through Highland deference, avoided such explosive comment to his host.

It happened that Maitland Mackie, later Sir Maitland, found me my first farming job as an Aberdeenshire 'orraloon' on Sandy Beattie's Gartly farm of Whitelums, just down the road from a cousin of the clan, John Mackie. An able chief, as befits a Mackie, John eventually found himself a chairmanship with the farming co-operative of North Eastern Farmers. Fifty years later, as a colleague of John on the Secretary of State's Hill Farming Committee, he reminded me, with dry Doric wit, of my shortcomings as an apprentice 'orraloon' at Whitelums.

One evening at a dicky-bow opera performance in Aberdeen, I was able to thank old Sir Maitland for his sound choice of my training ground. Many years passed and I sat alongside his equally energetic son, 'Boy Mackie', on the Farmers Union's General Purposes Committee. His views on dividing tomorrow's countryside between recreation and chemical food production I heard with horror matching that of old Alec MacRae viewing a stack of nitrogen bags. Maitland became the loquacious Chairman of the Board of Scottish Agricultural Colleges although, as Brian Pack, boss of the major auctioneering firm of Aberdeen and Northern Marts once remarked, 'Amongst all Maitland's ramblings there is always a nugget of truth – the trick is finding it.' In the rural world, using by-names was once a pastime. Maitland merited 'The Genius'.

Even in the early days as a committee member of Aberdeen's College of Agriculture Advisory panel, under the despotic Professor Raeburn, doubts were growing. I began to fall out of line with farmers and their college-promoted methods. Fresh from shepherding hills, chemical crop production and intensive livestock systems were not my style. I watched agricultural output spiral to new heights, as the worship of artificial nitrogen and the adoption of genetically selected plant species designed to mop up its applications grew uniform fields of ryegrass. It threatened my belief that the preservation of environmental stability depended upon biodiversity.

I had witnessed blanket afforestation provide a feast for the pine beauty moth and the aerial spraying designed to correct the stupidity of monoculture. Daily observation told of the crash of wild bird populations, skylark and corn bunting to name but two. The treating of cornfield flowers as weeds ensured that car windows were kept shut to keep out the stench of sprays. Only when clovers and daisies and little blue speedwells returned to the fields of Breakachy was I happy with the system of farming I'd begun to adopt. Nature Reserves and the Sites of Special Scientific Interest, proposed by desk-bound biologists, I regarded as political whitewash – oases where scientists fiddled whilst farmers with government support surrounded them with a decimated ecology.

In short, I believed in a holistic approach – a farming practice involving a high degree of symbiotic balance and society having regard for other life forms, as it subscribed to a vital understanding of the biological interdependence necessary for its survival. The day of organic interest was still to dawn and my outlandish views were smiled away by most colleagues on various committees. Back to cave and loincloth living? About as naïve as Rousseau's 'noble savage' turning down the offer of an electric blanket. I agreed – it takes more than a pipe dream to keep you warm.

As for sprays and pesticides, humble instinct, never mind the smell, warned me to avoid them in my farming operations if I valued my own and the family's health. My hunch was underlined at the time by a chance conversation with Edward Hulme, cousin and enzymologist at Cambridge University's Cavendish Laboratory. I spoke to him of the death of a Beauly farmworker. 'Youngish chap, cancer of the throat, worked for a local farmer, big in the tattie and veg business, supplied most of Inverness. Poor bloke, he did all the crop spraying each season.' 'Um, that figures,' came the biologist's observation, over forty years ago.

Agri-college approach to its subject in those years centred on a concept of the 'rustics' aiming at a viable farming entity based upon specialist interests. Mixed farming? Waste of time and motion. Pull those hens' necks, sell that handful of ewes. Fat cattle? Never paid. How about all arable? Sack the shepherd. Or try dairying. So many cows per acre, all yielding so many gallons. New milking parlour? Hay? Rubbish – never beat the weather. Ten tons of silage an acre – you'll need to double the size of the pit. Slurry? Yes, that's another thing – another pit. Don't fall in. Ha, ha.

The ideal agri-college system was always just out of reach but egged on by advisors assessing the required production one's land must achieve to supply a balance sheet healthy enough to maintain the bank overdraft without paying tax. Ever hopeful of reaching this relaxing goal, farmers grabbed chemicals, cheap energy and mechanical innovation with the same greed as any pressurised species seeking to survive and prosper. An abundance, and often excess, of food in developed countries resulted in long-run producer prices falling in real terms. Stacks of washed bags of water called potatoes would appear on supermarket shelves at suicide prices to the grower. Produce what the shopper demands or dive into the slurry pit. The western customer has become a spoilt brat.

Any possible residual contamination of the eatables, and perhaps its longer-term implications for the nation's health, which might result from agriculture's wide chemical and antibiotic usage, was largely ignored. The effect of repeated chemical applications on the living soil, its bacteria and earthworm populations? So what? The attitude towards wildlife? Summed up by the case against Mr Mole. Menace to modern machinery. Kill 'em with strychnine. An unpleasant poison, causing death by violent muscular spasms. Government grant, naturally, its regulation supply of the substance by a pen-pusher plotting mole heaps on a map.

Political wisdom had already stepped in. 'Submarines? Yes, damn close thing for the nation's food supply, PM. War's over of course, good effort on the whole – still we must boost home production, PM. Country should maintain ample food reserves, keep up nutritional values – orange juice, cod liver oil, all that sort of thing. Did kids a power of good. Health of the nation, you know.' 'Don't be foolish, Geoffrey, the nation must be free to choose what it eats and where it comes from. Anyway, children can't be molly-coddled any longer. We've already stopped school milk – wasteful and expensive. The war's over.'

Enter fast food, cheap outsourcing, big mark-ups, big adverts, big time, school bus, fat children with asthma. Back in the kitchen, staple foods gradually become cheaper to consumers, demanding a decreasing percentage of the household's disposable income. To-day, about one-tenth of the average family's expenditure goes on the dining table. 'Sorry I'm late, darling, traffic jam. Yes, accident, five cars, three dead. No time to cook. Shall we try that new, what's it called, The Taste Bud?'

Pop-star gimmicks to space stations, the edifice of modern society could totter on a food base of dubious long-term stability. The effects of planetary warming will kick in just as the burgeoning populations of the developing world hitch aboard the bus heading to consumerism. Meanwhile, the ingenious techniques of chemi-cally orientated food production pose as the only intelligent solution to feeding the masses. The possible costs in human health, and certainly to the environment, are well masked for those with the fullest bellies are in charge. Who could possibly dream of a Wimbledon without strawberries flown halfway round the world? Full trolleys at the checkout allow an increasing proportion of human activity to be environmentally deleterious. For the affluent west, playing on the planet is replacing the necessity of its respect.

Given the global advance of soil degradation and water pollution as a result of these intensive chemical systems, plus the eventual salination of many fertile coastal areas due to rising sea levels, will there still be space for growing enough to feed a probable doubling of our species to twelve billion mouths by the middle of this century? Admittedly, beyond then, a decline is forecast by falling birth rates – it may be hastened by other means.

So far we use only 1 per cent of the sun's energy falling on the planet; there's plenty spare, yet we choose to pump out and pollute our home base with carboniferous sunshine and nuclear radiation. The methods by which we use the sun's energy are man's most critical activity. 'Biodiversity is a major factor influencing environmental stability. We are modifying the environment at a rate outwith the genetic adaptive capacity of many species and ultimately perhaps our own.' Since I wrote that paragraph forty-five years ago, other major factors which may affect survival in our present form have been added, never mind the immediate situation whereby some nine hundred million of the world's poorest people currently depend on there being adequate levels of biodiversity for their day-to-day living.

Noted scientist and the UK's Astronomer Royal, Martin Rees, in an article in *New Scientist* writes, 'Society could be dealt shattering blows by the misapplication of technology that exists already,' for example lethal 'engineered' airborne viruses; powerful bio- and cyber-technologies; the escape of new pathogens into the environment. He highlights the work of ultra-energy science, the creation of 'quark matter' and the not-quite-zero chance of events with an almost infinite downside. He ends, 'Humanity is more at risk than at any earlier phase in its history.'

Shoot the gloom-and-doom messenger if you like, so far we've managed to feed the masses – Malthus needn't rub his hands just yet. Old Mother Hubbard trots to the cupboard and, while for some it's bare, for the bulk of us it overflows and supporters of chemically intensive agriculture insist more would face empty shelves if their systems were curtailed. Enthusiasts for chemical-free mixed-enterprise agriculture claim their approach can match the output of artificial systems and is also sustainable. Wisdom would investigate the validity of these assertions. Short-term expediency was ever the politicians' dilemma but, as the public sharpens its awareness of dangers ahead, those whom we voted into minding our best interests might choose to ignore commercial bandwagons for a change and commission detailed research into the biodynamics of organic farming and nitrogen fixation by bacterial action in root nodules.

The government is indifferent and keeps organic subsidy inducement to a minimum. No Ministry health promotion commercials advise eating organic produce. A carcinogen identified in cows' milk didn't hit the headlines probably because, at the time, we were too busy bombing Afghanistan. Organic farming is seen as the pastime of a few Luddites – harmless 'hayseeds' trying to market carrots with fly holes. 'Let those organic freaks be market-led' is current Whitehall thinking, 'Who knows, PM, all their bugs might kill 'em off. Organics – just a fad of the chattering classes, won't catch on. We in the Ministry must take a wider view.'

Should the 'green' view prove well-founded, it would behove the government, already expert in treating farmers to carrots and sticks, to take a positive attitude and guide agriculture in that direction. At present, an organic diet is more expensive than its mass-produced equivalent and tends to be eaten only by enthusiasts or those who choose to afford it. Demand for organic food is rising and a utopian hope would see interest in healthy eating spread across all income levels – at a price range to match. Both society and eco-stability could gain.

For the moment, the wealthy may soon prove the exception. We must all die of something and almost one in three humans will now develop some form of cancer in their lifetime. 'It's not an epidemic, is it doctor?' 'No, we don't say that. Do sit down. You see, the condition has multiple causes, complex biochemistry is involved, a faulty Ras protein remains switched on, forces a cell to keep dividing, and of course there's the vascular endothelial growth factor required to provide the tumour with a better blood supply, then viruses sometimes . . . ah, I know it's not easily grasped – best leave it to the specialists.' Superior smile, professionally reassuring. 'How's my old ticker doing, Doc?' 'Ah you're in luck, the latest polypill coming on the market is a mix of five well-tested drugs, plus a dash of vitamin, set to reduce heart attacks by 88 per cent, adds ten years on to the proverbial. Now take these tablets, three times a day, please, and make an appointment for next month. You haven't a policy with us? Please settle at the desk, thank you.' Trust in me.

Personal health handed over to private-enterprise witchdoctor dangling a stethoscope frees you from responsibility. Elixir pill, whoopee! Cancel that direct debit to the Health Centre and let's get back to the old lifestyle – you know, the one which produced a need for this wonder pill in the first place. 'Shall we walk, darling?' 'No, we'll take the car.' 'Does my bottom look big in this outfit, darling?' 'Er, not really – delightfully shapely, I'd say.' Oh the bliss of a good panty girdle.

A worldwide rise in non-infectious diseases – cardiovascular and respiratory; diabetes; cancers; and obesity-related conditions – accounts for 60 per cent of today's deaths. Unhealthy diets, smoking and sedentary lifestyles carry much of the blame. Refined sugar and excess salt are the basis of the junk-food industry's appeal. The party political donations by such monoliths as the sugar giants render it difficult for administrations to frame policies which challenge the corporate right to supply voters with the 'goodies' which company television adverts ensure they demand. Nor should the public's liberty to eat as it chooses be subject to legislation. Individual common sense should operate. Does it?

Few experts for the moment suggest any blame for these health statistics could attach to a chemical analysis of our diet. Have agricultural mono-culture and the subtle pollution of soil and water supplies a case to answer? Genetic predisposition is a known factor but the widespread use of antibiotics by the medical profession and intensive farming units are playing into the hands of virus in the wings by depleting gut bacteria, weakening immune systems and opening the pathways for viral invasion of our cellular DNA. We search for a cancer cure – are we looking through the wrong end of the microscope? Is not a critical look at farming practice and the food it produces, at a molecular level, overdue? Not all cancer victims smoke fags. Most eat and drink.

Quoting Martin Rees again, 'The long-term consequences of genetically modified plants and animals for human health and the ecological balance are manifestly uncertain: a calamitous outcome may seem improbable, but we can't say it's impossible.' My 'be friends with the environment' approach, on the analysis of bankers, politicians and economic pundits, mirrors the sage remark of ex-PM Thatcher: 'It's not cost-effective.' One unquestionable effect of this exciting attitude has been to squeeze farmers to less than 1 per cent of the country's population. An average age heading for sixty; working alone; his wife part-time at the checkout – oh my, it's

declining income; economic pressure; a son damned if he'll fall into
the trap; and an industry sliding steadily into the hands of major
commercial interests specialising in shareholder satisfaction and
heavy political leans.

Genetically modified seed, the march of Monsanto and already
an area of the globe the size of Spain is under GM crop – mostly in
the US, Canada and China. Is there a whiff of the blanket
afforestation principle? And, wait for it, cloned high-production
livestock; fields full of Daisy the dairy cow; identical hens by the
billion; robotically handled – there's even a microchip to take the
sweat out of the cloning trick. It's likely to be more than morning
dampness on the hayfield for an 'old timer' wishing he had the
horses back. The pounding hooves of progress may be the best way
to elevate the drudgery of growing food. Allow more time for the
good things in life – holidays, playing on the internet, becoming a
pop star, doing nothing in particular. Is it bikini beaches or a cliff?

As for the 'townee' tending his window box – millions to a city
and not an acre of ground amongst them – will they become
dependent souls asleep on the cushion of multinational magnanimity? International corporations strive to control the two ultimate
essentials – food and water. Add in the patenting of staple seed
genes, the human genome and many bacterial DNA sequences, and
the plot thickens. The control of food, air, outer space and real
estate on Mars used to come under science fiction.

◆

Back in the plodding days, before current upheavals, the agricultural colleges had their own jobs and organisations to protect. One
measure of their success was amplified by their holding on in the
face of the decimation of farming's workforce. Their advocacy of
intensive methods, when coupled with succeeding governments
thirled to cheap food imports, aided the erosion of farm-gate prices.
The day of 'hayseeds' leaning on a fence to watch the cows for a
moment became 'not cost-effective'. Flitting vans pulled into council flats. Ruddy faces found jobs tending the gardens of village
incomers, occupying the farm cottages and steadings the rustics had
just vacated. Escape routes opened into the countryside for those
who made good in trade, commerce and bureaucracy.

City affluence and, in some cases, the swelling ranks of pen-pushers running agriculture from a computer brought a fresh culture to the village. Farms within commuting range of the 'office' made building space available for architectural extravagances and 'Flymo' lawns. Five-day weeks, two cars and daughter's pony jumps in the fenced-off paddock. The incoming Community Councillors growled about wandering sheep, cattle dung defacing the road and talked of buying the local woodlands for amenity. Heaps of horse droppings were splattered without comment as the local agricultural show became more of a gymkhana.

Farmworkers were soon followed down the road by the smaller farmer. Government schemes of the sixties aimed at stemming the flow from the family, ten cows, two hundred ewes and Fergie tractor units, gave way to the Farm Amalgamation grants. Farmers gobbled their neighbours' ground. Untailored taxpayer subsidies to agriculture ended up benefiting the larger units. The Farm Manager, BSc Agric., running a city-financed estate from maps on the wall in an air-conditioned office is the latest trend. And one shouldn't forget the jolly band of bureaucrats bent on telling the remaining few farmers what to do. More importantly, coming in twos checking any shortcomings. 'Dry day, we'll just nip out without warning and do a spot inspection. I see Thomson has the red cross on the top of his file – he'll do.'

Perhaps the most overlooked, yet simply stated, social change to affect society, mentally and physically, in the past thousand years is a move away from the critical discipline inflicted on family life by the responsibility of producing its own food. My grandmother spoke of childhood hours and days spent gathering stones, following the corn scythe or as a mobile scarecrow. No pay given nor expected and no option. A bent back and five acres plus the chance of an empty barn succumbed before the 'enclosure' of common land in England and the abolition of the 'runrig' system in Scotland. Today, an industrially developed society, gradually removed from the land, pay-packet-dependent for its number one staying alive item, doesn't feel cornered or uneasy and doesn't apply too much 'do it' discipline to its children.

Until a hundred years ago, many families had some connection rooted in the land, understood something of granddad's warning to 'beware of taking more out of the ground than you put in'. A pair of hands was for other than a laptop and mobile phone – they could handle a plough; kill and skin a sheep; knock in a nail. Old-fashioned independence, self-reliance and the snag of going hungry on occasions, required a practical approach to daily living. Common sense grafted on to hand-me-down experience, sound judgements on soil and stock, an eye for the best and easiest approach to contingencies. Common sense rarely sits at a computer – it doesn't have to. Food is something which appears – you don't need to know about it, just find the way to your mouth. Phone for a takeaway and let out another notch on the belt.

The rapid breakdown of a homogenous rural structure has led to a widening gap in sympathy and understanding between the nouveau country addicts of 'It's my playground' and a dwindling band of 'flat caps' driven to ground by economic stricture, without a more obvious bolt-hole than supplying the urban populace with a means of passing their leisure time. Disneyland apart, old boy, a jag of hedonism is no bad doctrine but some of today's versions involve the wildest trips into natural domains. White-water rafting is mild by comparison to some antics. Wildlife is on the run from more than the shooting fraternity, with fewer corners left for shelter. Hedgehog lovers may squeak in protest, birdie-folk pile seed outside the kitchen window. Innovative thrills and spills – playtime on the planet is one colossal new industry.

Can a natural environment sustain the expanding whims of urban 'playtime', the ubiquitous seep of industrial complexes, more homes occupied by fewer people per house, the excesses of an extractive, 'toss it in the waste bin' civilisation? Tourism, concrete dough and six-lane jams have the loudest shout on land use. Can we continue to produce sufficient food by anything other than emergent technologies? Is there space enough to return to sustainable farming methods? Is a return to organic methods just pushing dung uphill?

Space isn't the problem – there's still plenty to turn over to less intensive methods. Under the folly of modern farming, a tenth of this country's arable land is set aside from production, a sizeable area is supported by subsidy payments and most of the remainder cropped by piling on fertiliser and pesticides. Nobody suggests returning to a pig rooting in the midden and hens on the doorstep but the will to devote more research and incentive towards a more sanely balanced approach seems beyond the common sense of politicians and their lily-white-handed advisors.

Unfortunately the problem is vastly wider. Extinction rates of planetary species are spiralling to heights not known since the dinosaurs waved to an incoming asteroid. Global warming, genetic tinkering at all levels, a new generation of mini-nukes on the drawing-board, ideologies locked on to outdated beliefs but switched on to the latest means of mass destruction. With philistines leading the world's superpowers – say no more – the race is on. Will we wake before the nest gets too dirty or drown in our own defecation? In days when the village headman was an idiot only his tribesmen fell into the cesspit. Today it's a global village. And a wise headman? Nowhere in sight.

Still, for the man on the Clapham omnibus, there have been incredible payoffs. Scientific endeavour has seen off many killer pandemic diseases and given us the means by which lifespan is extended and leisure enhanced. We are now aware of the dangers of a self-indulgent lifestyle, widespread obesity, children diabetic at four, longer queues at the surgery and so on. Specialists look up our social navel – eat less fat, do more exercise, don't drink more booze than two units per day. Yet more people are becoming dependent for health, food and water on a corporate-controlled 'democracy' and scientific research is far from immune from its influence.

Jean-Jacques Rousseau, who finally went insane, touted the back-to-nature, 'noble savage' ideal. Few imagine such a state of pristine, worry-free 'you Jane, me Tarzan, we take clothes off; eat banana' idyll ever existed outside Pinewood Studios, but recent Norwegian studies do find a positive correlation between stress levels and certain types of cancer. Instinctively, many hark for a less complex life – a longing for fresh air and a blink of sun hides behind the slackened tie of the office conscript taking his lunchtime sandwich in the park. Modern life doesn't stack that way – it builds complexity and consumerism out of the widening cost-ratio between the food we need and the newest, see-through phone we don't. A need creates a touch of worry if you haven't got the very latest gadget. But it side-steps the fact that, given a decent roof, good food and health, happiness is a simple fraction – expectation divided by realisation.

Sadly for the world's poorest farmers in Africa and Asia, the much-vaunted Green Revolution of the 1950s has ensured they are now even poorer. Thus finds a recent report by Robert Evenson of Yale University to the Consultative Group on International Agricultural Research. New rice and grain varieties, plus fertilisers and sprays, boosted yields and created gluts so that prices fell and only farmers who could afford to buy next season's seed stayed in business. A damning conclusion states, 'Some farmers experienced real losses from the Green Revolution.' Back in the UK, our college advisors called this theme 'achieving a viable unit'.

Moreover, the world's poorest 5 per cent lost a quarter of their income between 1988 and 1993 whilst, in the same period, incomes for the wealthiest 5 per cent grew by 12 per cent – perhaps not such an obvious trend in Britain, but a globally accelerating division between two extremes. The connecting middle class is fast disappearing. The developing world, without industry, robbed of oil and mineral wealth, struggles to become a food exporter and its poor are egged on to buy the baubles paraded by wealthy nations – the very trinkets and non-essential trash which create cash flow into Swiss Banks. Not a recipe for social stability.

Empires used to be confined to portions of the globe; the Romans stuck mainly to Europe, the Brits, on the back of the African slave trade, did better. As far back as 1932, Aldous Huxley, in *Brave New World*, suggested applied science could keep a lid on the behaviour of the 'plebs'. Will the global village headman manage to hold off the Huns? The means by which one section of world society and its mantra seek to control opposing divisions will move from the self-defeating, gun-slinging crudeness of atomic warfare to more subtle applications – taser guns and behaviour-bending biotechnology, for starters.

Turn society upside down, inside out, take any quantum leap you will, the first universal principle, be it galaxies in space, children in a ghetto or politicians on a soap box, is survival. Success in the survival game, as B. F. Skinner, the US behavioural psychologist, pointed out, is speed of learned response – good old punishment and reward. His laboratory rats soon picked up the idea of pressing a lever for the pleasure of food. Rate of change is the critical factor – our ability to adapt in time is survival.

Skinner went on to point out, 'Society sure has got its foot mighty hard on the good time lever right now, an' those producing food sure ain't getting much reward. Darn it, they're right at the bottom of life's lil' old pile. In the old days, pardner, when the going cut up, like real rough, all yer needed to call the survival dice was a good woman, five acres an' a rifle.' Future survival systems may be rather more cunning, though possibly less fun for the masses.

Such prognostic debate is a far cry from being part of any college curriculum and farmers, who are not so inclined, require to believe in old-fashioned common sense. In Aberdeen's agricultural cloisters, they did at least hang a memorable 'Goodbye to Farming' painting on the boardroom wall. A gift from the late Lord Glentanner, it depicted a 'nicky-tammed' ploughman and a pair of arch-necked Clydesdales ploughing harvest stubbles under a monster cumulus sky which hinted at more than passing showers. Although I worked a pair of horses in my Aberdeenshire 'orraloon' days, years later, I did decline the offer of a College Governorship. I trust the painting hangs on.

## 10

# 'The Finest Little Farm in All the Highlands'

Pander to a sweet tooth, build a factory in Liverpool, bake imported flour along with Caribbean sugar, add whatever else it takes and, bingo, you get Crawfords Biscuits and cash. Amalgamate your company with that of a Morayshire baker and the result? United Biscuits, a Forres Chairman, Sir Hector Laing, the friendship of Prime Minister Thatcher and lots of cash. Mind you, all this company extravaganza was before I met Archie Crawford, the shareholding biscuit director from Beatledom responsible for arranging the UB's deliveries of one of our nation's favourite addictions.

Tucked deep amongst Surrey's exclusive foliage, its rolling countryside, canopied lanes and leafy bank accounts was an 'Anne Hathaway' home of house martin, eave and creeper-covered stonework. I was collected from Heathrow and driven to this stockbroker-style retreat by Martha, there to meet 'hubby' Archie, the placer of ginger nuts beside your morning coffee. An accountant to trade, now a mildly aspiring farmer, Archie was a grandson of Crawford the Liverpool baker with the bright idea. A sign 'Rare Breed Station number 69' on the steading corner bolstered first impressions and, given the thatched Merry England tenor of the villages we passed through, I half expected to find a figure in doublet, pantaloons and clogs prancing round a maypole. Instead Archie drove up. Dark curly-haired and elegantly good-looking, he leaned an elbow in film-star fashion out of the largest four-by-four jeep I'd ever seen.

Over a cordial handshake my eye was drawn to a Jersey cow standing on top of a midden of dung staring intently through an open lead-lighted window which looked out on a cobbled courtyard. I could see this rarity lark extended beyond orange pigs, exotic hens and the tiny Dexter cattle which appeared to roam the Crawfords' estancia. My engaging hosts were indeed hatching a plot, a 'get away from it all' exit from stiff shirts and peck-order parties. The pretensions of England's pin-stripped commuter belt had them planning, if not quite to don boiler suits, at least to sport brogues and green wellies.

The bottle of twelve-year-old Highland Park which I produced accelerated our discussions in an agreeable direction. During lunch, the aspirants expanded on their dreams of a red deer farm some-where in the Highlands. Life in shiredom was claustrophobic and boring. That I could believe – neither of them fitted the image of 'strap hanging', soft handed, office wallflowers. The mooing of a Jersey cow tended to underline my superlatives on the merits of Inverness-shire as the Mecca for seekers of the bucolic idyll. Her face had filled the open kitchen window most of lunch. More moos. One of Martha's clients arrived for her daily lesson in hand milking. After years of kicks and three-legged stools, I'd discovered pressing bottle tops to be safer, though less romantic, than pulling teats. It now appeared fashionable with those who yearned for the feeling and smell of nature. 'Tie your cow's tail to her leg,' I advised, 'saves her swishing *au natural* round your neck. And keep your knee between her kicking weaponry and the pail,' I added. 'They generally let fly in more ways than one when the pail's full.' A lack of smile suggested my tips were not in Martha's teaching manual.

Archie and I warmed their dream of the Highlands and our nether quarters between another 'clinky, clink' and a log fire which blazed up the lum of a commodious inglenook. Yes, I had a farm, with house, which could get them started and, yes, I might consider selling. We talked. Conviviality surrounded the dark refectory table. Affluence oozed from Jacobean corner-pieces, comfort lolled in

chintzy armchairs. Cosiness dozed under oaken beams which could
support a life of genteel ease and idleness. I pictured kitchen hooks
hung with cured ham, onion strings and dried herbs, the smell of
new-made treacle cake awaiting lantern swinging carol singers on a
snow-bound doorstep. Long winter nights, warm slippers, a book, a
dram. *Wind in the Willows* and the hibernating snores of Badger's
snug parlour.

I contrasted this with the house which I had in mind for
augmenting the Crawford dream, the one to which Betty and I
had flitted twenty years before when beginning our farming career.
Rat holes round the skirting boards, no electricity or sanitation,
double-burner Calor gas on a chair, water from a well down the
yard, two young children and half a mile of steep track. Snowed up
every winter, but a superb view over the Braes of Kilmorack, our
neighbours' crofting efforts, Lord Lovat's estate and Ord Hill above
the Beauly Firth. In short, a testing ground for bio-stamina, thermal
underwear and the elasticity of an unwary bank account. I waved
aside any talk of terms for it was, I assured them with a suitably
moistened eye, 'the finest little farm in all the Highlands'.

A follow-up letter underlined my glowing assessment. Solicitors
acted with unaccustomed alacrity. By November the deer-farming
pioneers were into their first taste of well water and driving snow
sizzling on Tilley lamps. The Crawfords and their four boys rose to
the challenge both physically and financially, hauling caravan,
chattels and load after load of red deer, Martha at the wheel, up
the eight hundred miles from southern England to their castle in the
air. Idyllic, though perhaps a tad primitive, a hefty application of
cash performed a dramatic transformation. Old Cluanie house went
into shock, the dilapidated steading became a slaughter house-cum-
shop for the venison trade, six-foot deer fencing criss-crossed the
land and even the torturous road was tamed, all by grateful local
lads whom I pointed in their direction.

Such was the Crawford enthusiasm for Highland life that, by
another twelve months, they bought, lock, stock and barrel, all our
farming enterprise. Goodbye to a farming lifestyle into which Betty,
the children and I had invested eighteen years of happy hard work
and government subsidy. Miles of fences tight and new, ditching
and tile, each field drained and a swinging gate. Concrete yards,

swept and tidy, beat winter mud. We built barns, silage pits, a sheep fank, loading bank, crush and cattle pens. Fifty head of pedigree Aberdeen Angus cows grazed flower and clover swards or organic grassland. Our bees filled their garden hives, honey all round. On the 30th of November 1979, my forty-sixth birthday, crumbs fell from a United Biscuits barrel – an appreciable sum of money changed hands and the Crawfords owned Tighnaleac of Breakachy.

The hardiness of the newcomers was equalled by their resources. Six hundred freshly purchased hinds soon took to checking the march fence on Breakachy hill. I warned Archie that here and there its wires were a fraction droopy. Copying the example of Hugh MacKenzie, my predecessor, repair work had never been a priority. As a tenant, prior to ownership, a discreet disposal of the resulting crop of incursive stags had neatly equalled my Breakachy rent. In law, deer belong to the owner of the ground upon which they stand, and jestingly I hinted that come the first blizzard the Crawfords' newly acquired property would fill with Lovat Estate deer seeking shelter. A quick fix of the fence, all the animals they needed. Legal – just the price of the wire. Craftier arrangements had been a feature of deer forests in times past.

Archie frowned. No, no Highland sleight-of-hand. Quite right, I soothed. Come spring the situation reversed. A fair proportion of Surrey-bred confines at £300 a head sniffed the winds of freedom. Skyline bound, they were spotted by the Beaufort keepers romping over Lovat land with Martha and a pail of nuts hastening in pursuit. Tame, expensive? My, my, the Estate promptly made the legal position plain – no enticing deer off our land, thank you. Undaunted by set-back, driven by dreams, Archie and Martha set about arranging the Breakachy Dutch barn for the first auction sale of red deer ever to be held in Scotland. Crawford entrepreneurial skills were by no means confined to baking biscuits.

Helping to this end was my last effort. For their deer sale, I built straw bales into tiered seating within the Dutch barn. The sides of bull pens were heightened to shield the hinds from bobbing human heads. A drafting race constructed down the centre passage would guide the animals gently into a sale ring. All was ready. A herd of unsuspecting deer corralled in the steading munched hay. Land Rovers bounced up a supply of plus-foured keepers; Volvo estates brought the tweedies and flocks of 'darlings' in headsquares and green Barbour outfits. Wicker baskets and wine appeared on tailgates. A herd of Scotland's finest red-deer fraternity munched salmon pâté sandwiches.

Into the yard blazed a Bentley open-top tourer and out jumped my sparring partner of after-sale jousts behind the 'green door' of Perth Auction Mart, Macdonald Fraser's special effects man, Roley Fraser. I hastened him into the 'side room' to limber up his auctioneering elbow. At one o'clock on the dot, his hammer fell. The first auctioned hind in Scotland was sold.

The sale erupted in applause. The tin roof rang. Enthusiastic bidders leaned, the seating bulged. Would it jettison the top row of headsquares and net tights into the ring? Kicking, squealing, up on their hind legs, clawing the rails, punching the air, the deer panicked, as did Archie, but refrained from clawing the pen. Martha kept cool. Squeaking deer fought to stay out of the ring, fought to stay in. Eyes jumped out of sockets, tails shot up, pellets flew. Bedlam ruled – egged on by waving catalogues and Roley's masterly equilibrium on a straw rostrum.

A triumph for balance, if not for price, so voted those who repaired to the 'side room' after the sale. Martha beamed at Roley. Archie checked the accounts. The beginning of the Crawfords' Highland obsession was carried on a tide of success. Fun to ride the flood. Awaken to the ebb? Today, Archie has two steel hips and a young wife; Martha farms alpaca in Chile; and the boys, hardened off on the heights of a hill farm, are engaged in various international businesses. Biscuits behind them, they remain a pioneering family of much enterprise and charm.

◆

My only achievement in the Farmer's Union, whilst still farming Breakachy, that I deemed of any consequence was the setting up of a Land Use and Environmental Committee. Late afternoon flicked slats of sunlight over snoring delegates. I made the case quietly, no hell-fire organic preaching. Much mischief has been done, I opined; from *Bambi* to *Watership Down*, public sympathy now lay with birds, butterflies and all things furry, certainly not with the horrid 'run rabbit run' farmers. No more screaming and kicking against banning the gin trap, Union members must lead the way, engage a tame ecologist, meet the 'green wellies' over a pint of real ale and tell the 'woolly hats and sandals' that, with government assistance, all our ecological sins could be absolved.

Repent, I told them. No more ripping up hedges, draining bogs and spraying daisies. Stop poisoning the postie's bees. Make friends with the badger that's undermining the top field. A friendlier reception at the 'local' could be ours if only we took to creating bits of 'birdie' wilderness round our fields and, anyway, the Department would get round to the idea before too long, once their political masters cottoned on to an urban vote catcher. To Scott's amazement, the motion passed without debate, a feat he attributed to the delegates' need to consider the plight of farming in more congenial surroundings.

Feeling pleased with this minor victory, after dinner that night I joined in that breath of animation wont to waft over the 'sons of toil' when freed from the care of their loved ones. The name of our elegant hydro accommodation passes memory but the day's success justified a tune on the 'box'. Fingers, notes and tempo slightly at variance, tunes blasted out until, tired by emotion, the performer drifted up to bed. At some point, an unlocked door let in a crowd of what must be described as 'rugby types' from the Black Isle. They pulled the accordionist upright, strapped on the 'box' and led him back to the spacious lounge. Shouts of 'Scotland the Buff' brought salvos of chords and wild applause. A Nairnshire dairy farmer, Geordie Phillip, praised me at breakfast. 'What a musician, Thomson! You put a swing in the tunes with more than your toes.'

All that a-swinging thirty years ago. Not being trusted as a true fertiliser bag farmer or in case any of my bizarre ideas got out of hand, the convenership of this new committee landed on John Hay, a major potato grower of the most modern techniques from the Perthshire direction. John, an amiable man of polished intellect, smart suits and a theatrical voice, drove to meetings in an immensely valuable vintage Bentley. The committee, seen as a drain on the Union's dwindling funds, lasted two years and was abolished. Man the ramparts, farmers were fighting a rearguard action and the war chest was running low.

Disillusionment set in. Certainly the membership at large

considered any airing of this environmental nonsense, especially in public, only tempted the anti-farming lobby to put in the 'green wellie' boot. Beyond stimulating such possibilities, a degree of frolicking on a Union ticket had become a shade public. Sunshine, quoting his favourite poet, William McGonagall, decided his organisation needed more 'tone' and less buffoonery on the part of one of its office bearers. Farming politics were not for personal entertainment. Curtains were coming down.

John Cameron, tolerant friend, also headed towards the end of his second term in office. Always popular, plain speaking, wily and able, never pompous and ever the ordinary farmer's man, his last presidential stunt was to arrange for the gift of a horse-cart full of farm produce to be trailed through Glasgow streets en route to an old folks' home. Whether to emphasise deprivation in the diet of the elderly or the give-away price of farm produce seemed unclear. No matter, the parade was to leave, ten sharp, from the West End, grand piano in the lounge, Grosvenor Hotel, where 'us lads' had spent a night coping with the misfortune of falling returns.

We mustered down in the backyard next morning to find a Clydesdale nag with sunken eyes and brown teeth straining at an immense load of swedes and cabbage piled pyramid style on a cart with flat tyres. Cameron grabbed the head collar. Soon eyes were a-popping and a tail alifting with staccato bursts of energy – the horse's, not our President's, I must emphasise. The procession moved westward in fits and starts. We pushed from behind, striving to avoid the RSPCA, cameras and salvos from loitering urchins provided by way of a trail of fallen cabbage.

John stood down, donned his train-driver's cap and went to shovel coal into the firebox of his pet steam loco – excellent limbering up for his Chairmanship of ScotRail. His two vice-presidents fought for the honour of stoking the farmer's cause: George Anderson, amusing if a touch droll, every acre a farmer, his skill and a spacious farm outside Laurencekirk breeding top Simmental cattle; and Iain Grant, son of a noted Aberdeen Angus breeder at The Thorn near Alyth. Handsome, debonair, polished speaker and reluctant raspberry picker, Iain's eloquence, well-cut suits and a commanding presence pulled the votes. He became an imposing President and, even better, good company after hours.

As a last fling, I stood for Union Vice-President, a move driven by a combination of vanity and a desire to further a hidden environmental agenda. The rank and file weren't fooled. After a rollicking pre-election night in the Pitlochry Hydro which ended in a bedroom-chair-under-the-doorknob tussle with Inverness-shire's Colin Hugh, his rugby-playing pals, some feline screams and a lacerated face, I got three votes – my own and two chaps who'd misplaced their specs.

# 11

# Engulfed by Experts

Well, as they say, when one door closes, another one traps your fingers. To the surprise of more than myself, courtesy of a whisper from Sunshine in the halls of power, I clambered onstage again at Scotland's prestigious Countryside Commission. It crossed my mind, 'Did the dear boy harbour a grudge towards this harmless organisation?'

This well-meaning band of mildly influential people, ranging from uni profs and the Glasgow Provost to trade union officials and the ex-boss of Scotland's biggest fertiliser company, would sound off on matters rural under the beady eye of a small power-packed chairwoman, Jean Balfour. Once a month, after sifting through a host of earnest applications, we voted modest dollops of taxpayer cash to enable the general public to enjoy hands-on visitor centres with lavatories and wooden walkways tacked over with wire netting to stop them slipping into bogs. Any connivance to hasten the civilising of Scotland's grandeur and encourage trippers not to pass a craft shop or stray fifty yards from their cars was on.

The Commission's comfortable, Virginia-creepered HQ outside Perth relaxed amongst the shady parklands of Battleby Estate. I was shown around office with map-papered walls by Tom Huxley, a close relation of the *Brave New World* author, Aldous Huxley. Brains are far from a random gift and Tom displayed monumental intelligence tinged with a smattering of intellectual arrogance. Soon after my arrival, the reign of Jean B. gave way to that of Sir David Nixon, a highly professional chairman who cut through 'waffle' quicker than a nifty ghillie can gaff a ten-pounder. His company happened to buy the salmon fishing on the Ross-shire River Conon for a rumoured ninety thousand. In spite of this extravagance, he seemed to enjoy poaching yarns – perhaps a reason for his tolerant attitude towards an ex-shepherd.

Given a couple of years, the migratory urge for a more progressive appointment came over Sir David. He left us to chair the Confederation of British Industry and thence to prop his feet on the desk of Clydesdale Bank. At David's farewell dinner, I sat beside Commission Secretary, Bill Prior, and passed the meal regaling him with the story of the embarrassing theft of Winnie Ewing's presentation goblet at our outlandish Strasbourg luncheon. 'How awful,' he remarked. To my delight Bill considered the debacle with the pained expression of a dedicated official, for I'd noted a package lying below his chair. 'See that parcel,' I spoke to the waiter out of the corner of my mouth, 'move it quietly under the chair on the other side of me and help yourself to a double.'

Sir David rose at coffee and liqueurs, sad his stay amongst such an enlightened bunch had been so short. We were destined to do great things for Scotland's countryside – litter bins in every parking glade, signposts to the latrines. He wished us success and sat down to well-deserved applause. Up stood our incoming boss, Roger Carr, factor to Willie, Lord Mansfield. David's shoes would be difficult to fill – much had been achieved during his term of office; we would continue the good work, inspired by his departing leadership. 'And now, Sir David, as a token of our esteem . . .' Roger nodded across to Bill. Hand gropes under chair. Nothing. Down on his knees. Nothing. Poor Bill. Minutes pass. Silence. Roger flushes scarlet. I bent. 'Is this what you're looking for, Bill?' 'Thank you,' he snarled. It turned out to be a Caithness glass goblet engraved with gratuitous appreciation and a leaping salmon. 'That one nearly got away.' The look on his face suggested Bill wasn't a fisherman.

Roger Carr led us on many entertaining junkets monitoring the countryside environs. A fine chap, he truly had the interests of the common man at heart – not an area in which to display sympathy for anyone wishing preferment. Under his leadership, we cheerfully opened visitor centres which inflicted scars on the landscape, gazed at wall charts of birds which our clientele was helping towards demise, lunched at ski-slope restaurants, admired their artificial 'runs', dined at functions for the opening of country parks and, on one occasion, a charabanc edged a load of us along the single-track road to Achiltibuie and into the spellbinding territory of farthest Wester Ross.

Strolling down a sunshine morning with three collie dogs came Kenny 'The Manager', combined flockmaster and West Coast timekeeper. At his Ullapool wedding, the church was full. We all waited. Half an hour passed. The head-swivelling congregation by this time included Margaret his bride. This reversal of ceremonial etiquette resulted from Kenny, full regalia down to white heather buttonhole, delaying at the police station to fill up his regulation sheep dipping papers. Wedding day apart, 'The Manager' spotted me in the front seat of the Commission bus and flagged us down. Our conversation – he mixed Gaelic and English – began with lambing disasters and prospects for the clipping season. His dogs, sensing an interlude in their shepherding duties, climbed aboard, tail wagging and licking. Commissioners, who preferred country living through a window, moved aside. A collie's welcome could involve leg lifting.

By contrast to this pastoral idyll, we journeyed, professors, scientists, pen-pushers and me, around Glasgow. The gardens of Bearsden sloped to the sun, gardeners bent over rose beds, all was a-glitter, two coats of blue paint every third year. The Joneses were alive and well. Downhill took us into the land of twenty flights up and battery living. Fifteen up, a pair of elbows on a window ledge propped an empty face gazing across five hundred acres of green belt. 'Why not turn an area into allotments? Give the folks something to take a pride in – a small rent, a gardening society, self-regulating and prize marrows,' I pressed a City Planning Officer. 'You must be joking – they winna even keep a lobby tidy!'

The era of fish farming dawned. Each month a batch of applications to take up the rental of seabed rights from the Crown Commission was attached to our agenda. In the main, applicants were multinational interests. Prospective sites began to dot the western seaboard of the Highlands like spots of fungal infection on a caged salmon. Our Commission applied the rubber stamp – each one passed, most without comment, apart from the vociferous exception I took each month. Two grounds merited dissension: the opportunity for any locally based enterprise was being snapped from below the nose of crofters whose land bordered the sea lochs of proposed development; and, secondly, I regarded salmon farming as yet another environmental rip-off with major pollution implications for both wild fish stocks and other forms of marine life. My objections failed to reach the minutes.

Furthermore, as an admirer of the writings of naturalist, Seton Gordon, whose book *The Charm of the Hills* gives an eloquent account of the diversity of plant and wildlife which once favoured the Cairngorm plateau, I doubted if an infusion of 'toorie bonnets' and clumping boots would enhance the delicate balance of this fragile area. The skiing fraternity were not to my taste. The encroachment of tow wire hoists clanking uphill to reach the aroma of a burger and chips café when passed off as environmentally sympathetic seemed to me an overstatement. A sanctuary of life forms unique to Scotland was being swept under the avalanche of leisure.

Salmon or skis, neither pose was popular and seen frankly as reactionary prejudice. The latter not upholding the spirit of a government body whose aim lay in assisting a populace, disinherited by choice or otherwise from a countryside legacy, to enjoy something of its amenity. The views I peddled did reflect a selfish, insular era and the Commission's attitude was more enlightened. Anyway, a female official from Scottish Office sat in on our meetings, taking notes in a furtive manner. A second three years as Commissioner ended with a letter of thanks and a pleasing watercolour painting of Battleby House.

So to a seat on the BBC Rural Affairs Committee, swish lunches at their Glasgow HQ and more copybook blots. After repeated TV showings of a dairy cow slipping horribly on a concrete yard when infected with the so-called 'mad cow' disease, I accused the Corporation's news desk of presenting a vegetarian bias and implied that, at every opportunity, they landed the health and hygiene record of the red meat industry on the cutting block of adverse crit. 'Specialists' in avoiding bacteria, I claimed, filled the screen with dire warnings and faces of deathly test-tube pallor. Pot-bellied professors in need of a ten ounce sirloin steak and fresh air pontificated on healthy diets and exercise. The old adage of 'a little clean dirt keeps you healthy' swilled down the sink. Any suggestion that a wide spectrum of gut bacteria enhanced the immune system was met with vigorous hand scrubbing. As a toiler at the dung heap and breeder of Angus bulls, a bellow of disapproval seemed justified. The chairperson thought a ring in the nose might steady her meetings. Goodbye to fine wine and media cronies. I was running out of committees.

By now, I was down to the Scottish Department of Agriculture's Secretary of State, Hill Farming Advisory Committee. For many years, it guaranteed first-class fun around a table of witty colleagues. Border Sheep Barons, Tom and Billy Elliot, George Murray, the lady charmer from Rogart in Sutherland, two ex-Farmers' Union Presidents, the old buddies, Messrs Cameron and Ross, and, from my Aberdeenshire 'orraloon' days, John Mackie of Gartly. To add scientific weight they threw in the boss of the MacAulay Land Use Research Institute, precise Prof Jeff Maxwell and honest Jim Seaton, the 'I despair of farming's future' College Advisor from Inverness. Latterly the Sex Discrimination Act brought in two female members which cleaned up Tom Elliot's after-dinner jokes, to a degree.

October meetings involved death moans over the government's mishandling of farming affairs. We were all doomed – sheep prices slumping, wool barely worth a-sharpening the shears. Not that impending disaster showed in the quality of Billy Elliot's Cheviot Tweed tailoring, but then he'd been Chairman of the Wool Marketing Board since the day it opened. Calves were barely worth hauling to the mart. Fat cattle? Butchers were all vultures – we wouldn't bother feeding the public if it wasn't for the bank overdraft. A catalogue of tribulations ending in a tear-jerking plea from George Murray for Department support at the Lairg Ram Sales, an event at which, by a stroke of coincidence, his tups happened to feature.

At each meeting, my chief entertainment lay in contradicting

John Cameron and propounding the merits of organic food production – it irked both him and the committee no end. A certain
level of jocularity and a measure of irreverence towards our
bureaucratic masters might be tempered a touch when the current
Secretary of State felt obliged to show up for a grilling. The most
obvious benefit of such in-depth 'face-to-faces' we observed to be a
vastly improved lunch with less orange juice.

Spring pilgrimages into the 'sticks' to see how the 'ferma mannies'
were doing merited three days, five-star digs, an executive coach
and wellies. Over the years, no corner of our nation was left
unscathed, no issue safe from discussion. Beyond imparting considered opinions to the range of high-flying officials who accompanied our 'progress', there were humble advantages. On one
venture, I picked out a shapely Angus bull from Orcadian Colin
Davidson of Skaill whilst committee members wandered away to
ponder the tillage practices of the Bronze Age settlers of nearby
Skara Brae. A certain languor was detected amongst committee
members, perhaps because of the sea air or our late-night 'discussions'. Colin dispensed a liberal pick-me-up of Highland Park and an
Orcadian knees-up was only avoided because of our sense of duty.

Latterly our chairman, private secretary to his nibs, the Secretary
of State, was another of the Cameron tribe – Tony this time. A fine
lad, shy and sharp-faced, he has since moved to the post of boss of
Scottish jails. Not his exact title and there is no reason to enquire
unless a spell in the 'slammer' threatens. However, I'd known TC,
as we called him, since a night on a Brussels jaunt when we pestered
the pianist of our swanky hotel to pack up Eric Satie and give us
'The Dashing White Sergeant'. With such memories under wraps,
Tony guided the committee's exhaustive investigations and each
evening, after dampening the day's dust, he held council as we
reviewed the salient points of our forced march.

So it transpired, on a day of face-colouring sunshine, that the
winged Isle of Skye turned its back on winter's sadness and
welcomed the month of May with the greenness of sweet grazings
on the castellated heights of the Trotternish Ridge. From basalt-
columned Flodigarry Island, tucked under weathered cliffs, the
waters of the Sound of Raasay carried speckled blueness beyond
the rock-naked Isle of Rona to a placid Minch on which a pair of

circling lobster boats lifted their creels. Mainland hills ran north in a perspective that faded into the first of summer's haze. Scenery stretched in breath-catching splendour.

Equally stretched, in breath-catching gulps rather than splendour, was a column of committee members toiling upwards, wiping foreheads and wafting midges amidst the lava flow landscape. We were there to inspect the degree to which erosion endangered the stability of the magnificent Trotternish Ridge. Excessive tramping, it was thought, might topple The Old Man of Storr, a pillared rock extrusion of remarkable size which stands out from surrounding buttresses at an angle much admired by tourists of a suggestive mind but equally, much respected as an area of mysterious happenings by the older natives who experience the terrors of its 'wee folk' after closing time and by younger locals who experience its more magical effects after dark in the viewpoint car park.

That evening we gathered. The exertions of the day embellished the faces of all but our lone teetotaller whose moribund pallor rivalled that which extends naturally to professors of biology, keep-fit addicts and the administrators of health and hygiene regulations. We were engulfed by experts, 'ologists' of varying disciplines whose concerns for this Skye landmark ranged from the minutiae of its botany to the average size of a tourist's boot. Opinion as to the means of the ridge's desecration, outwith Flockmaster Cameron and myself, settled upon an excess of local crofters and their inclination to graze too many sheep. George Murray added that all Skye sheep-men should buy their tups in Lairg – these thrifty animals, notably his own, ate less and went about on tiptoe.

By and large, preservation of the high, wide and lonesome was the theme. Thin out the crofters, fence out their sheep and encourage hillwalkers to wear lighter boots. Why not a funicular railway, I suggested, up one end, along the top, down the other – they'd get a better view and it would eliminate footprints altogether. Facetiousness only sounds clever sometimes – every shift in attitude towards a saner treatment of the environment, however tiny, counts – but, with a mind wandering from global warming to its future impact on world food production and weary of experts, I pipe up, 'Well, Mr Chairman, the way the world is ticking, I don't think it matters a damn if the Trotternish Ridge slips into the Sound of Raasay.'

Far enough. An Orcadian spree finally knocked the props from under the stage. Next season, as we gathered at the end of a day spent considering the needs of the islands, the vivific qualities of twelve-year-old Highland Park intruded. Paperweight policies were parting company from practical farming, I pronounced – common sense rarely sits at a computer. The tourniquet being applied to agriculture by letter boxes stuffed with onerous regulations actively expanded the influence of a bureaucratic heavy mob who, at the same time, controlled our incomes via a costive subsidy system. Farmers were losing heart – the laxative of freedom to farm as they wished was needed to get the industry into motion. I warmed the theme with similar outbursts of incendiary assertions which led finally to the unkind analogue of a parasitic dog. 'When the load of parasites his body can carry reaches a critical level, Mr Chairman, the dog calls it a day. Farming can only carry a certain load of parasites. Lordy help us if pen-pushers ever have to roll up their sleeves.'

Official eyebrows closed ranks, scowls showed through five o'clock shadows, farming members smirked behind hands. It wasn't friendly comment. Tony, Scottish agriculture's de facto boss at the time, always stood his hand – a good lad. Over bacon and eggs next morning, Jim Seaton, chief dispenser of agri-college advice to decimated Highland farming, made a point: 'Calling them parasites is one thing – you might have left off the "bloody".'

A final indiscretion – my last committee. Bye-bye to traffic jams on Princes Street, visiting art auctions on George Street, listening to Radio Scotland in tailbacks on the Forth Road Bridge – 'They're all out of step but our Johnny'. Anxieties over what I felt were the flaws in modern farming had me marching on the wrong foot. Details of piddling Brussels regulations became boring, major issues were being gagged. Debate on the underlying forces propelling farming and the countryside towards rapid change and possibly cataclysmic challenges? Taboo.

Any plea I made in committee for government interest in organic principles or for the adoption of realistic conservation attitudes to aid wildlife survival and most eyes reached for the ceiling. I was an enemy in their midst, insinuating subversive doctrines. To salve any public unease, the Agri-Department set up a ridiculous Farm

Assured Scheme – another whitewash ploy which I bitterly opposed. It allowed chemical agriculture to continue with government blessing. Worse, almost, was that the scheme's implementation involved 'on-farm check-ups' by yet another batch of inspectors as artificially minded as the methods they monitored – a brigade with far less understanding of the countryside than the old moustache twirling buffers. Office-bound bureaucrats and their spying inspectorate were becoming a new form of gentry – de facto land controllers whose capital was not in acres but index-linked pensions.

Enough of the bogus altruism of politicians, professors so erudite I wouldn't trust them with a supermarket trolley, experts without instinctive feeling for the land, pipette and computer farmers, detail peckers who could ignore the average 70 per cent fall in many wild bird populations of the past twenty years and see a field of wheat without a poppy as part of putting nature in its place. Control and extraction merchants were obliterating the May song of the corn bunting and the summer blooms of the tiny blue speedwell.

The reservoir of people who farmed because of a love of working in tandem with the land, who believed that other species had a right to some room on the planet, was drying up. The advance of environmentally concerned bodies, Greenpeace and Friends of the Earth in the van, had chemical farming hiding behind government support for its malpractice.

Residual know-how and self-discipline, vital requisites when people's dinner depended on their own skill, were fast eroding. Home-grown common sense was evaporating like steam off a September river. The artificial world, a concrete rat trap, claustrophobia its hidden illness. The hills were back in business and the sun made circles on the sea.

## 12

# The Edge of Time

Clear as the air in a corrie streaked with winter snows, the song of a ring ousel carried through a silence which lay heavy on the hills of dawn. Mountain blackbird, herald of days in a distant glen when northern lights fade only into twilight and the first hint of sun draws puffs of mist to the hillsides with all the promise of a fine day. Handsome bird of tumbled scree, glossy black wing, broad white chest, it nested above my corrie camp in a frost-split cairn where rowans left the burn and grew dwarf and twisted amongst the blaeberry crannies. Early that summer I made a campsite home high above Glen Cannich, domain of deer and eagle, far from intrusion's steady tramp.

I wakened at the ousel's call and turned my head on a pillow of shirt and tweeds. Stillness. Canvas roof a-glow, beaded with droplets. Nothing breathed or stirred. No sound. Then again, the ousel's song amongst the crags. Shrill then mellow, pausing to catch an echo, swelling from an upturned throat, filling the hills until every stone rang with its lilt.

The curlew speaks of melancholy, the solitude of places lost, a black-throated diver in long flowing call tells of moorland lochans, treeless and remote, but the melody of ring ousel sings of the richness of the first flood of yellow light which brings the green of sheilings to a land of stretching horizons. I lay. Listened. Time, unmeasured and mine. Wakening, as crisp and fresh as a night that spins the crackling stars.

Retreats of driven snow softened into pink. A tip of sun for the briefest moment put its golden halo on eastern ridges. Through an open tent door, shadows hurried from hills far across the loch. High snows deepened into orange. Great spangs of yellow lustre crossed the corrie. The ousel fell silent but, high on the buttress above me, a harsh croaking told a raven took wing. The cough of a hind nearby flattened her calf to the ground as she began to graze. Insects made tiny whirrings on their heather knolls and, from a gully of hidden pools where we washed and swam, the tinkle of their falls grew in the waxing light.

Steps of day on the crochet moss of spider banks, emerald and moist. On spray glistened ledges, on the upturning leaves of dripping birch. Shining, transforming. Hollows wet with dew lost their chill. Mankind huddled under skins worshipped the first rays of sun, origin of all our myths, our beliefs, our invention of a God. The goodness of light and warmth banished the prowling night, saved them from its evil terror. Breathing the soundness of sleep under canvas, I waited, snuggled in the contentment of lying on the ground, knowing the early sun made haste to leave a distant horizon, for already from the cotton tufted flats away below my camp its drying air brought the scent of wild hyacinth.

Sudden brightness lit the canvas. Sunshine. Shiver and tingle. Life in the open, ruddy, rolling, rollicking, skipping, free, it raced in a delirious shock. Flap of the tent, a droplet shower, ice on the back, grass, cold to the feet, air clean and keen. Sun on the skin, head over heels in the romance of a corrie camp I scampered to fill a kettle from the opal pools of morning.

◆

Hidden amongst the hills I knew from shepherding days were sounds of a past, memories from a world which once held a wholesome lifestyle. Many's the morning I climbed the ridge above the camp and looked over the emptiness of Strathmore, bygone hills of dogs and gatherings, our home under hydro waters, and I began to write *Isolation Shepherd*.

Deer tracks took me to the tops, I walked the long smooth summit of Riabhachan, swam in the lochan below the white peak of Sgurr na Lapaich, crossed again the hills that were windows on a shepherd's way and, by the light of a summer's night, we lay and listened to the music of Dylan Thomas in the wistful lines of 'Fern Hill' and I wrote and wrote.

One afternoon, after a deal of careful spying with the 'glass', I marked a jumble of stone to which the brown female ousel busily flew with food. Accompanied by the churring alarm call of both birds, I clambered up the cairn and, after much peering into crannies, found a large, grass-woven nest tucked under the shelter of a leaning rock, quite a few yards from the spot I'd judged it to be. Clever birds, they protected four pink-skinned scrawny chicks which, all heads, yellow beaks and closed bulging eyes, filled the nest. So ugly only a mother could love them but next year, with luck, they'd be as bonnie as their parents. At my movement, or perhaps my shadow, four weaving heads craned up and wide red throats emitted a chorus of squeaky notes. Singing lessons lay ahead.

That evening, at the turn of the day, as the old folks would have the summer solstice, I crouched beside the cairn of the mighty Sgurr na Lapaich. Peaks surrounded me. Many I had known in daily work. I lifted my telescope. Familiar stones on nearby hills came to me and I recognised the shelter retreats of a day of rain or sleet. The shoulder of Bidean an Eoin Deirg, high top of the Strathmore sheep ground, filled the lens. An unfailing spring bubbles summer and winter below this graceful summit. At a gathering, the ewes, drawing their lambs fast along the face of Toll a'Chaorachain, would have seen dogs and me in hot pursuit and I'd dip my face and gasp at the chill of its pure icy water.

North of the ground I thought of as my own, the hills of Fannich shone bright and verdant in a falling sun. Sheep and deer, home of the Ross family, shepherds and stalkers – a vanishing style. West a little, I spied at the glowing red screes of Torridon's ancient sandstone rock. A barren cascade, revealing some of the world's oldest fossils, it slipped winter by winter under erosion's grind from the heights of Ben Eighe and the long ridge of Liathach. Torridon's ownership, also suffering erosion, slipped from the Earls of Lovelace to the Scottish National Trust in the 1960s to provide enjoyment for tourist and walker. Lucky folk – a week's tramping the ridges, admiring views, spotting an eagle, down for a pint over their maps – but could they guess the depth of a shepherd's feeling for his stock and his hills? Could they know his day-to-day work in the remoteness of lonely places imparted an affection for the hidden waterfall where he might pause on a lambing round? Could they feel the familiarity for a stone which took his back as he turned a 'spyglass' on roaming sheep? Could they imagine the pleasure of a sun-facing corrie where he dozed with the dogs by his side? Did they understand his revulsion for screaming jets that panicked the deer and shattered the wisdom of silence? Did they feel the sanctity of lofty 'tops' which opened horizons in the mind?

Dusk brought ochre shades to the distant tip of Slioch, a fire to its weathered buttress. I knew the gentle evening would see the great hill's reflection on the stillness of Loch Maree and stealthy oars in the lee of its ancient burial isle would allow of a late cast on trout-rising waters. Around me mellowing rays tinted the greenness, touched each blade, put a sheen on hugging carpets of crimson moss, bathed western slopes in the last of a day's warmth. Arch-necked hinds grazed the moistness of an early dew. Stillness carried the click of a hoof on stone. Step by step they moved, flicking ears, ever but one head raised and watching. Below the shoulder at my back the corries fell to gloaming and in the mauve of evening's tread the pines of Caledon were darkened.

I turned the glass. Luminous sea twined in its lens, a silver thread amongst the islands – sun path over waters. Islands of the west, I heard their music calling as the cry of the geese that pass each spring.

Vaulted clouds curved into serried ribs above me, the cavity of some great surrealist creature. I sat at its heart. Gold seeped into vermilion crept over a dying form. Sunset bones. An orange shaft split the waters of The Minch. Palest peach sank to mauve. Hills into blackness, headlands lost. The circle of the sun grew round, its shade a darker hue. Far out, as far it seemed as twilight at the edge of time, the Hebrides slipped beyond the horizon and into dreams.

Down to the lochan, the ridge was steep and broken. I ran in failing light. Clammy white air, a whispering breath, swirled across a dangerous track. The weather was breaking, I reached the motionless water below the peak. Lifting mist driven by buffeting draughts became tentacles of crimson cloud, lustrous in the fierceness of a sunset hidden by the looming summit. Over ledge and precipice writhing arms raged skywards. Ridges and heavens blazed above my head. At my feet the lochan's water thickened into blood, a dark blood red.

Next morning I struck camp. It was high summer, the sun in the north, my hollow by the burn bright with flowers. Yellow celandine, purple milkwort and tiny radiant blue plants I took to be violets. Dowdy pipits made fluttering flights on the knolls about me – homely little birds, lacking any grandness. On my wanderings, I had come on several of their nests, shallow grass bowls under a tussock, nutmeg-brown eggs, usually four and a hen bird that sat tight until you almost trod on her. I didn't seek out nests, just walked the hill quietly. A pair of curtsying wheaters with their black eyebrows had nested close by my tent and I found their beautifully built home in a stony outcrop one morning, but the dipper that bobbed on our kettle stone kept the secret of his brood.

The hinds looked up without apparent fear as I left. Most now had calves at their side – many still spindle-legged creatures with dotted birthday coats. I sat on the shoulder which led out of the corrie. A family of stoats appeared amongst the boulders. A large one, probably the female, and three darting russet curves, the young ones. Each stood a second, poised on hind legs, showing their creamy chests before an even faster vanishing trick. I mingled again in strolling days and the pleasures of a shepherd's life.

The corrie camp, a green hollow surrounded by nostalgia? Bogus simplicity sheltering from the trap of complexity into which life had fallen? Maybe, but it was an interlude which allowed me to sketch the end of an era in a Highland glen when time and machine were not master and the hills meant more than a playground – they were home.

◆

The previous winter was my first visit to Shetland. I stayed with John Scott of Bressay, over the bay from Lerwick, where he had a farm and the farthest north Georgian house. We sat on a long sofa in his grand sitting room taking our tea and scones with the farm lads. Laird and loons – I liked it.

Next day John took me across the ridge. We looked down on the Isle of Noss. Wind of the northland, fjord and ice floe, slanted seabird. Emptiness, white topped and turquoise. It drew me, held every sense quivering, a passion unfolding, compelling, mesmeric as the secret lodestone of life draws us down a path of fantasy, stronger, more beautiful, predestined as the surge of the tide.

From the beach the little red-haired girl ran again, laughing, her turquoise dress fluttering, matching the sea of a western horizon which has no ending. At the edge of the tide, flesh white against rock black, I saw the Seal Woman – auburn tresses in a turquoise sea.

Untwine the double helix, decode its formula, trace your Y chromosome two thousand years, it will tell you home, explain affinity. I needed no science. The wheel of time spins slowest at its edge. I carried my pack from the corrie camp down past a loch straddled by the concrete of a boasting hydro dam and headed west to seek a boat.

## 13

# 'A Great One for Drinking and Girls'

> Build me straight, O worthy Master!
> Staunch and strong, a goodly vessel,
> That shall laugh at all disaster,
> And with wave and whirlwind wrestle!

These rousing lines open Longfellow's poem, 'On the Building of a Ship' – they ring still as I hear my mother's voice reading a five-year-old to sleep. And sometimes it was Masefield:

> I must go down to the seas again, to the lonely sea and the sky,
> And all I ask is a tall ship and a star to steer her by . . .

The power of poetry sows the seed of lifelong influence.

> A wet sheet and a flowing sea,
> A wind that follows fast
> And fills the white and rustling sail
> And bends the gallant mast,
> And bends the gallant mast, my boys,
> While, like the eagle free,
> Away our good ship flies and leaves
> Old England on the lee.

I listened, a young mind aflame with pictures. Poet Laureate John Masefield sailed the windjammers:

> . . . for the call of the running tide
> Is a wide call and a clear call that may not be denied;

A command for those who hear it, who feel it with the pangs of homesickness.

The sea suffers no fools – it demands practical people with a straight eye. The Vikings proved their capabilities. Open boat and epic voyage, deft axe and hammer strokes, the building of the longship – the *dreki*, the 'dragon ship', named for their figureheads. Raging eyes and flaring nostrils, fearsome pride fashioned into a symbol of terror. Their timbers cut from the forest oak with more female than male flowers made ships into 'she', denote a seaman's love of his ship to this day. Each longship would be adored, cared for as a living being. Sleek seaworthy vessels, often exceeding sixty feet on the waterline with a narrow sixteen-foot beam, they were given an oaken keel for stability and overlapping planks of red larch for strength. The dragon prow, curving high and pointed, lifted the ship through combing crests; her stern shaped likewise rose easily before a following swell. Graceful, buoyant as a feather, they skimmed the sea, flexing to the waves, breasting a shoulder, swooping through a trough as a fulmar will at the merest tilt of wing. Ocean thoroughbred, the longship made as light of its element as a tree dancing to the gale.

The single rectangular spread of drawing canvas set on a mast mounted amidships was controlled from the stern by ropes fashioned in hemp or platted sealskin. A loaded longship might easily weigh eighteen tons and, though highly manoeuvrable under oars or sail, the strength to steer her by a massive oar pivoted from the aft starboard, or 'steer-board' quarter, without mechanical advantage beyond the leverage of the helmsman's arms, meant muscle and no namby-pamby diet. Ten knots in blow, ship and stamina in rippling skill, crashing to windward, man and boat in balance, bare feet on wood, legs braced, rush and plunge, they waltzed with the sea.

The Norse merchant ship, known as a *knorr*, lacked the leanness of a longship, their duties being markedly different. To give greater stowage amidships, these trading vessels were shorter on the water-line with a much wider beam. The design made for a fullness of bow line, upsweeping and beautifully rounded, befitting a rover's thoughts on solitary watch. In its genitival form, the word *knorr* describes a woman of ample shapely bosom, an attribute said to be appreciated by lusty lads, home from sea.

Without push-button satellite positions, getting home safely required more than luck and the press of carnal desire. The early Greek astronomer Hipparchus drew star maps and estimated the distances apart of the earth, sun and moon. The sailors of Portuguese – Henry the Navigator, with his five-acre sundial, and School of Navigation on the Algarve coast – were encouraged to explore and reached Madeira and the Azores. In between these eras the ability of Viking seamen to track oceans far beyond the pilotage of headland transits was quite a skill. What was the trick? Did they follow the Alban walrus hunters?

Common sense and some form of calendar might have given those voyagers an understanding of latitude by the altitude of the sun. A latitudinal course might be steered over days by checking the angle between the boat's lubber line and the setting sun. They may have used a flat horizontal board marked off in degrees with a pointer swivelling from its centre. Keep the instrument horizontal to the horizon, sight from stern to bow along a mark representing the lubber line, and the pointer would give the angle of a sun about to vanish. The night sky, rising moon and planets might complement sun shots. Put land hull down on the horizon and an acute awareness of the motion of heavenly bodies gets a grip, I assure you.

Longitudinal distances we know from the Norse sagas they took as so many sailing days, east or west from a known position. To aid 'land ahoy', telltale clouds often settle like a cap over a land mass and perhaps the floating Arctic Mirage, that weird phenomenon of northern latitudes, would indicate a destination far ahead. Use of the terms 'ship's log' and her speed over water measured in knots comes to us from their expedient of running out a piece of wood on a line with knots at a certain distance apart. Twenty knots, a yard apart, slipping through your fingers in ten seconds is one hundred and twenty yards in a minute and around four miles in an hour, but how did they measure the time factor?

The sages say, during foggy or overcast weather, the properties of Icelandic 'Sun Stone' came into use. This translucent piece of calcite rock, called Iceland spar, polarises a light source by its crystalline structure and could pinpoint the direction of an illusive sun. Had the secret of the magnetic lodestone been discovered? We don't know. There seems little told of their navigational methods – maybe they took it as everyday knowledge. Excavated longships such as the graceful Gokstad ship taken from a burial mound in south-west Norway give no clue. Had the Viking an inborn sense of direction, similar to the Native Americans? Boldness would not be lacking – nor perhaps beard scratching when unrecognisable land appeared on the bow.

For a helmsman under sail, the feel of the sea under the hull is his continuous monitor. He watches the set of the waves – the curl of their tops tell the wind's strength, help him spot bank and shallow. He notes the sea's changing colour when nearing land, sees the flight of bird life and knows the habits of the marine creatures which share it with him. The lore of the sea is in his blood. To the Viking's innate navigational ability, their knowledge of tidal currents and each season's prevailing winds add a deep affinity with the rolling swell and the headlands of an island home emerging through the smur of an ocean dawn. A love of the sea follows the generations.

◆

The Viking age of plunder and expansion began around AD 800. Population pressure forced land hunger and the innovation of the longship aided business greed. These were just two features of a phenomenon whose impact on Europe, both ethnically and behaviourally, put its mark on us to this day. Their settlement of the Atlantic islands, coasts and estuaries of Europe shaped our intellect, our traits of aggressive domination and stubborn grit. Norse mindset, prone to wanderlust and spring fever, sought the fresh gale and took a grip on living with the vigour of a helmsman running his ship before a nor'easter.

Icelanders consider Ingolf Arnarson in 870 to be the first Nordic coloniser of their volcanic terrain. A statue in Reykjavik honours this precursor of the islanders' extremely narrow genetic base. It's possible both Alban walrus hunters and Irish monks beat Arnarson to the island by a few hundred years but toppling a monument won't prove it. No doubt exists concerning Thorvald Asvaldsson and Eric, his red-haired teenager son. Thorvald's unsociable attitude far exceeded that of brawling ruffian and, by AD 960 he'd been outlawed in south-western Norway for 'multiple manslaughter', a refined description of mass murder and probably a not-unusual indictment given the appetite for blood-letting which permeated Norse society at the time. Father and son, taking a view on this delicate situation, caught the first wind to Iceland.

Twenty years pass and Eric Rauda, our history books' famously seafaring Eric the Red, has carved out an Icelandic farm, married a local girl and is fully maintaining family tradition. A landslide, accidental or otherwise, engineered by Eric's slaves, engulfs the steading of his two neighbours, Eyjolf the Foul and Duel-fighting Hrafn, who, one might suspect from their names, are not a mealy-mouthed pair and quite liable to protest. They do and are promptly 'taken out'. More murders follow. A summary execution is pending and sword-happy Eric hoists sail.

Wife, chattels, Lief, his Icelandic-born son, and Eric hit the sixty-fifth parallel. Two hundred miles puts them in eastern Greenland. Not all glacier and barren rock, valley bottoms bloom with meadow grass in the short high summer days. Fjords might jostle with icebergs but they teem with fish, an ideal Viking bolt-hole, remote and pristine. Given a politic interval, Eric returns to Iceland, calls for volunteers and leads a fleet of twenty-five ships to embark on the colonisation of Greenland.

The population rose to an estimated three thousand as the western seaboard was settled but they were not, according to saga, the earliest Vikings to discover these demanding shores. It was already known to Icelanders as Gunnbjorn's Land. Christianity may even have found a foothold. Eric, not given to self-effacement, swanked about the colony in the prestigious role of First Settler and now steps up for our historical Oscar. Ruthless and untameable, the hardness of granite, he was not a man to notice hacks on his hands, nor even blood.

No less forthcoming, his son, Lief the Lucky, takes the credit for exploring Baffin Bay which separates north-east Canada from western Greenland. Following a nose hooked on plunder, Lief sailed down the bay's eastern inlets and called in on 'Vinland', a name translating to grassland rather than the more desirable concept 'vino'. There are sources, notably the tales of Thorfinn Skull-splitter, Earl of Orkney, yet another whom nobody hurried to contradict, which indicated that today's Newfoundland was already known to Atlantic seafarers both as Hvitramannland, Land of White Men, and, interestingly, Albania.

Christianity had already spread north from Ireland and the term 'White Men' suggests robed Irish monks may well have settled the fringes of North America. The Latin text, *Navigation of Saint Brendan*, written around AD 1050, recounts his legendary skin-boat voyage to a land of saints far to the west and north. Saint Brendan, an enthusiastic founder of monasteries, County Galway's Clonfert being one amongst a number in Ireland and Scotland, would have been no stranger to pulling ropes and praying for a fair wind. Old maps place Saint Brendan's Country west of the Cape Verde Islands, a wildish stab but at least out in the Atlantic.

Greenland saga has it that, around AD 1000, Leif, inspired by the sword-brandishing of Norway's evangelist King Olaf Tryggvason, also found Christianity to his liking and tiny chapel ruins discovered a short distance from Eric the Red's Greenland homestead at modern-day Brattahild, may relate to this preference in salvation therapy. Was Leif Erikson the discoverer of Uncle Sam? How far south did he explore? If Leif was America's founding hero, how fitting that the land of homicides should honour the family of such gifted exponents of the practice.

◆

Whilst Eric and Leif were dodging icebergs, much of our western seaboard from Shetland to the Wirral, from the Isle of Man to Dublin, came under the Norse Crown. Tactics? Shock and awe. From ocean crossings to overland portage, the versatility of the clinker-built longship did the trick. To add more to the Sea Raider's kingdom, Magnus Barelegs in 1098 set a sail, sat at the helm and had himself dragged across the Kintyre isthmus. The boats' shallow draft, just a couple of feet, made them especially suited to navigating river systems, a facility which permitted these specialised operators in terrorism to paralyse every estuary in western Europe and well beyond. To name but two, the cultured Saxon trade centres of Dorestad on the Rhine and Antwerp on the Scheldt were torched to screams of reckless killing. Fearsome death followed by anguish. Assorted priesthoods, as is their wont from time immemorial, blamed or justified these tribulations on the population's propensity for sinning. Either way, not a time to be opening the door to strangers.

Whether or not his name implies a style in plus fours is of small consequence by comparison to his actions. In AD 845 Ragnar Hairy-Breeks sailed up the Seine with one hundred and twenty longships. Frankish king, Charles the Bald, marshalled his huge army on the river bank. If not previously hairless, he soon had reason. Ragnar swiftly dealt with the advance troops. Over a hundred prisoners were promptly hanged on an island in full view of Charles and his main army. Unnerved by twitching corpses, the Franks called it a day. Ragnar sailed on, emphasising his disdain for Christians by sacking Paris on Easter Sunday. It cost Charles, by now the Bald, seven thousand pounds of silver to persuade the Vikings to pull out for an agreed six years. Not being adverse to adding deceit to blackmail in their business arrangements, they called back after two. For wealthy Anglo-Saxon England under Ethelred the Unready, a byname any king might prefer not to bandy about, peace amounted to a yearly payment to the blackmailers of 'Danegeld'. Belying his title, Ethelred found 'the readies' through a tax on his subjects. A notion still applied with political gusto.

For decades no coast escaped. The Bay of Biscay, Moorish Spain, into the Mediterranean – pre-tourist traps were ravaged. A trip up the Rhône, more than bikini blondes, took the Norsemen to the Balearic Islands. Their leader, Björn Ironside, had Rome in his sights. Possibly sacking Pisa as part of this excursion, he sailed on to Europe's religious heart, the Eternal City, Rome of the Seven Hills and gleaming white Carrara marble villas. Whether the Vikings achieved their aim is uncertain but it gave rise to a yarn of the type which had the longship boys rolling on the bottom boards.

A glance from the sea at Rome's impressive fortifications convinced the Vikings that onslaught by storm was not practical. It had to be subterfuge or nothing. They sent a messenger. 'Our chief is old and dying and wishes to be baptised in your true Christian faith before his death.' Roman ecclesiastics were flattered. 'By all means.' Next day's message, 'Our chief died overnight and his last wish was a Christian burial in your Holy Cathedral.' 'Bless him, of course he may,' – a converted sinner was top value. Resplendent in mitre and gold-embroidered vestments, the city's clergy turned out to escort the coffin with its wailing mourners to a vault. Much praying and chanting. Remains about to be committed. Up shot the coffin lid, out sprang the dead chief, slew the officiating bishop and flung open the city gates to his comrades awaiting a Norse-style night on the town of blood-letting, rape and pillage.

This tale strikes an authentic note. There can be little doubt that the arrival of a fleet of galleys, with snarling dragon figureheads carved on their prows, which discharged a horde of screaming, sword-waving vagabonds, would be a trouser-filling prospect for any pastoral villager. The universal fear of the Viking can be soundly attributed to their main business enterprise – a rapacious line in slave trading. Human cargo – women, teenagers and children – was the sought-after booty. In typical raids, many able menfolk would be killed during the onslaught. Old or wounded were dispatched on the spot – too much trouble in transit.

Dublin became the Viking slaving centre for a network of human misery stretching from Iceland to the Near East. Negro slaves from North Africa, dubbed 'blue men', reached Ireland. Southern market preference, however, inclined to fair skins and blue eyes. Handily for Viking slavers a source of ideal material lay on their doorstep. The fifth-century about-turn of Roman garrisons from Britannia had allowed the Germanic Jutes, Angles and Saxons to nip across the North Sea and set up temporary independent states. Before long, Egbert of Wessex ran the whole show. Angli, the Latin word for English, was paving the way for England's 'God Save the King'. In spite of Alfred the Great burning cakes and building Angli's first 'Hearts of Oak' navy, consignments of Anglo-Saxons continued to top Viking trading requirements and were shipped to slave markets in White Russia, Constantinople and Rome. Viewing a string of blonde, blue-eyed children from Angleland tied leg to leg for the convenience of preventing escapes, one Pope remarked, 'Not Angles, but angels.' Whether he made a purchase is not recorded.

Heavily pregnant women and babies found no demand, the former they slaughtered but suckling infants the slave trader used for 'sport'. The baby was flung high in the air. A circle of warriors armed with spears demonstrated their skill in catching the child on a spear point and tossing it across the ring to be impaled on the weapon of an opposite player. At the end of a 'game', the mother, forced to watch, would then be raped in a berserk manner and transported into slavery without the hindrance of a child clinging to her breast.

Viking bestiality – no animal would descend to such depravity – fully justified condemnation, perhaps ignoring the degree to which the level of brutal hardship from birth to death in a society fosters latent cruelty. Five hundred years on from the Viking slave trade, Cornish cousins Drake and Hawkins, made fortunes. The latter, believing he gave the blacks a better life, named his African slave ship *The Jesus*. Humanity has an uphill fight.

Warfare topped the Norseman's agenda. Operational battle kit, laid down by law, was: sword, axe if preferred; spear; bow and three dozen arrows; iron hat (not tin helmet); mailcoat or protective jerkin. Attennn-tion. All weapons to be inspected annually by local royal officials. Weapon training, weekly. Swords to be sharpened regularly. Dismiss.

This was no Dad's Army but a body of bloodthirsty fighters who lived by the sword. Slash and parry, no other weapon matched its glamour. Often ornamented with gold or silver, patterned on the blade to impart magic properties, beloved and given a name – 'Fire of Battle', 'Lightning Flash of Blood', 'Leg-biter'. Many celebrated a deed – King Hakon's 'Quern-biter' cut a quernstone to its centre! The older they were, the better they killed. A prized possession, the aristocrat of weapons.

I had a ceremonial sword myself whilst a trooper in the Horse Guards. On one parade, on the order 'draw swords', my horse made a side-step as I flicked up the weapon, its point took the neighbouring trooper, an inoffensive Cumberland lad named Skeleton, under his right ear. 'Lug-clipper's' call to action cost me ten days' CB (confinement to barracks) and several pints.

Long-handled axes wielded with skill and power epitomise the Viking at his fiercest and most brutal. The axe's flared head gave a

wide cutting edge. The weight and length of its shaft gave it momentum – only a brave man would face the onslaught of a screaming fiend
swinging such a weapon. The wounds inflicted were horrific. Head, leg
or arm were the favoured targets as decapitation or amputation
avoided the extraction difficulties which could be encountered by
an axe head stuck amongst one's opponent's ribs.

Invariably those picked for the kingship during the heights of
Viking supremacy were imperious fighters, leading from the front,
hard-jawed and able, living side-by-side with their followers, fighting hand-to-hand beside their men in battle. King Eric Bloodaxe of
the tenth century was one such. Generous with food and drink,
clothes and weapons, he was more daring, bolder, craftier and
braver than others. King Magnus, described two hundred years
later, fitted the same mould:

> Easy-going and light hearted; much after the fashion of young men, a
> great one for drinking and girls. He enjoyed games and liked to be
> better than everybody in agility and dexterity. His physical strength
> was also above the average. He was generous, but he would have his
> own way, and he was eloquent in speech. He was boldest of all men
> in battle. Much of a dandy and showy in his dress. He was rather tall,
> a muscular man, slender waisted, with well-proportioned and sha-
> pely limbs. His face was handsome save for some irregularity about
> the mouth.

And he was born eleven hundred years too soon for a Hollywood
hit.

This same chap led his men into battle dressed in a fine red and
white tunic, carrying 'Fish-spine', his famous sword. He enjoyed his
last fight and was killed at twenty-eight. Another King Magnus,
dubbed Magnus Barelegs, stated 'a king is for glory, not for long life'
and proved the point. He too was killed raiding Ireland in 1103,
aged twenty-nine. Turnover in Viking kings was high – they led
from the front. A marked contrast to the bravery displayed by
today's warmongering politicians, draft dodgers hidden in nuclear
bunkers, deploying fighting men then emerging for a handshake
television shot when the action dies down.

Film-star blondes, blue eyes and tall men, together with the lasting names on hills, islands, bays and headlands, remain the most identifiable legacy of the five centuries during which the littoral of northern and western Scotland lay under the shadow of the Raven. The Old Norse language in its Norn dialect survived to be widely spoken in Orkney and Shetland as late as the 1745 Jacobite Rebellion but a seaboard of salt-laden gales did not best preserve the Vikings' material possessions.

A crofter's cow meandering amongst the dunes of Uig Bay on the west coast of Lewis in 1831, defying midges by throwing sand over her back, dug up a twelfth-century set of carved chessmen. Luckily she didn't chew her find for the Uig chess set is now regarded as one of the finest of all treasures recovered from the era of Norse settlement in western Scotland. Imaginatively carved in walrus ivory, probably a product of the Scandinavian colonies in Greenland, their painstaking carver presented the back-row pieces, king, queen, bishops, knights and rooks, as a medieval monarch with his courtiers. The ranks of pawns defending this royal entourage, doubtless modelled first hand, he styled as 'berserk' Viking warriors, biting the edge of their shields, eyes a-pop in fighting frenzy. This IQ-testing board game, of Indian origin, took a thousand years via Iran, Italy and Spain to call checkmate on the edge of the Atlantic. Not every evening ended in wenching or brawling beneath a table.

Many fine artefacts, often elaborately carved, have been found. Memorial stones depicting ships and mounted warriors, horse collars, axe heads, caskets and, intriguingly, tortoise-shaped brooches. Portable scales for the weighing of precious metals, horse-riding stirrups, coins, pinheads, jugs and drinking horns – any object justified a motif. Interlacing patterns of animal bodies coil into fierce faces with darting tongues; ships' stem and stern posts become snarling heads and swishing tails. Norse artistic skill combined flair and stunning quality with blatant ostentation. Be their ornamental art practised on humble bone pins or the opulent gilding of weaponry, it suggests pride and vanity, if not arrogance – characteristics difficult to divide.

Undoubtedly these Nordic peoples were of a creative, independent turn of mind, their concept of life swayed by the thrum of the tide on shores of transient light, by a summer horizon suffused with midnight glow. A race inborn with respect for the hand that spins the seasons, an ear to hear the auburn scurry into autumn, thoughtful eyes to watch the arc of sun shrink to northern lights, velum black alive with aurora, red and green on winter snow. A wind to cake the drifted birch, a frost to crackle with the stars, put blue in flames of firelit tales. Adventure and daring, saga-stirred, told by old, until a torch of sun brought blackbird song and catkin yellow to river's edge and the milk-blue melt from ice-capped hills put longships back to sea.

Each season moulded beauty in the perspectives of sea and space, filled their days with a tapestry of shape and colour, flitted through the recess of lively minds which saw, in the hollow wave, a cave of green, in the wind-twisted branch, a waving arm, a clawing hand. Images hovered, cogent to them, surreal to us, flickering souls in the latitudes of counter-light and shadow. Ideas came alive as the scent of earth turned each spring by a creaking plough, clear as the air that drew their sails, sharp as a taste of the sea in a spray-filled gale.

Small wonder Viking society revered a poet's mastery of expression as the divine gift of their pantheistic heaven. The sagas of multiple gods reflected their own wars and voyaging. They bequeathed to us in runic inscription, poem and storytelling, tales of valour and tragedy unsurpassed in sharp description and elegant style. The accounts of their boisterous achievements bear favourable comparison with the Homeric epics – surpass them in soaring imagination.

Inspiration, life force and drive. Demands on fortitude aplenty. A race pitted against the elements: survival on the Arctic Circle. It bred vitality and an eye for beauty.

## 14

# The Rover's Bride

Wrath – the ultimate in violent anger; Cape Wrath – the ultimate in the fury of sea. It pounds on to the north-west shoulder of Scotland. Arched backs of Atlantic power whelm its gullies, tear at sparse cliff-top turf and fling their spray over a lighthouse of singular isolation.

To voyaging Norseman, it was neither Wrath nor rage but a vital landmark – a cliff fortress given to wheeling bird and climbing wave. They knew it as the Hvarf, the turning point – an easy corruption to Wrath. Languages and their accents ever adapt and entwine with cultural flow. Today, as a bombing range, this sentinel cape still reflects violence. Jets scream in, birds scatter, cannon and rocket blast a tiny island beside the point. Twelve hundred years past. Twist that steering oar, haul for the Hvarf, unfurl the Raven sail. Northland men, there's work for your swords tonight. Harry south, plough The Minch. The killing wind's on the quarter, foam is blood to the dragon's teeth.

Tucked behind the Hvarf are the limpid shallows of a forsaken bay. Shipwreck and silence haunt this home to cliff-nesting raven. Once the mewing of the white-tailed eagle would mingle in the stillness. Long gone, it provided sound haul-out and fresh water for ships that weathered the Cape. Sand-water, Sand-vatn to the sea robbers, describes perfectly a bay where cloud and light play upon the thin shimmering trickles of water which follow an ebbing tide. Today's corruption, Sandwood, is meaningless, yet this bay, tide-spread and lonely, left to a guardian stac and the flight lines of greylag and diver, calls through its buffeting sea winds for the beaching of the longships.

'Top of the tide, run out the ships. Treasure for the taking, boys.' South again, drawing sails, dipping bows. Handa, the Sandy Isle, Point of Stoer abeam, Rubha Reidh on the horizon. 'Helmsman, swing her to port, run for the Hawrarymoir.' The 'Hawrarymoir', Islands of the Haven, the Norsemen named them well – they offer the finest anchorage on all the western coast, safe from the thrash of The Minch, many's the longship snug.

Fifteen heather-topped islands, booming cave and seal-haul skerrie, guarded from the south by jagged islets, black and bare. Worn incisors jutting straight from the sea. Long settled as a sheltered retreat, these are today's Summer Isles. Across the Dornie Sound, the weathered heights of Ben Mor Coigeach turn the east winds of March from this kindly archipelago, its wide base curves above the village of Achiltibuie. Houses and crofts, whitewashed and straggling, a beach of rounded boulder heavy with the kelp which at a time past filled pony creels and made fertile the lazy beds which grooved the bending hillside with long days of spring labour. Distantly the shapely An Teallach shows its peak over the green waters of Loch Broom and the ferry ships of Ullapool follow yesteryear's sailing winds to the Outer Hebrides.

Dutch fishermen founded the herring industry of The Minch in the fifteenth century and used the anchorage at Tanera Mhor, the largest of the Summer Isles, as their base. The Cromartie Estates of Easter Ross during that period were the owners of these islands and also a fair chunk of the adjacent mainland, but their clan participation in the 1745 Jacobite Rebellion resulted in confiscation by the British government. A subsequent sale by the Forfeited Estates Commissioners was to an English company with fishing interests. Subsistence crofting obliged with a ready supply of labour.

Cheap hands allowed the Tanera fish-curing station to develop. By the 1880s, a population well in excess of a hundred lived and worked the islands, giving rise to substantial buildings, a jetty and an export trade to Dublin to feed the peat-digging Irish. Soil returning as ships' ballast was spread on a field called the Little Irish Park. More ambitiously, Summer Isles salt herring soon featured on the menu of black slaves hacking sugar cane under a Caribbean sun. The fish were cheap, healthy and nutritious for men losing sweat and needing salt – indeed for all the labouring classes. Hardly suitable for the silver and linen dining table, they were particularly relevant to ex-Highland crofters holed up in Glasgow on the Friday-night-is-pay-night regime. The modest cash injection sweetened many a labouring family's tea with demerara sugar and, by way of reciprocation, thanks to Stephen Foster, they voiced 'Old Black Joe' and 'Swaneee River' 'ben the room' with an inkling of plantation poverty round a Sunday evening's holy Victorian piano.

Salt herring for the masses caught on. To further an industry of apparently endless free resource for sustaining Scotland's blast-furnace coolies and also to gainfully occupy their idle crofter cousins back home, the British Fishery Society in 1780 built the 'grid plan' town of Ullapool beside a shingled anchorage in Loch Broom. Herring on the doorstep, a whiff of the sea, a pier full of oilskin and creels, a frontage of pubs. Wild men, wilder nights, two hundred years on and it's still the Klondike of the Highlands. Yes, something of a frontier feel, it seemed the place to find a boat.

◆

Three miles north of Ullapool, with the Summer Isles peeping in sight, I pitched tent at the Ardmair Boat Centre and from Peter Fraser bought a sixteen-foot open boat – tiny cabin on the bow, six h.p. outboard engine on the stern – and called her *Mrs Seal*. A tame enough name, less pretentious than *The Raven* for a *Peter Pan* pirate intent only on a modest plundering of the islands without wearing a black eye-patch.

Preparations were simple – three gunmetal ex-army ammunition boxes, minus live rounds, a packed tent, food and the 'meths' cooking stove. Spare clothes and sleeping bag went into a sea-chest covered in yellow canvas which, when jammed under the for'ard thwart, served as a table. Bottom boards made sleeping quarters. A heavy green tarpaulin spread over lashed oars would form an awning. Spare fuel, compass, ropes and anchor aboard, an unfolded

Ordnance Survey map on the thwart and, whoopee, it was the first time ever on salt water in a boat of my own.

Isle Martin, an ex-herring station, shelters Ardmair Bay from the west and is named after Saint Martin, a chum of proselytising Columba. The remains of this pious follower, Martin, are reputedly below an imposing stone, marked with a cross, which lies in the island's walled burying ground. So, not a day supplying piety or pilgrimage, the sun poured brilliant light, bounced a spectrum of summer green islands on a cushion of sea blue haze. Isle Martin appeared pleasantly deserted.

Two pulls of the starter cord, a goodbye wave to shore and I tootled over the sheet of varnished water with a laugh to match *Mrs Seal*'s ebullient wake, all dancing bubbles and glittering froth, churned by a giant whisk. Off with the shirt; the day, the sun, the dazzle, the bliss of irresponsibility. A whoop of spirits, a blast of voice, 'Oh say you were never in Rio Grande?' and 'The Mingulay Boat Song'. I wasn't heading for either although it felt like it. I could be drowning the roar of the outboard. Hunch-necked cormorants, black and missionary, clamped to even blacker rocks in the centre of the bay looked grave – the legacy of Saint Martin?

'No landing, no landing,' an English voice in white shirt and shorts hurried down to the island's jetty waving arms to a sign which repeated the welcome. I throttled back and coasted. Bernard Planterose, warden for the Royal Society for the Protection of Birds, viewed his job with a terrier-and-bone enthusiasm. Perhaps considering me deaf and illiterate, he caught *Mrs Seal*'s painter. I smoothed hackles and was kindly taken up for tea in a cottage built for the island's last crofter. Society policy excluded wayfaring sailors and any crofting activity on their property. Tillage and grazing would enhance the feed base for a more varied bird population. Who should tell the experts? The island's last crofter family could have done – they were old friends and knew the system. But this was a Royal Society sitting on an insular egg and eschewing a crofting lifestyle.

Fighting bark-stripping rabbits with net fencing occupied Bernard, ornithologist and artist extraordinaire, who busied himself living on Isle Martin defiantly planting native trees. Equally hardy, his wife Emma bore the first baby born on the island in more than

1. The Castle Bridge, Inverness,
prior to planning Blitz

2. The old *Moray Coast* on the North run,
Liverpool to Leith, via the Pentland Firth

3. Margaret meets the boys. Left to right: John Cameron, President, SNFU; George Anderson, Vice-President; Bob Bain, Orkney; Tom Brady, Secretary SNFU; Margaret Thatcher, PM; unknown; author; Willie Mainland, Shetland; Peter Cheyne, Easter Ross

4. Proud Priam of Breakachy at Perth Bull Sale

5. The Corrie Camp,
Glen Cannich, Inverness-shire

6. Stac Pollaidh ahead, Wester Ross

7. Landing in the hidden bay

8. Home-making

9. Mrs Seal tucked in

10. The Doll in a Boat

11. Heading west, *Rhum* leaves the Caledonian Canal

12. *Ring of Bright Water* Gavin Maxwell's bay

13. Loch Hourne, the haunt of his otters

14. Scrub down and paint at Ardmair, Ullapool

15. An evening sail to the Summer Isles

16. Moidart and Castle Tioram

17. Callanish, Isle of Lewis

18. Into Castlebay. Barra and MacNeil's Kisimul Castle

19. Sailing and camping at Sanday

20. Left to right: Barra Head, Mingulay, Pabbay and Sanday

21. Barra Head and the Isle of Geirum Mor from Mingulay

22. Mingulay Bay, *Rhum* and the *Boy James* at anchor

23. Gathering sheep on the west side of Mingulay

24. No false step here when gathering above Mingulay cliffs

25. A gathering makes to the schoolhouse, Mingulay

26. In from hill and cliff to the ex-playground

27. Archie and author on the shears. Neil checks the style

28. Mingulay schoolhouse dipper. Archie, author, Sandy, Donald Beag, Iain Rory, Roddy, Calum, Neillie, Iaghan and John Joe. Sheep check the privy

29. Gently, gently. Frightened lambs, steady men

30. Little by little, down the ledge

31. In behind the sheet. Neillie, John Joe and author

32. Lambs beside the tide. Archie and author, catch and throw

half a century. Infant Sam was kept in a plastic fish box, which, given handles, holes and no ready supply of nappies, seemed a triumph for common sense. The Planteroses became good friends. Years later they rented a cottage further north at Scourie, from Jean Balfour, ex-Chairwoman of the Countryside Commission, and began a business propagating native Scots pine. I called – car but no sign of life. I looked into the byre. An eight by twelve foot canvas covered the floor, an abstract painting of circles and lines in the loudest colours. No artist? A distinct plop and a red blob spattered on to one corner. Ten feet up, Bernard, balancing amongst cobwebbed rafters, flung down dollops of paint with a definite knack. A pioneering couple with a novel approach to life, eventually they bought a pinewood plantation on the side of Loch Broom and reared their family in a home-made tree house.

Adventurous but more conventional, Roddy and Mary Boa took the crofting tenancy of Isle Martin in 1940 for £12 a year rental from a less conventional Commander Vyner. Two cows, furniture, implements and a family of six children from nine years down to six weeks were ferried across to a house boasting the novelty of electricity. This surprising perk resulted from the retired Commander introducing a flour-milling industry to the island. The machinery driving this outlandish choice of enterprise was powered by a massive and temperamental diesel engine whose single cylinder required coaxing into life by the application of a blow lamp until it glowed red-hot. Bread wheat, transported from Liverpool, was a regular run for a graceful three-masted schooner, the *Penola*. She arrived monthly with her cargo stowed in hefty 2¼ cwt sacks. A derrick on the jetty hoisted the tonnage into bogies which, on a light railway from pier to mill, were pushed by the men. Four or five days of dust and milling and the *Penola*, loaded with flour, sailed for Liverpool. She must have been one of the last vessels trading under sail and sadly she struck a German mine off the Firth of Clyde and was lost.

This mystifying enterprise, mothballed by the Ministry of Food for a period during the war, finally closed in 1949. From his 'Big House' across the bay, the Commander ordered the mill's demolition. The Boas left that same year, cattle and chattels, the school closed and, ultimately, the island fell to Bernard and his bird-friend bosses.

Evening approached as I headed *Mrs Seal* west from Isle Martin's scalloped bay, skirting the rocky dykes of a Viking fish farm which the longship lads managed without cage or chemicals. A heron, tall and deliberate, poked food into waving beaks which showed above the edge of a heaped nest of knitted stick on the island's sheltered corner. No cattle to eat down areas of rough and so make space for wild flowers; no claps of dung to buzz with insects for the birds; no hay nor harvest, scattered seed and mouse grass nest. No Highland bairns to sneak afloat with home-made sails and flegg their mother, crofting's turn of phrase and pastoral lifestyle left with the indigenous folk. An office-run island as dead as its sod-bound Saint.

The sea meant shaded eyes. Angled rays, green through the lens of rippled mounds. Moments alight. Swelling and flopping, the lazy beat of waters slack between the tides, warning the danger of submerged rocks. The fractured point of Horse Island drew abeam. North-west now, the motion of the boat a roll, long and easy. The glare of day was past, yet its warmth came to my cheek in hollows between gold-tipped waves. Puffs of summer, lured by the last of sou'-west's breeze across a hyacinth blue. Ahead, in the Norseman's eye, a longship floated, low and dark on the winding shroud of mist and memory that bound the islands to the centuries, the halcyon voyage and a landfall in the sail-stowed Isles of Summer.

To starboard, the hill lengthened in that way settled weather will have of making heights seem low and distant. Hay-ripening slopes flattened below the mauve of heather ridges. Whitewashed cottages, strong and simple, glowed pink against the darkening fields. An engine had no place in evening's hush. *Mrs Seal* quietened her bubbling wake. Heads broke surface and followed, seal eyes watched, round and wet and knowing. I dipped the oars. Quietly we slipped through a dripping haze and into the bay of Tanera Mhor. Viking refuge, Hawrarymoir, 'Islands of the Haven'.

Lights from Tigh na Quay, the Tanera house, winnowed over the water. I pulled alongside a tall-sided jetty built of hefty pink sandstone, its blocks neatly fitted and sound. During Hitler's war, a leading ecologist, Frank Fraser Darling, owned Tanera and, as part of the war effort, he rebuilt the herring station pier, very much with the assistance of his wife. Modest sweat through the spreading of shell sand – minus any tolerance for what Darling described as the West Coaster's untidy sloth – also put his farming theories into practice. His treatise, 'A West Highland Survey', though admired by academics had little relevance for natives whom he considered not always meriting his advice. He became Sir Frank.

'You're busy, boy.' And then, 'It won't rain tonight.' The remark drifted to me as I pulled *Mrs Seal's* awning across the lashed oars – a local voice. Sandy 'Bootie', otherwise Sandy MacLeod, grinned down. His people crofted the island until its small community dwindled as the herring boom waned. This MacLeod family subsisted for a few more years and were the last to work its meagre tillage – the last, that is, until the knighted ecologist rejuvenated the abandoned farming with subsidies from the government and his pen. 'You'll have blisters on your hands and your backside if you've rowed from Ullapool,' Sandy laughed. 'Come over to the house when it suits you.' And later, suitably equipped, I did.

Glasses smiled between us. We yarned away. The Bootie told of his grandfather – or was it great? Doesn't matter, long past. This chap, a MacLeod anyway, skippered a dashing schooner for a Tanera man of freebooting inclinations, one Captain MacDonald whom, with the bloke's stravaiging habits in mind, the locals called 'The Rover'. And what did the Captain call the pride of his heart? *The Rover's Bride*. Through Sandy's story, she sailed trim, sleek on the water, twin masts, a long bowsprit, and boy, boy, the name – what a name! The story paused to refuel.

'Well, Thomson, for the sheer joy of sailing and other business matters, The Rover would visit Brittany on an occasion and, whenever he returned to Tanera, a boy would be posted on the hill to watch the headlands.' Sandy held his glass to the light, two twinkles met – eyes and whisky. 'One morning, the loon arrived at Captain MacDonald's house, panting fit to bust, 'There's a strange sail just rounded Rubha Reidh.' Now *The Bride*, as they called her, lay at anchor in the bay, fresh up from France and her down to the plimsoll with kegs of brandy. 'Ah dhia, it'll be the Revenue cutter,' says MacDonald, 'sure as a seagull puts a splat on your Sunday cap.'

'Damn me, in hardly more time than I'm telling you, boy, didn't The Rover have his schooner under sail, gunwale awash, reaching north – lucky the wind, every stitch of canvas singing tight. He cut Cape Wrath by a coat of paint. Inside that rock, you know, the

cutter was closing. They'd be running light, you see. Orkney's on
the horizon, wind on the beam, Old Man of Hoy, – Revenue
officials signalling 'Heave to!' and waving fists.

'Heave to? *The Bride*'ll no' lie over for you, bastards!' And The
Rover, under full press, took a narrow channel between two islands.
Not a chart. Oh, man, he knew the coast. The customs skipper
hadn't the bottle – luffed up for the long route north about. And I
tell you, Thomson boy, by the time the cutter made Kirkwall Bay,
*The Rover's Bride* was bobbing in the harbour, light as a bride on the
night of her wedding dance.'

# 15

# The Phantom of Consciousness

The closeness of the hull brought to each fresh sound a clarity as curious as the voice of the sea in a shell at childhood's ear. *Mrs Seal* ground her keel gently on the shingle. A grating sharp and harsh above a murmur that grew in caverns deep where swaying weed and crawling pincer lived and rocks were pink and clean. Muted first in a soft crooning, then the faintest babble, then a jibbling, jabbling clamour uncurled in the vespers of an ebbing tide. A bay on the brink of sleep. Little by little, the voices hushed, lulls grew longer and the imperceptible swell of a sea was at rest, pillowed the listening night.

Snug on the bottom boards, bedroll and sleeping bag, head on a bundle of clothes, through the open end of the awning I'd slung over the oars, a gleam of light traced the horizon. A stretching shape filled the bay. An immense shadow rose portentously from the tendrils of mist which crept along a far-off shore. A lordly hill reached to the stern of my boat. In mirrored dimensions it quivered – animistic, the antithesis of a materialistic solution to its power. Stealthily I knelt, dipped a hand into thick dark water. The brooding figure slid away – an impalpable realm lurking behind the phantom of consciousness.

Stars flickered in and out of existence, photons of incandescence scattered on a velvet cover. The velum of space, membrane of some immense expanding cell, with planets its electrons, suns its atoms, spiralling into galaxies – the skeletons of matter circling the cosmos, universe orbiting universe. Above me, the apogee of truth, a hunched figure of primal rock, coalescence of ultimate elements, synthesis of all conceptions in the throbbing system we strive to understand. Arc of insight, its angle of vision encompassed the boat in a blackness, a blackness elemental, absolute, reaching into an abyss greater, deeper, more penetrating than earth's paltry night.

An abyss, spinning, spiralling, faster, tighter, faster, faster, tighter ever tighter. Captured light crunching mass to energy. Energy, heavy, heavier, crushed to a density beyond the laws of science, a heat beyond the nth degree. Time ground to an instant tinier than a measure. Speed of light bursting into limitless dimension. Fission or fusion, the forge of creation? Matter, antimatter, attraction, repulsion. Unending expansion or contraction beyond oblivion? Dualism eternal? War of the oscillating universes? Dark energy or gravity? Victory or annihilation?

No. In the domain of quantum gravity, infinite density warps time into space, space into time. Speed of spin defied by the crush of gravity. There exist all futures, the matrix, the womb of universes eternal. There exists the rotating orifice throughout which all has passed, through which all will pass, infinitus, the arrow of time.

Energy imbalance heats the magma of singularity on the anvil of understanding. Boundless knowledge, God of the Universe, powerhouse of the heavens at the heart of infinity.

Darkness settled into stillness – the tangible pressure of a silence beyond the pitch of hearing. A paradox surrounded me, the closeness of endless space, a space of spinning, screaming electrons slowed to the hush of an age before the birth of life.

Somewhere, far behind the instance of man's emergence, somewhere in the memory of the stones, came a call, clear across the waters – the whistle of a redshank: 'Teee,ou,ou,ou, teee,ou,ou,ou, teee,ou,ou,ou.' Three notes, lingering notes, harking in sorrow back to a place where they existed in the beginning – by a bay at the edge of time when newborn hills looked down upon the seashores of creation.

The air on my face came cool, put the taste of the sea in my mouth. A falling tide uncovered the tangle of the Summer Isles. A last plip-plop of water jostled under the hull and *Mrs Seal* settled herself quietly beside the jetty.

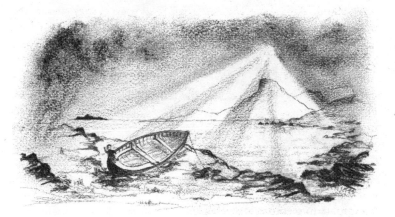

16

# The Doll in a Boat

An impatient scrunch, the rattle of a running tide on shingle. The first stab of sunlight burst over the bay. *Mrs Seal* nudged the pier. A wee tug on her stern line pinged beads of dew into a tiny rainbow. I knelt with the sleeping bag about my loins and looked over the gunwale. Along the jetty's foundation stones, pink anemones clung in scores, tiny flowered tentacles waving at each passing swish of breakfast. Shoals of cuddies darted in unison, twisted together, in shade, tails flick, out, in, out, mottled backs a moment, then a flash of silver.

Blackbird bugle – reveille from an oak tree by the ruins of the old fish-curing shed. 'Up, Thomson boy.' I threw back the awning to a bursting cantata – a pert-tailed wren in pier-head willows, 'chaffes', hill pipits, a dunnock chorus twittering about the buildings. Boy, oh boy, life is luxury. Everywhere, ringing and singing. A rollicking shoreline of waders: 'wicka, wicka' from the 'seapies'; 'curr . . . lew, curr . . . lew', faster and rising, from the wily curlew. All a-whistling, a-probing, a-flitting and feeding on the rim of an encroaching tide. Wide awake, day on the make, heart lifting, light and sound. I stood, naked, toe wrinkling, arms stretching sunward till muscles cracked with wellbeing.

Oatmeal and boiling water – brose, the breakfast fare of plough-boy days, couldn't be bad for a would-be sailor. Wash up over the side and ready. I rowed between two nearby islets which sheltered an inlet named by locals 'the cabbage patch'. Oar-gripping weed rendered progress more akin to rowing through rhubarb as I pulled towards a stone jetty.

Streamers of green slime clung to a landing stacked with rusted chain piled in kipper boxes. Orange fishnet floats peeped through brackens marking a trail which climbed towards a corrugated shed claiming, by its tarnished sign, to be an 'ost Offi'. Behind me hill and channel were transformed to a polychrome study fit to front any VisitScotland calendar. Who, the whole length of our stamp-licking realm, could be so lucky to frank letters before such a vista?

This outpost of Royal Maildom offered yet more Highland grandeur. Captured on sixpenny Dixon postcards, it hung in bleached curling strips down a window-cleaner's challenge. Up-turned bluebottles littered the window ledge, sets of Summer Isles postage stamps under stained cellophane depicted gliding Rosetta terns guarding three mottled eggs on a sandy beach – gems to any passing philatelist. Ranks of purple lupins and lady's smock, the cuckoo flower, guarded a door in little danger of being jemmied. I forebore to knock on such engaging neglect.

By mid morning a launch-load of tourists from Ullapool would circle the islands consuming canned beer to the loudspeaker commentary of Desperate Dan MacKenzie, nocturnal salmon investigator and part-time pirate whose one eye took in more than many blessed with two. His converted Admiralty launch would soon be cutting a wake between the skerries, entertaining curious seals to curious humans and taped music.

Dan, whom I'd met at Ardmair Point as he applied 'expertise' and paint to the sale of yet another bargain Admiralty launch, blew out an eye with an exploding twelve-bore shotgun as a boy of twelve. He'd sold house and croft overlooking the Summer Isle for forty pounds at the end of the war and needed but a patch to place him on the cover of *Treasure Island*. No tourist was safe from his charm.

*Mrs Seal* threaded out of the weedy anchorage. Where to find a writer's retreat? 'Head north, boy.' None to contradict, I rounded the point of Tanera Mor. Seal-calving islets lay to the west, black skerries, battered sanctuaries green-topped with sea bent. The channel between Isle Ristol and Eilean Mullagrach opened. Bog cotton cloud sailed a lazulite stratosphere; I sailed its blue reflection. Islands pranced on the skyline, hill tops quivered, sunshine's ardent call. Stravaiging.

The promontory of Reiff ran bare and shelving from sheep-shorn hill pasture. I skirted cliffs of white-streaked ledges. Ruffles of tide lapped into boulder-piled crannies. Late-nesting cormorant beat back and forth. Family gatherings of earlier broods sat on the sea, heads up, eyeing *Mrs Seal.* Too close, up and over, minutes pass, a hundred yards off, a line of black corks bobbed to the surface.

At Rubha Coigeach I turned east into Enard Bay. No landing opened, each winter's northerly 'whitebacks' burrowed into the coast. Ahead was Stac Pollaidh, its hacked-out corries narrowed to weathered pinnacles, steep and angular from a base which spread into empty moorland. A large shallow inlet appeared to the south. Dunes and sand. Houses, crofts, a road. I sailed on, closing the shore. Jumbled rock and keel-grinding boulders, stunted birch on white spindled legs poked out of bracken-fringed banks. No shelter, no landing. Stac Pollaidh on the bow, a mitre turret, my eye searched for a break and then, a last moment, yes, an opening, turning abruptly to starboard I slipped into a hidden bay almost at its foot.

Evocative as the imprint of homeland hill and wandered sea-shore, I'd found a circled bay of sheltered water secure from the swell of The Minch. Tucked into sloping westerly banks, above a line of shingle, nestled the ruins of a salmon-netting bothy, remote and unvisited. One sandstone gable remained, red and mellow, the roof long given to the northerly gale, a front wall of lintelled doorway and window socket faced the bay. A summer home, abandoned to moss and nettle, but there was fresh water from a burn which fell by a tiny waterfall on its southern shore. The anchor settled into clean sand. Ripples drifted on water, lens to a burning sun. Stripped in seconds, I dived off the stern and swam ashore.

Abandoned? At once a curlew sped to a watching stone on the headland, its call sharp and distressed. Rabbits scuttled about on the polished turf which surrounded the dwelling. Oystercatchers, noisy and bolder, brassy as their orange bills, held their ground. A wee sandpiper, white-chested, discreet as its dainty trill, scooted to a safe distance and bobbed at 'white man' dripping in the sun. A reproving heron balanced sedately at the mouth of the burn. *Mrs Seal* sat in a reflection suddenly broken by a round black head. Dark questioning eyes. Seal studied seal. Laughing, I made to the bothy. Pipits complained from where the bank ran into heather clumps. Abandoned? The place was alive. Below the ruin, an area of beach had been cleared to sand and shingle. The heaviest stones, heaved and levered, made a rough jetty. Here a salmon cobble had lain to unload white-bellied beauties, mouths agape, tails a-tapping the bottom boards. 'Silver darlings' hauled from cork-bobbing nets strung beyond the headland in the path of homing travellers. Fishing station times were no more. The ruin? Vacant possession? Nobody knew or cared – neither voice nor soul.

The tide was making its first gentle roll. An undulating carpet curled round the headland and flopped on the sand at my feet. The change of tide moved the air, a honeyed scent of crimson bell heather stirred across a moorland barrier. Disused peat cuttings made moss pools into spongy foot traps of orange sphagnum. Midge and cleg dens, frogs' delight, hoverpads for blue-bodied dragonflies and the rashy shelter of crouching chicks under a tumbling and fretting plover sky.

Helter-skelter I ran back into the sea, dived into yet another world – green fronds waving, limpet-encrusted rocks, sun-speared pebbles of gold. I swam wide-eyed, breath-bursting, cool and silent. Below me a crab scuttled on puppet legs. A world within worlds, connected but unknowing, stupidity thinks we near the end of knowing. I turned on my back and hand-flippered over to *Mrs Seal*, body brown basking on a sun-dancing sea.

Shell-encrusted jetty stone meant shoes. I carried the ammunition boxes of kit up from the boat to a home-making in the ruin. A childhood book returned – *The Swiss Family Robinson*, a tale of shipwreck and island home-building. Long consigned to a dustbin by the violence of computer games, it remained one of my mother's favourites in her nightly readings to me. I realise now how much a child may be shaped, dreams implanted, aspirations engendered by the impact of suggestion on heredity.

Scrapes of the spade showed a dry cobbled floor. Once cleared of nettle and fallen timber, I took the boat's tarpaulin, weighted stone on its ropes and drew it over the front wall and gable. Two spars and a lashed crosspiece propped centre and back. I prowled the scatter of valuables abandoned by high water. Wooden fish boxes nestled in the bracken. 'Crones Kippers. Return to Lochinver' they demanded. Not today. Instant furniture. The bothy became an airy dining kitchen. The rations were stowed in a spare box by the time steam poured from the little sooty kettle perched on my 'meths' stove. Tea. I leant against the gable. Its stones held the warmth of a cloud-free sun. The day slanted west. Presently I rowed *Mrs Seal* out to anchor. She turned her bow to the flow, a happy boat. She did me proud.

Under the bank at the back of the bothy, long grown with green slime, I came on the well, a small circle of built stone. What more? The ground beside the gable, dry and grassy, made my tent site. A peg into the wall at the empty window hung a shaving mirror, a strung mooring rope the clothes line, I was set up. Supper – sardines and tatties. Washing up – a rub in the sand at the water's edge. Round to the waterfall, toothbrush and towel, the season dry, yet slanted ledges still threw out a spray. I sat under. Cold. Boy, boy. Toes curled, breath shrank, testicles vanished. Three minutes, I pranced on the bank. Alive? Blood raced into corners it hadn't reached for years – a sunburnt body quivering with energy, a mind bursting with ideas, legs that could spang to the moon. Irrepressible, irresistible freedom. Yes, yes.

Last thing, I leant an elbow and looked out; the tent door faced the bay. Busy, I must have been the first to turn in. Rabbits munched just yards away, twitching noses, ears flat, their cheeks full, snuffles quite loud. The heron in great arching wing-flaps alighted at the end of the jetty, a haughty silhouette against glowing waters. A jerky-necked cormorant fished not far from the boat. Birds whistled and skimmed about on private business and the sandpiper, with a graceful lift of wing showing its bonnie white oxters, paused a moment on the sand and sang in lisping little notes.

And the tent, tight and close, the smell of the earth at my head, and the scent of the sea, oh the sea, the hugging sea, at my door, in my head, in my mind. How the waters shone, returning to the skies the light of a glorious day. And *Mrs Seal*, not to be outdone, showed her bonnie white lines on its luminous stillness.

◆

Softly, then again, the boat stirred, the day stirred, the sea stirred, sparkled before eager hills, nubile, beckoning. Warmth wakened with the breeze. A turning tide spread dimples round stones, glittered sands to treasure troves. The merest swell, unhurried from the south, floated fronds, strands of weed, up on a breath, down with a sigh. From the boulders of the night, her tresses gently wakened, combed by the tide to a toss of pride.

The Seal Woman turned, limpid eyes of a turquoise sea. Her sunlit hair rose and fell, caressed by the fingers of morning. Each thrust of the sea spread her auburn bliss, wet and glistening amidst a flurry of spent white froth. The bay was life. Life in love.

◆

Windswept and bleak on all but days of cloud-free skies, when a torpid Minch strung mist-edged islands out to dry, the rock-strewn *bealach* cut over a ridge which set me down the road to Achiltibuie. Undulating moorlands of stagnant peat cuttings and black hill lochans were left behind. Snipe nested on each rashy fringe, their bleating calls followimg my walk from the hidden bay. Sheep sounding bleats, wavering on evening's quiet warmth, a close and soft warmth filled the breath of a sea far below. I caught the dark shiny leaves of bog myrtle which grew by the road and rubbed them in my fingers – their fragrance was of wild places and pureness of shepherd's hills, unspoilt by human voice.

Let the road wind its way. On the *bealach* here I would sit awhile, on the gunnel of a broken boat. Southward, Ben Mor Coigach, cool and louring, lay before the departing sun. Beyond, imperious Slioch was mist-woven and orange-warm in the pine lands of Loch Maree, its sienna shades tapering from the Gairloch hills to the harsh promontory of Rudha Reidh and a lighthouse, marker to the mouth of Loch Ewe, the gathering ground of war's Atlantic convoys. I would put the sun on my shoulder and gaze northwards. Storr Point, the lume of its lighthouse would be showing on my homeward trek but, on the reflecting sea of evening, its land glowed with the green of winter geese and the white of circled bays. Grains of time ground from Suilven's peak across lochan moors where divers, black and red, tended dappled eggs and throated their wailing cry. And, held in these headland arms, I looked down on the 'Islands of the Haven' – coral sand and heather hummock, tucked in the safety of Loch Broom.

Beyond this island scatter, lay Skye and Trotternish and Quiraing, the fairy ridge, sharp against the western sun. In the Old Norse tongue, *quiraing* meant 'crooked cattle fold' and, to the squinting eye, a chiselled spine reached out to the cliffs of Rubha Hunish and over the tide-rip sound to the sheiling Isle of Trodday – Skye's northern tip and said by MacBrayne skippers of the one-time Kyle to Lewis run to be the roughest seas in all The Minch. For emboldened Norsemen, Minch, from *megin nes*, the 'great headlands', referred to Cape Wrath and the Butt of Lewis, where seahorses mount the land and seamen under sail know relief in safely rounding. These waters are broad, demanding and streaked with current – a corridor of snapping canvas since longships sheeted hard took seas on a starboard quarter and their loose-footed lug sail descendants, all sixty feet of double-ended lines, the great Zulu ketch of the herring boom days, raced Ullapool–Stornoway, six hours in a nor'east press.

West, against the indigo of Harris hills, breasting the force of constricted wind and current in the throat of The Minch, three islands seemed merged into one. The Shiants stood clear – round humps to bending gale, shunned by glacial power to a turmoil of tide, their rocks seldom without the taste of spray. Author Compton MacKenzie, their owner for a few years after the Great War, rebuilt the only house. Abandoned isles at the turn of last century to the seabird fishers of The Minch, in times of faith they were a hermit home. I vowed some day a visit, for the spirit of great emotion would haunt them still.

Away northward, by crimson cloud the Eye Peninsula of Lewis hid the Rocks of Holm. A shipwreck and drowning of Lewis young of which my father spoke. Sea-dug grave of homeward men from Flander's fields, trench and poppy red. Pensive homes of croft and creel, black in setting light.

At last I stirred. A breeze that follows round to evening's sun is a friend of settled days. From the drying orb it came and made crinkled veins where upturned clouds had sailed their way uncharted. The Minch drew in the hollow of the night and I followed west the flight of hill and cliff, steps to thraldom, golden down the sunset isles.

◆

My seat beside the road was a cracked, back-broken boat, its wind-peeled planks of faded blue, thwarts of flaking white. Nail and rib sprung from its gunnelled memory, timbers ground by the mighty coitus of the land and sea. Strange it lay so far from home, up there upon the heights.

Each evening as I passed summer into autumn, auburn haired, dress sad torn, turquoise as the sea, raised arm waving, a tiny dimpled doll, a child's doll, sat propped against the stern. Nothing, nobody, not child nor gale, moved her, took her home. Did she wait a childhood lost? The sun would set in hazel eyes, unblinking eyes, unfocused on the present, a stare which held the past, and we spoke, the doll in a boat and I.

My bay-ward late met waving hand, put moonlight in her hair, a dewdrop crown on auburn dark. In eyes so bright with memory's light a turquoise day saw children play beside their dune set bay, and spirits laughed to see them count each treasure shell of childhood's golden spell.

◆

One night as the season waned and a sated land poured musky warmth like balm upon the sea, I rowed beyond the bay, into the darkness below Stac Pollaidh, boat and the Seal Woman, together. Nothing marked shore from hill, no sound, no curling surf. The sea slept and, from its dreams, spilled cascades of life. Specks of phosphorescent glow, seconds each lived their golden radiance in the ripple of our wake.

The tip of oars made pools of gentle rowing, each move a sequinned trail. Dipping hands caught the glittering trickle, living silk in lingered fingers, bejewelled moments touching the lustre of moon-flesh, yielding moon-flesh. Soft the embrace of a milk-flesh moon. An autumn moon that, on the blackest pillared hill, placed her saffron crown. A harvest moon, who down the pathway to fulfilment suffused a sea which through her light saw the birth of our reality.

◆

Lochinver to the north was my source for supplies. I decided on a last sail – the weather might turn, another moon was waxing. It seemed natural living without a switch to note her every phase and humour, her ability to foretell the weather and mine to read the forecast. That night she stood high, icy crisp, crater-pocked, clear-edged. The air was thin and shadows short. I stood by the tent for a last look at the bay before turning in. The moon floated on its surface, a saucer of brightness within impenetrable outlines. The boat lay to her anchor, motionless, a white swan. For a second, a glinting light aboard her cast across the water. It vanished. I stared dumbfounded, listening without breath.

And from somewhere over the quavered water there arose a wailing chorus, many voices, high pitched, then fading into stillness. A sound mournful, beseeching. Beyond sepulchral grief. I caught my shepherd's stick and walked gingerly. Rounded boulders clicked. Each step staccato sharp, dead bracken rustled at my knee.

The unearthly sound grew again, mingled with the moonbeams. My breath coiled damp and white into a frost-tinged night. Beyond the headland, out on the rocks, silhouettes against a moon-green sea, weaving, swaying. Slender pointed heads, limbless profiles, dark vibrating throats strained towards the carnal temptress.

I shuddered. The probing sound came again, a long wavering siren throbbing into the very pores of night, trembling with the chill of an opening of sea-locked graves, of a drawing forth of souls set to endless wander – of those who loved and perished by the ocean moon's imperious call. The People of the Sea were singing. But, as I listened, their voices faded, died to a crooning. The drowned, weary within the chrysalis of their sealskin tombs, offered a coronach before the ensnaring moon.

◆

Next day, I made the supply trip to Lochinver. The islands which marked my route, Fraochlan and Soyea, had lost their heather blush. The birches of Inverkirkaig straggling towards the massive

Suilven were lemon-leaved. The great ben itself was a grey carbuncle protruding from an endless morass of matted sedges and diver-flown lochans. Sailing back, the sea felt restless.

I beached *Mrs Seal* beside the rough stone jetty, knowing the tide would be full by mid morning on the morrow. After supper, I swilled the dishes at the water's edge. The candle glowed from my green tarpaulin kitchen. Its tin was filling with grease. Nights were closing. I lay in the dark tent, the sounds of the bay muted. Last thing, as always, before the solid sleep that comes wrapped in a natural world, I stepped out and felt the weather on my skin, the moist chill of a change. In the bleak light a northern sky set studding clouds.

Dawn held a rawness, without heat a salty dampness seeped into the tent, my clothes and, more importantly, my writing paper. Wad upon wad of Scottish Farmers Union press releases, unread but clean on one side, I used for all correspondence plus the almost-completed longhand copy of *Isolation Shepherd*. I peered out. *Mrs Seal* would float in a couple of hours. Winter quarters were needed.

I made a last cup of tea. All packed and loaded aboard, the empty bothy reluctant as myself at parting. Foolish the attachment that grows for worn stone and a sturdy gabled shelter in lonesome one-to-one living. My hands round the cup, the wind sharp, ruffling the bay, low over the headland flew eight large birds and skimmed on to the water. Dark backs and long whitish necks, they paddled about with a slight jerky movement. Their heads were beautiful. Black crests, a dagger bill and white cheek feathers which shaded into bright chestnut above a black ruff. Slavonian grebes? They were strangers to me. Ttravellers south before the storms?

Gauntness hung on Stac Pollaidh, the coat of autumn's apprehension. Gone the summer's medley. Soon birch would lean, the season would be about their feet and a north wind would fill the chinks of the gable with the sound of winter. I poled away from the jetty. Hunched gulls were turning the tide wrack, fretful and peevish. The bothy, roofless and doorless but, in the bay, the dark eyes of the People of the Sea. *Mrs Seal* turned the headland into a rising swell, grey and cold. The hidden home, a lost place.

## 17

# 'Phone, Darling, For You – it's the Russian Embassy'

'I was planning to call the coastguard, Thomson boy. We watched you rounding Reiff point, in and out of sight when a big one came, close thing. Anyway, the nearest lifeboat's in Stornoway so we downed tools and hurried here to be sure you made it.' Their careful choice of observation post was the window of Achiltibuie's Am Fuaran Bar. Concerned pal, Murdo William, accordion maestro and doyen of the County pick-and-shovel squad, looked seriously into his dram. I'd booked one of his Summer Isles panorama chalets for the winter. 'Aye, a fair push, Murdo, but, look here, it landed me in at a handy time.' Relief at my deliverance from the deep was already spreading over several faces.

As I entered the north channel into Old Dornie Harbour, a ponderous run of waves over the sandbar threatened to slew *Mrs Seal* broadside and join me in the boat. My predicament, clearly visible from the window of a bar with an equal propensity for slewing the novice, caught the attention of accountant Bill, retired London 'shredder' and lately displaying a marked fixation for a Fuaran stool. Speechless, he'd laid his head on the counter, preparing for grief. Pat, his wife, ex-shipping lobbyist to the House of Commons, who'd viewed *Mrs Seal*'s possible foundering with a gravity suited to the loss of the *Titanic*, was now rejoicing. 'Thank God there'll be no insurance claim,' she twittered continuously. Nor was it every afternoon that the Achiltibuie Roads Department was given an opportunity to prepare itself for snatching a man from the jaws of the sea. Moreover, the road engineer's departure for Ulla-pool had been noted two hours previously. Oh be joyful. A nod to barman owner, Andy, ensured the yellow oilskins gathered solici-tously about me downed something more to their liking than a shovel.

◆

Two or three nights a week, with a sheaf of *Isolation Shepherd* tucked in the back pocket, I'd spanged the fourteen-mile round trip from my hideaway bay to Achiltibuie and back, *en passant* to indulge a round or two of Guinness as I sat doing bookish corrections, head down, low profile, in a corner of the village's cultural heartland, the inestimable Am Fuaran.

Quaint name, quaint old but and ben which, when elevated from croft house to public house, became the polished pride of Andy Wilson and his wife. Quaint? The word required redefining. The quality of whimsy extended far beyond its name and the establish-ment's capricious selection of nautical curios. Exhibits varied. A ship's boiler with brass bridge to engine-room controls took pride of place before a bulbous, screw-on, diving helmet which, in extremis, could be adjusted over the head of any client requiring oxygen. Wall and ceiling were festooned. Navigation lamps, lobster creels, sails, flags, models, maps, oars and lifebelts, the gleanings of wrack and wreck, a pint-pulling mermaid wiping froth with her tail would not have raised an eyebrow.

Each summer ripened its tourist miscellany. Over half shandies, varicose veins in shorts and full-blown bottoms in tight jeans, interspersed with macho muscles and twiggy popsies, exclaimed at this extempore collection of salty mementoes. Not without a touch of envy did they mingle, sniff, nay even savour, the egalitarian scent of prawn fishermen up from cleaning their catch at Old Dornie jetty and the Havana whiff of accountants relaxing from the stresses inflicted by their imaginative profession. A compound of inventors and subversive poets sprinkled the general cacophony with erudite remarks whilst 'double snooter' shepherds passed as unnoticed the offensive skirt-lifting habits of their collie dogs' noses.

Despite its Gaelic name – *Am Fuaran*, translating as 'The Well' – there seemed little to suggest water played any significant role in the expertise displayed by the establishment's numerous exponents of the art of avoiding a view of the ceiling after ten-thirty. Seasoned campaigners to a man, not to mention a comely selection of ample ladies, they, when nudged by the elbow of emotion, would embrace Am Fuaran's inflaming dose of tartan dance music and Scot Nat. politics.

By twelve each Friday, as a result of the dispensary's prescription of Famous Grouse, Jimmy Shand and the fiery cross, the mawkish 'Flower of Scotland' had bloomed three times and Proud Edward's Army had dropped swords to cover their ears. Tourist throng and local fervour alike would be weaving arm in arm amidst the nautical trappings to emphasise the brotherhood of mankind, whilst chanting, heedless of any incongruity, for the freedom of a nation enslaved by the English yoke. Non-pacifist sentiments, fist waving behind the security of a single-track road and a hotline to Ullapool which would afford timely warning of any possible peak-capped impediment to such spirited aspirations.

Short only of a loudhailer to convey one's order to the bar, this cocktail of abstraction powered a shoebox premises with an element of fantasy difficult to locate elsewhere in the Highlands. In short, a suitable training ground for those of revolutionary tendencies and certainly a premises of sufficient educational merit to propel the youthful David Green from road-gang navvy to Convenership of Highland Regional Council. Furthermore, its cramped parking facility provided a convenient stance for Murdo William's digger when not engaged in opening drains and its bilateral front door the friendship of old-timers like Donnie the Drover, when not engaged in finding them. Above all, for the few not swayed by the view of its internal novelties, the tiny bar window snapped a 'wish you were here' postcard print of the Summer Isles.

Tucked behind the diver's helmet, I scribbled corrections, mindful of my duty to the pen, elevated to a higher calling as it were, in keeping with the attitude of some fellow scribe whose advert I'd spotted on the 'For Sale or Swap' notice-board: 'Poems written, any subject, any length, 10p per line, apply Les.' Roughly a sonnet a Guinness. A well-reasoned calculation at minutes to eleven. I checked my stock of verse. The approach of an exhaust-free Land Rover with a window full of yelping terriers, drowned even Donnie the Drover's continuous rendering of 'Fear A Bhata'. Raucous laughter, occasioned by one of Tam the Painter's more questionable jokes, dwindled to a snigger. 'Marie's Wedding' exhaled from the Sinclair lassie's bagpipes. Margaret, the dark-haired barmaid, our 'Bonnie Lass o' Fyvie O', blushed the blush of a fluttering heart. In burst 'Kenny the Manager'. Ah, sweet the romance when eyes meet through a smoke-blue mirror behind the optics.

Dedicated flockmaster and proud wearer of his calling's professional insignia which hung unfailingly on a thong round his neck in the form of a dog whistle cut from a Heinz beans can, 'The Manager' seemed invariably en route to, or returning from, a fox den. Am Fuaran served as the pivotal point of much nocturnal rambling in the name of vermin control. He smiled at Margaret, pints appeared, pen and paper slipped out of sight and, in moments, he and I were picking over the financial and political entrails of Scotland's pastoral industry. More my style. Never a writer of consequence nor inclined towards the literati circuit, I preferred the banter of a sheep fank and the clack of working shears to the click of a typewriter.

◆

Bill and Pat, a cultivated and entertaining couple who fitted the Fauran's eccentric ambience well, had purchased a sea-fronted croft house as far as one could go if heading south from Achiltibuie. Their à la mode renovation – open plan, open house, log fire and always the same half-finished watercolour gracing an easel by the front door – viewed the wide scenic entrance to Loch Broom. In due season, an invitation, if not a summary proclamation, was issued throughout the five parishes of the Coigach Peninsula indicating a New Year extravaganza, tempered with a measure of decorum befitting London ex-pats of some social standing.

Sadly the tenor of their croft-house idyll had, for several months prior to the summons, been marred by uncomradely intrusion from behind the Iron Curtain. Assorted flotsam, lewd music, song and certain used unmentionables, all this uninvitingly spiced by the stench of gutted mackerel, drifted daily to the foot of their garden. Lights blazed and heavy diesel engines thumped, night and day, through a fug of blue fumes. The croft-house windows and Bill's powerful binoculars looked out on some twenty-odd massively rusting Russian fish-freezer ships which had dropped anchor in quite pre-emptory fashion just off the sensitive couple's newly-planted shrubbery. How could one possibly prune the roses?

Every boat capable of staying afloat was in the trade, furiously tipping The Minch's mackerel treasure into the floating Volgavich deep freezers of these latter-day Klondykers. Every evening speeding launches plied an equally furious trade. Taxi-loads of Inverness ladies embarked, only to realise, after their first exhausting night spent in furthering the cause of Scottish-Russian relations, that fifty thousand roubles, which exchanged at four shillings and sixpence, was scant recompense for their ministrations, notwithstanding, on the morning's limping departure, the crew's generous gift of a box of gutted mackerel.

That misfortune apart, letters flew from the croft. Captain MacLeod, the Ullapool Harbour Master, the Minister of Trade and Industry and the Russian Ambassador were but a few of those appraised. Such was the exposé of one fourteen-page diatribe, sent by registered post to the Ministry of Defence that spies abounded, Trotskys plotted the shelling of a load of tourists aboard Desperate Dan's *Summer Queen*; and secret agents sang hymns at the Fisherman's Mission. Reds under the bed? I tell you, an alarmed Cabinet felt moved to consider a resumption of the Cold War. To say the couple were outraged: *Dieu et Mon Droit!* Such indeed were the outpourings of fulminous correspondence, that three of Bill's finest fountain pens now had crossed nibs. Our nation stood in peril. Further, and equally seriously, the Fuaran's clientele endured a daily pint-curdling tirade of vitriolic displeasure.

New Year's morn dawned with a clarity enjoyed only by the abstemious of Achiltibuie – the massed ranks of whom would not prevent the door of the village's phone kiosk from closing, nor, I must add, would 'Bill the Shredder' number amongst their under-subscribed fraternity. His trembling hand strayed from head to curtain, the absence of any external throbbing a puzzle. His hand knitted a moist brow. He feebly unknitted it and reached for dark glasses. Loch Broom opened up. Ship-free, fume-free, only a spiral of gulls squawked over sinking guts. 'Hallelujah,' he bawled. A careless response, it conveyed both a false image to his dozing spouse and a searing flash, not entirely of insight, to a head which fell back upon feather pillows. Vindication at last, his Parker pen was proven mightier, er, mightier than, mee, aarr . . . 'Oh, my God!' Bill fumbled for the commode.

A singing cavalcade jostled its way along the single track that night. To Kenny the Manager's Land Rover and its standard consignment of terriers were added: ourselves; Margaret, 'The Bonnie Lass of Fyvie O'; Jack Thomson 'the Inventor'; Tam, 'the paint slapper'; a crop-spraying contractor; and several unidentifiable bodies. The little bijou croft house welcomed us with blazing lights and a thick coil of peat smoke from its stubby lum. 'Guid New Years' and embraces were freely exchanged, some a shade juicier and less inhibited than met the approval of lady wives. Beyond certain frowns, through a 40 per cent haze and peat-fire warmth came the tinkling notes of our host's rosewood boudoir grand as it brightly entertained more than a sprinkling of long dresses and the two inches of cuff influentials of Wester Ross.

Tuxedo and bow tie, Bill was an Ivor Novello buff, a passable pianist and knew all the words. To his rendering of 'We'll Gather Lilacs', a few of us of a musical taste gathered admiringly round the piano. The majority busied themselves gathering sausage-roll dainties and admiring the drinky cabinet – prior, that is, to closer inspection. A casual query, 'Is there a spade in the Rover, Kenny?' A nod. In moments, from a perch on the back shed, a couple of divots covered the puffing lum.

Bill's recital had reached a warbling wartime favourite, 'Keep the Home Fires Burning' when the smoke attack struck. He sang manfully on, his voice reduced to a croak, his hands and the keys now invisible under billows of a throat-gripping reek that engulfed the drawing room. People lost sight of their drinks, there was much groping, not all in search of glasses. At that moment Pat was heard calling hoarsely through the smog, 'Phone, darling, for you – it's the Russian Embassy.'

Bill's chest swelled. He coughed. 'Yes, I thought they might contact me.' And, catching the phone, he said, 'Hello. To whom am I speaking? Ah good. You obviously received my letters.' Long pause. The fug was clearing from the room – unlike Bill's brain. A quick flip of the divots had left nothing more than an aroma reminiscent of the home's origins as a 'black house' and Pat's tapestry drapes in need of dry cleaning.

Good manners failed and we all listened intently. A guttural voice with just the smattering of a lilt crackled along the line. Bill's rise to Second Lieutenant in the Pay Corps shone through. 'Look here, give me the Ambassador.' More grunting, and, faintly in the background, the strains of Jimmy Shand. 'Evening, Ambassador,' Bill, meticulous to fault, was allowing for continental time as the mellow chimes of the couple's stately Harrison timepiece struck 1.30 a.m. 'Thank you, Ambassador, for having your fleet removed. A revolting experience, d'ye hear me? Yes, revolting – an outrageous infringement of our privacy, you understand, out-ra.' Crackle, crackle. 'Yes, I'm prepared to accept your apology – preferably in writing.' Crackle, more Jimmy Shand, and more than a hint of the Fuaran. 'Oh, oh my! How kind of you, sir – yes, so kind, yes, of course, sir, of course we will, sir. I shall acknowledge with the greatest pleasure. Thank you so much. Goodnight, sir.'

'Darling, darling, we're invited to lunch next week at the Russian Embassy!' And, racing back to the piano, Bill launched into a rousing salvo of 'Rule Britannia'.

Some weeks passed before 'Bill the Shredder' was to stare at a puzzled letter from London bearing the Hammer and Sickle and a second-class stamp.

# 18

# 'There's Something Menacing Us'

On a winter's day, sallow with feeble sunlight which tinged the mists that prowled along a coast of fingered edge, we walked from my hidden bay where gale-shorn turf lived only by its tenuous grip and the pink flowers of summer thrift had long huddled in their roots. The booming caverns which snuffed a swell were empty and silent, for the sea that day was without feature, grey and shapeless, and the gulls, which drifted here and there amongst the pockets of yellow fog upon its surface, were strangely mute. Not by accident it might now seem, we came upon a tidal passage through a gash in the cliff which opened into a tiny perfectly sheltered cove. Invisible from the sea, it formed a retreat into which some small boat might, by plucky helm, be swallowed by the land.

A wooden bothy beside the cove indicated times within memory when tarry-seamed salmon cobbles would vanish through the cliffs to land their catch and booted fishermen filled boxes tide by tide when the fish were on a run and nets were scrubbed and hung to a muttered cursing of the seals and their damage. Now isolation lay dank and heavy; no mewling bird to cry on sombre air. A mist without motion, thin and remorseless, entwined the bracken fronds which folded dull and bent about the hollow. We wandered into a place of abject seclusion. Only for those who lived before the fishing times, who strove by lazy bed and creel, did green hummocks lie in rows, a reminder of survival toil.

I stood looking. 'Almost graves.' I spoke quietly. An involuntary comment, a statement forced as though before the thought. I felt a slight unease. Stillness carried the melancholy of an oppressive void, penetrating as the invasive mist which refused to be shaken from the face of the sea, cloying as the first pangs of a tangible foreboding.

The bothy door scraped open. Disuse gripped its hinges. We sat on the dusty floor to have Christmas cake and a dram. I hesitated. The unease grew compelling. 'Do you find anything strange about this place?' Words barely uttered before my stomach turned to clamps of dread. A tingling sensation of intense apprehension, some force jangled through my nerves. A chilling malevolence surrounded us. Some sinister motive, threatening, as though to strike. I shivered violently. The Seal Woman looked shaken. 'Yes, I do – very, very. There's something menacing us – really close. It's in the air – it's horrible, evil.' She jumped wildly to the window. 'This is choking! I'm frightened – let's get out of this place.'

Thoroughly alarmed, we ran from the hollow on to the moorland to find the evening sky clear and cheerful, the bracken glowing chestnut on the dunes beyond the distant sands of Garvie Bay. We sauntered down to the wide expanse of solitary beach. Flocks of wintering knot, plump and grey-feathered, scurried after the fleeting tide. A little run, a probe hither and thither and a short flight on rapid wings brought fresh probing and, as they alighted, their soft lisping voices floated to us across crimson pools of setting sun. We watched them into the darkening, until the beams of Storr light were cast over a sea no longer enswathed.

A year passed. We motored one clear January night by the shores of Loch Maree. Tall pines darkly outlined its holy burial isle across waters stilled by a turn to frost. The heights of Slioch flitted between the wayside birch. I admired its soaring power through an open car window. And then for some reason, 'Remember our uncanny visit to the wooden bothy?' As I spoke the hair rose stiff on the back of my neck. Never before had I known such an experience. Evil, force or spirit, whatever form, it flowed about us as though obeying a predestined order of happenings incorporeal. For moments the intensity of dread returned.

Our friend, Willie Muir, rented the salmon stations and netting rights which stretched around the Coigach Peninsula. Few knew more of the ways of wild salmon. His disgust at them being farmed in cages had no bounds. The introduction of this practice to the Summer Isles across from his window he viewed as environmental rape. Sophisticated intellect marked a man also tempted to a modicum of sophistication in dress and habits. A visit to his pine-panelled house in Achiltibuie where rifles hung above a computer screen tended towards recondite conversations requiring much mental digging. My half-remembered theories of Karl Popper, the Austrian philosopher whose David Hume-style statement that 'science is not certain knowledge but a series of conjectures and refutations approaching, though never reaching, a definitive truth' appealed to Willie no end after several malts.

Such a visit to him transpired the night after of our unusual journey beside Loch Maree. Smoked wild salmon and malt whisky were blending when I mentioned that a year previous we had discovered his wooden salmon bothy at the secret cove east of Garvie Bay. Our bizarre experience of that twelve months past, now much underlined during the lochside drive, I carefully avoided recounting.

Willie poured another malt before commenting, 'Did you find anything strange about the place?' he queried, looking sharply at us. 'Yes, we did.' I didn't disclose more, just waited for comment. 'Well,' he said after a pause, 'I never got any fishermen to stay the whole week in that place – they simply refused.' Ominous stillness struck the room, I was alert and tense. Willie spoke quietly, 'Old record has it that a band of MacLeods from Lewis, ex-Viking type, sometime in the 1500s, found that cove and put its family to the sword – man, wife and children.'

Had we touched a realm where great emotion leaves its imprint? An energy wavelength which conquers time by 'entanglement'? As science unravels the behaviour of subatomic particles, does their role in the electro-chemical exchanges in the synapses between the neurons of our brain echo the mysteries of the occult? Wavelength and energy are inseparable – the energy of a photon dictates the wavelength of its emission. Einstein's special 'space-time' relativity is under pressure. The speed of light may well turn out to be proportional and variable to its energy source and, within such a frame, the quantum particle moves in mysterious ways – can spin both clockwise and anticlockwise simultaneously, can exist 'entangled' in two places simultaneously over incalculable distances.

◆

The son of a Scottish bookseller was to turn the Cavendish Laboratory of Cambridge into the world's greatest research institution. By extending the electromagnetic theories of another Scotsman, James Clerk Maxwell, and using Wilhelm Röntgen's discovery of X-rays, J. J. Thomson gave us the electron. Two thousand times smaller in mass than the lightest known atomic particle, the hydrogen ion, Thomson's experimental deduction is regarded as the greatest revolution in physics since Isaac Newton. Under Thomson's brilliant direction, his student, Ernest Rutherford, together with Niels Bohr, gave us nuclear physics. The concept of the atom as a miniature universe in which the mass is concentrated in a nucleus surrounded by planetary electrons placed scientific research en route to atomic disintegration and the phenomenal energy release of shattered uranium.

The force binding an atom is ten thousand, trillion, trillion, trillion times stronger than gravity yet the interplay twixt micro- and macro-energies is a continuum. Theory suggests the force of 'dark energy' accounts for at least 70 per cent of the universe's mass. Its tug-of-war with gravity may determine the time scale of our present universe and the volume of its mass. The physical relationship of human thought to an evolving, changing cosmos has expression through great emotion, in the elegance of mathematics, music and the arts.

Hydrogen atoms represent three-quarters of the detectable mass of the fifteen-billion-year existence of this universe's cycle. Chilly interstellar space at twenty Kelvin is the common birthplace of most stars. Five billion years back uneven densities in swirling stellar dust felt the grip of gravity. Space gave birth to our sun, built a furnace, fifteen million centigrade at its heart, blasted hydrogen into helium. Carbon atoms coalesced, grew the bridge between inorganic and organic. Water, an oxide of hydrogen. Wavelengths of sunlight, catalyst of the earliest terrestrial molecules. Three billion years and single-celled organism discover sex via the trick of protein synthesis. The sea, home of the first reproducing cells, had our fish-like amphibian ancestors sunbathing on the Palaeocene beaches of moon-drawn tides. Homo sapiens' ancestors, a stripling species swinging in Olduvai Gorge two million years ago, ate condensed sunshine, their bodies but decelerated energy distilled from universal elements; their consciousness, electrons whizzing around atoms in the synapses between the neural molecules of sensory detectors. Our sun has just ten billion years of hydrogen supplies left in the kitty, short, that is, of being accidentally dragged into an accretion disc and sucked down a black cosmic plughole – time enough surely for the force of imagination to act on insight and redesign the universe. After all, 90 per cent of the 1 per cent of genes which differentiate chimps from humans dramatically increased activity in the human brain. Are we on the brink of an intelligence expansion?

Information, its storage, transfer and usage, is the basis for the next technological explosion. Scientists argue over the speed of digital information transfer. Günter Nimtz of the University of Cologne believes that encoded microwaves can be transmitted through a tunnelling device at 4.7 times the speed of light in a vacuum. At the University of California, Raymond Chiao showed that pulses of light pass through a filter made up of thin layers of titanium oxide and silica glass at 1.7 times light's vacuum speed. A team in Milan's Technical University recorded pulses travelling five times faster than the cosmic speed barrier. For the moment the researchers suggest their results may be an illusion. A pulse contains many light waves of slightly differing frequencies. Nonetheless, their work leads to the frontiers of space-time.

The ancient Greek, Euclid, believed that there are infinite prime numbers. Zeno and his hare and tortoise paradox showed that the concept of infinity is something which your maths teacher can't do without. Infinity makes mathematics tick – as Leibniz and Newton discovered when inventing calculus. Raise infinity to the power of infinity. Do we get a larger infinity? Mathematicians are teasing out more than one kind of infinity by playing with numbers. The size of a number, no matter to what power we may raise or decrease it, must be related to, or simply reflect, the speed of its calculation as a continuum. If we count at the speed of light do we reach infinity, a paradox or just a process?

Graph the growth of processed knowledge over a planetary time scale. How steep could the curve become? Would vertical point to the instability of infinity? Could the universe exist and still contain the concept of infinity? If the universe merely reflects the rate of change of an energy imbalance, can infinity exist?

The hunter-gatherer circling a water hole twelve thousand years ago didn't ponder on differential calculus or the options afforded by genetic manipulation, yet their possibility must have existed. Prowling the solar system is stalking at today's water hole – looking back through time as a means to see into the future, probing the universe for the possible, seeking the Holy Grail of cosmology, an ordered system of knowledge, the Unified Theory of Everything.

Is such a theory possible, improbable or impossible? It depends on proof of infinity. And if this can't be proven? Joseph of Arimathea reputedly used the cup of Christ's Last Supper to collect the blood that flowed from the Crucifixion. That Holy Grail has yet to turn up. If either were found, would they undo the beauty of a metaphysical world?

# 19

# This Supreme Act of Sexual Ecstasy

Sunrise, the male erection of morning's glory, a rising moon upturned, the graceful spread of curving limbs. Venus, the evening star to bless a coitus bond. Unruly planets to outpace the stars. Circles and heel stones to align procreation with each season's vital journey. Lunar month and menstrual flow dictate mankind's succession, give power to the female principle. The wild arc of the moon's nineteen-year cycle, alluring in mystery, fickle in the difficulty of its prediction for the ancients. Feminine wiles set before the steady sun of seedtime, summer growth and autumn fill. Male sun, female moon and planets to play the very mischief with our fortunes and disposition. Maybe naïve fancies for most today, compelling truths to our stonemason ancestors.

These celestial attributes are the origins of theological conjecture, the core of prehistoric worship. Two geocyclic features, their profundity impacting upon primitive survival, connecting mankind to something above and beyond, creating his superstitious nature, prompting enquiry into the mystery of life and consciousness, fuelling a search for some predictable hedge against death and booking a goodbye ticket into unknown oblivion. The might of nature frightened primitive minds into supplication, into the worship of an omnipotent sun who held the trump cards of each season's bounty, who sired the swelling moon's flow of fecundity. A masculine world of feminine compliance.

Simple observation grew to belief. The supernal character of these life-sustaining phenomena provided the safety of day, the danger of night. Light and darkness became the concept of good and evil. A virtuous Creator versus a malevolent Devil. The dualistic reasoning of Zarathustra, a desert prophet to the Persians from the foothills of Afghanistan nigh on three thousand years ago, whipped up this theme. At a final battle, with shades of Armageddon, he forecast confidently to his Zoroastrian followers, purity and good would triumph, a new world order would emerge – standard gloom and doom leavened with a dash of hope. A variety of Messiahs were soon waiting in the wings for their stage cue. Cultural religion was hotting up, splitting a sun god into various polarised versions of the 'truth', each claiming absolute validity. Priesthoods, in multi-powered forms, all with a monopoly on 'truth', stepped into the sunlight and a shadow fell between man and his supposed maker. 'Truth' was no joke but a specialist activity.

Monotheism, the belief in a single, invisible, indivisible, all-powerful God, resplendent throughout all eternity who deals in the ultimate destiny of man and the universe, is, for the masses, the most influential theory so far conceived by human mind. The effects of this concept permeate the behaviour of Western and Middle Eastern societies, historically and politically, to the present day.

Religion, as we describe this phenomenon, easily got a grip on societies susceptible to the forces of nature. Nor should it surprise today's generation of transcendental meditators that such elevated theorising three or more thousand years ago involved the highly probable use of hallucinatory narcotics. Indulge their usage in a situation of wide horizons and isolation – a mountain top or desert will suffice – and you produce a powerful form of mysticism, a sense of communing with some all-pervading power.

◆

Hidden in the desolate mountains of the biblical land of Edom, an arid area to the south of the Dead Sea, the Edomites, a sect of the Hebrews, had a hand in the origins of monotheistic worship. High on a sacred mountain, perhaps Mount Sinai of the Ten Commandments but certainly above their oasis city of Petra, Edomite stone tablets depict the worship of a masculine sun lying between the horns of a female crescent moon.

A concentrating of the Edomite sun god's power was achieved by deflecting the first rays of sunrise with a highly polished disc of gold or silver on to an altar sacrifice in their holy shrine. Its shaft of light, focused on to the ritually slaughtered lamb or calf, imbued the meat with the spirit of God. Priests partaking of the resulting meal enjoyed a similar infusion of divine spirit. A cracking good theme which later developed into the communion ritual and the mysterious Holy Spirit of the Christian's New Testament doctrine.

Growing on the sun-baked soil of the Edomites' holy mountain is an extremely hardy desert shrub, the thorn apple. This bitter fruit when eaten produces an extreme burning sensation which induces hallucinogenic visions. The priesthood of the Edomites used this fruit when worshipping before sacrificial offerings on a stone altar with carved horns. Moreover, they were certainly connected to the biblical foundling Moses – he of the basket in the bulrushes story and the stone tablet of Commandments from God given on Mount Sinai. Nice one, but did Moses indulge? Was this mind-bending apple the forbidden fruit of the Garden of Eden? His burning bush the Tree of Knowledge? An apple a day would definitely allow any priest or prophet to communicate with the visionary world. Not an indulgence for the laity.

Perhaps the most appealing aspect of Edomite belief was to be found in their egalitarian attitudes. They treated women as equals and were democratic even down to the collective ownership of property. The mercenary proclivities of their fellow Jews they detested. Above all they valued mercy, peace, compassion and forgiveness. Slavery was abhorred and, most unusual for a society of high mysticism, the pathway lay open for anyone wishing to train in accessing the glory of their God. For the Edomites, God was to be reached in the mountains, His spirit sought in the seclusion of remote and lonely places by a self-denying contemplation and His presence entered into even by the naughty hallucinatory effects hinted at in St Matthew's Gospel on the occasion of the transfiguration of Christ on the Mount as he ascended into Heaven.

Around this period of Edomite indulgence, the so-called 'Heretic

Pharaoh' Akhenaton, King of Egypt in 1370 BC, also used a technique of directing the sun's rays in the temples which he built specially for his monotheistic solar cult. Moreover Akhenaton who, by the way, was involved with Moses – he of the famous exodus from Egypt – depicted himself as being bisexual. God incarnate and no carnal nonsense. Mankind's shift from hunter-gatherer to herdsman had created a healthy respect for Ferdinand, his horns and penis power. The sacred bull of great antiquity whose horns mimicked the new moon presented the attributes of a hermaphrodite and was deemed suitable by the pharaoh to represent the emergence of the human race. The Old Testament's fashioning of Eve from Adam underlines this infatuation with androgynous creation in Hebrew thought. Bulls constantly feature in biblical texts – golden statues to the God Baal, killing the 'fatted calf', the bull myth covers all Middle Eastern civilisations. A shade passé for Moses, up from the Nile and bursting with ideas, it all got a thumbs down from this theological entrepreneur from Pharaonic Egypt. He set about a revamp.

Ra, the archetypal Egyptian sun god, was closely allied to the grain god Osiris, probably the most significant of the Egypt's pantheon. Osiris, by their way of it, met with a touch of misfortune. Seth, his jealous sibling, after a particularly boozy session together, stuffed the comatose Osiris into a coffin, nailed down the lid and turfed it into the Nile. Their sister goddess Isis, after much searching, found the washed-up body, breathed it into life and impregnated herself with her brother's semen. A notable feat for the times.

Miffed by his sister's knack with AI, Seth regained the remains of Osirus, hacked them up and re-dumped them along the banks of Nile, taking malicious delight in flinging his brother's penis to a passing crocodile. A low trick if ever there was one. A sobbing sister Isis, searching once more, buried all the bits and pieces at various Holy sanctuaries, excepting of course the crocodile's lunch, which lamented private member was to become the focus of a highly popular Osiris cult for, in remembrance of the missing phallus, Isis modelled herself a somewhat exaggerated replica, copies of which are not unknown to this day to devotees of such aids to pleasure.

Isis became the mother of the god-kings of Egypt. Her portrayal with a crown of cow horns encircling a sun disc was an image later to enamour Greco-Roman culture. They called Isis Stella Maris, 'Star of the Sea', and represented her as the North Star. Researchers show that this Isis cult much influenced the portrayal of the Virgin Mary in transition of Roman pagan religions to Christianity. Arcane cults exist today which are traceable to these mythological origins. Could it be that Zarathustra or Ancient Egyptians thought up monotheism and, via Moses, Edom and Rome, provided the backdrop to Christianity's one god theory?

Threads lead us to the myth of Isis. Worship of the Black Madonna, still found in the Languedoc of Southern France, points to Isis, the goddess of a dusky hue and consort to the great god Osiris, who died and rose again on the third day. Black Madonnas were worshipped both as fully experienced women and as holy virgins, the fullness and power of the female principle and the sacredness of the sexual act represented for pagans and certain Christians alike. The remains of Mary Magdalene, discoverer of the empty tomb of a crucified messiah and considered by the Gnostic Gospels to be the lover if not the wife of Jesus, are said to lie in the Languedoc area. The mytho-poetic theme of the sexual union of heavenly gods and an earthly female as a sacred act lies behind Greco-Roman Christianity and though airbrushed and sanitised by two thousand years of misogynous attitudes, it kept women subservient to a male-dominated religion which invented its own prejudicial rules.

◆

Intriguingly, a French secret society, the highly exclusive Priory of Sion, records Leonardo da Vinci, painter of two of the world's most revered works, as one of its Grand Masters. In this context the *Mona Lisa* and *The Last Supper* are perhaps not what they appear. Why is Mary Magdalene at the meal? From the beheading of John the Baptist, the lost Holy Grail, cup of Christ's farewell supper, to the Knights Templar, Freemasonry and the sacred Egyptian geometry of Jerusalem's Temple of Solomon, an underworld of fact and fable relates Scottish alchemy to the Pyramids and to certain esoteric beliefs which considered they represented the incarnate motives and thinking of some Supreme Being.

A few miles outside Edinburgh is Rosslyn Chapel, built about
1450 by local laird, Sir William St Clair, as the Lady chapel to a
larger building which he planned to construct on the design of
Solomon's Temple. The symbolism of the chapel's carvings link the
Green Man, pagan Celtic god of vegetation, the Babylonian
Tammuz, a god who died and rose again, and his Egyptian
equivalent, Osiris, who achieved this same feat of resurrection.
Authorities believe the Rosslyn crypt once contained the statue of a
Black Madonna. The St Clair, now Sinclair, were Norman-Viking,
their name deriving from the beheaded Scottish martyr. As Tem-
plars, they became the hereditary protectors of Freemasonry in
Scotland during the Middle Ages and also the guardians of gypsy
groups who were active in pagan goddess worship.

Scholarship shows that, unwittingly or otherwise, Christians
believe much which shadows the oldest ceremonies lying at the
core of the human psychic's attempts to lock on to a supernatural
wavelength. Sunday worship, day of the Sun, and the east–west
orientation of churches are simple examples. The cry of Christ on
the cross which puzzles many, 'My God, my God, why hast thou
forsaken me?' is the result of altered translations. Some bystanders
believed he called on the prophet Elias, but one of the earliest New
Testament sources has him calling Helios, the name of the sun god
whose cult remained widespread until the fourth century. This
would equate with the period of darkness at the moment of the cry
and certainly fits the cult's central tenet of a cyclic sun god. Egyptian
Osiris, killed on a Friday, rises again on the third day and the sun
turns black at the moment of his death.

The name Jesus was by no means exclusive in the Palestine of
New Testament days; indeed it was as commonplace as John is
today. Lord, as a title was a standard term of respect and did not
denote at that time the supreme Lord of All which it became under
Christian influence. The enlightened outlook of the Edomites and a
sect of religious zealots, the desert-dwelling Essene, of whom John
the Baptist and possibly Jesus were followers, appear indistinguish-
able from the beatitudes of Christ the Messiah's Sermon on the
Mount. The wisdom and humanity of the theme did not depend
on the views of one man but rather were drawn from early Greek
philosophy.

Recent analyses show that, behind the accepted teachings of Jesus and his possible rival John the Baptist, there lies ample evidence of Egyptian mystery religion. To a backdrop of myths, it played on miracles, magic and occult powers as being inseparable forces. Christ, probably not Jewish, was classed in contemporary writing as a sorcerer. The miracles he performed – raising the dead, for example – were standard to the repertoire of the Egyptian magicians of the occult schools of Alexandria. One macabre aspect of this crossover lay in the worship of a severed head. Here the beheading of John the Baptist takes on significance, particularly for the highly secretive rites of the Knights Templar. Their stories of the Holy Grail deemed John's head both sacred and magical and rumoured of Jesus's hypnotic or otherwise magical enslavement by the Baptist. A severed head kept in the Egyptian temple to Osiris had, according to his priesthood, the power of prophecy.

Underlining this hybridisation, the Lord's Prayer was not composed by Jesus but originated as Egyptian supplications to their god Amon. Many of Christ's best loved sayings – 'In my Father's house there are many mansions', for example – are direct quotes from the Egyptian Book of the Dead whose god Osiris, killed on a Friday, was resurrected after three days by his consort goddess, Isis. Textual research indicates that rites of ecstatic sexual union, acting out a dying god who rose again empowered by copulation with his divine goddess, lay behind the relationship of Christ to Mary Magdalene, the practice of baptism being the prelude to this supreme act of sexual ecstasy.

Harking back to feats of escapology commonly performed by Egyptian mystics, many believed at the time, and some still do, that Christ did not die on the cross. Several traditions exist claiming to account for the disappearance of the crucified body from the tomb and, as we are told, Mary Magdalene appeared first on the scene and there was a strong assertion that she took him dead or alive to the south of France. This might account for the beliefs and practices of certain highly secretive cults of that area which, however, remain at variance with the majority of Christians who credit Christ's disappearance from the tomb as his physical ascension into Heaven.

The Turin Shroud with its flowing blood suggests the body of

Jesus was alive in the tomb. Investigations of the relic by carbon dating indicate its more recent origins. Believer or agnostic, humble credulity or dangerous scepticism, hidden superstition whispers, 'Believe. It's safer, just in case.'

Perhaps our most significant connection to past beliefs is through the communion taking of bread and wine – the symbol of Christ's Last Supper in the Upper Chamber and his gift of a Holy Spirit. The ancestry of this all-pervasive act is traceable via burnt offerings on a stone altar adorned with bull horns to the sublimity of the mutual orgasm of human love mirrored in celestial ecstasy by the sacred coitus of old world's gods.

Far-fetched fundamental religiosity thrives. Pentagon-backed Lt General William Boykin, Deputy Undersecretary for Defense, in charge of tracking down the Muslim fanatic Osama bin Laden, said, 'War against terror is a battle with Satan, we are hated because we are a nation of believers, a Christian nation.' A two-thousand-year-old speculation gripping a nation whose citizens are ten times more likely to attend church than their European cousins. American religious culture, wealthy and television orientated, is building mega-churches the size of football stadia to hold congregations of forty thousand. The dichotomy of God and the Devil bogged beside its companion dogma of 'my beliefs are right, yours are wrong'. The clash of culturally-embedded monotheism inspires the humanely altruistic and the demonically destructive. There's a distinct lack of Mother Teresas. The world bleeds for lack of humane leadership.

Religious intolerance lies behind the outrage of 9/11. Apart from outright techno-war effort, pre-emptive action by the USA is taking many forms. At the University of St Louis, Mark Buller, with US government funding, has created a genetically altered cowpox virus via the technology used to design a 100 per cent lethal form of mousepox which does for Mickey, vaccinated or not. With cowpox being a first cousin to human smallpox, the implications are plain. As a step in between a new strain of monkeypox is proposed, it's to be tested on simian patients. Buller states his work is necessary to check on what bio-terrorists might get up to.

Is it too late to ditch monotheism? Through today's razzmatazz of coquette hats and ostentation in the name of humility, from yesteryear's mish-mash of myth, Greek philosophy, Gnostic writings and New Testament obfuscation, there still shines a man of supreme caring and tolerance, a defender of underdogs, a humble symbol of humanity that deifies the pomp and dogma of concocted deities. Jesus of Nazareth – just a decent chap.

20

# 'Soon They Will Be Wringing their Hands'

In an object lesson on the phenomenon of homage towards religious certainties, our original deity, the sun god, is now demoted from a golden disc which could impart the succulence of roast lamb with power of the Almighty, to frying nudists on a Spanish beach. The mighty solar discs of Egypt and Edom are reduced to halos adorning holy heads – heads which enjoyed the origins of their power by courtesy of the sun's undeniable influence on this planet's transcendental affairs and, more especially, around heads to which spin-doctoring and tampering with contentious documents were religiously and politically expedient.

In the fusion between the Old and New Testaments, the roots of Christianity entwine deeply into the fertile mythologies of Babylon, Egypt, Classical Greece and the social beliefs of the Edomites. The Babylonian myth of the Garden of Dilmun supplied man's biblical fall from grace; the Gilgamesh Epic provided Noah's flood; the water goddess gave us the New Testament's belief in a virgin birth; and so on. Examples are numerous of the cobbling together of fresh ideas which the common man would swallow with a dash of the old belief left in to make it palatable.

The appealing idea of a Holy Trinity stands out. In one form or another it is common to many ancient doctrines, often as delightful allegories which reinforce the ideal family syndrome: mighty father figure, law enforcing, a touch tyrannical but kindly behind the scenes; mother, beautiful and saintly with the knack of handling the old boy; and son, a good egg, who looks after the underdogs of this world and helps keep the devil off their backs. Beware the instability of belief – seemingly incontrovertible ideas end up grinding on the shoals of fresh insights. Even that bedrock of physics and cosmology, Einstein's general theory of relativity, is heading the way of the phlogiston theory.

Be that as it may, the so-called Sermon on the Mount's line of preaching provided a humane backbone to Christianity. Only Stoicism, a classical school of Greek philosophy taught by Zeno of Citium about 300 BC and doubtless known to Gospel writer the Greek Saint Paul, equals this unsurpassable Sermon's strength in preaching human brotherhood and tolerance. Whatever may be fact or fiction in the religious business, when stripped of myths, doctoring by spin merchants and the pomp and power of bigotry, Christ's Sermons are the best recipe so far for human survival.

◆

Away from desert tribes, stone tablets, holy tabernacles and the Jewish patent on God and Palestine, in Mediterranean climes, a bath in the blood of a sacrificial bull let you into the cult of Mithras. Roman soldiers especially enjoyed this warm and colourful baptism. Mithras, the Persian God of Light and the power of goodness, had reputedly killed the Sacred Bull from whose blood all life sprang. More importantly, the cunning Mithras promised forgiveness for sinners after death. Roman Legionnaires understandably felt the need of a safety net in the afterlife as, throughout their ranks, it was by far the favoured religion. Eventually the Roman Empire was to become the conduit for a new line in atonement – yet another promise of being let off the hook in the next life. What puzzled the troops – and, more recently, Messrs Bush and Blair – was a theory of passivism giving one a leg up into eternity and a 'just war' achieving similar results for the assailants.

Anyway, the guy to straighten out a hotchpotch of pagan Roman practices and unify his spiritual control over the rank and file was the wily Emperor and politician, Constantine the Great. Proclaimed Emperor whilst in York, he decided his victory over a rival claimant in AD 312, which gave him supreme power in Rome, was the work of this new miracle-working Christian God. Struggling advertiser of the latest religious brand, Pope Sylvester, assured the Emperor this was undoubtedly the case. Constantine issued a decree forthwith, baptised his troops by marching them through a river, struck Christians off the lion's menu and overnight Christianity became the official faith throughout his vast Roman Empire. Spain apart, bulls were pleased and Mithras sulked off.

It took a committee meeting to finalise Christianity's main framework. In AD 352, Emperor Constantine called the heads of this nascent church to the Council of Nicea at a city in Turkey. Into a theological blender went Christ's humility, the uncomfortable prospect of a Day of Judgement, a suffering Messiah and our atonement through his death – overall a concoction of Middle Eastern legend and Greek philosophy cobbled together with plenty of gory bits left in to make a good story for folks denied the pleasure of dining alongside their favourite lions digesting a Christian.

Most Christians subscribe to a belief that the New Testament reflects a degree of divine inspiration. The rejection by the Councillors of over fifty other books, many of equal claim to authenticity – including the Gnostic Christian Gospels discovered in 1945 at Nag Hammadi in Egypt, the Gospel of Thomas and the Gospel of Mary, the latter not the Virgin Mary but Mary Magdalene – implies a subjective approach. Amongst much else which smacked of feminine influence, the Gnostic Gospels openly proclaimed Mary Magdalene, not Peter, as second in command to Jesus. Not on – religion was too grave a matter to be run by women. The Gnostic books were ditched and Saint Peter upgraded. By a voting procedure, the Conference decided the nature of God. The Holy Trinity was composed and approved, Jesus Christ promoted from a prophet to 'The Son of God' and the Holy Spirit made the driving force for believers.

The most contentious item on the Conference agenda turned out to be the matter of the Eucharist. Harking back to the old idea of the sun's rays on a meat sacrifice, it was deemed that, at any Holy Sacrament, the actual flesh and blood of Jesus were consumed. This feat of imagination, not surprisingly, stretched credulity to a point which ultimately caused much dissension within ecclesiastical ranks.

A self-righteous religion rolled into business. It ignored the Jewish rights on a covenant between God and His Chosen People, usurped the Jew's Ten Commandments, featured Christ's beatitudes and forcefully insisted upon one merciful God, split three ways – Father, Son and Holy Ghost. Out of the Council meeting emerged Romanised Christianity and, with a little arm twisting, it took off. Intense passion marked the proselyte, cruel intolerance the professional. From then on, for over a thousand years, any freedom of philosophic thought and expression became subsumed by a divine law, revealed and confidently interpreted by an oppressive elite. The privilege of divine insight could not be squandered on the lower orders.

Along with theological power came wealth aplenty – a tricky one, given the products from the carnal inclinations of various pontiffs down to humble priests and nuns were liable to chip away at the treasure trove and undermine central authority. In AD 1139, the Vatican hit on the idea of celibacy for all ranks as the best solution – it appeared to work in several eastern creeds of ascetic persuasion. Marriage to the Church should sort out the inclinations of the flesh, natural or otherwise, it reasoned – a contention with increasingly questionable, if not expensive, results.

For many centuries, suppression of scholarly endeavour was ruthless – witness the attempt to prevent any translation of the Vulgate Bible from the dead language of Latin, accessible only to ecclesiastics, into the English of the common man. The gifted translation by William Tyndale, working from Holland in 1532, led, seventy years later, to the elegantly poetic King James Bible. Tyndale's efforts were rewarded by burning at the stake. Although the scholar was afforded the mercy of strangulation prior to lighting the faggots, the executioner made a botched job and the Bible's translator was consumed alive. A number of similar heretics were to hear the crackle of the flames. John Frith, a priest who questioned the truth of transubstantiation, a belief that the Eucharist transformed bread and wine into the actual body of Christ, met his fate at Smithfield, his death being rather slow due to a fresh wind fanning the flames away from him.

Priests and scholars alike went to the stake for siding with Tyndale. The authority behind a number of such burnings, Sir Thomas More, Lord Chancellor of English King Henry VIII, incorporated stocks and a whipping tree in his comfortable Chelsea home to assist with enquiries. Though ultimately More was executed for opposing Henry's divorce, he was beatified in 1886 and canonised in 1935. More recently, in October 2000, as an added honour bestowed by the Pontiff, he became Patron Saint of Politicians – a warning to our current heads of state about 'the absolute priority of God's judgement at the heart of public affairs'. Much beneficial effect is yet to be noted.

By dethroning the Papacy and appointing himself to the job of God's earthly right-hand man, 'Bluff King Harry', Henry of the six wives, effected the political rupture between Rome and the English monarchy. Not any doctrinal change but no ex-communication. Henry's son, Edward VI, aided and abetted by Archbishop Cranmer, pulled off a Protestant coup – little change in pomp and grandeur but no mandatory auricular confessions. Cranmer's elegant writing of the First Prayer Book and much else provides the basic form of service for the Anglican Church of England and the Scottish Episcopal Church, the latter known north of the Border as the English Church and thought rather more the frequenter of a better class of hat.

Edward died young and his half-sister, Mary, succeeded after Cranmer's engineered debacle of Lady Jane Grey's brief queenship of twelve days. The nation, Roman Catholic at heart, rejoiced. Their rightful Queen Mary was enthroned. A chronicler wrote, 'Now they are ringing the bells, soon they will be wringing their hands.' Mary, soon to be styled 'Bloody Mary', emphasised England's return to the true faith. Protestants burned by the score – three hundred for starters. Nothing burned better than a detested Proddy. Cranmer, consigned to the Tower, watched the flames from a window, recanting his Protestant bias appeared the coolest option. Mary decided on PR. Contrite on paper, yes, he might still be Protestant at heart. Cranmer must burn. On the stake, fire licking his feet, the Archbishop retracted. Thrusting his right hand into the flames and holding it there as it burnt off, he cried, 'This hath offended. Oh, this unworthy hand.'

The counterattack on Roman Catholicism was harsh. Mary's half sister, Elizabeth I, otherwise 'Good Queen Bess', didn't delay in passing various Recusancy Laws aimed at Catholics who stuck with the old faith. Fines and property confiscation escalated to life imprisonment, transportation, torture and death. Some thirty-odd thousand were disposed of by the blessed 'Virgin Monarch', mostly by hanging and disembowelling. One busy day at London Tyburn, with eleven Catholics in the queue, the crowd barracked the hangman after his first five chokings for cutting down the victims prior to their disembowelling whilst they were still fully conscious.

With King James, the Scots Protestant implant to the English throne, came the infamous Gunpowder Plot, a conspiracy to which his government was privy, if not its originator. It backed an excuse for further anti-Catholic legislation. Guy Fawkes, racked until his leg sockets sprang, was hanged as much as a warning to other Catholics considering insurgence as for attempting to blow up his king and the Houses of Parliament. Religious discrimination remains on the statute book and features in the trappings of this country's highest social fetishes.

The years from Bloody Mary to Lord Protector Cromwell and his soul-cleansing, hymn-singing 'Ironside' troopers illustrate the fulcrum upon which the two ends of Christian doctrine balanced with difficulty. The beauty and brilliance of the Renaissance art, music and church-building of Roman Catholicism contrasted starkly with the bareness of the Puritans' whitewashed walls, black hats and iconoclasm. The tenets of faith stretched accordingly. On the one side, glories of stained glass and holy statue were objects of deepest veneration and in some cases gifted with miraculous powers. For the other, artistic icons were idolatrous objects a priesthood placed between man and his maker.

North of the Border, Christian Scots had the benefit or otherwise of John Knox. By the 1540s, the Dutch Lutheran Reformation was lapping Scottish shores and Geneva-based Calvinism was challenging Roman Catholic authority. Knox, who'd kicked off from St Andrews in Catholic orders, fell for the preaching style of Montrose schoolmaster, George Wishart. Less attracted was Glasgow's Cardinal Beaton who arranged Wishart's burning for his airing of the Greek New Testament. Calvinist supporters saw to it that the

Cardinal was duly 'taken out' and Knox along with the murderers holed up in St Andrews Castle. Their surrender to the French after some months enabled the captured hellfire-and-damnation preacher Knox to perfect his rowing technique as a galley slave.

Eighteen months on, calluses on his hands, splinters in his bottom, Knox secured a reprieve from the rowing bench thanks to England's Protestant pair, Edward VI and Archbishop Cranmer, who applauded the preacher's pulpit-thumping style. With their blessing, Knox set about a fire-and-brimstone round of the English shires. Converts were filling the aisles when Edward died at sixteen, to be succeeded by the horrors of his half-sister Bloody Mary. Recalling the misfortune of his mentor Wishart and not a man given to privation, Knox concluded the furtherance of his soul-saving mission merited immediate departure to flame-free Switzerland. From the relaxing shores of Lake Geneva, he penned heartfelt letters to the converted results of his English rantings, urging them to stand firm in God's faith before the flames. Many did.

Preacher Knox, by now a mate of Calvin, comforted himself by writing *First Blast of the Trumpet against the Monstrous Regiment of Women*. A diatribe of such venom as to make misogyny appear a harmless caprice, it condemned any woman, queen or commoner, who meddled in politics, strayed from the sink or disported herself beyond the marital bedchamber. The latter, strange to say, would seem an area outwith the compass of his displeasure. Two sons by his first wife, three daughters by a second, married as a slip of sweet sixteen, the flame of love burnt more appealingly than the flames of martyrdom.

Inspired by inflammatory renderings of the Old Testament, Scottish Protestants got their act together, sent for Knox and, geed up by stories of the 'Chosen People' smiting the Philistines, the 'Lords of the Congregation of Christ' galloped about the country-side fomenting religious insurgency against the 'Congregation of Satan' – i.e. the Roman Catholics. The *Confession of Faith* and the *First Book of Discipline* were drafted. Doses of Knox's fulminous wrath poured from the pulpit of St Giles' High Kirk. Acts of Covenant were sworn in a 'glorious marriage of the Kingdom with God' – a black-and-white, no-compromise formula hastening doctrinal-cum-political upheaval and civil war. Yet another exclusive Covenant with His Chosen People had the Almighty puzzled.

Following the death throes of Divine Kingship under Charles I, religious action in Scotland moved to a hammering by Cromwell at Dunbar. The Scots army under Leslie 'cleansed of ungodly elements', a phrase relating to the standard wenching and swearing of professional troops, became 'an army of clerks and ministers' sons'. A Bible-chanting downhill charge met 'Ironside' discipline. Three thousand dead and ten thousand prisoners proved in practical terms that sword and pike outdid prayer.

Assorted skirmishes and battles betwixt Episcopalian authority and Covenanters saw the murder of Archbishop Sharp of St Andrews for his savage treatment of Presbyterians, an act giving rise to the brutal 'Killing Time' retaliations of 'Bonnie Dundee'. Finally a Presbyterian settlement in 1690 ushered the common transgressor on to the 'cutty stool', the sobbing teenage girl renouncing her pregnancy before a sanctimonious church and the prayers of the 'unco guid' as portrayed by Robert Burns in the words of Holy Willie.

◆

Outside Scotland's sectarian squabbles, philosophic minds within the papal 'closed system' had attempted to surface. Giordano Bruno, a Dominican friar about 1570 believed the universe to be infinite, containing a countless number of inhabited worlds moving within an uncentred space composed of minimal particles. In Friar Bruno's extreme pantheism, God, nature and eternal matter were identical. His was a 'holistic' approach, light years ahead, which influenced such diverse thinkers as Galileo, Isaac Newton, Shakespeare, Spinoza and Karl Popper. Sadly for him, his illuminated vision fell short of keeping his mouth shut. After a seven-year trial by his Church's Holy Inquisition, Bruno was burned at the stake in Rome.

Polish astronomer Copernicus, whose publication *De Revolutionibus* suggested the sun to be at the centre of the universe, got off lightly by dying as it rolled from the press. Galileo, the Italian astronomer and natural philosopher, picked up the idea. He'd already beaten Newton to the theorem of the equal velocity of falling bodies, apparently, it's said, by dropping objects from the top of the leaning tower of his home town, Pisa. Further to this schoolboy trick, by perfecting the Dutch invention of a refracting telescope, Galileo launched astronomy into orbit. Moon mountain and valley appeared. The Milky Way, he pronounced, was a track of countless stars, four satellites of Jupiter showed up and, from the sun spots, he inferred its rotation. The Vatican, with its own private lunar observatory busy sorting out the Julian for the Gregorian calendar, had a notion Galileo was on to something. Hauled before the Inquisition by Pope Urban VIII in 1632 and given a courtesy inspection of the torture chamber, with its ingenious array of opinion-changing equipment, he decided, on reflection, his discoveries merited classification as condemned documents and went to jail as the softer option.

Religious inertia versus scientific investigation – little changes. America's FBI, a modern version of the Inquisition, have launched a post-9/11 crackdown on scientists and institutes involved in work with various bacteria. A climate of fear is developing amongst researchers in many fields, their work subject to inspection and control. Microbiologist Thomas Butler, of Texas Tech University, dutifully reported the loss of thirty vials of plague material from his lab. Arrested and charged on sixty-eight counts in a contorted case, the sixty-two-year-old faced one hundred years in the slammer. Although he only got a two-year sentence, Butler was framed as a warning, maintain his fellow scientists.

When the instructions of state or religion can't swallow the fruits of science, these same bastions deal with the scientist by any means at their disposal. As the complex results of research set out their stalls of elixirs and their under-the-counter envelopes of mass destruction, many argue for control. But how and by whom? Who will assess and arbitrate? The talking dollar or some altruistic saint? Science without morals could be mankind's poisoned chalice.

Back in 1740 it took the breadth of a Scottish brain to place logic, morals, philosophic criticism and politics on an enlightened pathway. Edinburgh-born David Hume, the greatest of eighteenth-century philosophers, broke the stranglehold of doctrinal dogma. The Hume, or Hulme, family clan trace their origins to the Norman Conquest – Vikings by the back door. It suggests the attitude of this pivotal Scots intellectual and friend of Rousseau perhaps owed something to the innate scepticism of his Norse antecedents;

empiricist and agnostic that he was, his *A Treatise on Human Nature* unveiled fresh horizons, opened a vista which questioned reality.

Suggestive of turning the handle on a 'What the Butler Saw' peep-show machine, Hume's statement that mankind 'is nothing but a bundle or collection of different perceptions, which succeed each other with an inconceivable rapidity, and are in a perpetual flux and movement' was a milestone on the freeway to a twenty-first century where the mystery of organic consciousness wrestles to understand the inorganic cosmos though a medium called thought, as it taps into the abstraction of mathematics with the tools of insight and imagination.

21

# The 'Angel of Death'

Guessing what may follow death is a game central to past and present society. Survival in this life, a secure food and water supply, effective procreation and a plea to some 'intangible power' for the promise of an everlasting 'good time' after popping one's clogs are strands common to Western and Middle Eastern cultures – not forgetting, of course, the ancient codicil of help in doing for one's enemies. Inside knowledge of this supernal mind was generally imparted to a selected person or group by divine tip-off – the launch pad of a religion.

A certain character and attributes were assigned to the 'omnipotent one' and much onerous ritual applied. Exclusive paraphernalia accumulated to support entrenched positions. Holy sites were set up, messiah mementoes cherished and the whole process of promotion and growth was undertaken in a style paralleled in its operation by the current expansion of a multinational corporation. Cultures bloomed around the 'in' religion of time and place, each belief tending towards the triumph of hope over reason. It led directly to excellent grounds for hating one's neighbour and the curse of mankind – religious rivalry.

Constantine's imperial order from Rome and a spot of disciplinary persuasion amongst legionary ranks ditched Mithras and set the Gospel message tramping smartly north. The first recorded Christian hot-gospeller to tackle the Celts of southern Alba in AD 394 was the Roman-trained son of a British chieftain, Bishop and later Saint Ninian, who preached from his mission church at Whithorn in Galloway. Power-sharing amongst a host of Celtic deity was out; monotheism, with little mercy shown to non-believers, had pagan diversity on the ropes.

The idea flourished on sound strategy. Irish noble Saint Columba and his fellow salesmen sought out those in authority to achieve their results. Tribal chiefs and kings happily embraced a swish style of Godhead – not least because it incorporated the Almighty's consent to 'The Divine Right of Kings', and their heirs, to rule. A congenial arrangement for the top brass, it provided an additional grip on subjects through a pyramid of spiritual control. God, Pope, kings and clergy – it was a power system grown on the vine of the Roman Empire's flare for the legislative machine ripened to a centralised religious bureaucracy. Temporal advancement entwined with saving souls. Land, wealth, politics and comfort featured highly amongst the hierarchy's interests.

An objective view should not detract from the deep and genuine belief on the part of so many down the ages who furthered the cause of humanity in the true image of their faith. The early followers of Columba in Scotland were to suffer. His Iona monks watched their monastery burn and crash. Generations of work lost in a day. Buildings, learned manuscripts and Gospel books went to torch and flame. The Holy Order stood in turn, throats were cut. Pragmatic, pagan Norsemen exulted and carried off the loot.

The illuminated *Book of Kells*, lovingly crafted on calfskin vellum, a supreme achievement in Celtic-Christian art, transferred to a monastery in County Meath, escaped this destruction. The four great eighth-century Iona stone crosses survived. Spiritual strength survived. The sanctity of Columba's memory lives as a shrine of unceasing pilgrimage. A burial site of kings, Irish, Scottish and Norwegian, Iona Abbey, several times destroyed by the Vikings, was rebuilt out of faith – that inexplicable intoxication, illogical visionary phenomenon, faith. The belief, a single caring God without tangible proof, remains the cornerstone of Christianity.

The possibility of a vision or a voice from the Almighty being auto-suggestive, an attack of schizophrenia or deliberate wishful thinking, is dismissed as being counterproductive to any priest-hood's PR programme. From the booming voice of Apollo at the Oracle of Delphi, to Moses on Mount Sinai, through assorted prophets, to Lourdes-type miracle sessions, the list of those who've had a hot line to heaven is impressive. It's too easy to deride such as Joan of Arc, the Maid of Orleans. Through her conviction that voices came from on high, she led a French army. The English, less than convinced, burnt her at the stake. Such is man's inclination towards blind faith and simple belief, scepticism requires courage.

In all their plundering of Western Christendom were the Vikings merely inhumane sceptics, carefree of gods, boorish pagan vandals, the Antichrists of the Dark Ages, sent by Satan to test the faith of the true believers? Were they immune to the wanton sufferings they created? Merciless barbarians without principle? Who were their Gods?

Ritual human sacrifice, so many bodies per festival, seems the earliest means by which Nordic society secured its 'future hope'. In the hangover from hunter-gatherer days, spirits haunted mounds and waterfalls. Stone talisman must be carried to bring health and luck. Foretelling events involved visiting groves by night to awaken the dead men or 'mound dwellers'. Less ghoulish was magic chanting, the malevolent use of hair and nails, images fashioned in clay or dough and the 'evil eye' possessed by some local hag. Shibboleth and soothsaying in Norse society gradually gave way to the pragmatism of sea rovers who, though highly superstitious, abandoned shamanistic rituals. Trust in their own proven abilities, mental and physical, was more dependable – plus a dash of faith in the gods of their trinity for good measure.

The concept of any divine trinity is the allegorical representation of a human family. The Viking trinity cult was no exception. Odin or Woden, from whom we take Wednesday, stood as the father figure – God of war, fighting to ensure his people's survival on an alien earth. Ultimately came the pay-off when, along with his fallen warriors, feasting and drinking in the heavenly Halls of Valhalla, they prepared together, nursing diabolical hangovers, for a Last Battle – the Doom of the Gods.

Doom. We're all doomed. Melancholic preoccupations on the

part of Odin involved the occult, dark forebodings, dire premonitions, the not-unfamiliar sandwich-board rantings of hellfire and damnation. When not depressed, Odin thirsted for knowledge. The quest of a spiritual or temporal version demanded suffering. Odin sacrificed an eye and, in order to discover a secret alphabet, stabbed himself several times before hanging on a tree for nine nights. His tendency towards masochism revealed the runic script – sixteen letters of a magical code to be used on memorial inscriptions or to fool an enemy with secret curses.

Odin's course on enlightenment secured a degree in ultimate knowledge. Thereafter, he became the font of all wisdom – God of the Nordic belief in poetry as the sublime art, the invasive scalpel with which to peel back man's innermost conjectures and glimpse the world of abstract thought. At a political level, on his shoulders perched two ravens, Huginn and Muninn – Mind and Memory, alias MI5 and MI6 – who surveyed his subjects with an informing eye.

Odin's wife, Freya, or Frigga, in whose honour Friday is named, was lusty, busty and womanly, wanton in the arts of love. Frigga was not to be confused with frigid. The lure of her titillation took in both wizardry and mystery. She exuded femininity and possessed the child-bearing beauty of commodious hips so beloved by artists the world over with a penchant for comely bottoms. This curvaceous line in feminine pulchritude the Norse extended as a fecund backdrop to fruitfulness in nature and the harvest field – a theme which I suggested as a heraldic device for the Scottish Farmer's Union.

Frigga's brother Frey found himself a welcome guest at wedding ceremonies. Something akin to a male kissogram, he posed in the imagery of animals of supreme potency. As a wild boar or stallion, he is portrayed quite unabashed, wielding in a somewhat boastful manner a gigantically proportioned phallus erectus. This earthy sense of humour typical of sailors and rugby clubs would bring blushes of nervous speculation to a virgin bride and bashfulness to the bridegroom, as well as affording many a suggestive quip to the party. More poetically, this untamed male accoutrement gave embodiment to the delightful Norse myth whereby a burst of spring sunshine deflowers the frosty maiden of winter.

Thor is mightiest of the trinity. Protector of the Universe, patron of seamen and farmers, the defeater of all evil, he doubles to us as Thursday. Carrying Mjollnir, his hammer of supernatural strength, Thor rode the heavens ruling tempest and storm. The Earth shook as his anvil blows of lighting rent the clouds. Thor's long-shafted hammer, we are told with a wink, doubled at weddings as a fertility symbol. Following the example of their Gods, booze and carnality took centre stage at any Viking festivity.

Insight or wisdom, the Vikings made no attempt to force religious belief upon others – they were entrepreneurs, not sainted evangelists. Norse character bore the hallmarks of fierce individualism. A party of Vikings campaigned in Normandy. 'Name your leader,' shouted the opposing French from the banks of the river Eure. Back came the reply, 'He has no name, we are all equal.' They cooperated as equals and held a questioning and often dismissive attitude towards authority. No flunky forelock-tugging à la Anglo-Saxon society, hamstrung between feudal barons and prelates. Leadership in foray or war was generally by consent. The will of the people, or at least a major section of society, ruled through a form of democracy. The 'Ting' drew together an assembly of 'freemen', who decided and decreed on leadership, law and matters of regional or national importance. An egalitarian ethos prevailed, its fallout still socially and politically discernible today the further north you travel.

Kings were chosen by popular vote. Franchised and proles alike expected the incumbent to nurture the honour, safety and well-being of his electorate. Nor, in contrast to many European kingships approved of by the Vatican, did Norse kings think of themselves or were thought by their people to be identified with the gods, far less regarded as a divine incarnation. Canute or Knut, the son of Sweyn I, 'Forkbeard' Haraldsson, and Viking King of England, Denmark and, by 1030, also of Norway, proved to be a man of sterling worth and ability. To his conquered Anglo-Scandinavian empire he brought justice and peace and a generous tolerance towards the native churches, their priests and saints.

Fawning Saxon courtiers deemed Canute to be divine. In exasperation, to prove them wrong he had a chair set before the rising tide on a beach down the Thames at the Isle of Sheppey. 'Go back,' Canute commanded and sat until the wavelets lapped about his knees. Floundering courtiers clutched at dripping robes. Satisfied they were cold and soaked, Canute announced, 'God, not man, controls the tide.' Divine origins may now pass as fancy – delusions of grandeur never fade. Canute fell for neither. Nordic intelligence prevailed.

Any shortfall in a Scandinavian king's performance could see him deposed or, in an extreme case, during days of pagan belief in the offering up of a king to promote the wellbeing of his people, the erring monarch could be made a sacrificial offering. The system possessed attractions.

In spite of the Nordic common-sense approach to regality, William 'Rufus', eleventh-century King of England and son of the Norman-Viking William the Conqueror, fell to his death in the New Forest from an arrow fired by his 'favourite', Sir Walter Tyrell. An intriguing incident, passed off as an accident, but whispered, with due head-wagging, to be connected with ritual sacrifice. William 'the Red' was actively anti-church. His red hair, the colour of blood, harked back to days when red-haired men were burnt and their ashes scattered to 'quicken the seed in the earth'. Pagan rites centred on a May–November cycle, the breeding cycle of cattle and sheep, but in particular they highlighted 'the Gule of August', the great 'witch' festival and the giving of the first fruits at Lammas-tide.

The year 1099 hung with superstitious dread – the end of a century. An unprecedented tide inundated the Thames valley; people, villages and stock were taken by the Great Dragon of the Sea. In May of that year, William's nephew, Richard, met his death by an arrow shot in the New Forest. Accidental? At sunset on the morrow of 'the Gule of August', William 'Rufus' is deep in the New Forest, a glade of pre-Christian holy worship. He stands under an oak, sacred tree of the Celts. His slayer stands below an elder tree, the tree of doom, said to be the wood of the Calvary Cross and the tree upon which Judas hanged himself. Tyrell is commanded by the King, 'Shoot in the Devil's name or it will be the worse for you.' Rufus fell. Royal blood dripped on the earth the entire journey to Winchester they whispered. The blood of a divine victim, shed to bring bounty from the soil?

Or was it just Viking retribution applied to a king who failed his people? Doubtful. Rufus saw himself as divine. His favourite oath, 'by Saint Luke's face', had hidden connotations – its ecclesiastical symbolism meant a bull, the Great Bull of the Mithraic Oath and slaughter. Fertility worship? He died in the guise of a stag. Was it the theme which passes through Calvary back to Osiris, the King-God whose blood must flow for the life of his people? Or was it the older Dianic cult with its forest sacrifices at full moon? After all, ecclesiastical legislation had attempted and failed to stamp out this ancient practice since the seventh century. Who knows, old beliefs linger to this day. The leaves on an autumn oak are last to fall.

For certain, William the Red's outrageous, irreligious rule, not to mention his homosexual habits, were an abomination to the ecclesiastics: an attitude that was reinforced for them when, soon after his burial below their fine new tower of Winchester Cathedral, it collapsed on his sarcophagus.

◆

In daily farm life throughout their fjord homelands, Nordic peoples would pass close to the newly dug earth of Grandpa's burial mound. The old buffer's spirit hovered close, a critical eye on life about the croft. Each generation of children viewed their forebears with interest and respect. An atmosphere pervaded by the supernatural, by spooks, magic, health-giving stones, runic charms or curses and be sure to avoid the bent old harridan of the evil eye. Appropriate deference to the 'other world' was serious stuff but, for 'late-night' entertainment, the villagers erected 'penis poles', an amusement banned once Christianity inflicted its more seemly superstitions.

Belief in the 'dead walkers' as people who could return from death to plague the living required a corpse to be treated with care. Nostrils, mouth and eyes were closed. Death confirmed the beginning of a journey to an existence in another world. Many, especially the wealthy, were buried or cremated at the helm of a prized longship made ready to sail. Into the funeral ship, along with objects of daily use, went their warfare gear, horses and sometimes a slave woman. A ninth-century chieftain's galley excavated in the Isle of Man revealed a woman interred face down over her chief, her skull smashed from behind.

One description of funeral rites tells that 'at a chief's death his family called for a volunteer amongst the slave girls to accompany him on his journey'. Once found she was plied with drink and carefully watched. A week of lamentation might pass before cremation day dawned. A grim woman, the 'Angel of Death', dressed and embalmed the corpse. To precede its farewell sail, the intoxicated volunteer provided sex for six mourning relatives in a carnal prelude during which each moaned, 'Tell your Master I do this out of love for him.'

Heaped with wood, the ship was ready. The girl, given more drink, was led aboard. She cut off a hen's head and threw its body into the boat. More drink. The assemblage beat their shields. Screams were drowned. The hag directed her to 'lie beside [her] Master'. The six men took her, two held her legs, two her arms. Two placed a rope around her neck. The 'Angel of Death' stabbed the strangling girl through the heart.

A flaming torch held by the chief's nearest relative lit the pyre. The gathering came forward, each with a burning branch. Flames swept corpse and slave girl to paradise. Purification through fire. Cremation, the Viking short cut to the 'hereafter' – short, that is, of a glorious death in battle.

## 22

# 'To the Glory of our Creator'

Immortality-seeking monarchies throughout Europe of the Dark Ages hit on land grants to the Church as their possible fire escape from eternal damnation. Rapidly growing ecclesiastical wealth resulted in a programme of church building. Christianity acquired a solid material status. Chosen sites generally overlaid those of pagan worship, often vantage points of prehistoric ley lines. The penis pole and female legs akimbo of sites which worshiped the reproductive cycle became the twelfth-century soaring Gothic cathedral tower and arch, more acceptable to a clergy married to their religion and eschewing distractions of the flesh.

Patron saint of pen-pushers and Europe's greatest bureaucrat prior to the advent of the EU, the Frankish King Charlemagne had himself crowned Holy Roman Emperor by Pope Leo III in Saint Peter's Church, Rome, on Christmas Day AD 800. Installed on earth as next but one on God's right hand, he set about persuading Saxon Europe to agree a Christian viewpoint. The destruction of a Frankish army by a revolt of Saxon objectors gave the Emperor opportunity to celebrate his title by beheading four and a half thousand pagan prisoners. Their leader, Widukind, spotted the advantage of becoming Christian and opted for baptism. A revamping of Europe's spiritual values banned ancient ritual, stamped out moonlight incantations and labelled Celtic shamanism as heathen witchcraft. Fresh beliefs and dogma were drafted in, carefully blended to achieve credulity amongst the illiterate masses. Charlemagne's last battle in AD 810, before being called to take up higher duties, was against the Danish Vikings.

The strength of the Church's centralised Vatican administration regulated royal successions throughout European Christendom by the novel idea which decreed that a king's authority was by divine gift, derived with Papal consent, from one God and one only. Monarchies in tandem with the Papacy built a spiritual power structure of mutual consent which skirted around such irksome New Testament teachings as poverty, humility and turning the other cheek. Christianity and feudalism went hand in hand. Kings invariably quarrelled, overbearing prelates were murdered, progress within senior administrative ranks required poison and backstabbing. Popes competed, Vatican versus Avignon, but, for the soul of the common herd so embroiled, the route to salvation passed through Rome.

Transition from Scandinavia's polytheistic traditions to control by a religiously fostered southern oligarchy which enforced monotheism took a couple of hundred years – a conversion process largely forced upon the north proles at the point of an evangelical sword. Nordic democracy went to ground. Christianised Norse kings usurped the traditional leadership by selection. Dynastic ambition neatly complemented Christian subservience. Authority, not to mention wealth, was enhanced by the teaching that a convert's first duty lay in obedience to his Divine Royal Lord. It guaranteed the enlightened believer both a temporal and spiritual boss – a fair damper for free-thinking lads who enjoyed a frolic.

At all levels of Viking society, the Church made slow progress – particularly in matters of drunkenness and sexual laxity. Early Scandinavian churchmen played the party-pooper. No brawling, bloodshed or the purchase of drink and women for entertainment. Of King Sven Estridsson, a cleric lamented to Rome that he was 'an obedient son of the Church in everything except feasting and women, and the latter weakness we regard not so much as a personal fault as an inborn propensity of the Danish and Swedish nations'. On the Scandinavians' weakness for the sport of horse-fighting, clerics remained silent. An in-season mare, tethered at the edge of a ring, in sight and smell of two stallions, goaded the animals into a biting, squealing, kicking fight which usually resulted in one of the animal's death. Owners behaved in a similar fashion – it added much to the general air of festivity.

◆

Vikings who, by the ninth century, fancied kindlier French climes followed the son of Norse-Orcadian Earl Rollo in a sail up the Seine to besiege Paris. A few days stravaiging about the countryside, a night or two on the town and Charles III of France was persuaded to grant Rollo and his desperadoes the province of Normandy. Rollo's huge size, beyond the carrying capacity of any horse, earned him the name 'Hrolf', the 'Ganger' or walker. By the Battle of Hastings in 1066, Rollo's direct descendant turned out to be William 'The Conqueror'. Vikings in the guise of Norman knights swarmed north, the White Settlers of their day.

Without doubt the appraising eye which fashioned the curvaceous longship could admire the trim of a handsome woman and, given a touch of ecclesiastical propaganda relating to the parlous state of the Holy Land, the noted Viking weakness for the fair sex flowered during the early Middle Ages into the chivalrous code of the Crusading Knight. Norman-French hero Roland, a knight of Charlemagne who gave rise to the saying 'a Roland for your Oliver', inspired this aristocratic craze of valorous chivalry which is epitomised by the illustrious romance, *Chanson de Roland*. The stirring words of the poem's battle cry, trumpeted fortissimo, 'Infidels are wrong, Christians have the right', had aspiring knights composing heraldic slogans and squeezing into their armour. With a veneer of Christianity barely covering both predatory inclinations and such bygone blots in papal eyes as the massacring of the Lindisfarne Monks, Norman Vikings naturally found Vatican-sponsored rapine and pillage which encouraged a crack at Muslim heretics defiling holy shrines in Palestine to be right up their street. Typical of this pious call to arms was Rognvald, a swashbuckling nephew of Saint Magnus who arrived in Orkney from Norway claiming a pact with God which involved building a great cathedral should the Earldom of Orkney Isles fall his way. Along with the local bishop, he embarked on a Crusade easily mistaken as a piratical expedition for, whilst they journeyed to the Holy Land, the financing of their outburst of saintly zeal necessitated the capture of fellow Christians, cashed when passing Muslim slave markets. Home and basking in his earldom, Rognvald began the building of the magnificent Kirkwall Cathedral from leftover takings.

The Third Crusade, endorsed by a pontiff who banned the use of the deadly crossbow except against the infidel host, attracted Richard 'Coeur de Lion', King of England, Duke of Aquitaine and of direct Viking origin. Together with his homosexual partner, Philip, King of France, their extravaganza got off to a good start by occasioning much bloodshed in Scilly and Cyprus on passage. Arab leader Saladin and his Muslim followers, by comparison to Viking brutishness, were a cultivated and learned people who could claim a sophisticated civilisation when northern Europe pranced in skins, but their occupancy of the Palestinian seaport fortress of Acre blocked the gateway to Jerusalem, the Christians' Holy of Holies.

Richard and Philip set about the siege of Acre. Hefty stones, dead cows and bucketfuls of latrine content featured in the material lobbed over the defenders' walls with the aid of a huge wooden cantilever contraption, dubbed with affection by the marksmen, 'God's own Catapult'. Beaten by starvation and smell, the Arabs surrendered. Celebrations to mark the Crusaders' capture of this strategic fortress included chaining together and lining up three thousand Muslim prisoners on the road to Nazareth. Starting at one end, they were killed, men, women and children, each watching their turn approach – jubilant thanksgiving in the form of throat slitting. It took from dawn till dusk. A witnessing chronicler devoutly observed, 'They died to the glory of our Creator.'

During this Crusading period, Vikings had the run of the Mediterranean. Crack unit of the Byzantine Emperors of Constantinople at the time was the Varangian Guard. As Viking mercenaries on a par with today's SAS, they followed a certain Harald Sigurdsson. A top-class ruffian with the deadly amalgam of courage, cunning and greed, he played a cloak-and-dagger part in Byzantine royal intrigues. Deposing the unpopular Emperor Michael necessitated his being blinded. Sigurdsson gleefully performed the valedictory eye gouging. Ultimately loaded with wealth, Harald and his cut-throats left for home but a massive iron chain strung across the Bosphorus blocked their escape. By loading his ship to the stern, rowing hard, then racing the crew to the bow, she slid over the boom defence and into the Black Sea. Up the Russian rivers, they made it home with enough loot to claim a share in the throne of Norway.

Schism split the Roman Church, Pope and anti-Pope, and Crusading as a pastime ran out of steam. The eight Holy ventures achieved little more than fly-blown heaps of bodies and lasting hatred. The era of Viking supremacy was fading. Superfluous knights of minor nobility kicking their heels in England turned north. They took land in the Borders and eventually by infiltrating the Highlands became the blood stock of clan chiefdoms. Frasers, Chisholms and Sinclairs stand as examples of this migration of 'pushy' families who imparted to the leftovers of Pictdom an overlay of a Norman Frankish gentility which lingers to this day in the manners of those of Highland descent.

Crusades and chivalry. Indifference to barbarous cruelty, treachery and self-interest had proved paramount, yet certain ideals were fostered. The victorious jouster doffing his plumed helmet to a bevy of palpitating ladies fluttering hankies from the grandstand epitomised a gallantry of spirit, a courtesy and supposed devotion to the faithful childbearing womenfolk. Admirable principles and pious religious motifs were emblazoned on the Black Knight's escutcheon. Elevated thoughts flowered. Clicking the lock on a chastity belt strapped to the little lady back home was merely common sense – proof of one's progeny. In a man's world, the Christian God was masculine. Emancipation for the fair sex was not on – not theologically, politically or from the kitchen sink.

Christians arose throughout Europe. Initially the persecuted underdogs but, infused with the power of their Holy Spirit, a proselytising fervour spread The Gospel, often by methods totally contrary to its humanitarian teaching, once on top, pomp, intolerance, torture, pogroms, mass murder and much warring ensued.

Only the 'Black Death' boasted a finer record in population control. In three days, the massacre of Saint Bartholomew dealt with seventy thousand Protestant Huguenots and so on. The ability to turn a benign, 'blessed are the humble' theology inside out lay with the egoism of its operators. Hypocrisy excelled; hatred and baseness ruled – vainglorious pomp and religious intolerance. Claim and counterclaim – each offering definitive routes to celestial certainty, glory and forgiveness. Naïvety deifying intelligence.

Thankfully there were, and are, within the Christian and many other beliefs, those who did, and do, uphold humanitarian concepts like self-denial, pacifism and consideration for the poor and less fortunate. More than preaching in fancy-dress outfits and being well fed, warm and dry, they get stuck in where once the lepers fell apart and now where children tread on the leftover detonators of cluster bombs.

In the northlands, Christianity and its set of superstitions succeeded when Scandinavian kingships saw it as a useful power system enjoyed by the wealthy southern monarchies with whom they traded. For Norse warriors, sceptical and perhaps a touch agnostic, Christian belief remained skin deep. They were more liable to trust to their own might and main, scorning a Saviour who, as they saw it, had suffered without a fight. A race ingrained with a sense of individualism but far from irreligious, they claimed freedom in thought and action and were prone to seek a direct and personal approach to their Creator, unimpeded by sanctimonious middlemen. Nor did they willingly bend a knee to that element of importuning required by the monotheistic dogma of a desert tribe subverted by politico-religious manipulators.

Whatever the horrific brutality of the Vikings, they had a clear code of manliness and stirring ideals of conduct. They showed equanimity in the face of danger. They were trustworthy and magnanimous rather than shrewd and mercenary – independent and self-reliant, yet fatalistic even to the point of melancholy. 'What will be will be' found them stoical in hardship. Resignation in the face of natural disaster and human foibles masked an inordinate pride of race which elevated physical bravery to its ultimate virtue. The touchstone of a true Viking.

Above all of them were gifted minds which roved the seas of

imagination, sailed the winds of creativity. And, in dreams, theirs
was a mind strangely addicted to flights of fancy, to the meander of
abstractions which took them beyond the realms of the cosmos.

◆

Whatever may be the religious belief gripping a society and however
unswerving its followers' adherence to its principles, history suggests
all deities have their day. The human psyche fashions its god or gods
in forms which attempt to infuse the incomprehensible with some
tangible relationship to our experience of reality. An unprejudiced
assessment of history from the earliest records illustrates that the
theological constructions we place on some possible 'omnipotent
force' become outdated as fashions of new thinking emerge. Has the
hubris of monotheism run its course? Today's exploring mind
snatching at the latest revelations which seek to unravel pattern
and purpose may well hit on 'insights' that stand for the 'truth'.

Truth, like the Loch Ness Monster, is a shadowy form in a cold
dark current which many claim to have glimpsed. Should it exist
and mankind shout 'eureka', still his version of truth may die with
him, an ill-fated conjecture, the dodo of a universe which seems to
exist by eternal change.

However staunch our faith in present gods, a blind refusal to
concede that ideas may evolve to alter religious allegiance, in spite
of ageless pundits of divine certainty and the countless priestly
purveyors of spiritual inertia, past record indicates that the god of
today is doomed to become the myth of tomorrow.

Had Odin, in his doom-laden prognosis for the ultimate fate of all
gods, caught the hint? Did Norse intelligence and insight, their
contemplative thought, borne to horizons where sea turns to sky,
carry the nascent gloom of nihilism? Most profoundly influential of
modern philosophers, Nietzsche considered the belief in any god to
be the naïvety of a weak mind, destroying its naturalistic values.
Free-thinking Vikings would probably have agreed.

Not unlike the Australian Aborigines walking their 'Songlines'
into 'Dreamtime', the Native Americans and their totemic affinity
with nature or the forest pygmies who dance with the moon, Celtic
pagans considered every feature of their natural environment –
from soil to sky, rocks to rivers, flowers to trees, all life forms –

contained a supernatural element. The human ego existed as only one integrated element in a multi-spirit world. Strangely, the current interest in a holistic ecology, with its concern for mankind's environmental impact and its symbiotic outlook, has shades of Celtic lore.

Monotheism and its Egyptian–Judaic derivation took a diametrically opposite stance. It set mankind apart from nature, above the beasts of the field, and supplied him with the moral right to dominion over the planet – its exclusive usage was for his own ends. It is an egocentric view which complements human greed. One-god religion, politics, science and business acumen backed by the parable of the talents joined hands and danced towards global exploitation and degradation, towards the multinational rainforest stripper, the shaman oncologist, the test-tube manipulator, the patent holder of our genes. Neuropharmacology and Mr Clone are poised to alter the natural forms of man's behaviour and its allied emotions – a deliberate redesigning of human nature, a restructuring of intelligence, the fulcrum of enquiry.

Will the boundaries of our imagination grow with the forces of an expanding universe? Although a mass-less photon of light is the fastest energy source so far discovered and it outpaces the speed of thought, are there pathways within which emotions and the corpus of knowledge may exist, may travel and communicate at wavelengths and speeds within dimensions which await our understanding? Is there some overall vein of knowledge into which we tap little by little? Do human enquiry and understanding expand exponentially? The more we know, the more we suspect there is to know.

Insight advances, doctrines decay for all but those in the sheltered cloister. God the Scientist, defeating death. A religion reborn on the promise of immortality on Earth, not in Heaven, but cash down. Can Messiah Mk III reach beyond the creation of mass out of energy? Has he got a unifying force up his sleeve for the next trick? Is good old God obsolete, finished? Was he just a helpful creation, a figment of human consciousness, an illusion as real as mankind's next theory?

Is the power to imagine, to construct theories, to experience a flash of insight, the driving force of creation? What may still emerge, evolve beyond the human brain? Perhaps the universe does not exist to pander to human thought. Maybe the organic arrangement we call consciousness is a dead-end aberration. Just as stars are born and face rapid death within the maelstrom of a black hole's accretion disc, so some fresh amalgam of atoms may yet blossom from the quasi-particles which jostle in the interstellar vacuum created by the implosion of a black hole. Could other arrangements of atomic function emerge that are not carbon based?

Was the big bang beloved by cosmologists the mega-mega explosion of a super-massive black hole? Is the orbital speed of the stars in a galaxy as it revolves related to the mass of a super-massive black hole at its centre? As a black hole swallows its neighbour and grows more gravitationally powerful, slowly the presently expanding energy of the universe might begin a phase of contraction, be compressed to the point at which suddenly the bonds of gravity burst in a flash of radiation – an instant ignition, the trigger that creates a universe. Will the black hole of Sagittarius swallow our present universe, perhaps to create another?

The German physicist Heisenberg, discoverer and articulator of the uncertainty principle in quantum mechanics, is reaching beyond Einstein. He uncannily resurrects Aristotle's idea of 'potentiality'. The atoms and elementary particles of the universe are not seen as real – they form a zone of 'possibilities' rather than one of things or facts. If all things are possible in an endless procession of uncertainty, then this statement cannot be true. This is not the path chosen by a mind of reactionary belief but the adventurer on the highway of imagination.

Of the universe's quartet of forces, the waves of gravity are said to be the weakest. Physicists hunt the elusive graviton – their carrier. Weak it may seem but gravity binds the universe and it may draw it once more to the edge of infinity where thermodynamic laws are yet to be dreamed, the laws of a force which creates infinity. Our minds stumble over the words creation and infinity. 'In the beginning' is as far as we've got for the moment. That may change.

But do the mechanics of human thought, which the current arrangement of consciousness calls reality, leave an indelible trace of 'interference', however infinitesimally weak that may be, upon the changing turmoil of energy that is our present universe? We are but what the heavens made us – the curve of space-time, our measure of movement; accumulated knowledge, its short circuit. Is imagination a wavelength in space, an arrow whose flight carries us beyond the constraints of time? Has the force of emergent thought the hidden strength of gravity, the power to build a universe?

## 23

# The Wing of Odin's Raven

Ferry bows rise and fall, froth spreads white and clean, thump and swish, the momentum of a gale. Crests are topped and V-winged gannets spike shoals below a herring sea. Gulls slip past the rail, greed in yellow eyes. Kelp and shell on a zip-up wind. Then there's salt to laughing lips, hair to bonnie strands, and a face full eager-eyed for a land that oft-times hides. The westerlies ride a bulwark, a hundred miles or more, scarred and treeless, old and hard, exposure rules, elements grind the shore.

But, in the days of turning hay, a mist will lie on the Sea of the Hebrides, a dripping circle, stem to stern where flagpole gulls stand mute and, below the sun-green sky, a form will hide, to be the isles. Gentle isles, summer-soft in a land of pleated sea, until the bursting sun spreads curving peaks and carries headlands into cloud, into blue beyond horizon's end. 'The Long Island' ever in the mind.

The Outer Hebrides, in native lore 'The Long Island', claim five hundred islands from the Butt of Lewis to Barra Head. Their settlement harks back to the knapping of flint tools and the masonry of chambered tomb, to a people whose meditations on the heavens raised monoliths and circle stones. Probing minds of moon and planetary movement by the western seaboard of the

Isle of Lewis built the riddle of Callanish. Thirteen pillared stones, hewn from the hardness of Lewisian gneiss, encircle a fifteen-foot monolith. Avenues set to the cardinal points. Rock of three thousand million years, half the aged earth, raised for worship or question, on a prominence of water-skirted moorland, open and bleak.

A midnight late in the year and the beat of the Atlantic clear on the cool air which flows before rain. Sheep cudded in the lee of Callanish, their coughs sounded on a night which grew to coldness. Stars told land from sky and we sat long, at a little distance from the stones, the Seal Woman and I. Away to the south-east, a sliver, then a matronly orb, breasted the hills of Harris. It glazed the sea, humbled crouching islets. All about us, moorland and peak, each bead of heather dew, instantly beset with silver sheen and as sudden, in outline, against her orange circle, fangs leapt from the mound, stone incisors gnawed the sky. Or were they handless arms of beseeching dead that rose from torture's grave?

We walked into the circle, stood beside the menhir, touched its grated surface. Stillness felt of a lost awareness, cloaked some great enigma hidden within the hiss of silence, the answer to the riddle of reality. Close, the standing forms towered. Bronze Age tools had cut slim bodies to a gauntness infused with the age of the earth. The moon on our shoulder lit each figure, flitted slowly, face by face. Shadows moved. Tall. Emaciated. In measured step, down to the gleam of Loch Roag. Gradually, upon a pillar scoured by salt, wind and rain, but uncarved, unmarked by other than the pureness of lichen growth and the grain of mica seams, there glowed three shapes, their heads as though bending in prayer. And, to their left, the outline of a prone skeleton.

◆

Three thousand years passed and a belief in the afterlife of the body led the Beaker folk of the Western Isles and perhaps elsewhere in Europe to mummify their dead. An archaeological site at Cladhan in South Uist provided the first evidence. Gutted bodies were buried for an allotted period of months in the all-preserving peat. Ironically, the rot of sphagnum moss into peat, by a chemical face-about, ensured that the preserved remains, albeit stained and leathery, could be exhumed after due immersion, dried and brought home to stay with the family. Rituals centred on these mummies – the power of the dead over the living.

The earthenware pottery of these Iberian Beaker folk, their distinctly bell-shaped vessels stamped with a zigzag pattern below the lip and their expert working of bronze into brooch and sword were to become obsolete before the spread of Celtic ironwork. Outdated also became their belief in the resurrection of the body through mummification. With a breath of Reformation greater than Lutheran Protestant displacing Roman Catholic, Celtic belief in the head as the host of conscious power saw sacred Bronze Age mummies dumped back into bogs which first pickled them. So in turn were the Celts of the Western Isles to find the fences which they built from human skulls set on poles did not protect them from the evangelising bunch that paddled up from Ireland.

The Atlantic coasts of the Long Island are lee shores without mercy. Gales in mid ocean roll mountains of sea on to cliff and shoaling beach, heap water into the tide-rip sounds which separate the islands. At the tip of the Outer Hebrides is Barra Head, monitor of calm and storm, a disciple of the sea in all its teaching. A square-rigger driving home from the New World, sheeted hard and clawing south, her skipper watching the sea's crawl on to this ocean crag, he would thank his Maker to weather Barra Head. Two islands lie to its north, twenty miles from the shelter of Castlebay and the Isle of Barra. Mingulay and Pabbay were to become outposts of the new faith.

Unique to Western Europe because of their topography, these tiny islands, difficult of approach, became the retreat of ascetic Christians – contemplative austerity far from the spirals of embroiling dogmas and self-enhancing pomp. Mingulay had its earliest chapel dedicated to Saint Columba, his sacred mass stone still in local memory, and north by a channel, an island upon which proof rests in its Norse name – Pabbay, a priest's isle. A little above this island's landing bay is the large, man-made, conical mound of sand from which a Pictish symbol stone was unearthed. Its markings indicate a graceful moon-shaped crescent with wide eyes and a mason's right-angled mouth above flowing lines suggestive of prancing sea creatures holding a setting moon between their tails. Over pagan imagination had been incised the blunter message of a cross, one certainty succumbing to the next. Moreover the mound bore a burial whose skeletal face covered by a clam shell betokened the remains of a Crusader.

Holy places they would have been when Viking pragmatist Onund Wooden-Leg, the plunderer of Barra and its southern hermit isles, hirpled ashore from his longship fleet in AD 871. Five galleys slid into harbours galore and ready-made fertile soil. Summer warfare and jocund Barra winters were his style. To guard against cold feet when north-east gales lifted the blankets, local marriages took place and slowly the enticing fallback of rollicking Valhalla faded into the strait-jacket of Christian morality. Proof of this defection from Odin lies in the tiny rough stone church on the east side of Barra. Cille Bharraidh, ancient and abandoned, in the keeping of humility, sees the sunrise over Minch and mainland summit. To a Norse runic inscription carved on a gravestone has been added, on the reverse, a cross for the deceased. Odin's Viking and Christian local? Pagan or Pope, whichever you may prefer, it matters little, for still upon the remote isles of Mingulay and Pabbay, in the soughing winds that ever speak from the wave-cut sloc and the empty shore, that winnow through hillside cleit and fallen gable, that whisper in hermit caves before the setting of the sun, there live the spirits of emotions past.

◆

The gleaming axe gripped by bare muscular arms paused high above a humble head bowed in prayer. The giant of a man stood square, blonde hair flying, chest heaving, ready to strike, berserk for the scent of blood.

The man of God, kneeling before the entrance to his shrine, raised a wooden cross in brave skinny hands.

Eyes for an instant met. Viking blue, crazed with killing lust; Celtic brown, shining with the deep intensity of forgiveness.

In one swing, the axe split a skull down its centre. A cross fell to the sand, red and slippery.

The man from the north wind turned, looked back through his life, back to the sea. Did the man of God step before him on to the pathway of life? Down in the bay the tide had turned. In the immensity of the day, would it flow again?

A north-westerly breeze had brought clear brisk air to a morning early in May. Vigour and elation lifted the day. A young boy helping his father to cut peats out on the hill was first to sight the sails. Five, he counted, square on their masts, aslant and drawing, they rounded the headland of the neighbouring island. The father scrambled up from the peat bank at the boy's call. Billowing in bright sunshine, the outstretched wings of the great black birds on the sails were alive. The boats, long and low, flew over the sparkle of the sea. Man and boy ran breathless to the village.

A line of hurrying families climbed the shoulder of the island's peak. Below, the galleys slid easily on to the sands of the bay and helmeted men leapt over gunnels, waist deep, hauling lines.

'God speed and save you and your children,' the holy man had blessed them. 'I will stay.' The last fleeing man saw in horror the slaying of their priest.

Out on to the Dun they fled, to the fallen fortification of ancient times, across a narrow bridge of land with sheer cliff sides which held it to the island. Atlantic rollers echoed in the cave they reached.

The sea robbers came. The island men fought. The tools of the croft were their feeble weapons; the neck of land their lifeline.

Sweep of sword, crash of axe, splintered bone – one by one the bodies of the islanders were flung contemptuously, dead or alive, to the crunch of the rocks below and the hunger of a waiting tide.

Only the women and the girls trailed weeping back to a village by the bay. Night's chill and the steadfast star of evening lay upon an echoed sea. The holy man, a crumpled, cloven head, a trickle red, a drip on ashen death. An old woman in anguish knelt and sucked its last, 'All the sand that ever blew on this island is not worthy to drink one drop of blood that was born in Christ.' Her simple act the bridge between a dying Celtic creed and the Cross of Calvary.

Fires glowed, the starlight dimmed. Long sleek galleys lay safe, drawn above the tide. Leather hogsheads of ale were broached. The men of the north had need; the women were comely; that night, they lay beneath the raven's wing.

And so, through the fulfilment of lust, a generation grew, manly and brave, wedded to the strength of the sea, and they christened the island of their ravaging, Mingulay. But in the hearts of the womenfolk lingered the loss of the holy man and his teachings. And, little by little, his words and ways brought the rough men to pathways of new thought.

24

# Euthanasia but no Morning-after Pill

Deep sea lochs cut the eastern seaboard of 'The Long Island' – safe retreats from The Minch, that put boat and creel to the foot of crofts, whose spade-won soil is acid and thin, as it falls in hollows between glacier-scarred ridges of Lewisian gneiss. Heather tops are the communal grazings of scattered townships. Hardy blackface sheep clip a coarse wool which, carded and spun, sets hand looms in the back shed a clack-clacking into hairy tweed, lanolin-oiled and smelling of peat, fit to turn the angled rain. Homes of a lifestyle on the quicksand of change. Yet windows, from where the spring sun marks its north-bound progress on terraced mainland peaks, take in turn each morning's ruby edge.

Western seaboards are the machair lands. Flat and spacious, they shelter behind dunes of shell sand; lime-rich and stone-free they put a sweetness on the meat of their grazing stock and bring a profusion of summer flowers to skylark tussocks. Here the ocean scent is strong and, of an April night, when south winds turn to warm, pinions beat against a crescent moon and, above the geese calling machair their north-bound cries leave a falling tide to solitude.

These oceanic islands were to provide a homeland for an established Nordic lifestyle which enjoyed a simple balance between crofting tillage and inshore fishing. The semi-open society which the

Vikings brought with them lacked the flummeries and pretensions of overweening monarchies and the pomp of religious devotion. Piratical jaunts passed summer days for the lads and left homestead, hoeing and hay-making to the women and slaves. Individual freedom was a man's watchword.

Not so for the slaves, or thralls, upon whose labour Norse society depended. Working chattels on the narrow ribbon of arable land surrounding a fjord coastline, the typical farm of twelve cows and two horses would be run by three slaves. A labour requirement and social position little different to my days as an Aberdeenshire 'orraloon'. There is no record of castrating male slaves or, surprisingly, 'orraloons'. Freedom to breed in servitude was permitted. Food supply versus labour requirement dictated their numbers, control being chiefly by killing off the old and infirm. A night's deep frost did for old crones and excess infants were dispatched by exposure to the elements. Out of earshot? By singular acts of bravery, slaves might become freemen minus pedigree. No taking egalitarianism too far. Bastardy amongst the freeman classes, though a legal impediment, was of little social stigma; indeed it could be deemed to breed that zip for life which results when genes encoding for headstrong passions are paired in the privacy of the uterus. Ancestor pride, whether legal or from behind the haystack, the Norse would never swallow.

Whilst stravaiging menfolk slit throats and kindled monasteries, dutiful womenfolk kept home fires burning, ordered the slaves, reared offspring, cooked, made clothes and embroidered tapestries in their spare time. Milking the house cow was also their responsibility, right up to my crofting days. The long house, sometimes hall-house, over which the guid wife presided, often measured eight by thirty metres and was usually at the centre of a grouping of byre, smiddy, stables, hay-barn and store sheds. It afforded surprising space and comfort. Wooden furniture existed fifteen hundred years before Ikea; walls were hung with draught-excluding tapestries; as there were geese, so there were eiderdowns and pillows; and, keeping sheep meant something to warm feet on earthen floors. Luxury faltered before the smoke from a central open fire.

A little distance from the main complex was a vital building – the steam bath. Far removed from being lice-scratching scruffs, the

Vikings took fastidious pride in appearance and cleanliness. Full beards and flowing locks received much combing and attention; underpants and knickers saw frequent changing. Better than our plodding Saturn Day, commemorating the Roman God of farming, the Scandinavian word for Saturday derives from their old language and means 'hot springs day'. I find it heartening to note that the fondness of Norse maidens for communal saunas au naturel, followed by a roll in the snow, has never waned.

Compared to our swivel-stool fizzy-drink junk-food craze, their wholesome diet would shame us: home-killed meat of all types; fish in every form – raw, pickled or smoked; pints of whole milk, frothing from an Ayrshire-type cow, cream and cheese; cultivated peas and beans; wild vegetables and fruits; herbs, garlic and bio-flatulence. Every farmstead had its straw bee skips with comb honey sweeter than Tate and Lyle. With salt from boiled sea water and iodine from seaweed soup, the ladies' skin had a shine and vitality that would make the results of 'vanishing cream' appear like applying axle grease. No tossing back vitamin pills, no vegetarian scruples. Extra fibre before the advent of All-Bran? They kneaded ground rye into a coarse loaf stuffed with bran which, for weapon-wielding power, they bequeathed to the Aberdeenshire 'orraloons' of an enslaved youth in the form of porridge eating without end.

Steaming curls rose from cauldrons of stew, larger chunks of meat were spit-roasted or boiled in a wood-lined pit. Hot stones from the fire dropped into water could boil a hundred gallons in half an hour and no oven gloves. Mead, brewed from honey, had the potency of parsnip wine; ale, brewed from bog myrtle, apples and cranberries one better; but beer malted from barley filled a barrel any brewer would happily roll out. Ardent uptake of the latter slaked a national thirst facilitated by the use of the Norse drinking horn, a vessel which demanded of a' man' the quaffing of its contents in a 'oner'. Made from the sweep of a cattle horn and therefore, by virtue of its shape, impossible to stand upright, this feat not infrequently reduced the performer to a similar state.

Kicking or carrying a comatose husband to bed might be standard duty for the womenfolk but it gained them few judicial rights. Some areas of Norway prohibited their bringing of a law case against any man, no matter the crime. As widows, no uncommon status, women did however enjoy full rights of inheritance and many became rich and powerful. Gaining independence, either by plotting or the loss of hubby, some were noted leaders. Witness a Viking tigress of the tenth century – 'The Red Girl', who terrorised parts of Ireland. Her ferocity when sallying into battle, a screaming banshee, eyes ablaze, red hair flying, watered the knees of bravehearts who valued their privates on hearing her cruelty had an obscene 'originality'.

Other ladies became cunningly vindictive. One particular wife, seeking atonement for a past injustice perhaps, went a little beyond even the norm of Norse lifestyle. Premeditation is reflected in a poem, *The Lay of Atli*. No bedtime story, the verse tells of the 'good wife' Gudrun who suffered the murder of some of her kinsmen by Atli, her husband. Atli lies full-bellied, eyeing Gudrun as she gloats before him. 'You have chewed them, carcass-bloody, sweetened with honey, now you can digest their slaughtered human flesh. You will never call the boys to your knee again.' The incensed woman has tricked her husband into eating the hearts of his two freshly killed sons. With more than symptoms of dyspepsia, Atli slouches drunk and despairing, contorted with horror and grief. Gudrun takes the kitchen knife and stabs the 'dipso' to death. To round off, she seizes a fire brand and ignites the house, cremating both hubby and evidence. Readers of Sunday tabloids will be familiar with similar outbursts, though they're rarely set to poetry.

◆

Guarantees of virginity in pre-Christian Nordic society reflected a watchful eye – the family name and pedigree status must be uncompromised by the ardour of the village lads. There was to be none of your Celtic 'handfasting' and a couple's twelve-month living together trial. The honour of one's daughter was to be highly respected as it underpinned her value in any marriage bargain. The debutante must be untampered-with – a condition tantamount to a general certificate of demure behaviour or possibly indicating her skill in avoiding detection. Thanks to the elevated status of poetry within Norse communities, any love poem not leading to a formal proposal of marriage could involve bloodletting by her father or brothers. A touchy matter, family dignity was easily dented so enamoured poets were necessarily cautious in committing undying lust to paper.

A suitor's knee was first bent to the father-in-law-to-be who forthwith busied himself checking the aspirant's fighting prowess and health of wallet. If satisfactory, thence to an agreement on the 'bride-bargain'. A witnessed handshake between the two negotiators sealed the girl's joy or misery. The groom's contribution to the arrangement – cash, property, boat or livestock – had some bearing on the bridal dowry which a suitor might expect. His minimum liability for the marriage to be legal and their children legitimate was twelve ounces of silver, an amount known disparagingly as 'the poor man's price'. Clearly any negotiation discounted the impecunious swain who would be promptly instructed to 'sling his hook'.

At a fixed time after a betrothal, the wedding was solemnised. Guests gathered at the bride's home – formal feast, speeches flowed, frequent liberatory extortions. Evil spirits banished, now to the promotion of the couple's fertility – a subject quite ineffectively addressed without repeated 'bottoms up'. Depending upon one's point of view, merrymaking, or an unseemly 'drunken bash', continued until swaying well-wishers voted to prepare the innocents for the nature of matrimonial duties. Prone, protesting, shy or immodest, a ceremonious undressing and plonking into the nuptial bed might lead to hilarious guffaws for the menfolk or an admiring eyeful for the ladies. Whatever the sighting, a traditional 'bedding' climaxed a ceremony only terminating days later when drinking horns and much else lay horizontal.

Sad to say, women were not to be trusted, men were deceivers and what follies could unfold when called upon to explain hayseeds in the hair. Love, infatuation or unbridled lust, legal realism suspected much 'nooky' lurked behind the byre door in the thrust of 'mighty passion' as Norse poets described it. Attempting to defuse widespread licentious behaviour, the laws of Gotland imposed fines for touching a woman prior to marriage. Placing a careless hand upon wrist or comely ankle, in proven cases, cost the perpetrator four ounces of silver. Let your straying fingers touch an elbow or leg between calf and knee and you were done for two and two-thirds ounces. Breast fondling – singular or plural, not stated – and lawbreaking in terms of pleasure became cost-effective at only one ounce. Distract the lady's attention with a searching hand above her knee, a dishonourable grope called the 'fool's clasp', and the heavy breather suffered no penalty at all – at least not financial. The law reasoned that, when a hand had explored thus far unhindered, then a woman invariably enjoyed any further progress – a legal ruling framed by an empiricist.

Few wives went knickerless or threw bras in the air, for adultery on the part of a wife, in a society where the menfolk spent long spells at sea, constituted a heinous crime. Any husband chancing upon his spouse in flagrante delicto had the right to kill both her and the chap attempting to flee with his trousers about his ankles. However a man keeping a concubine or producing children outside his marriage incurred no penalty and illegitimate offspring could be legitimised at a ceremony of induction to his family. A girl in every port – hey ho, double standards in the seafaring spirit.

Legitimising informal leg-over results required agreement by his legitimate heirs and, of equal importance, a specific brewing from eight bushels of malted grain. Skin taken from the hind leg of a three-year-old bullock slaughtered for the ceremony was fashioned into a leather shoe. The father, taking his youngest legitimate offspring into his arms, led the bastard child forward to step into the shoe. In a Cinderella procession the whole family tried on the slipper. Simple, bureaucracy free, little impediment to the Master of House multiplying his genes or, in common parlance, putting it about a bit, nor, need it be said, to an application of home brew.

Population control, warfare apart, hinged on thinning out the least useful family members. Fjord-land topography limited cultivation and, hence, food supply. Short growing seasons hinted at harvest and head-count. This was self-sufficiency – no namby-pamby menfolk pushing supermarket trolleys, no morning-after pill, no condom vendor in the Gents. At the birth of each child, before it was suckled, the father made a decision as to whether the baby was worth rearing. Deformed babies or one too many for the household economy and a mewling infant was put out to die. Once suckled a child could not be killed without penalty. The old, infirm or otherwise unwanted were persuaded to opt for a night in the deep freeze. No hangers-on – harsh reality, a society on its toes.

Naming each safely delivered baby deemed worth keeping required special attention. Viking tradition, superstition if you will, believed in the direct interplay of a first name and such personal qualities as the parents might wish to instil in their offspring. They believed in the psycho-dynamic impact of a carefully chosen name and the role its connotations might play in shaping the recipient's subsequent behaviour. It might influence faith, pride, heroics or loyalty but, most importantly, it should express family genealogy and cultural belonging.

A male child would be especially studied. Length of leg, strength of bone, hair, his lustiness or lack of it – no wasting a good name on a weakling. It reminds me of days as a pedigree cattle breeder when a sturdy calf with the makings of a champion would be grandly christened. A classic case turned on 'Proud Priapus of Breakachy', a name suggesting an arrogant penile performance. The bull took a Perth Sale ticket and became an unstoppable breeder and, as any observant stockman will tell you, a good bull knows it and holds his head with pride, high and haughty. The mental impact upon the holder of a name, gifted or inflicted, is ripe for study. The alpha male is unlikely to be called Marmaduke or Eustace.

Rebirth through a particular name following down the generations affected the Norse deeply; it complemented an abiding respect for their ancestors. Departed family members lived in fireside stories. Great-grandfather grew to be the hero who influenced a wide-eyed childhood listener gifted with his name. Forenames followed the generations, a first son invariably being called after his grandfather. Another son might receive the name of a dead kinsman; reincarnation shadowed their thoughts. This practice of family nomenclature made byname usage imperative.

Christian conversion, foisted on the people at the turn of the first millennium, saw the names of saints creep into usage. New Testament gospellers were compounded with those of heathen gods. Hybrid versions of Thor became popular – a sensible precaution should missionaries be peddling a bogus system of beliefs. John and his brother James, known as Sons of Thunder were the tough guys of the Twelve Apostles and fishermen to boot so they came top of the pops.

Jon is still the commonest Christian name in Scandinavia but this slavish recital of Christian naming is retreating before the charisma of celluloid 'phoneys', film idol worship to set old folk scoffing. Fifteen hundred years on and 'sen' or 'son' following a forename – Anderson, Thomson, Johnsen – is straight Norse. 'Mac' preceding a second name denotes older Celtic influence. Many surnames in the Western Isles mix the two cultures: MacAulay, a simple hybrid, son of Olav, King of Man and the North Isles in the 1200s; MacIver, son of Ivar; MacAskill, son of Asgeir and so on. A thousand years of interbreeding and the appearance of many Highland folk can be traced on face and stature to racial origins that came north by coracle or south by longship.

What's in a name? How far does kinship's affinity stretch? Run five hundred sheep, a milling, bleating mass, down a drafting race and they follow through in families, never mind dogs and stick-waving shepherds. In an established herd of cattle, peck order counts. Offspring of dominant families invariably stay at the top but all the way down the pile they have their pals and relations, animals with whom they graze.

I started a pedigree herd of Aberdeen Angus with two Balavil heifers brought from the local vet, Jimmy Stuart. After Jimmy's death, his herd was dispersed in Perth and I bought another Balavil heifer to join the fifty strong Angus cows then at Breakachy. This animal, though related, was too young by several generations to have known my two original Balavil purchases. I let her off the float. Next morning, she was grazing alongside the two Balavil cows. Kinship? Coincidence?

One sunny Aberdeenshire afternoon, we pulled in to picnic. A lay-by near a burying ground, trees, moss and peaceful, on the hill road out of Rhynie, never before visited. I unlatched the iron gate and stood looking through the shade to curve-topped headstones leaning with age. Moments fused. I became conscious of an un-explainable sense of familiarity – somehow I was acquainted with this place, its surrounding country of dyke and field in a flush of warmth as at the unexpected meeting of some friend of like mind.

It passed but affected me strongly. I turned. The Seal Woman stood beside me. 'Strange, I feel at home about here, in this neck of the woods, for no reason.' We entered. Many, many gravestones bore the name Thomson.

The burying ground at Walls, headland and voe on the west side of Shetland, is full of Thomson graves. Consanguinity, strong and reassuring – blood down the centuries. I belonged.

# A Serious Attack of Sea Fever

Glamour sways in many ways. Havoc can be wreaked. A man's emotions, his lifestyle, his bank account. Ah me, the syncopating hips of a black jazz singer, the rolling eyes of an Aberdeen Angus heifer, a sleek-prowed yacht lifting and falling with the skill of a professional seducer. Mercy me, there's danger.

Take a glitzy London Boat Show – sniff the crispy smell of canvas, grasp a tiller, wink at the come-on eye of a compass and your dreams are swinging in the rigging. Ride the swell from a pint or two of Guinness, taste the trade winds in its froth and a mistress of the ocean is planting a palm tree romance on your fantasy beach. Your wallet is about to be holed on the waterline. Ten thousand down, my name is on the sale note of a brand new blue-water Nicolson and my foot landed on the deck of a yacht for the first time in a farming life.

Barely back from London frolics and dedicated landlubber Griffin caught my drift. An urgent meeting with John MacGillivary was flagged up. John, a man of multiple enterprise, manifested in youth by his hoisting of a pair of girl's knickers on the flagpole of Inverness Royal Academy, is respectably known to the city's Rotarians as 'Gigs'. Enthusiasm for yachting, plus grants from the Highlands and Islands Development Board, provided an excuse for John to become the proud owner and Flag Admiral of Loch Ness Charters. Each summer his fleet of sailing cruisers plied the dour loch of the monster, strange to say, without ever a sniff of its multimillion pulling wheeze. Tiresome rescue operations revolved around Gigs – a yacht perched on a rock, the odd ceased engine. The Admiral began to tire of his ploy.

Monday morning, down at the Caledonian Canal with forty-five-year-old memories of model yachting trips in mind and there, warped to a pontoon by the tow path, lay a tall-masted Bermudan sloop, white-hulled and sleek, a sheer at the bow, lift to her counterstern, no hard lines, she would flow on the sea with the grace of a lady, a Rival 34, the classic of blue-water yachts. 'Welcome aboard *Rhum*,' boomed up the companionway. I slid open the hatch. Havana smoke swirled round a bottle of brandy, uncorked and smiling up from the saloon table. The Admiral reclined on the cabin's best couch-cum-bunk. The heater glowed. Likewise Gigs, in top selling mode, and his fleet's flagship no less. I fell for bottle and boat, never to regret it.

A fortnight aboard, a cheque to Gigs and *Rhum* was mine, ready for sea, complete with instructions from John on the art of sailing her. 'You're fairly intelligent, you'll soon learn.' Shepherding togs doubled for a sailing outfit. With telescope and wellies, sleeping bag and towel, *Rhum*'s Volvo Penta blew a cloud of smoke and victim and his ocean-going yacht chugged away from a canal pontoon beside the irascible Lord Burton's fish-pond. Masefield knew the symptoms – a serious attack of 'Sea Fever'.

The east wind of March lingered long enough to fill the jibs'l and flutter an L-plate. I nipped about the deck discovering which ropes to pull or not to pull as *Rhum* swooped down Loch Ness past Urquhart Castle, a decrepit pile captured by Edward of England, the 'Hammer of the Scots' and later blown up by the troops of arch-chancer, William of Orange. Excitement. Shiver me timbers! Given a cannon on the bow I'd have finished the job and treated the tourists to a salvo.

Fort Augustus Abbey, mauled during the '45 Jacobite Rebellion, presented grim towers to an evening sun slotted between the hills at the head of Loch Ness. Dr 'Dictionary' Johnson wrote to Boswell after their visit in 1773, 'The best night I have had these twenty years was at Fort Augustus', an ambiguous remark for a word practitioner but, it being after closing time for the canal, worth checking on. I moored to a pontoon and made for the lockside Guinness haven. Sure enough, a couple of Inverness nurses were keen to sail to Fort William and, by midnight, round the world as well. Dictionary be damned – the Doctor had a point.

Between oak and ash and the daisy fields of lambing crofts, winds Telford's masterpiece – his Cape Wrath-beating canal which was built between 1804 and 1822 complete with ample water, sturdy lock gates and gravity for free. Smart buildings, black-and-white-liveried at each set of locks, hydraulic rams in place of muscle-bending levers and *Rhum* was lifted twenty feet at a time by sluices with the swirl of a mega washing machine. Lock-keepers caught ropes as next morning we climbed into Loch Oich and motored down Loch Lochy. Ships'-mast larch, still tinged with the pale russet of winter needles, reached from skimpy shorelines into grey scree and the dark pleated skirts of Forestry Commission woodland. Ben Nevis grew momentous in height and girth and shed its grandeur into motionless green water where mighty hills balanced on their heads and fledgling clouds loitered. Against a duck-egg sky, the Great Glen opened its gateway to the west.

Above Inverlochy Castle, a rich man's dream sat abandoned. A yellow funnelled steam yacht, sporting many portholes, lay keeled against the bank – a toy of the late Mr Hobbs, one-time owner of both castle and the Long John Distillery. Hobbs's enterprise had poured the Ben's 'enlivened' waters down eager throats and the by-product of the process, in the form of draff, over the 'thrapples' of a thousand-head herd of cows which roamed over his Great Glen Cattle Ranch. When death took the controls, his fortune appeared to have vanished into cattle dung.

Fort William's combination of holy spires and a failed wood-pulp mill stood amidst some of the finest arrangements of mountain-scape and sculptured estuary to be had – a discordant mix of man and nature, grating as a bum note in the middle of *The Messiah*. The canal's final flight of eight locks and a drop of sixty-four feet took *Rhum* down 'Neptune's Staircase'. I'd reached Banavie without a bump. Gigs, bent on my navigational instruction, and the Seal Woman, bent on adventure, joined ship as I tied to a jetty outside the sea-lock. Salt water below the keel and I'm able to throw a coil of rope.

> All the nice girls love a sailor,
> All the nice girls love a tar,
> For there's something about a sailor,
> Oh, you know what sailor's are.
> Bright and breezy, free and easy . . .

I forgot the next bit, but trilled the last lines:

> When you think he's in the pen,
> He'll be off to sea again,
> Ship ahoy, sailor boy.

There might be something in the old song.

Before April dawn put sun on the late snows of Ben Nevis, mooring lines were aboard and ripples round the bow. First taste of sea lay beyond the Kessock Ferry. Loch Linnhe on the ebb swirled us through the Corran Narrows and, down by Glencoe of army days and rock climbing on Buachaille Etive Mor, railway tracks reached the slate quarry village of Ballachulish. The remains of MacIan, victim of Glencoe's lamented massacre, rest on the Loch Leven burial islet of St Munda, a little west of the old ferry crossing. Many years before its replacement, I rowed across and spent time by MacIan's grave – the enormity of steep pressing hills centred on his islet resting place, the silence of their heights broken only by voice of nesting gulls. An old man done to death by political machination had a finer soul window than all the marbled pomp of the mighty.

*Rhum* heeled to a breeze that funnelled down the 'Glen o' Weeping' and for a brief space we glimpsed the box-girder Meccano monstrosity which presently rips through the curvaceous backdrop of the Pap of Glencoe. Perpendicular hills crowd the straits of Ballachulish where for many years a gibbet dangled the wired-together bones of James Stewart, an innocent man hanged for the murder of Campbell of Glenure on the Appin braes in 1752. The woodlands of Lettermore, scene of that mysterious gunshot, reached to the shore in spring green birch and sombre oak. We slipped quietly by for the great hills muffled a southerly breeze.

Rising over the bow, blessed in shape and song, was Mull of the cool high bens. Bacon and eggs drifting from below, the long, croft-dotted Isle of Lismore came abeam. Trim sail, tighten the main, belay ropes, Gigs asleep on the Admiral's bunk, proof of his belief in delegation. 'Drake's Drum'. 'Cap'n, art thou sleeping there below?' – the great poem for real. Pencil lines appeared on charts from cross bearings taken with a hand-held compass. I plotted our position and relayed the result to the Admiral.

The Sound of Mull poured westward, an enormous Minch-bound river. Duart Castle, pride of the Lords of the Isles, and twin lighthouses command its entrance from the Firth of Lorn. The tidal Lady's Rock upon which a MacLean chief staked a superfluous wife was just showing as we rode the current, keeping to the north shore. It's believed this side once was Henderson domain, for the old name of the Sound, Cuan mhic Eanruig, may translate as Henderson's Sea. The intense green of Mull's huge smooth hills shone on water speeding us round castellated headlands. A quick view into Tober-mory Bay behind the shelter of Calve Island, a multicoloured waterfront and the Mishnish Hotel of accordion maestro, Bobby MacLeod – I was to know both, MacLeod being of Wester Ross origins. Do Spanish doubloons from an Armada galleon wreck lie in Tobermory mud? More treasure dances over the Mishnish counter to the sound of pipe tunes. Bobby would appear late, half-ten maybe, climb on to a tiny stage, nod, and pick up the 'box'. His arthritic blue roan spaniel curled at his feet must have known every tune by heart. I would be in the cramped space by the side bar which doubled as a dance floor and the track to the Gents. The lilt of his music, the lift he gave it. Off with the wellies, to hell with splinters, dance and dance until he would come down for a 'wordie' about the Highlands.

CalMac's *Claymore* and a steamer rail of faces were Castlebay bound. A peak-capped, white-shirted figure appeared on the wing of her bridge and waved both hands. Greatly flattered I waved back. Gigs stood on our stern locker and held up the kettle. 'That's Iain Dewar, her skipper,' he said, 'you'll meet before too long – he'll come for a trip with us.' In moments her wake was flip-flapping our sails and the kettle, restored to the galley, was whistling away – time for Oxo.

Ardnamurchan Peninsula thrust westwards from the mouth of Loch Sunart. This beautiful sea loch curves its way inland to the hills about Strontian. When not inventing the miner's safety lamp and discovering the laughing gas effects of nitrous oxide, Sir Humphry Davy, the English chemist, prowled this mineral-rich area and by applying electrolysis to the pale yellow metallic substance he came upon, also discovered and named strontium. For the amazement of those attending Guy Fawkes Bonfire Nights, the salts of this element add a red flame to fireworks. Less frivolous are this element's radioactive isotopes – $^{89}$Sr and $^{90}$Sr. They represent some of the most dangerous fallout from nuclear explosions and the unhealthy by-product of nuclear power stations. Some might consider life safer had Sir Humphry confined his amusements to laughing gas.

Along Loch Sunart and its shores of limpet bay and evergreen islet, the oak woodlands, still without leaf, were darkly etched below the strikingly lit shades of Ben Hiant. Under this hill's shadow is a red granite pillar marking the grave of a St Chiarain and carved with a cross said to be the handiwork of Columba. Maybe so, for Iona is no distance south. We tacked a heading wind as the small Tobermory ferry left Kilchoan Pier, a stance from where those who care may view the fate of thirteenth-century Mingary Castle. A notice reads 'Dangerous ruin. Keep out'. But it would have been a more dangerous prospect in its heyday as a seat of the MacIains of Ardnamurchan who held the peninsula for some four hundred years.

The castle's sea gate leads on to rocks and here MacIain had his raiding galley painted black on the port side, white on the starboard – its target the plundering of 'Far Lochaber'. From the Loch Linnhe shore, a white boat sailing east, armed, a black boat returning west, laden. Once too often? The fallen ruins of MacIain's 'nest' look over the Bay of the Spaniards, a name given to it after an equally resourceful Lachlan MacLean of Duart laid siege to the castle using Spanish soldiers he'd borrowed for the occasion from an Armada galleon which lay recuperating in Tobermory harbour after fleeing Drake's fire ships via the Pentland Firth. MacLean didn't succeed; it required the weight of Clan Campbell. In 1624 they laid waste the whole peninsula and had a go at demolishing Mingary Castle. Many MacIains hurried to a cave on the north coast. Careless footprints in the snow gave away their whereabouts. The Campbells pounced, held the entrance until a huge damp fire filled the cave with death-choking smoke – MacIains no more. And today? A crofting and fishing lifestyle dying of holiday-home disease.

Gigs reclined on the Admiral's bunk, perusing the Admiralty West Coast Pilot, and considered the terrors of Ardnamurchan Point, now up ahead. This wave-beaten junction at the mouth of the Sound, claiming to be the most westerly tip of the Scottish mainland, has been imaginatively translated. 'Promontory of the Sea Dogs' and 'Promontory of Sea Villainy' are talented stabs and then there's 'High Point of the Great Ocean' and, appealingly, Aird nam Murdhuchuchan, 'Height of the Sea Nymphs'. We rounded close in under a lighthouse of impressive girth and reassuring stance. South wind and tide, full sail driving, seven knots. The Seal Woman, bare feet braced to the helm, laughing eyes, sunshine hair, rainbows in the bow spray. Skim the last sea-exploding rocks, suddenly a skyline bursting with the gabbro pinnacles of volcanic days. Green-black waves flashing with dabs of white raced before us into the abounding blue of the Cuillin Hills of Rum and Skye. Shapely hills whose name may have come to us through the eye of Viking imagination and their word *Kjollen*, 'Keel-shaped ridge'.

Fine to port, sharp as a charcoal sketch, the blue-black Sgurr of Eigg. Its precipitous east face and summits of weather-torn notches give the island its Gaelic name Eilean Eige, Isle of the Notch. Yet another saint, this time Donnan, together with his followers, ended their days as corpses in a sepulchral urn. Hebridean traveller, Martin Martin, had it excavated. Bones but no skulls – decapitation was ever a Celtic fashion. Much later and another cave-burning exercise dealt with the native MacDonalds, possibly in retribution for their massacre of Sky MacLeods by burning a church full of worshippers or for their affront to a MacLeod chief whom they tied in a boat and set adrift on The Minch for his having played havoc amongst the Eigg maidens – it's not clear. Either way, the MacLeod galleys pulled up and the Eigg MacDonalds retired to a secret cave. Not secret enough, for shortly the damp thatch from their houses was producing deadly smoke. The bones, when found, were in family groups. Subsequently assorted owners have tinkered with the island. Notable in recent years was a Dutchman whose acrimonious divorce case opened the door to an invasion of a different people with little Highland connection.

Fertile and well farmed, Eigg's neighbour, the Isle of Muck, probably takes its name from the porpoise or, in Gaelic, *muc mara*, 'sea swine'. Around the Small Isles, as this group is known, the currents which flow were well stocked with fish and shoals of these trusting mammals would be arching their backs and rooting the sea lanes. Although the natives escaped thinning out by the smoking cave treatment inflicted upon the folk of Eigg, the poverty years in the 1800s saw them packing their bags for Nova Scotia. MacLeans held the island until the last of them, back from the American War of Independence and sporting a Yankee wife, became Deputy Lieutenant of the Tower of London but couldn't fund the lifestyle. The then owner of Eigg, Thomson MacEwan, added Muck in 1879 and set about building a model farming unit with sheep, tree planting, dairy cattle and cheese exporting – a man ahead of the game.

Forms of sea transport hold fascination for many and few more so than a seventy-foot converted Admiralty launch named *Shearwater*. It was purchased by Murdo Grant, owner of the Arisaig Hotel across on the mainland, from my one-eyed pal, Desperate Dan MacKenzie, in Ullapool. Dan the pirate, amongst other activities not unconnected with salmon, dealt in second-hand boats which he bought at naval auctions in Plymouth and proceeded to coax home prior to refitting for sale at Ardmair Point. The *Shearwater* – other than the sea, her name bore little relation to *aqua* but rather more to *vitae* – was commissioned by Grant for circulating the Small Isles with a licence for dispensing alcohol, in addition to the accommodation of passengers. Her fascination for the natives seemed never to wane and, on arrival, they would crowd aboard. For watch-glancing tourists, departure time from an island was pure speculation.

For us though, an azure day held the same intensities of colour which stimulated the intuitive art of Cadell and Peploe. It also matched the blue ensign that rippled with a superior flap from the flagstaff on our stern, denoting a Commodore of the Fleet was aboard – in our case, the owner of Loch Ness Charters. Up ahead, off the island of Eigg, prowled a naval vessel, her peashooter guns covered with canvas bags. 'Admiralty ship ahead, skipper,' I shouted down the hatch and, noting a crewman lowering her white ensign, added, 'I suspect her captain has just died.' John bounded on deck, grabbed our ensign and dipped it with a flourish. The grey vessel responded by raising her ensign and altering course to give us a clear passage. Flag etiquette and a courtesy manoeuvre towards a superior rank – standard navy regulations.

More to sailing than just zero one zero, magnetic, which steered us up the Sound of Sleat and into Mallaig to tie for a night alongside herring boats stacked three out from the slimy harbour wall. Lads in Arran jerseys caught our ropes – fishermen who named their boats with more than a hint of the drama of a trade not for weaklings. From *Ocean Maid* to *Morning Star*, they were proud boats all, scrubbed and clean with derricks lashed down and boxes stowed against their gunnels. We clambered across their decks and I read each vessel's registration number, INS, an Inverness boat, PD for the east coast port of Peterhead and, in against the jetty, CY5, *Boy James* – a Castlebay boat which I was to set foot on again. Up the vertical iron ladder and on to semi-dry land. Melting ice trickled under pyramids of creels, fish marinated with salt air and the quarrels of one-legged gulls. Bowlines on to bollards, our ropes criss-crossed with those of working boats. A mite abashed to be amongst real seamen but at least none of your white ducks and 'yachty' caps – just wellies and jackets. A day on the waves and we wobble-legged it up the town for a dram with the oilskin boys.

The northbound flood up the Sound of Sleat plus Gigs had us on deck before dawn and any possibility of a sailing breeze. Loch Nevis and Knoydart were shadows to starboard – a remoteness magnetic to eccentric landowners and government agencies alike. In the thirties, Nazi sympathiser, Lord Brocket, entertained Hitler's hierarchy to flunkey sporting days. By 1948, seven local lads, home after a taste of the Führer's megalomania, attempted to claim their Inverie crofting rights from Brocket and found themselves visiting the Inverness Sheriff Court for their audacity. War or no, the 'Seven Men of Knoydart' soon discovered who fired the bullets this side of the channel. A peninsula of mournful solitude, dogged by taxpayer grants and absentee owners, its indigenous people had been shipped to Nova Scotia in 1853 by a Josephine MacDonell of Glengarry. Given a false promise of land waiting for them in Australia, they willingly went aboard unaware of their true destintion. Knoydart has exchanged its cultural identity for an adventure school playground and tourist jaunts from Mallaig.

◆

The redness of dawn brought a warning flash to Sandaig light and a chill, grey awakening to the dew-soaked hills of Loch Hourn. Savage in a triumph of isolation, hidden from the world of overspill, these hills gave peaceful seclusion to shallow bays and grass-topped islets which Gavin Maxwell of the otters shared with millions of readers in his beguiling *Ring of Bright Water*. For me, Loch Hourn prompted recall of both an uncanny meeting and the disquiet of reading the birthday copy which, on publication, arrived from my mother. Its impact didn't fade. As with those twists that may follow some ordained process, I came to spend many weeks with *Rhum* at anchor in fjord-like surroundings. On the loch's southerly shore is a small island of deep heather and rocky outcrop upon which the noonday shadow of the immense Ladhar Bheinn would fall. Here was shelter from the shrieking winds that lift the waters of a loch whose name is said to mean 'Loch of the Underworld'.

In my time nobody walked the shore or came to the Eilean a'Phiobaire, the Island of the Piper, and the gulls found freedom to fill it with their nesting – heather tussock shelters, scrapes amongst shingle grit and their bonnie dark mottled eggs, point ends to the centre and a constant crying that rose to a crescendo when the great black-backed gull would alight. And *Rhum* would rock a little at the turn of the tide and I was privy to their world of concern until the golden shafts of an evening sky would reach into clouds which lay behind the fading Cuillin ridge and the terns would dip and weave their way out to fish the Sound and crimson light would fleck their smoky trail. Days into weeks, time was mine to stravaig each hill and bay and into the highest corries to watch a hind give birth and see the raven, with its keen sense of smell, strut at a distance in the hope of a gorge on her 'cleansing'. And only for me was there to be the silence of the hill in a hollow of sunshine and, far below, motionless *Rhum* beside her island and the Seal Woman asleep on the shore, for there was none else.

With times of the great herring runs long past, Loch Hourn and its margins knew native peoples and, at the headwaters, the shoals were so thick as to stall a sail boat and fishing for them was by the bucket. There was no other boat on a quiet day when we sailed between islands to a tiny bay on the north side. It lies beyond the end of a stone-made path which the locals of Arnisdale built as payment in kind for their supplies of famine relief. We anchored *Rhum* in this little bay and climbed through the scent of birch and bluebell to a crystal lochan and swam in the heat. A sun towel-dried us and I lay and spied over the lands of Barrisdale. Away on their far shore a low-lying island of sand and emerald grass held the grave-stones of clansmen. My lens filled with the twisting flight of terns. Others sat tight amidst the pink blooms of sea thrift and I knew they nested. A huff of breeze for a moment cooled the pouring warmth and took their strident cries to us and to the mind came the echo of a day when the old gnarl-rooted Caledonian Forest grew about Barrisdale House and Coll MacDonell with the handsome men of Knoydart took up arms for their 'Prince' in the calamitous '45.

After Culloden – or Drummossie Moor as the Highlanders preferred it – MacDonell returned to Loch Hourn on the strength of information he provided to Cumberland concerning the where-abouts of the fugitive Stuart. The Prince was in Perthshire, Coll avowed. A false trail. The retributive trail to Barrisdale House by Ross-shire militia proved certain. His old home ablaze and Colla Ban, as he was known, boarded a French man-of-war heading for France. Bonnie Prince Charlie, not content with the slaughter of Highland men he occasioned by his own suspect claim to a crown, also doubted Colla who, as a result, stepped ashore into a French jail. Escape to Edinburgh brought only a second captivity and death to a man who could but contrast the freedom of his native Loch Hourn with the folly of following another man's myopic ego.

The Loch of the Underworld knows squalls of a fury not experienced by many sheets of water in the Highlands. One September equinox, I cast off from the Piper Island bay leaving a large white fender as a marker buoy bobbing on the end of my anchor rope. A wind, light but uncertain, took *Rhum* quietly down to Maxwell's Camusfearna at the head of the loch. I rowed ashore and walked beyond the rusting iron of his shark-hunting boat the *Polar Star* and across rabbit-eaten croft-land to the faint remaining trace of the Sandaig home which he had ordered to be demolished after its gutting by fire. Below the woodland which hid the steep access road, a whitewashed croft house seemed unoccupied. The waterfall in the grotto where he wrote so movingly seemed indifferent. Did Maxwell die with the pain of dissolution, the sadness of seeing the beauty he described crumbling as surely as his own dreams were to do?

The wind fretted – puffs here and there as I motored down to a nest of islets which hug the north shore. Here was the playground of otter families. Angular boulders marked the shoreline, moss-topped and resting, tipped from the slender peak of Ben Sgriol high above me. Lined clouds accentuated the jagged Cuillin as I put down *Rhum*'s kedge anchor on the west side of Arnisdale bay and made my supper. A phone call kept me long after dark and I walked back from the kiosk to the first howls of a gale tearing through high corries and up the loch. Exceptional night vision was my blessing – I needed it as rain pelted out of blackness.

Dinghy down the stones, no toy oars, no 'futtering' with an outboard, an eight-foot pair of sweeps fit for a hard pull. The yacht veering wildly to her bar-tight kedge rope, surged at me. I caught the gunnel, one swing, aboard, one slip, um. The dinghy ran out astern on a hefty painter. Engine on, slow ahead. Step to the bow. Rope in, hand over hand, anchor clanked aboard, lucky it held. I swung *Rhum* away from a shore plain by its angry white edge.

Yeee, yeee! The alarm was screaming from the cabin. Engine heating? Sharp glance over stern – no water coughing from the exhaust. Stop engine or cease it. Stop. In seconds *Rhum* wallowed broadside. Shore a hundred yards. Hang on, up for'ard keep windward side of boat, jib lashed to rail, sail ties off, billow of sail. Shore close now. Mast, jib halyard, haul for your life. Hang on, hang on, back to the cockpit. Hard over the banging helm. *Rhum* brought her head off the shore, thirty yards? Maybe. Depth? Not healthy – six feet by the sounder. I steered into the open loch. No lights – lucky me, one good eye.

Without warning, the squall hit. I turned my head to get breath. Dinghy, airborne. *Rhum* heeled. A wild angle almost threw me over the side. I swung her through the wind. She steadied, jib backed. Wind twisted, hurricane and whirlwind in a oner, water lifted off the sea about me. Black as tar, salt eyes, I couldn't see. Jib crashed back, filled. We shot ahead again, heeled, surging, a furious rate, my foot against the cockpit side, port gunnel under, solid water battering the spray hood. Tearing across black Loch Hourn, nine knots, fifty-yard wake, only working jib. How to stop?

Waves flung on to the west end of Piper Island; I picked them out, eased the helm. Had the white buoy I'd secured to the anchor rope broken free? No buoy, no anchor pick-up, face this hurricane? I'd never tack out of here, the rocks for boat and me? The roaring of the gale on the ridge above the island was a fearsome sound. There's the legend of the Bull of Barrisdale, a supernatural creature with a thunderous bellow, and I was hearing it. Torchlight robs vision. Night eyes sought a dancing white float at the lee of the island. *Rhum* ran on. 'There's it,' I said aloud, sighting a white bouncing dot. Split-second judgement. Let fly jib sheet. Threshing, clapping sail. Leap to the bow, no safety harness, hang on to pulpit rail. Boat hook, ready. *Rhum* drifted fast, down on to the buoy. Lucky jab, buoy and rope end thump aboard. Quick, watch fingers, two turns on the Samson post and *Rhum*, in moments, true sea boat that she was, swung her head and bowed as gracefully to the anchor as I did – thankfully.

Next morning Ben Sgriol had a 'dossen' of September snow. The hills were not overheating, nor seemingly was *Rhum*'s old Volvo Penta which ran sweetly without any ear-blasting whistle. The water inlet couldn't be clogged – the rubber impeller which drove the cooling system was intact. Early on in this sailing lark, I'd learnt three rules: do thirty 'press ups' a day for strength; on the foredeck, stow the biggest anchor you can lift aboard by brute force; and have a sail lashed to the for'ard rail ready to hoist in an instant. A sail in need is a friend indeed. Never trust a smelly engine.

Many years before that particular incident, I browsed Thins bookshop in Inverness and became aware of a man in dark glasses staring at me. White polo-neck jersey, baggy trousers – nothing extraordinary about that. He was a tall man, angular face and features. We looked at each other for some minutes. The effect was unusual, as though each clawed at subconscious recognition. When he turned away, I questioned the shop girl. 'That's Gavin Maxwell,' came the reply. Nothing passed between us but a look, yet I see him clearly as I write.

On the twenty-fifth anniversary of Maxwell's death, the privilege fell to me of presenting a BBC documentary which gathered together those who had been closest to him in his writing days beside the waterfall at Camusfearna: Magdla Stirling, cousin and comforter of a mind often in turmoil; the two chaps who came from the south as school leavers to be otter keepers at Sandaig; Jimmy Watt, now living quietly at the ferry house by the Kylerhea crossing; and Terry Nutkins, the widely known TV wildlife presenter. Terry, himself badly bitten by one of the otters, told us, 'We might be out exercising the otters down at the bay and Gavin, in the heat of writing fervour, would shout for more whisky. We had to hurry with that order.' Royalties, fame and film rights followed. For the writer, a shower of cash, coupled to the constant knocking on the door at Sandaig by enchanted readers, destroyed a simple life which his art in writing had driven him to depict. Acclaim became the canker.

Richard Frere, himself author of several books, travelled across from Drumnadrochit to the celebration. A hardy man who canoed round the north of Scotland in his sixties, he became Maxwell's weary factotum for several outlandish enterprises. At Raef Payne's whitewashed cottage, the authoritative biographer Douglas Botting also joined our group. Each evening, Raef, as Maxwell's friend and neighbour, had read the latest outburst of writing. BBC Inverness was fortunate in having Ann Bates as editor and programme maker. Her crafting made a worthy tribute, no less of an insight, to a man and his idyll of the otters.

As we sat talking by an open log fire, a dram in hand doubtless drawing Maxwell's approval, it brought to light the torn mind of a poet who had suffered the dark side of failed relationships. The curse put upon him by the cries of poetess Kathleen Raine clinging to the tree of the rowans on the night of storm, when he turned her from the door of Camusfearna, affected Maxwell deeply. In a poem of love, she gave title to one work, a *Ring of Bright Water*, into which he poured his longing for the simplicity and freedom of wild places – writing in which Maxwell came closest to his inner loneliness.

Kathleen Raine, spurned soul-mate, and her curse at the rowan trunk began his slow, often angry, lapse into disillusion, a mind-play on dreams searching for yesteryear's elation. The joy of which he had written became the touchstone of a success which turned happiness into dross. Gavin Maxwell, creator of a legend for the masses, couldn't live with its collapse.

I looked beyond conversation. The tiny cottage window framed the otter bays, the small lighthouse on Sandaig point, the black Cuillin in its topmost pane and a man, tall and in a white polo-neck jersey, stared up from the beach. Thirty-five years had passed since my mother's birthday present.

◆

Many's a thread twining through those live-aboard years on *Rhum* found its origin within patterns of thought and behavioural traits which, for better or worse, lead towards the outlooks and attitudes of forebears, inclinations one inherited in privacy and innocence. Whilst our bodies may be cellular mongrels, may contain cells from your mother, your siblings, even your grandpop, due to the phenomenon of microchimerism whereby cells flit cheerfully between a mother and her foetus in either direction, we are, for the moment, genetically predetermined to prefer certain things or, without doubt, a particular type of person. The banker may know you're heading for bankruptcy; the lawyer, he's seen the will; the quack, your piles – but, short of committing a crime, your genome is relatively private and tamper-proof, so far.

Step in commercial population genomics. Cloaked by the proposed benefits of epidemiological studies but other perhaps more intrusive chromosomal assessments, national genetic databases may well be another pathway for state power to dismantle what remains of the private individual. How far is your genetic inheritance private property? Would you care to have Grandpa's genome unzipped for inspection? Maybe yes, if it meant avoiding deformity or dysfunction in your offspring. What if the state were to decree your personal identification by DNA profile? What if there were leakages for commercial or political ends?

In Iceland, where producing a national gene database is under way, the old Viking love of individual freedom is fighting its corner.

Clear limits have been set by the Icelandic Supreme Court as to how far commercial population genomics and biotechnology can intrude into the private life of the island's citizens. Norse settlers founded a republic and a parliament in AD 930 and complete independence for Iceland was secured through a referendum in 1944. I fear their spirit to be a guttering beacon.

The east–west religious volcano rumbles on. Eruptions of brutality down the ages would have any messiah with hindsight wishing he hadn't been so assertive on only subjective evidence. The standard thousand-year-old formula never fails in its political, religious or an unholy combination of both. Induce fear in your population. Justified or not, it's the key to handcuffs, trial without jury and a control system with jail, or worse, arranged for dissenters. It's a standard dilemma of democracies since Socrates drank hemlock. How far can a 'free' society remain 'open' without being undermined by those who differ, blow whistles and risk high treason, by those outwith the system whom it must exploit or oppress to maintain its freedom? One man's terrorist is the other man's freedom fighter. Meantime scientific advance provides techniques to help with the problem – DNA 'identikits' and GPS electronic tagging for starters. Surely an improvement on three hundred years past when Scots Presbyterian power hanged Thomas Aikenhead, a nineteen-year-old theological student, for the blasphemy of doubting the Trinity and calling Christ an impostor? Bonfires and torture in the good old-fashioned religious style will soon be forgotten, their beliefs fade into benign fairytales. As this century's politico–scientific experiment with the human genome takes off, freedom may not even lie in the mind.

Forget your nth grandpa's genome, forget the double helix, the supposed stability and elegance of Watson and Crick's model DNA with its polymerase enzyme unzipping and zipping up each matching pair of 'bases', a flies-down, wham-bam, knickers-up, at a molecular level. DNA too can be a sexual gymnast, twisting into many different structures, triple-helix, tetra-helix, cruciform, novel arrangements which may play their role in or even control our gene expression. The so-called 'jumping genes', which are responsible for gene duplications and mutations, may hold the key to the evolution of the human brain by setting up the raw material for providing new proteins, hence fresh and accelerating patterns of gene expression. Sifting through the human genome for the coding region of genes whose rate of change is beyond chance throws up many genes active in our brains which bear this mark of fast evolutionary adaptation. All-out molecular warfare, and this without even mentioning polarity, spin and swallowing the host of exotic compounds our ingenuity is now spawning. Natural selection at DNA level, inside those twisting strands –it's a gene-eat-gene jungle, boyo.

Our most rapidly evolving gene since we parted from chimps is called Morpheus. Geneticists have still to work out what it does to pass the time. They are not snoring on the job. A handful, with a hint of philosophy thrown in, suggests that a person with a particular set of genes has a particular type of consciousness. Who knows? Anyway, from the novel twists of our DNA, through the twists of our behaviour, to the twists of 'fate' within human reality unzipping and zipping amongst a helix of universes, where lies the connection? Morpheus, the God of Dreams, needs a nudge.

◆

Greyness separated into land and water, the Sound gathered light, the whitewashed beacons on Isle Oronsay and Sandaig Point now stood out clearly to either side of a narrowing seaway. Gigs found inspiration in the frying pan; I looked from cockpit to chart table through bacon haze. Narrows lay ahead. No break showed through the dim-lit range of hills. Father's ship, the *Northern Coast*, led convoys through this passage without navigational lights in the 'blackout' days of war. U-boats lurked and ships went down. He hugged the coast, took inside channels and knew each skyline. Hebridean waters were home, the ways of the sea an instinct.

Land flew past as *Rhum* gathered speed without apparent effort. Kylerhea narrows opened abruptly, a grey slash twixt Skye rock and the mainland – little wonder the myths of Fingal. A dogleg of a channel, close and racing, you don't dawdle when seized by nine knots of spring tide in full cry. A pouring current, a coiling, sinuous demon, it swung *Rhum*, dipped her and twirled her. The rudder barely kept course. Water tumbled over and vanished in foam. Whirlpools corkscrewed, black, curly plugholes. A bubbling mass of moon-tugged energy throttled by land – an artery of the sea with high blood pressure. Unconcerned cormorants popped up, beaks hung with a fish breakfast, one gulp over and down. John handed up a bacon roll.

In cattle-droving days herds of the Skye 'doddies' browsed their way to autumn trysts in Crieff or Falkirk and would swim these narrows at slack water tied head to tail. By 1820 some seven thousand head were making the crossing annually. Years ago, for a TV spectacle, a team of latter-day drovers tried to emulate the trick. Despite thrash and shout, the Highland bullocks wouldn't wet their feet and instead chose the comfort of the ferry. In shepherding days, when swimming a herd of cattle across Loch Monar, we'd catch a young calf and row out with it in the stern of the boat. High-pitched bawling tugged at the bonds of motherhood. Into the loch would plunge the distressed cow and, to our glee, the remaining herd. No blowing nostrils in sight, *Rhum* sped round the corner and reached, under full canvas, towards the Kyle of Lochalsh, a ferry crossing that hummed 'Over the Sea to Skye' in the minds of thousands of tourists.

King Haakon of Norway, sailing his Viking fleet to their defeat at the Battle of Largs in 1263, couldn't have known a finer day to cast his name on the strait – Kyleakin, derived from the Gaelic *Caol Acain*, translates as 'the strait of Haakon'. His Viking galleys had lain anchored beside Sgier na Cailliche, the Carlin stone, to await the south-going tide. Perhaps they knew of the golden-haired Norse princess who rigged a chain between the headlands to extract a shipping toll and whose spirit is said to look down from its burial cairn on the summit of Beinn na Cailliche. We only dodged blunt-nosed ferries shuttling back and forth. Streams of cars queued on a slip below the ruinous Castle Maol, stance of the blonde ex-toll keeper. Less glamorous 'over the sea to Skye' is now via a high-span bridge. Although the toll penalties, inflicted on motorists using the bridge to the benefit of a Yankee bank, have been abolished, the view is still despoiled for free.

◆

Funnelled winds and tide often meant a lively chop when sailing past the lighthouse and out of the straits. Years on, *Rhum* and a yacht from Ardvasar were chartered by Gordonston Summer School. We sailed each week on the heels of their sixty-foot yacht *Sea Spirit* with a fresh young crew of wealthy parentage aboard to provide a vacation pursuit for Little Lord Fauntleroys and the nouveau riche – something of a cross between character building and corrective training. Saturday mornings and Kyle Pier staged each crew changeover. That chore accomplished, the Lochalsh Hotel beckoned. The other yacht's skipper, Jim Boyd, Irish to his Liffey Water, and I would repair there to much frowning by our fleet's grand captain, T. T. and English to his epaulets. Returning one mid afternoon, delayed by a chance session with a jovial Black Isle farmer, Buckley Morrison, I looked down on *Rhum* and into the upturned faces of six Chinese boys.

Carefully, rung by iron rung, I arrived gravely on deck. They stood round me, smiling yellow faces, albeit tinged with apprehension. 'Right, oilskins and safety harness on now.' A sharp hand clap and they jumped to it – no language barrier. I lined them along the coach roof, hooked each to the safety line and, quicker than I write, set the main, cast off and heeled *Rhum* into a very smart lick. Up and down we went with spray pouring over them. They certainly didn't like it but Jim and I had always agreed the short sharp start to each trip prevented mutiny at a later date. Half an hour and from my shelter in the cockpit facial demarcation became plain. Out of yellow oilskin jackets peeped little green moons. It wasn't kind. I hove to and took them beside me in the cockpit. It turned out, of all the different combinations which sailed with me that summer, French, Italians, Germans, Dutch, English and goddamn American, the Chinese boys were by far the most pleasant, well-mannered and hardy. Many of the rest were spoilt brats in need of discipline. Witness a rumpus in the fo'c'sle one evening when anchored in Plockton and I had to separate a boy from his knife.

◆

Gigs plugged in the autopilot and went below. The galley kettle whistled. I took coffee and sat on the forepeak hatch. Taut sails drove us, just the slightest heel and the constant chatter of waves on a lustrous spring air. I lay at the bow, looked over and listened. Voices came at each dip of her forefoot – *Rhum* talked with the sea, sailing herself, happy, just the odd 12-volt tweak of the helm to keep our course. I rolled on my back, rose and fell in foetal content. The

round-bellied royals of a homecoming 'windjammer' sailed on a sky
that took on the curves of our canvas. Light streamed from a
blueness that was made more intense by the purity of its clouds. I
turned my head to islands at deck level: Pabbay with its flat fields in
the olive green of early grass; Scalpay, houseless, empty and austere
against the dark Isle of Raasay; Raasay, tree-girt sgurr, mentor of
Sorley MacLean's searching poems:

> I'd stand forever by the waves
> renewing love out of their crumpling graves.

Islands all, made young each spring in lapwing tumble and the
soft growing rain and, beyond, old in the Celtic legend of Cu
Chulainn and his loves long by, the red Cuillin of Skye, harsh to the
ptarmigan sitting eggs through the flurries of snow which tipped
their cone-like peaks. Shade and layer, shoulder and corrie, white
flecks on the grey scree told the wind blew chill across the dormant
heather, rich brown amidst greening pastures which sloped to lines
of tide-marked rocks where I guessed the last fjord-bound migrants
might pause, for these shores were little walked. Perhaps the easily
approached turnstone would be flicking pebbles, confident of
blending his handsome chestnut feathers amongst the orange
wrack. Or, shyer and wilder, the dark mottled whimbrel, in whose
cry is the call of Arctic solitude. We sailed a living D. Y. Cameron
landscape over vivid blue waters jostling into Loch Carron with
merry white tops. I made back to the cockpit, eased sheets and laid
off to pass astern of a red-hulled lobster boat working creels. And the
boy on the hauler paused and lifted his hand.

A steady westerly, main and working jib, northbound on a
seaway I'd spied from stately tops on days that gave shepherding
a pause for breath. Sharp eastern ridges above the softer hills of
Plockton, the green summits of Strathmore, cool in the breeze of a
summer gathering. On up the Inner Sound, Applecross peaks to
starboard, dwarfing the speckle of cottages surrounding their horse-
shoe bay. Raasay broad to port, its black sgurr modelled by
weathering to resemble the conning towers of the nuclear submarines which fire their torpedoes on the surface or lie doggo at eight
hundred feet in the glacially-scoured potholes under our keel.

Ashore on Raasay, a MacLeod stronghold, the lintel-less ruins of Brochel Castle which once upon a time controlled this passage with oar-flashing galley. Tools of violence evolve but the steady dip and swish of a bow on the undulations of the sea remains and so too do the loch and hills of Torridon, lacquered with sunlight and the rocks of Red Point, kind and rosy in their white-duned seclusion.

◆

Stalking estates rise abruptly behind Loch Gairloch from sanded bays and headlands of bog and snipe moor, past hollows and trout-ring lochans, up through the humid air of warbler-song woods with their leafy scent of oak and birch. Flowerdale and Fisherfield emerge in steep clean Landseer hills. Mist-damp corries where a royal stag will lie cudding on the dryness of a rumble of lichen-covered stone, his fine spread nodding slightly at each chew, the glaze of security in a blue-brown eye. About him, the outpost crags of weeping moss down slivered gullies once were plentiful with golden eagles and Dixon, the chronicler of old Gairloch days, boasts, 'Our game-killer, Watson, had a good day with eagles, producing three splendid birds from a day's shooting, besides two young birds also killed.' Clearly delighted, he recounts, 'The chicks, having got more lead for breakfast than they could digest.' Blasted to a puff of feathers in their eyrie, the brave deed of a forelock-tugging keeper, the ignorance of a social fetish sacrificing wildlife to emphasise superiority.

The original lairds of Gairloch came of the Viking but Allan MacLeod, in the 1400s, married a sister of Hector MacKenzie, the Laird of Kintail, and they had two little boys. No MacKenzie blood was to foul that of a MacLeod of Gairloch, vowed Allan's two brothers. They murdered the laird, their brother, as he slept in the summer heat on a knoll beside the River Ewe and in a frenzy of hatred cut off his head. His two infants, torn from a screaming mother, were slain. She pleaded for their blood-stained shirts and, that night, hurried east to Brahan Castle. MacKenzie of Seaforth, her father, barely believing the crime but for her blood-soaked evidence, had influence with the king in Edinburgh. Hector MacKenzie, Seaforth's brother, duly made plea and received a commission of fire and sword against the MacLeods. By 1492 a Crown Charter was granted for the lands of Gairloch which the MacKenzie family hold to this day.

An Tigh Dige, simply the Moat House, was the Gaelic name for what was little more than a turf 'black house' with a protective ditch which served the MacLeod times – a name preferred by Osgood MacKenzie, writer of *A Hundred Years in the Highlands* and creator of the subtropical Inverewe Gardens but lacking a certain flavour. Flowerdale House was built and so named by the estate's successful lairds. I came to know descendants of this ancient Highland family when shepherding for Sir John Stirling of Fairburn at Strathmore, beside Loch Monar. Sir John's wife, Katie, was the sister of the last of the MacKenzie male line, the bachelor, Sir Hector MacKenzie of Conon and Gairloch. Flowerdale included, the estates passed down the female line to John Stevenson, who took the name MacKenzie on his accession. A tearaway boy, I remembered him from his visits to Strathmore with his father, Brigadier Stevenson.

Now it happens that at no great distance from Conon House, in the seclusion of native woodland by a bend of the Conan river, is a long-disused burying ground of iron-spike tomb and moss-encroaching slab – a natural mound, unusual to come upon. No creeper remains of a place of worship and what need? Chestnut and beech carpet each dank path into winter, lighten the yew-green atmosphere with the flutter of spring leaf, and unchanging at its foot is the pebbled mute of the river. One of my MacKenzie forebears lies below a slab perched on carved feet. Died Conon, 1801, aged 102, he must have known the '45 rebellion but perhaps stayed at home.

Many years had done little to mellow MacKenzie of Conon and Gairloch and we met over a noggin at a game fair. 'John, I have a favour to ask of you,' he began and, mentioning my connection to the burying ground beside his house, he indicated that I might wish to fill a vacancy in due course. He slapped me on the back. 'Iain,' he laughed, 'be my guest.'

More auspicious guests gathered at Flowerdale House in 1921. New York-born of Spanish father and Irish mother, Eamon de Valera, the republican fighter for Irish freedom, sentenced to death for his part in the Easter Rising of 1916, met with Liberal PM Lloyd George, social reformer and ace fornicator, for the negotiation of the Irish Free State Treaty. Secretary of War to LG, the 'Welsh Wizard', was Winston Churchill, master of rhetoric and dogged Englishness. Ireland was to be divided. De Valera refused. The Treaty went ahead.

It is intriguing that a man, who, only by the intervention of the US consul, avoided a British firing squad which executed his fellow 'terrorist' leaders in 1916, should meet with the man responsible for the application of this revolt-crushing prescription.

De Valera and Churchill were to deal again during Britain's 'We shall fight on the beaches' gloom of 1940, when the principle of uniting all Ireland was tabled in exchange for Eire's entry into the war. Irish PM de Valera turned down the offer in favour of neutrality. History-making is often the pawn of hubris and war leader Churchill was not a man to digest humble pie, but would Catholic Eire have joined the Boys of the Boyne in the saving of England?

◆

Loch Gairloch opened to starboard under an array of formidable peaks. Crofting in the back seat, from shoreline into hillock the assorted houses of a B & B economy spread around broad sand-castle beaches. A massive hotel of notable prominence, built by the LMS Railway Company for guests able to afford the high-water mark of luxury in the pre-coach era, added nothing to a natural splendour. Masts of fishing boats, whose crews preferred the down-beat conviviality of the Old Inn, poked over a wooden pier which had known the privilege of a daily MacBrayne's steamer service from Kyle. Prospects looked good. 'Ready about!' Boom across. I let out and wound in jib sheets to the metallic clicking of winch ratchets. John swung east for the run-in, wind on the stern quarter, an island at the mouth of Loch. 'Longa,' he shouted, 'that's where the first Viking settlers wintered, under their longships.' A romantic touch and, with no small skill and equal romance, he sailed *Rhum* straight on to her mooring in the little bay below the Badachro Inn.

Landfall in finest Wester Ross. Shelter guaranteed for boats by birch-lined promontories. For crews, Fred and Sheila's gregarious onshore facility which, though lacking certain mod cons, was much frequented by crofters, fishermen, jetty-side loafers and the like, who, with only minor prompting, were given to revealing the wit and unpretentiousness of bygone times around a clapped-out piano, a roaring fire and the tearful Gaelic songs of old 'Affie' Thomson, after hours. Impromptu ceilidhs sprouted from emptying optics, accordions and fiddles from under benches – as did, on occasion,

some of the participants. 'Loch Maree Islands' and such ditties as
depicted the scenic glory of the neighbourhood were treated to a
fervour, if not a tonic harmony, that suggested an undercurrent of
insularity rather than the embracing of any principles of union
extending beyond the parish of Gairloch.

The counter undulated with elbow dents. I tied up alongside yet
another namesake. This one, finding farming life irksome, now ran
a yacht charter business with a style and efficiency which saw little
need for straying far from polished mahogany and Guinness froth.
All the ingredients of friendship and bon accord, two pints down
and we compared notes on future ploys. Put in small compass, I
steered without deviation into a past-tense time warp which preyed
with disarming charm upon those hair-down longings that hide
deep within every poker-faced banker touring the Highlands.
Thomson, boy, secure the mooring lines. The Badachro Inn was
a rip-roaring waterside refuge from midges and, moreover, from its
window, a-swinging an' a-swaying in the bay, could be viewed my
glamorous home on the ocean wave.

Weeks later John sent for his admiral's flag. I dropped it off at
Caley Marina, Jim Hogan's Inverness boatyard. Nice timing, for,
out on Loch Ness, Gigs entertained important clients. A Shakleton
spotter plane flew slowly towards his boat. 'Watch this.' The blue
ensign was proudly unfurled. It straightened in the breeze – emblem
of a Commodore of the Fleet. The aircraft waggled its wings in
respect. The yacht's prestigious flag relayed a spray-on message
reading, 'I have seen the Loch Ness Monster.'

# 26

# Our Lady, Star of the Sea

To give *Rhum* a home which avoided the snooping of Crown Estate Commissioners claiming seabed rights, a case of royal audacity which no Viking worth his longship would have tolerated, the local lads helped me to put down a three-legged mooring round the corner from Badachro in Shieldaig Bay. Over the side of a work boat in a flat calm we lowered three anchors, each with thirty feet of heavy chain attached to a central shackle. A tug of the launch on the ropes we'd attached to the anchors stretched them apart. Although twenty-eight feet down, such was the clarity of the water that, when all settled, we could see them in position. From a lighter chain, secured to the seabed links by a swivel, floated an inconspicuous buoy with *Rhum* painted in small letters round its boathook ring. Invisible from the road, bobbing away, just on the surface, the clandestine privilege of shelter in an anchorage used by local fishing boats and the occasional yacht which missed the way to Badachro Inn.

We took up residence, a lone yacht surrounded by creel boats and bird life. Eider duck woo-oo-ooed their call over some wonder uncovered by their dabblings, handsome goldeneye, the energetic little green-winged teal, mallard of course and, to the north, under the cloven rock face, along the kelp-bound shore, heron, yellow wagtail, redshank and, each dawn, the alarmist curlews. One morning, wakened in the half-light by their incessant calling, I spied across to the shore and, by his white chest, picked out a dog fox standing at the water's edge, one front paw raised, nose in the air, his breakfast round – ducklings in danger. By day, I'd climb the blaeberry banks, rowan, birch, chiffchaff and redstart. Out to the heather ridge, a silent cuckoo flying low searching out a meadow pipit nest and sometimes the flap, flap of a mewing buzzard. *Rhum* seemed moored in the middle of a wildlife park without cages, keepers or tourist buses.

Still waters make a sounding board and often, before it came bright, through their coverlet of mist, the drumming of boat engines reached to sleeping bag and bunk. Local boats were away to fish the Sound or lift 'creel trots' from the shoaling banks north of the island of Rona. Herring gulls untucked their heads, stretched wings above their backs and off they set in pursuit with much harsh clamouring. Others with warmer bums launched themselves from the chimney pots of a hotel whose windows and soundproof drapes remained tightly closed. Do not disturb. No chinks to intrude from brilliant June mornings when our mooring chain hung plum and neither breeze nor tide undid the reflections. *Rhum* was printed backwards on the sea and from a knoll above feather-pillowed bedrooms sunrise pines pointed their heads towards her. The birch lands and sea thrift ledges which circled the bay were a racket of chirping and whistling – every bird without a sore throat from the previous evening's chorus was competing. My kettle joined the din. Porridge in the cockpit, I turned off the shipping forecast and listened to their predictions of a fine day.

For Shieldaig, read *Sild-Vik* or 'Herring Bay' – the Norse boys again, their activities long prior to a fine shooting lodge, turned up-market hotel. Tea-party lawns ran down to its shingle shore and somewhere quiet to park my inflatable within the walls of a roofless boathouse – the delight of the place. It was engulfed by rhododendrons, beech and oak to shade the fairest skin and there were oystercatchers inspecting curly worm casts before breakfast room windows. I christened this 'yes, darling' aid to pretension the DugAnn, in honour of Douglas and Ann Bertram, the pleasant couple who came to manage its 'Chesterfield' gentility. To great excitement the following year, its lease came on offer. Would I? Funds good, DugAnn keen. No, be content hanging its dining room and mahogany stairway with Victorian paintings – a mistaken ploy in which I fancied myself as an entrepreneur with Douglas the well-spoken salesman. Less polish, more to the point, fishermen-crofters, Donald Warren and his brother-in-law, Willie MacIntosh, gave me prawns and taught me something of the wiliness of The Minch.

And *Rhum* taught me to sail – the hard way, single-handed, plus frights. Witness a first jaunt down the Inner Sound from Shieldaig to Acarsaid Mhor, an inlet on the south end of Rona. Quiraing, the backbone of Skye, in fairy green above the Sound of Raasay, commanded attention. Not my first time admiring the ridge on a blistering day which wrote glorious from every pinnacle to the horizon but this viewing, even better, five miles off on a placid sea and minus the wheezing Hill Farming Committee. A hot weather squall off the heights darkened the surface away to starboard. Agitation marked its path. A white circle of froth – a helicopter downdraught. I did notice but failed to prepare. The advance was rapid. Woof, it hit. Water slouched down a lee deck, a fully canvassed boat in a wild heel. Instinct – hang on, hard over with the helm. Up she came and off – a seahorse tossing spray. Lucky, exhilarating but wrong – I should have reduced sail in time or, if not, let the sheets fly. Snap a shroud and the mast might have gone. Never lift your eye off the sea and watch the waves – they tell you much. I was learning – observation and caution.

I let the engine just tick over as *Rhum* glided past protruding rocks and into the almost landlocked harbour of Acarsaid Mhor. An isle sparse of grazing, its meagre soil is confined to gullies running up from the shore into peat and bare rock – a barrenness inflicted upon the crofters moved here from the neighbouring Isle of Raasay when it was cleared to make way for sheep. *Rhum* lay anchored in perfect shelter. No wave to clean the green weed from shoreline borders. Cliffs echoed with the evening call of a song thrush from a stand of fir trees which darkened the bay. Was the harbour too enclosed, no view to the west, or just empty of indigenous people? Maybe because I knew Rona's story, seclusion trapped a dejected island.

When the islands of Sound of Harris are stretched long and start across a roseate orb that puts The Minch a-glisten, its evening glory casts but a dark shadow of the Quiraing across the narrow Raasay Sound and on to the abandoned stones of a croft beside the shores of Acarsaid Tioram, the Dry Harbour. Sweet waters from the mineral backbone of Skye gather to falls which cascade over basalt cliffs near the clachan of Flodigarry, so different a taste from the brackish wells of Rona. A widow and her two sons kept this home on the island's west side and looked out to the lushness of Flodigarry. It was their fashion to take drinking water for the house from the falls. On a summer's evening the boys rowed over the Sound to fill their barrels. They didn't come back. Each night until she died, the old woman put a candle to her croft house window. Now each year the purple bell flowers of the foxglove hang beside the empty sockets.

◆

The chart table locker was filling. Schoolboy fascination had journeyed the globe by the pages of a world atlas, boyhood days unfolded Dad's Liverpool docks and the River Mersey on the kitchen floor and, each evening as *Rhum* lay to her Shieldaig mooring, so I sailed the Hebrides on Admiralty charts. Names were enough. Wanderlust, that old migration urge, a survival feature of many life forms, why should we escape the magnet? No instructor, examinations or qualifications, navigation lessons, sailing ticket or whatever may now be required bothered me – indeed, in years to come, I was offered a skippering job by John Ridgeway of Atlantic rowing fame. A three-mile walk-in reached his Sutherland-shire Adventure School at Loch Laxford. Lads with haversacks on their backs and tongues hanging out came jogging past. They seemed a little saggy at the knees. Ridgeway explained that part of the toughening-up and character-building for business executive material included three concrete blocks in their haversacks.

'Yes, I know the Hebridean waters and beyond but I've have no paper qualifications whatsoever,' I stated bluntly, viewing *English Rose*, the yacht in question, from the window of his Ardmore croft house. She lay beside a small island to which his clientele must swim, possibly to spend the first night's training striking their sole supplies, a box of matches, which had become damp en route. 'How many years have you been about these waters?' 'Eight or more by now.' 'Well,' he looked hard at me, 'you'll do, I haven't passed an exam in my life – doubt if I could. Survival and common sense go together with the odd bit of luck thrown in.' In case it involved swimming and matches strapped to my head with a shoe lace, I wrote thanking him for his offer and stayed with *Rhum*.

Shieldaig evenings and one chart was pulled out more often than others – Scotland–West Coast, Outer Hebrides, Barra Head to Greian Head. At its SW corner, the Seal Woman and I studied the island of Mingulay – liked the name and the song. Childhood fascinations sprang to a resurgence of interest in the Viking. For how long had they been prowling The Minch? Scandinavian rock carvings dating to the Bronze Age of 1000 BC depict ocean-going longships. Surely they reached the Hebrides? Back to the name Hebrides. The small Roman fleet circumnavigated Britain about AD 85 and, from them, Pliny, their man of letters, gave us *Hebudes*. What about the adventurous Pytheas with his Ebudae? Could these not be the phonetic rendering of the Old Norse *Havbredey*? Its three components are *Hav* meaning 'sea', *bred* 'an edge' and *ey* 'an island'. Got it – 'Isles on the Edge of the Sea'. Now that did fit the charts. And longships that made the journey? *Horse of the Gull's Track, Elk of the Fjords* and, grandest of all, *Raven of the Sea*.

Decision taken, a fair wind, off the mooring, out of Loch Shieldaig, Rubha Reidh Lighthouse and north about The Minch – destination Mingulay, by the Viking route. Summer days, nights that glowed in the north and the sea mauve to a morning sun which hid behind the great hills of the mainland. They filled The Minch, end to end, beyond our stern, their purple spread wide on the long furrows of a resting sea and proudest in isolation was Suliven, Pillar Hill of the Norse tongue. Sunrise brought breeze, shimmered the water to a deep red hue, just for moments, The Minch, an artery of sunlight, and we sailed on for Stornoway from the bird cliff Isle of Handa, once a burial ground of safety for the coast lands of the north-west when wolves would scavenge. The wind put the Isle of Lewis on the bow at the Eye Peninsula. Croft houses, whitewashed and sheep-bound, lined its ridge. Rocks closing in, marked by a red pole, were just awash. Brown weed clung to them – the Beasts of Holm. We turned for the harbour. My father told of their tragic association and, many years on, I was to hear of it again when making a BBC programme at the croft of Peggy Gilles, who had been a little girl at the time of her loss.

Haig's Somme advance achieved six hundred thousand deaths for a twenty-mile gain. Two hundred Lewis men, survivors from the insanity of warfare, saw the lights of Stornoway from the crowded deck of a small ship, the *Iolaire*. It was New Year's morn 1919 and joy and home were just a moment away. A force-eight gale swept seas over the Beasts of Holm and soon it was bodies. The *Iolaire* struck. With no life-jackets, all but a few perished. Peggy was silent and then said, 'We were told Dad was expected and we stayed up late till he would come. The table was set with all our best cups. We hadn't much but it was like a party. We were taking turns, my brother and me, to see the lights – if a car would come it would be him. When we wakened in the morning he hadn't come. Everybody was combing the beaches, my uncle at every tide. It was three weeks before they found my dad and they brought him home from Stornoway on a cart of straw and I remember that.'

'Peggy,' I said quietly, 'how your mother must have suffered. How old was she?'

'Twenty-six, yes, twenty-six but you know, Iain, she told me she didn't know where the strength came from but, before she died, she said to me, "Peggy, the Lord was never so good to anyone as he was to me." And, years later, divers found the *Iolaire*'s bell and my brother and I went to a service for those involved and I remember my mother telling she fell asleep waiting for my dad that night and she heard a bell in her dream and she said to my dad, "How am I going to manage?" And Father said, "That's what I thought when I heard the bell."' The bell which rang, 'Abandon ship.'

◆

South we sailed by the Shiants. Two islands split into three by a high shingle causeway lie in the centre The Minch and overflow with seabirds. Gulls, fulmars and razorbills crammed on the sheltered water between the islands and thousands clamoured overhead, wheeling and screeching. Puffins flew to rabbit holes, beaks hung with sand eels; guillemots on wind-up wing beats – low-flying squadrons out to dive the shoals; and, on slimy green rocks fallen to the shore from the cliffs, platoons of upright cormorants squirted white paint. On the air of these islands, ammonia hangs rancid and nose-pinching. It's an arena of bird life, a community of unceasing turmoil. Strident clamour echoes cliff to cliff giving eeriness to the doings of a lifestyle indifferent and uncomprehending as we are to the background scream of energy grinding matter into the music of the spheres. Amongst shoreline boulders, as elsewhere in societies, the rats looked sleek and fat.

Compton MacKenzie owned the Shiants for a spell before he discovered Barra, but an air of forgotten ways broods over these islands and in the name of the easterly and least approachable isle is maybe a reason. Eilean Mhuire, 'Mary's Isle', takes us beyond a naming by some holy anchorite who made it home to the mystical meanings of pagan times when the Great Mother Earth was wedded and bedded by the Sun. Hidden within the name Mary could be words for earth and sea and perhaps Mhuire – or, as we say, Mairi – means 'Daughter of Sea and Earth'. Set in loneliness as they are, under the sun, in a circle of sea, for those who had lived by the mercy of both, the small Eilean Mhuire would indeed seem to be the daughter of their power.

A passage from the Shiants to the island of Scalpay Harris faces the strongest tidal flow in The Minch – 'the Stream of the Blue Men'. That day a smart easterly breeze tormented the north-bound flood and it ran like a blue-green river in spate with white tops tumbling over water cliffs. Working jib, two reefs in the main and *Rhum* smacked her way across. With waves rearing from any direction and spray all the way, I could see why folklore claimed the Blue Men would join you in the stern and not for a chat. The strength of current crabbed us towards the Isle of Scalpay lighthouse. Stephenson-built and prominent in a dangerous part of The Minch, it is known for good reason as the Sailor's Friend. The sea settled as its tower came abeam and *Rhum* ran smoothly by Scalpay Sound towards the island's sheltered north harbour. A smart coaster, the *Shiant Isles*, appeared from round the corner steaming out to sea and the ferry cast off from her slipway bringing the daily benefits of civilisation across from Harris. Pass all vessels to port to port in confined waters – navigation rules deeply imprinted by Gigs. I put up the helm, went astern of the ferry and left the coaster to port. A hand wave from both bridges – did they twig a first-timer on a maiden voyage?

Croft houses perched on rocks around the bay. Not a inch of the island's thin land that would take a lazy bed or graze a sheep was wasted. The trim of the fishing boats suggested the bounty of the sea made amends. One sturdy example, the *Reibhan Donn*, lay at the pier and men were busy painting her wheelhouse. I stood off a little. 'OK if we tie alongside?' 'Certainly you may.' An elderly man took our ropes, authority in face and manner. John MacLeod, skipper of purpose and principle, was as dependable as his boat on a bad day.

That evening we were up at his house for a 'strupagh' – a word, once common in the Highlands, for a small drink, especially one from a well. 'She's a strong boat you have, John.' 'Yes, the sea was good to us. I bought her when pelagic fishing was at its peak. You know,' he smiled, 'they used to call Scalpay "Treasure Island".' And, after a pause, 'We were too efficient and I can't put it past myself either, too greedy. Drift nets and sail went to ring netting and echo sounder – the herring didn't last.' His speech was slow and deliberate, regret showed behind his eyes and the subject changed. 'Where are you making for?' I made no hesitation, 'Mingulay.' 'Well, this wind will take you down. Put into Castlebay first – you won't get landing on Mingulay until it shifts to the west. Mind, there's always a danger down there.' His eyes turned to the distance. The Minch had taken his old aunt's two sons. The people said it was carelessness but the boys came to her in a dream. 'It was the third wave that took us,' they said. 'The boat was swamped.' That day she went to the cnoc at the back of the house and sat overlooking the scene of their drowning, and she made her sorrow into the most beautiful of Gaelic songs, *'A nochd gur faoin mo chadal dhomh'* – 'Tonight My Sleep will be Restless'.

I looked out to the bay. 'Whose is the wee coaster that left as we came in?' 'That's the Cunninghams' latest ship.' We talked on. Mrs MacLeod put down needles that grew a sock almost as fast as you could pull one on and made fresh tea. A tale was coming on. 'You see, Pabbay in the Sound of Harris is very fertile – well the folk made a fashion of distilling whisky.' I caught the element of disapproval. 'Mind you, they were never caught. You see, it was regulations for the ferry to carry a number at the peak of her sail but, if the Excise were aboard when she left Leverborough, a special number warned the Pabbay folk and all their kit went below the sand. Whisky or not, the evictions about 1843, landed twenty-eight families here on Scalpay. Well, Iain, they took badly to the change of island so the authorities brought in a family, Cunningham to name, to teach them to fish and handle boats. Now the Cunninghams were ambitious – very – and John Cunningham had three sons and they went to Holland and bought the *Sybal*. She was eighty feet, stern to stern, and they sailed her back here to Scalpay in three days with just a compass. At that time they got the contract of supplying coal to all the lighthouses from Barra Head to the Butt and Skye and Kylerhea and such like places.' The cup at his elbow went cold. 'She carried eighty tons – yes, eighty tons – and they took ten or twelve Scalpay men with them to manhandle the coals up the rocks above the tide. And the herring fishing was at its height – there were nine curing stations in those days – and they ran her regular down to Runcorn near Liverpool for salt for the curing. The first engine to come to Scalpay went into her in 1916. Then they got two coasters, the *Shiant Isles* and the *Cooshie*, and all through the First War they ran kippers to Mallaig but it's coals that kept them. They towed two barges over from the Continent for bunkers – you'll see them across the harbour. Now the boys, two generations down from John of course, have a new *Shiant Isles* – the one you passed coming in – and they have the Calor gas contract and carry explosives and ammunition and all that sort of thing. Oh, I'll tell you, the Cunninghams had a lot in the making of Scalpay.'

'What happened to the *Sybal*?'

'Well the tide's low just now and, if you take a walk, you'll see her on the mud at the mouth of the burn just below the village.'

White zigzags on wings beat away to the northern gloaming. Redshank had been feeding. 'Too-ee-ee-ee' followed their flight. The air held a softness that comes from the nearness of a great ocean at peace. Pools filled with darkness. One by one, the tide encircled each rib. Weed hung in braids, clung to blackened timbers – the last strength of a buried spine. She'd been double-ended in her day – sensual curves, a lover to the sea. She blended into night. I watched a longship and saw the *Sybal*, a worthy child, born again to the ever jealous Minch.

◆

Ropes taut and not a crease in her canvas, *Rhum* leaned to starboard, driven by the wind that MacLeod had promised. Waves
jockeyed in her wake. Twenty miles to port marched the Cuillin hills
of Skye, a cloud topped rampart lifting and falling to the tempo of
boat and sea. Low slung islands popped from under the boom –
each a schoolboy adventure. Sleek curves of sand, home to timid
nesting ringed plover, space for the thieving black-back gull, machair green and turquoise shallow – the islands of the Sound of
Harris. We anchored at their edge in a bay below the rock thrusting
stance of Rodel Church.

Plastic North Eastern Farmers feed bags jammed holes in the
door and faintly see-through windows of a back entrance to the
Rodel Hotel. A plaque on the front wall announced Queen
Elizabeth, mark two, had stepped ashore from the Royal Yacht's
liberty boat on to the tiny jetty of a tidal harbour with complete
shelter from skirt-lifting breeze and cheering crowds. Hardly a
Viking invasion – German maybe. Alan MacLeod who served
our Guinness looked more the part – tall, deep-set blue eyes and
strong jawline. Sure enough he had a fishing boat and 'Yes, the
church is open, help yourselves.'

We wandered through an expanse of sun and sky, through the
leaning gate of age, up a bluebell path, past the eaten eyes that
hoped, that believed, they would see again the serenity of The
Minch under the majesty of the Cuillin. On the crest we sat, the
church at our back and before us the Hebrides – the colour, the
vibrancy, the scent, the seabirds' cry, the dream that went with
those who left in body, never in mind. And below us the islands of
the Sound of Harris were scattered on a shelving sea – Atlantic blue
into faintest green. Into naked pools, virile and fresh and young in
the curtained showers which followed the curve of the Uist hills,
fleeting showers, white tidal sands, granite hills, three million years.
Youth and age, the sun makes one, dries the other but always the
sun – the sun that bursts from behind a cloud and sheds its warmth
on islands of scattered life and ancient slab alike.

Plain grey in local stone, square-towered with a solidity of
foundation, the Church of St Clement, aided by its remoteness,
escaped the reforming hammer of the Protestant ethic. Clement
wasn't so lucky. Banished from Rome to the Crimea, he was flung

into the sea with an anchor tied about his neck. Thirteenth-century MacLeods, the Viking lairds of Harris, built this little church to his remembrance. Angled gravestones wound up to the simple door. Outside, warmth and glare; inside, the cool dim smell of Holy Sanctity. Tiny lintelled slits threw quivers of light across the nave. The intensity of white dune and cerulean sea poured over a beautifully carved effigy. On a stone pillow rested the head of Alexander MacLeod of Dunvegan. Clean-cut lines of face, chain mail, plate armour and sword and with his feet crushing a serpent, he was a man of action. Behind him, more carving – a castle, men with their dogs straining at a herd of deer and, perhaps to carry his soul, a galley under sail. Norseman Macleod built his tomb nineteen years before the long journey. As we turned to leave, a journeying sun fell on his face.

Evening light bounced off the Atlantic upon the west gable of the church, picking out a carved St Clement standing on the head of a bull. 'The Mithraic bull of pagan Rome?' I wondered. Was Clement caught by the early Christians worshipping Mithras? It might explain his anchor necktie. More enticing for secret adherents to ancient beliefs, the gable carvings also depicted a crouching nude mother with child. She displayed her engorged vagina to a male figure clutching swollen testicles. A precaution not without reason, for his phallus erectus had been shot off. A warning perhaps to libidinous worshippers tempted to any indulgence outwith that permissible by the Church in their duties of expanding the congregation. Nearby, at the grave of MacLeod of Berneray, the memorial plaque tells that the lair's incumbent, though past the prime of life, fought in the '45 rebellion and, a year later at the Battle of Falkirk Muir, hand-to-hand vanquished an English dragoon. Safe home, he married his third wife at seventy-five and, with one eye on the carving and the other on the butler, he sired another nine children before departing this world in his ninetieth year. Cause of death is unstated.

◆

An unnatural calm had settled on The Minch with a glittering smoothness upon which the north-bound current made trailing lines of white froth. We motored down the South Uist coast with heat, glare and a mahogany tan. *Rhum*'s progress landed ripples under the lighthouse cliffs of Uishanish Point. The autopilot took the helm and I stretched on a cockpit locker, rousing every few minutes to put an eye round the horizon. Without warning fins broke the surface, a dozen or more. Black sickles on immense dark humps leisurely moving, fifty yards ahead, giving an impression of gargantuan strength. Each rose for a few moments, scything the calm, showing a broad curve of back, then down – a great harmless mammal undulating along just below the surface. I ran to the bow. They circled about us – the basking shark of Gavin Maxwell's venture into the business of cashing in on the bounty of The Minch.

I visualised Maxwell of the otters and his henchman Tex Geddes preparing to fire a harpoon gun from the bow of their boat, the *Polar Star*. The same fins circling round on a bright day. The Uishanish lighthouse keeper shouting and waving directions. Maxwell on the trigger, Geddes closing. Cut engine. Fire. Crash. Barbed shaft, snaking rope. Thud. A hit, a flailing coil, a sounding shark with a barb buried in his spine. Quick, secure the rope end to a fifty gallon drum. A marker for picking up the brute when he's dead and the slaughter is finished. Full ahead, after the next, follow the lumbering school out of the spreading red bubbles.

Soay is a rugged little isle south of Loch Scavaig under the frown of the Cuillin. For a period after Hitler's war, Maxwell owned the island and the almost landlocked cove on its west side became the base for his shark-hunting operation. One evening, years later, I anchored *Rhum* in the bay on Soay's east side and rowed ashore to the croft house then belonging to Tex Geddes. By this time, Maxwell had succumbed to cancer and Tex had retired. I spent the evening with him on his island home. We climbed the broken track past his solar telephone kiosk to the site of their 'factory' on the west side and he described their shark-fishing escapade.

Maxwell took the idea from the Mallaig fishermen and also from a chap called Watkins, brother of Gino the polar explorer. Watkins set up an operation at Carradale in Kintyre and harpooned his first shark from a rowing boat with the bravado of a Nantucket whale hunter. To his surprise the brute towed him at ten knots round the Mull of Kintyre and out into The Minch and back again before dying. In that era, vast shoals of basking shark cruised The Minch and the Isle of Soay lay adjacent to their summer feeding grounds. Sheds and slipway were constructed beside the cove and the boiler of an ex-Great Western locomotive raised steam for rendering the blubber. Messrs Geddes and Maxwell mounted a hefty gun on the bow of the *Polar Star* and, after some experimenting and not a few wounded sharks, they perfected a harpoon which didn't bend or snap on impact. Tally ho! A-hunting we will go. Each thirty-ton carcass was towed through the slit of an entrance into the harbour, winched up the slip, gralloched and its liver stuffed into huge rendering vats – not a job for those of a delicate constitution. Guts, stench and countless gulls filled the cove for oil at £120 a ton. A good day would see a dozen barrels bobbing off Uishinish Point.

By nightfall we drammed away in his private den – wife not admitted on any account. Small, red-haired and wiry with a spark in his eye, Tex relished the account of their doings and, by and by, caught up the barrel of the harpoon gun from where it sat, pride of place, on a dresser. 'This is the little lady that did the trick,' he said quietly with a glint which hinted more than mischief and dropped it on to my outstretched arms. The weight was astounding and to say they sagged would be an understatement, but luckily I held it. I carefully lifted the barrel back on the dresser and his challenging manner diminished. We parted empty-bottle friends. I pitied any nosing inspector and wondered how many official types hobbled away nursing broken toes?

◆

After the flat calm and heat of the day, evening brought a rising west wind. We steered into Loch Boisdale to gain the shelter of its South Uist harbour. Down went the anchor, a couple of cables off the CalMac jetty. The ferry steamer *Clansman* lay alongside ready for her morning Oban run. *Rhum* soon danced to her anchor rope. Every port was a first and nowhere was snugger than rocking down below. With the stovetop a-glow, a westerly gale was a-twanging her stays and a-whistling its head off in the rigging. Who could sleep? But we did.

Daylight came with a crunch, a jolt and a shudder under the keel – not a pleasant alarm clock. Wind still howling, seven o'clock, and us in nature's pyjamas. Engine on, I leapt to the bow and signalled

slow ahead to the Seal Woman. A scraping below *Rhum*'s forefoot –
the reef again. Clear water astern? If not, she'd drift aground
anyway. Only minutes and the rocks would be grinding her towards
being a wreck. I cast off the anchor rope, raced to the stern, took
over the helm. Ease away to starboard. Steady now, *Rhum*. No
grating. Mercy on us – a really close one. We motored to the pier.
Faces along the *Clansman*'s rail had enjoyed the display. The Bruce
anchor, designed to hold oilrigs, can take a fair grip of the seabed
but not, as I discovered when collecting ours at the bottom of the
tide, if it drops neatly inside an old lorry tyre.

A summer blow and a little loss of dignity were in the way of the
west soon forgotten. By late afternoon, a straggle of clouds headed
east and *Rhum*'s white topsides were creating sunlit ripples. We head
south, close hauled to a handy breeze. 'Eriskay Love Lilt' and *Whisky
Galore* – there was no sailing past. Down sail and gingerly through the
narrow entrance into the island's oval harbour. Father Calum, the
Barra priest, once told me how he and his school pals would gleefully
watch incoming yachts clip the channel reef and their wealthy
owners land flat on their faces. An immaculate fleet of herring boats
lay side by side at a jetty of nets and lobster pots. Sturdy native ponies
had no marks of panniers on their white flanks. They were no longer
carrying peat or seaweed. Rotting thatch and fallen gable squatted
end on to sound modern houses, painted and prosperous. Hens
strutted at the remains of Granny's 'black house'. Slow but sure
transition headed for Eriskay, the quaintness of paraffin lamp and dry
loo appeals largely to the camera shots of passing tourists.

We walked Prince Charlie's Strand, his landing here in '45, the
Jacobite chancer's last stab for the UK throne and the Catholic
cause bringing only the misery of Drummossie Moor and final bye-
bye to a tottering clan system. Overlooking the village is the church,
its altar shaped to form the stern of a boat. Sea and religion are
bound together – the people of Eriskay revered both. I could
understand why. Behind the islands of the Sound of Barra, beyond
the edge of the Atlantic, is the Gaels' land of Tir nan Og – land of
eternal youth – a hope preached by a crimson sun which brought its
pathway of faith to the water at our feet. In a dimming sky, Venus,
star of evening, rested on the indigo outline of Heaval, the Viking
peak of Barra. Castlebay tomorrow.

Bare feet on a deck wet with summer dew and we slipped away from Eriskay in the flat calm of dawn. In a little, I cut the engine and we drifted with the south-running ebb. Far out on the eastern horizon, the Cuillin peaks floated above a pink band of mist which lay across their middle. Settled weather. More distant, the hills of the Isle of Rum were the dimmest blue. Sixteen oars a side, the longships would be sails furled and rowing. Their Old Norse tongue surrounded us: *ay*, 'an island', forms the ending of so many – Flodday, Fuday, Gihay, Helisay, all in the Barra Sound; and *mul*, 'a headland'; *dale*, 'a valley'; and *Mikil*-ay, 'the big island with its cliff-skirted hilltop', gives the bonnie-sounding, Mingulay. Hecla, 'the Hooded Shroud', still lay hidden from us by the hills of Barra.

Instead I spied at the ruined masonry of a tower which appeared as though grown by some natural process from the sheer sides of a rocky islet lying just off the tip of Eriskay. On the tiny Stack island, a MacNeil to name and apparently something of a mini-pirate, built himself a retreat – not as a place of contemplation, rather as a site from which a well-aimed boulder would go through the bottom of any unwelcome boat. The firing platform's remains are still welded by eight-hundred-year-old shell-sand mortar to the cliff edge. A room, little bigger than twelve feet by ten with walls five feet thick, is approached only by an ankle-breaking climb. MacNeil of Caisteal a Bhreabadair, less impressively 'of Weavers Castle', considered the difficult access no drawback: 'My friends will find a way; for others I'd rather they stayed away.'

Never mind whisky galore, here there were islands galore. They grew to starboard all quivering in the thermals of sun on sand – some marram grass and beach, others heather top and rock. Hidden coves and long headlands to sneak behind – a pirate's paradise for pieces of eight and buried treasure. French cash to fund the '45 debacle, supposedly aboard *Le Dutillet* when she anchored off Fuday in the Barra Sound to set 'The Prince' ashore on Eriskay, just vanished. Vanished? Yes, all 20k of it, they say. Get the spade – I could believe anything. Up ahead, more realistically, cormorants preached caution from the black rock of Curachan which sat on the sea like a bowler hat with a curl of tide for its rim.

A sweep of the telescope picked out the marker for Castlebay, the Bo Vich Chuan, a yellow pole against grey Muldoanich island, at one time the deer forest of the MacNeil chiefs. Barra sprawled beside us, reefs and rocky inlets, croft houses to the foot of Heaval. Round the fairway marker we sailed, west now, with the sands of Vatersay to port and the white pillared Dubh Skeir light on its tidal ledge. Swing to starboard, into a wide, village-girt harbour. Tide and weed, a castle standing in water, dismally grey beside the blue and orange of a lifeboat moored in its lee. Fishing boats, lobster boats, moorings, boats, boats and boats, all under the Viking hilltop Heaval, bonnie, green and shapely and on a cnoc dominating the hotchpotch of house, street, shop and timbered jetty, the Castlebay church, the Church of Our Lady, Star of the Sea. Travel the world, not since Shetland . . . Boy, boy, it felt like home!

## 27

# 'Utterly Barbarous'

If the spirit of Viking sea power is to be sought then no castle the length and breadth of the Hebrides better holds the essence of its romance than Kisimul Castle of Barra. A tidal rock commands a wide, secure, south-facing bay with room to manoeuvre under sail. Channels to the east, a passage to the west, Minch or Atlantic, and hill tops to scan them both. A fertile island, fish abound, handsome women with a flash of Iberian darkness, handy for raiding Ireland. What better base for a territorial take-over? Barra – more than a stopover. As expert joiners, these freelancers could throw a wooden stronghold astride a stone base on the rock of Kisimul in a season and speed of construction counted if the natives were being difficult. Perhaps the old spelling 'Cisamul' is closer to the Norse tongue though we have no evidence of Norse occupation on the islet, just a hunch supported by a name.

The sturdiness of the present castle, however, reflects the masonry skills of six hundred years ago. Wet feet would be a feature of its building phase, for only the bottom of a spring tide fully exposes the islet upon which the fortress stands. Stout foundations follow the uneven contours of bare rock. Wide, high walls, no toeholds and one narrow entrance which overlooks a weed-slippery landing. At the top of each tide, water completely surrounds its sheer walls and tower. No place to hang about should the inmates be winging missiles from the battlements.

Cisamul rings Norse as *mul* is a common ending to many similar sea-bound outcrops which dot these islands. No site throughout the western seaboard would have appealed more to the longship boys than Cisamul. There's even a freshwater spring arising between its rocks, though nothing indicates these lads were subject to such addiction. Nor is there evidence of Viking usage, but haul your sheets, boys, round the Dubh Skeir, swing your tiller for the top of Heaval, the tide is flooding, the wooden palisade of Cisamul rises from the sea. Only those lacking the tingle of adventure would doubt that the longships rode in its lee and moored under its commanding position. Cisamul – rock of the Viking, castle of a sea-powered kingdom.

A charter from Alexander, Lord of the Isles, in 1427, granted Barra and its islands to the MacNeils. Kisimul Castle was to become the islet fastness of the MacNeil of Barra, turbulence in its memory, haughtiness in the masonry, a home to one of the proudest of all clan chiefs. Each day, the 'cockman' would cry from the battlements, 'MacNeil has dined. The Kings, Princes and others of the earth may now dine.' – an injunction confirming the chief's eating habits and a relatively safe PR stunt as few of any consequence would be within earshot. One should mention two features incorporated in Kisimul's building plans supportive of MacNeil hauteur. A stone-seated loo is vented directly over the tide, and given a westerly breeze those metaphorically reading the morning paper would be provided with the cleansing effects of a bidet, though less desirably, perhaps, an attack of piles. Certainly less congenial was the efficacy of a dungeon hole into which were lowered those who incurred the chief's displeasure. Situated in the soundproof bowels of the fortress, a pitch-black incarceration included the twice daily effects of the tide, up to the neck. Few went more than four tides.

During the herring boom of the early 1900s when fishing drifters filled the bay and one might cross from Castlebay to the island of Vatersay over their decks, Kisimul doubled as a fish-curing factory. By the '30s, the tower had tumbled and its strongest defence lay in the smell. In 1939 the structure was purchased by a wealthy American architect, John Lister MacNeil, who claimed the 45th chieftainship of the Barra MacNeils and set about freshening up his family seat. With a sufficient time lapse to eclipse any precise record checking, the chiefs of Clan MacNeil claim direct descent from Niall of the Nine Hostages, a fifth-century High King of Ireland. Ah to be sure, a certain Neil did abandon the Emerald Isle for Barra early in the eleventh century, by which time, of course, longships were well up the beach and, one must presume, their crews busily involved in the pleasures of integration with all the Viking flair for ravaging women and property.

Onund Wooden-Leg's descendants had been stomping around the islands since the ninth century and how these pushy MacNeils gained a toehold is unclear. A religious ticket or perhaps between the blankets? Language was never a barrier to connubial comfort. Barra, the island's name, Irish or Norse? If the former, then St Barr or Erse legend has a claim. The latter, and *bara* to the Norse meant 'storm-tossed' or a 'wave billow' and may well equate with their naming of the Orkney and Shetland islands of Burray and Burra. At a guess, Barra probably set off with its Norse meaning, to be construed as St Barr when the cultural twist of society embraced Roman Catholicism and preferred an Irish connection. Proof of the strength of Viking name and blood on the Outer Hebrides prior to much Irish influence is indicated by mainland Gaels terming them *Innse Gall*, 'the Strangers' Islands'. By the 1400s, however, proof of Norse-Erse integration clearly emerged. Successive MacNeil chiefs achieved a reputation throughout Europe's western seaboard for an expertise in piracy and law-lessness – the envy of every Barbary Corsair and the leg-wetter of many a landlubber.

'The wisest fool in Christendom' mildly described the mentally crippled King James VI of Scotland. A perverted monarch, who took notes on human behaviour during torture sessions and re-garded himself as a serious scholar, deserves a more accurate description. All that apart, the self-styled 'Virgin' Queen of Eng-land, put aside the fact she murdered King James's mother, Mary, Queen of Scots, treated him to a severe wigging. Her particular displeasure was to bring the activities of Barra's leading exponent in the art of piracy to King James's attention. MacNeil of the day, 'Ruari the Turbulent' as he was affectionately known to his friends, had cultivated a weakness for fine French wines. To facilitate this addiction, he took to seizing English ships up from Bordeaux, consuming their cargo and leaving a line of bottles and the captured crew bobbing astern.

Fly MacKenzie, a Royal sycophant, styled 'the Tutor of Kintail', arrived off Kisimul and invited 'Turbulent' to what in today's phraseology would amount to a piss-up. MacNeil awakened in handcuffs, in the hold, and soon to find himself hauled before King James, a man with less regality about him than an organ-grinder's monkey but not a boy to cross. Ruari knelt. Jamie frowned, his attitude to Gaelic subjects far from reassuring, being summed up when the studious monarch penned:

> As for Highlanders, I shortly comprehend them all in two sorts of people: the one, that dwelleth in the mainland, that are barbarous for the main part, and yet mixed with some show of civility; the other, that dwelleth in the Isles, and are utterly barbarous, without any show of civility.

As an afterthought, he instructed his son to treat these 'barbarous' islanders as wolves or wild boar, an interim measure prior to ordering total extermination and settlement of the islands with English-speaking Lowlanders. This brainwave he described as 'My Kingcraft' and put into practice over in Ireland where the effects of his wisdom still remain.

Ruari expected the interview merely to be a prelude to the torture chamber, followed by a farewell speech to his entrails on the gallows. He put his mind to the problem. 'Hanging would be harsh treatment,' he assured the king, 'for a man who has done Your Majesty a great favour.' James raised an enquiring eyebrow. 'Your Royal Highness,' said Ruari, taking the measure of his monarch, 'I have enraged the woman who murdered your mother.' King James, a practising misogynist who personally supervised the torture of women accused of witchcraft and was to pen detailed instructions for a socket-stretching debriefing of Guy Fawkes in the Tower of London, seemed faintly amused. A limp wave of hand allowed MacNeil to bow his way out. A close shave. 'Time up' for piracy. Castlebay freebooters dropped sail before the spectacle of Jolly

Tars, all Heart of Oak and pigtails, dancing hornpipes on the foredecks of eighty-gun men-of-war. Britannia ruled the waves and Barra's sea trade sank into the inkpot of J. M. Barrie.

No longer did galleys glide from the shelter of Kisimul, set their lugsails to skirt the Dubh Sgeir and head out to plunder The Minch. Nor did the chief's 'cockman' trumpet vainglorious announcements from the battlements. Nevertheless, more than a tinge of arrogance dribbled down the generations to the last of the old direct line, the moustache-twirling General Roderick MacNeil of Barra.

Kelp-cutting and gathering required wading up to the waist in cold water before hauling the 'tangle' ashore to be dried and burnt in a kiln. The resulting run-off glutinous liquid, when cooled and hardened, could then be shipped to Liverpool for the extraction of iodine and soda. The market peaked at £22 a ton and three to four hundred tons left Barra each year – big cash flow and only forty years after the '45. The chief snag for the crofters was, in fact, their chief, General Roderick himself. He needed his cut – roughly 80 per cent. Obtaining it, simple. Retention of the holdings upon which crofters subsisted was subject to conditions of work imposed by their landowner. Fish The Minch and cut kelp for me or say hello to America.

Letters from the general to Barra priest, Father Angus Mac-Donald, the go-between, make it plain:

> They much deceive themselves if they think that opposition or obstacles (and I anticipate some) will turn me from what I conceive the best course – you will tell them all that any man who does not comply with my terms shall be turned off my Lands, and any of the young men who think it proper to voyage to Glasgow may there remain, for I pledge my word they shall never again eat a potato on my property, be they ever so penitent.

> The Bishop of the Isles is informed that 'Catholic Holy Days' are to be omitted if they occur during the kelp and fishing seasons.

> They are peculiarly grievous in the summer and although I have the greatest respect for the Catholic faith I think it hard that I should

suffer loss, and must candidly tell you that if I don't experience real
and effective co-operation from the Bishop, and yourself, I will bring
in Protestant tenants.

For General MacNeil, religion weighed light on the scales of self-
interest.

Curdling his theme, he writes again to an apprehensive priest:

I think it but fair candidly to tell you that the conduct and tone of the
good people of Barra whom everyday experience teaches me cannot
be depended upon, from their fickleness, idleness and stiff-necked
prejudice, has produced in my mind a decided revolution.

And, in similar vein, he continues:

To ensure myself an ample harvest (which if I live I have no doubts
of) I must have fishers and kelpers who will cheerfully do my bidding
. . . so if you mean to keep your flock together look to it, I can easily
fill up the vacancies.

A far from veiled threat. Oh dear, his job undermined by an influx
of Protestants with their inclinations towards cant. Poor Father
Angus, the scent of blackmail called for smelling salts and a lie-
down.

Veins swelled on noble temples. The general composed a proclamation to be read forthwith from the altar

You will tell the kelpers, that they have earned my utmost displeasure. They have not obeyed my orders – nor the orders of those by
me set over them, which I consider as disrespectful to me, as it is
disgraceful to them.

Next for a bollocking, the fishermen:

Their audacity and base ingratitude has quite disgusted me. That if
they do not within eight and forty hours after this proclamation,
bend their energies to the daily prosecution of their calling as

33. Dinghy fulls out to the *Boy James* in perfect weather

34. A deck cargo of lambs bound for Castlebay

35. Mingulay schoolhouse needs reroofing. Sandy at the door

36. Archie on the hauler with materials for the new roof

37. Sandy and author on the schoolhouse roof: no helmets, no inspectors

38. Marooned on Mingulay. Sandy skinning rabbits in the rain

39. Ready to load wool off Pabbay

40. Wool aboard Roddy's *Spray*. Roddy poles her off the rocks

41. Starting the Pabbay sheep fank. Sandy and author

42. The construction company relaxes

43. Just a hundred years past. John Sinclair's home beside the road from Mingulay village to the school

44. The Mingulay family of John MacLean at the beginning of last century

45. Donald MacLeod and John Joe MacNeil
secure a dinghy at the landing on Barra Head

46. Changing times.
A west coast skiff lands at Barra Head only three generations ago

47. A Mingulay crofter and his cattle above the village in 1905

48. The transport system for Mingulay in 1905.
Launching a boat from Traigh Beac

49. A fallen cross in the burying ground beside Mingulay village

50. St Columba's Church and priest's house on Mingulay
a hundred years ago

51. The work of the gales on St Columba's church once the slates were off

52. Church-goers from Vatersay
at Castlebay pier

53. Cattle sale in Castlebay, Barra

54. The late Lach Maclean of Craigston, Barra, clipping beside the burying ground of St Brendan on the Borve machair

55. John Allan MacNeil, the coxswain of the Barra lifeboat
who saved my finger, and Aonghais MacLean

56. At Mingulay schoolhouse, Archie MacLean, his son Aonghais and Donald MacLeod, son of John MacLeod (Iaghan), hand over the islands to the
National Trust for Scotland

57. D.P. Sinclair,
comrade at The Captain's Table in Castlebay Bar

58. The road to Ledaig, Isle of Barra

59. Neil Sinclair (Neillie Mhor) and author:
'For the good days'

60. A meal of fresh herring caught and cooked by Dol William after the
Fisherman's Mass on Castlebay Pier

61. Sailing down the Outer Hebrides in a west coast skiff
belonging to Iain Thomson, Badachro, Wester Ross

62. *Rhum* returns to the canal and sale.
Author with Robbie and Alasdair Thomson

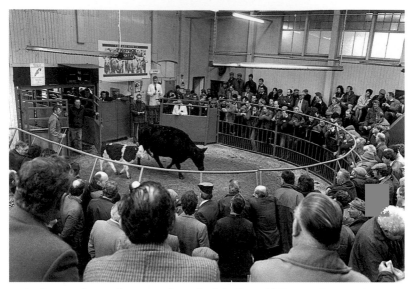

63. Buying Lovat Estate cattle at the MacDonald Frasers Auction Mart, Inverness, to begin Strathglass Organic Farms

64. Atlantic return, Fort William. Author, Jane and Katie, Ann Pilchour-Gough, Gigs MacGillivary and Rob Adam

fishermen, I shall turn every man of them off the Island were they steeped to the ears in debt.

Those waving goodbye to Barra get a valediction:

Say to those who are about to emigrate that I sincerely wish them well through it, and assure those who have signed and repented that their repentance comes too late. So help me God, they shall go, at all events off my property, man woman and child.

This none too friendly farewell rounds off with a volley aimed at piracy and any Norse leaning towards the insolence of independence which General MacNeil suspects still lingers in native attitudes: 'Lastly I shall exert myself to the utmost to crush all the disreputable trafficking and smuggling which has been too long tolerated.'

Father Angus MacDonald sees the light and decamps to Rome to become rector of the Scots College, leaving his successor, an equally hounded Father MacDonald, with the implausible task of collecting church dues from an island population already forcibly stripped of their cattle, sheep and ponies by the rent extraction methods of their good laird, the general. Woe upon woe. The people are banned from cutting tangle to manure their lazy beds as a large volume is required to supply MacNeil's latest soap- and glass-making project. A classic of bad timing. In 1836, due to Spanish competition, the kelp price plummets to £2 a ton, just as food prices rocket on the horrors of the great potato famine. Starvation is on every doorstep and death below the thatch. Each day the mass of the people rake the wide expanse of the Traigh Mhor for their food supply, the cockle. All by which time, General MacNeil is claiming his new clan seat as 'Barra House, Inverness-shire'. In a last flounder before bankruptcy, he attempts to hand over the priest's house, chapel and glebe to the Church of Scotland. Wisely they refuse.

Barra, its islands plus castle are flogged as a job lot for £36,000 under a sequestration order. Another military mind arrives to take charge – Colonel Gordon of Cluny. For a quick turn on cash down, he offers the island to the government as a penal colony. No thanks,

Australia is filling the bill and less chance of desperados swimming to nearby islands. Cluny, already a millionaire by extracting returns from his Aberdeenshire-based land investments – no mean feat from an area which made a virtue out of parsimony – now set about screwing the crofters. The kelp industry crash and what crumbs of a cash economy that went with it meant his factorial stringency spelled mounting rent arrears and summary eviction. Go to sea or settle in Newfoundland. After a spate of tearful goodbyes, the largest farm of Eoiligary at the north end of Barra fell to a William MacGillivary who maintained his self-esteem by having a couple of the natives run beside his pony and trap as he toured the island. Given the suppression of their language and similar demeaning regulation, even down to the laird claiming any large Clydesdale horse shoes, the crofter was left with little more than shellfish fishing, scenery or a steerage passage to breaking in land in Nova Scotia.

Fresh from exploits of colonial bravery such as testing repeater rifles against the skin shields of Chief Cetshwayo and his Natal warriors in the Zulu wars, by 1880 the spill-over from Victoria and Albert's Balmoral vulgarity trickled over to the Hebrides in the form of gun cases attached to advanced nasal strangulation togged out in red socks and 'plus-twos'. Writing at the turn of last century, C. V. A. Peel, Esq. finds himself trembling with indignation at the wilful affront to stiff-upper-lip dignity of the crofter's attitude:

> Much of the pleasure of shooting in the Outer Hebrides is spoilt by the conduct of the crofters. It is not conducive to sport to be followed by gang of men and ordered out of the country, nor is it pleasant to be cursed in Gaelic by a crowd of irate old women, even if you do not understand every word they say. They accused us of shooting their horses and sheep, filled the pits which we dug in the sand hills for geese, shouted to put up geese we were stalking, cut up the canvas and broke the seats of our folding-boat, and tried in every way to spoil our sport. They were especially insolent and troublesome in Benbecula and Barra. Taking them as a whole, the crofters are an ignorant lot of creatures, and the less said about them the better.

Unable to resist further assessment, he concludes, 'Their sheep dogs are far too plentiful, as they pick up many a nesting grouse, moreover, the gross cruelty of the crofters to their domestic animals is most revolting.' Keepers, however, are most helpful chaps.

His own shortcomings, if any, we are left to guess. As an Empire builder of some quality, he confines himself to describing the thrill of cocking his gun at the bird life teeming along the wide Atlantic coastline.

As for the Golden Plover, this grand sporting bird is a very strong bird on the wing, and requires very heavy shot. My best shot into a large flock with a 12-bore gun was ten birds, but to my mind the lapwing, or green plover, is one of the most sporting of wild fowl.

And on a day's outing with the great northern diver:

One I shot in North Uist led me a pretty dance in a sea pool some 200 yards long. When he dived to my left, I ran in that direction, only to find him 50 yards to my right. I raced up and down that pool for over three-quarters of an hour, when at length I got him with a shot through the neck.

Oh, well taken, sir! Great sport – pity about the crofters. The islanders regarded keepers in general as the lowest type of flunkey. They pandered to English toffs displaying their superiority by the fetish of a day's sport tramping over ground which the crofters felt they occupied with a whiff of the old Norse udal law – a land-holding system, by the way, which permitted any settler to enclose an area he chose to cultivate and hold it without obligation or service to any superior. Most irritating for the sportsman. This outdated Scandinavian law also gave crofters unrestricted access to the foreshore. How tiresome. Anyway, we have no word of his winging an impudent native which might account for the neck of C. V. A. Peel, Esq. remaining intact.

◆

Barra, an island with time for living, shunning the sanctimonious, side-stepping the pall of authority, smiling at the pretensions of those whose dignity needs the prop of affectation. A pulsating anachronism. To the elation of your step from a Twin Otter aeroplane into the brilliance of oceanic light on a white cockle strand must be added the attraction of its people – homely, friendly and hospitable, no standing on doorsteps, nobody to pass the door without a 'strubag' and to everyone a 'wordie'. Behind the islanders' ingenuous charm and quiet-spoken politeness, far from yokel naïvety, there hides a speed of mind which outpaces many a sophisticate. Good manners arise naturally in those of Highland breeding and the Gaelic is rarely spoken before those confined to English. An unassuming community, they are intensely and justly fond of their island and its beauty of aspect. There's a social cohesion in which consanguinity and ancestral respect play a cherished role.

In other ways, change strikes fast and nowhere more profoundly than in the usage of the land. Crofting townships with their common grazings of sheep and cattle still exist but communal clippings and stock handlings are dying out as the croft becomes a B & B base. A hundred years ago, little more, the crofter cooked on peats, burnt his black-house thatch and spread the ashes on the tattie patch. Now it's picture-window bungalows, central heating and a bag of tatties from Willie the Butcher. The same crofter, at that time, might still have been turning his ground with a *cas chrom*, the so-called 'foot plough', an Iron Age implement which put a Bronze Age digging stick on the shelf. A good man on its five-foot handle and iron-shod foot-piece could dig a tenth of a Scots acre in a day. Between World War One and Two along came the horse plough with crofters sharing ponies and tilling their holdings in rotational crop. Fifty years ago, as mainland tractors got bigger, the importation of cast-off second-hand Fergies killed pony power. Little if any land is ploughed and cropped today, few sheaves stooked and little hay coiled and, though crofting townships remain in principle, the children have a very different orientation.

Of equal consequence in changing attitudes towards the land is population shift. Amidst the influx of ethnic origin and background presently sweeping the Highlands, does Barra's being a small island make it a more secure, less pregnable culture, not so vulnerable to the rate of change on the Scottish mainland? Might Barra and the Highlands benefit from a blood transfusion, mix Jones with the Mac? Many strive to break in, learn the Gaelic, play traditional music, stand a dram. What of birth certificate and genealogy? Is it bloodline and mindset which for the moment bar the sanctum of belonging? The old style crumbles, subsumed by cheap food, furniture flittings and media influence – a sandbank eroded by farming efficiency elsewhere, population change and cultural evolution. Keeping up is a problem.

Meantime, for the migrant visitor, Barra is a bolt-hole for the careworn, a get-away weekend for pen-pushers, a hair-downer allowing 'pinstripers' to re-jig their perspective on life and, when the island's Castlebay Bar winds up the music on a Friday night, it affords devotees of a frolic the heady draught of uninhibited living. Arrrh.

Given a reflective moment over your second pick-me-up, more subdued attractions of Hebridean life wander below The Castlebay's windows. Heather hill and sanded bay focus around the island's natural scallop of sheltered water. When cloud clears from the west, a local boat, stern high with creels, will cut her wake to the lobster banks and dinghies will ply and 'yachties' flit. John Allan, the coxswain, revs the lifeboat engines for their daily test. A dinghy rocks beside the slip. Captain Sinclair, alias DP, sits on its gunnel awaiting his two o'clock castle visitors. A straggle balances aboard, clutching fresh air and cameras. DP hasn't lost one so far but has been known to leave a cut of them locked in, to be spotted later from The Castlebay Bar waving exhaustedly from the battlements. Sheep wander the street or graze the slopes below a smart new police station. It's a mix of crofting and fishing which can afford to ignore an emasculated castle marooned in memories of freebooting days and now reduced to plundering the tourists.

Occasionally a puffer will berth. Peterhead boats in from a fishing lie two by two against the piles and put the Doric tongue across The Castlebay's counter. Each day a crowd waits at the pier, loiters about 'Non' MacDonald's ticket office. Assorted knots of conversation and laughter, business and pleasure, a little gossip. Gaelic and English without embarrassment or effort.

Sheep are in the pens, unheeded dogs snap between the rails.
Round the Dubh Sgeir ploughs the steamer, red funnels and
eager faces. With a master mariner's eye from the bridge, she
manoeuvres alongside. Ropes snake out, men in boats since
boyhood move deft and deliberate. Bollards strain. People clatter
down the gangplank to handshake and hug. Home and away and
'You're home again!' – that's island living. Home to shades dark
on the bay, grey streaks of a shower that will lift to wavelets of
light mirroring the antics of a lively community in which many
bear the stamp of 'a character'.

Lively for certain but also a community with a thoughtful side for,
in keeping with the island's faith, tucked below the shapely top of
Heaval, the Norse-named hill which shelters the village from Arctic
winds, is a small white statue of the Virgin and Child. Of a
summer's day, families kneel at Mass, ask her blessing, her remembrance for the island tragedies, for those lost at sea, both near and
far. And, in the village, on a prominence above the curve of house,
hotel and shop, is a church of solemn atmosphere that binds the
people in spiritual security – the Church of Our Lady, Star of the
Sea. Tall plain windows stare beyond the bay to empty treeless
islands, home once on a day to many forebears of the people of
Barra.

◆

Religious faith, central to the island culture, is expressed in the tiny
church of Cille Bharra near the north end of the island. This rough
stone building looking out on the Sound of Barra traces to the
twelfth century and is dedicated to the sainthood of Finbarr of Cork.
A dedication of more recent origin may well eclipse that of Saint
Findbarr in general popularity, for amongst its graves is a plain
stone to the memory of Compton Mackenzie, the author who
portrayed his adopted island by writing *Whisky Galore*. Late-night
scribbling to hefty drafts of the book's guiding theme, partaken
whilst a local girl wound up '78 records on a His Master's Voice
gramophone, resulted in a worldwide best-seller and a hilarious
film. Both illustrate a relaxed approach to life and towards authority
in particular, an attitude which the island's populace finds little
difficulty in maintaining.

Those wishing to savour this era of unbridled pillage repaired to The Castlebay. Memory spoke from faded yellow walls hung with sepia prints of the early steamships that served the island. Passengers or lambs were loaded with equal facility. Photos depicted the herring boom of the 1920s. Sailing drifters stretched across the bay to the neighbouring Vatersay. The 'silver darlings' were gutted and salted by the local girls in curing sheds round the bay. Offal tipped into the tide put a shine on the coats of wandering village cattle. The pier filled with barrels as did the coffers of a certain Captain 'Blow' MacDonald who victualled the fishing fleet using rowing boats oared by a team of underpaid schoolboys. This wall-to-wall insight into an island life thriving on herring culminated beside the toilet door, perhaps of necessity if perused by peak-capped 'yachties', where hung an Admiralty chart depicting the exposure of surrounding waters to the weight of the Atlantic.

The public bar, necessarily spacious, featured two brown-painted iron pillars supporting a smoke-yellow ceiling. Cracked lino vanished towards dark wooden surrounds. Matching small brown tables, mostly requiring a fag packet below a leg to afford a pint any measure of equilibrium, were an excellent match. Incentive to stand at the counter was provided by cane-backed chairs. A large snooker table, carrying a 'no pints' sign, offered its legs to any collie dodging the crash of a swing door. Oilskins and overalls predominated and heads turned at each entrance. In the few steps to the counter, your needs were sensed and John the barman's hand was already priming the optic. Initiation over, slap down a note, nod to John, twirl a finger and another round appeared. He knew your company, knew each tipple, and the change lay at your elbow against further depredation. Little piles of cash waited safely here and there along the counter, some the store of those at the back pews who needed only to catch John's eye to ensure further sustenance arrived at their table. Magnanimity ruled, no grudging of rounds, drams arrived from down the counter. 'That's from Sandy.' Sometimes it needed a query, 'Who was that, John?' An inclination of the head in thanks. Slàinte.

For those who seek to ease the white man's burden against a polished surface, it emits an embracing, on occasion, an all-embracing ambience. No other drinker's domicile, world over, radiates such an aura. An uplifting haven whose name is synonymous with Barra – The Castlebay Bar.

◆

In bygone times, the fallout from a local cattle sale would fill the premises to overflowing. Tackety boots, sea-boot wellies and panting dogs eyeing each other from below table and bench. Crofters, relaxing after parting with bawling calves, waved auctioneer's cheques over quaffing heads and invested their takings in another round. Good prices spiced the conversations. The aroma of cattle was sharing equal prominence when in strolled a fisherman from Northbay – this village, while not exactly the opposition, was certainly at the other end of the island. He squeezed into a corner and sat with a bulge in his jacket pocket and his nose hoovering the froth off a Guinness.

The keys of a broken squeeze box wheezed a Gaelic air and the odd foot tapped the lino. The accordionist took it as a measure of appreciation in spite of a bum reed which, to his musical ear, ruined the tune and not just once. Exasperation gripped him. Crash! The instrument hit the floor and its bellows gaped. The musician climbed on the table, jumped and tramped until a last wheeze emerged from his box. He kicked it under the bench and sat down to resume his pint. Few paid attention – it was not outwith the general tenor of events in The Castlebay but, for the Northbay, man, it was the minor distraction needed. His eye stole over the rim of his glass, his fingers strayed to the pocket bulge – it had ears. The first dog to get a whiff of a liberated rabbit took the legs from under three chairs.

Whoosh! Whoopee! Wellies shot towards the ceiling, flailing arms caught tables, drinks flew, dogs leapt, men leapt for their glasses, the rabbit leapt for the pool table. Holes too small, it skidded below benches, into the ladies' toilet, screams, back into the arena.

In moments, the whole bar was cavorting in time to crashing tables, collies yelping and barmaids squealing – in some cases not for the first time, but that's a story for another day. The room rapidly grew a forest of legs – chairs', tables' and unsteady crofters' who'd slipped on their pints. The responsible grabbed for their dogs, those in shock for their drams and most for any unemptied glass within reach. This was not an emergency to be faced without fortitude.

Amidst a crescendo of bawling and barking, just a cottontail ahead of gnashing teeth, the rabbit, with the aplomb of a pole-vaulter, landed on the counter, skidded twice round the till, dodged a swipe of boss Big George's towel and shot through the back hatch, a point of egress normally reserved for the ingress of any local hand needing a 'nip' on the q. t.

Ah my, The Castlebay Bar – tolerant of fellow man's foibles, a test bench for a student's thesis on the human predicament. For the crofters, more fun than money in the bank; for seafaring men, the leading lights to the port of home. Cosmopolitan and convivial, oilskin jackets, hikers' hairy legs or the latest flock of tourists off the ferry. Gaelic and English, music with a lilt, much wisecrack and wisdom whisked to oblivion by the discretion of an extractor fan and, behind a row of sweating optics, the smiling mirrors of self-delusion. Happy days. If only mankind's greatest threat was the hint of closing time or a ditch when cycling home.

◆

*Rhum* lay in our view below the windows of Castlebay Hotel as we ate supper at its Puffin Grill. At the adjacent table a dicky bow and a lascivious eye hovered over the cleavage of a prize bosom. It strained to abandon an expensive London constraint and, who would know, perhaps gain a touch of naughty freedom? 'Tell me darling,' a note of petulance, 'is *this* the only bar?' A napkin nervously wiped precisely trimmed bristles, 'Well, darling . . . er, I'm afraid there is just the . . . er, the working man's bar . . . mmm, it's next door.' Steps and a swing door and we discovered the plebs were sweating at their evening toil. Barman John possessed divination. He supplied nods and glances without questioning their needs. No surprise when he stated, 'You're the skipper of the yacht that came in today.' And, between rounds, he quietly informed me, 'There's eight, no nine, ten, eleven men in here tonight with Master's tickets.' He indicated a table bearing rapidly emptying glasses and a group of ruddy complexions. 'There's four of them,' he grinned. 'Round the world and back here – they call it the captains' table.'

No gold braid, they flagged us over. 'Pull alongside, throw out a fender, sit in.' We scraped up chairs. John materialised with a glass on each finger. We'd berthed beside men no strangers to Atlantic storm or even the odd wave which from time to time swept The Castlebay Bar – two Sinclair brothers, Neillie and Donald Patrick, John MacLeod and Roddy MacKinnon, the latter whose preference for rum earned him 'Captain Morgan'. Neil had turned from fishing to lighthouse keeper on Barra Head but once the light became automatic he ran its maintenance boat, the *Bernera*. A good sea boat, powered by a thumping single-cylinder Kelvin engine, Neillie Mòr took her up and down the island chain weekly and, between times, kept her beautifully varnished.

Donald Patrick, otherwise DP, a retired deep-sea man who'd berthed tankers in the world's great harbours and, on one occasion, skippered his ship two thousand miles up the Amazon, now landed tourists on the castle slip. After the war, he'd skippered an Esso tanker on the Grangemouth–Inverness run. Yes, he knew the Coast Lines ships but hadn't met my father who would have been on the Mediterranean convoys and died as a result in 1946. Liverpool's Liver Birds? Yes boy, he knew them fine; also Captain Park, the man once keen to put a school-leaver to sea.

John MacLeod was better known to the locals as Iagan a'Dot. For him, Barra seas had been the western approaches – our nation's jugular vein throughout the early years of the Second World War. German submarines from southern Irish bases found it an easy stalking ground. After a reported sinking, Macleod put to sea with a rescue launch searching for lifeboats or those left to the waves. Now he and his son Donald Beag and their boat the *Boy James* were back at the fishing. Talk rolled on and friendships grew – nor has it slipped away. Rowing back to *Rhum* later, much later, the black stilts of pier under orange cones of light made gently moving shadows over silent water. I sat on the deck, each cool breath of air a taste of the sea. I lay back. The faintest swell of an incoming tide turned the topmast amongst the stars and, high above Heaval, the tail of the Great Bear on its nightly pilgrimage, pointed south.

◆

One way to see Barra is by bike and, next day, the hire of two roadsters took us round the island's single-track circuit. We pushed them on the long climb out of the village by the east side and looked back. The history of the islands spreads in the scene below. At its hub, the church. Not a grand building, just binding together the houses and crofts which ring a bay where steamer pier and a castle on an islet tell the story. South over the white sands of Vatersay were the clean lines of island upon island. No tree or building to soften or mar their skyline. Sea and land in a panoply of colour, drawn as though of some unsoiled beginning, a primitive environment at the mercy of the twenty-first century. There is no room for both.

Afternoon's warmth was on us as we pedalled the sandy track over hillocks of primrose machair to a burying ground which looks on the Atlantic. Sheep cudded in the shade of walls which kept out both their hungry mouths and the gales that blow from an ocean unbroken to this homeland of so many who left their kinship beneath the mounds about us. Sunlight shone off the sea and made tombstone names an easy read. St Brendan of the epic voyage is the rightful name given to a restive place which is never without the sound of the ocean – a lonely place to which the great flocks of migrant waders come each year. Spring and autumn they pass, beating wings on nature's way. They pause to probe the wrack which marks each tide on the sands below and then they are gone, calling in the night.

Many a lad from a torpedoed convoy was washed ashore on the midnight beaches of the Long Island. Flotsam of man's folly, they lie below the grey government-issue slabs of burying grounds beside the machair and always the voice of the element that took them – their names strange to the islands, some simply 'Merchant Seaman, unknown'. And each spring, to these sheep-cropped dunes, comes the skylark and, in her rising song, their hope is surely carried beyond the hush of each ebbing tide.

◆

It was no stretch to cycle on to the island's third hotel. A plaque on its wall indicated some architectural award for a building sitting on the dunes of Halaman Bay in evening light, enhancing neither and deliberately or otherwise denying public bar drinkers a view of the ocean. Friendliness by the barman made up. 'Where are you bound for?' 'Mingulay, tomorrow.' 'Well, there's the man to speak to,' he indicated into the gloom, 'he's one of those that owns the islands down there.' I turned as the man came to the bar, a bare forearm fit to turn the steer-board oar of any galley, a throwback to the longship lads! My impression stopped short of a sword and horned helmet. Archie MacLean nodded. His handshake a solid grip and our sea road to Mingulay.

## 28

# 'Homeward to Mingulay'

'That's them, the boys are away south,' I shouted into the cabin. My glass held steady on a blue-hulled fishing boat steaming across the mouth of Vatersay Bay. CY5 stood out – bold white letters on a maroon rail. I made out *Boy James* at the bow. The water drummed with engine power. Men angled their legs and leant against a varnished wheelhouse, two heads at the forepeak. The boys were hunkered amongst rope and winch tackle but not their white-collared shipmate, paws on the rail and barks at the bubbles creaming the bow, excitement by the eyeful. Boat and crew and the greyness of a callow morning on The Minch and the air rimy with wave-top salt whipped by a night's summer blow. It stung nostrils, sharpened the brain. The weather was settling, the sea was down, only a tap-tapping under the stern and east, on the steep, un-shelving isle of Muldoanich, only a cringle of dying swell. Far beyond, without warning, the sun burst between the peaks of Skye and orange segments danced on the curls of a southbound wake. My glass clicked shut. 'Come on, woman – they're away to Mingulay.'

The Seal Woman to the helm, me to the cabin top, along the boom, flick off sail ties. Now the mast, the main halyard, haul away, hand over hand. Up climbed the mainsail. Winch handle in its slot,

a last three-ratchet turns peaked the sail at the head of the mast. The
canvas filled and smoothed, sent a tremor through the rigging. *Rhum*
alive, an ocean maid, under my feet, through my legs, arms,
spinning the mind. Eyes a-shine, a shout to the helm, 'Sheet the
boom hard, keep her on the wind.' I stood at the pulpit. The plaited
anchor rope slackened. I hauled fast. Shackle, then chain, safe
aboard. *Rhum* veered, jerked out her anchor. Lean and lift. On deck
in a heave. 'Head her to wind.'

Flapping sail, another quick tighten on the halyard winch. 'Let
her pay off. That's it – put over your helm.' Across swung the boom,
'Slack your mainsheet, let her run, starboard a little, keep off the
headland.' *Rhum* turned her tail to the beach, drove out of Vatersay
Bay, bobbing to the sea. I balanced on the foredeck and lashed
down her anchor. Mast again, hold on, watch, she's heeling, rattle
up the jib. Back to the cockpit along the windward deck, winch in a
snaking jib sheet. Full away, sails and clouds, horizons blue. *Rhum*
embraced a sunlit breeze and the ripple at her forefoot began the
song of the sea. Who would tell me she didn't scent open water,
waves to be clipped? Boats and dolphins are born to play and we
were away to Mingulay.

◆

Two nights previous, at the Captain's table, John MacLeod warned
if it came to any blow then the holding west of the castle was not
sound. 'Soft mud and old chains, the one lets you away when you
want to stay, the other holds you fast when you're wanting away.' I
heeded his advice. The barometer said a summer low approached
and next afternoon we rounded under the eastern cliffs of Muldoanich to anchor in the shelter of Vatersay Bay. I was soon to learn the
short cut. Local boats, sighting on Heaval, the high peak above
Castlebay, aimed through the narrows beside the islet of Snasimul.

To the north of this rock-dotted channel is the tidal islet of
Uinessan, a burial ground in olden times. The faint ruins of a
church remain, Cille Bhrianain, or, more commonly, the Chapel of
Mary of the Heads. This lady-wife of a MacNeil chief who hailed
from the Isle of Coll favoured beheading as the cheapest method of
dispensing justice – hence her byname. She demanded to be buried
with a sight of her native Coll but, when rowing the corpse to this

supernatural vantage point, the oarsmen got fed up and decided Uinessan islet must do. Sad to say, were she to stand on ghostly tiptoe on a clear day, Muldoanich would intercept her expected view from the grave.

As we approached Vatersay, heavy clouds were assembling far to the west – round white heads and dark sagging bellies. From between their ranks, blades of sunlight swept the waters and, for moments, the whim of a cloudscape would turn the bay into a sheet of neon brilliance, winking and flashing with ultraviolet fluorescence. The Norse named the island Vatersay, 'water-island', and what water – clear as glass. *Rhum* lay in four fathoms but it seemed just a foot. Crabs made little puffs of dust as they scuttled, starfish idled and every grain of sand was plain to see. Only by the headland did underwater beds of tangle cling to hidden rocks and darken a luminous sea to purple.

By evening, the wind strengthened, twirling the spindles of marram grass on the carved dunes which sheltered our anchorage. We rowed ashore and crossed their backs to watch the Atlantic. Under a hodden sky, it rode on to the solitary sands of the Traigh Shair on the long dark humps of some far off disturbance. Crests reared into emerald curls of passion, each spacious lull an impending hollow which fell with a boom of sorrow for, in the blowing spume, there seemed no life. No lisping plover to dodge along its hissing edge or flit before us on drooping wing. Nothing to mitigate a desolation which cried in the gnawing wind, haunted the sand-blown gullies. We turned away and, when climbing back over the dunes, came upon a small granite monument. 'On 28th September 1853 the ship *Annie Jane*, with emigrants from Liverpool to Quebec, was totally wrecked in this bay, and three-fourths of the crew and passengers, numbering about three hundred and fifty men, women and children were drowned and their bodies interred here.'

Under the command of Captain Mason on an outbound trip to the New World, the *Annie Jane* was forced back to Liverpool for repairs after broaching in the fury of a gale which carried away her topmasts. They sailed again, families with potato famine and starvation imprinted on minds. Three days out and a roaring sou'wester, another Atlantic storm. The mizzen snapped, canvas blew and she sprang a leak. Passengers in relays manned the pumps and, for several days, she wallowed. A masthead cry in the last glimmer of September 27th sighted the terrors of a lee shore. The white glow of giant seas beat the cliffs of Barra Head. Weather it by the south? A desperate bid. They were driven back. The night howled with the glee of a devil. Out of thundering blackness, the jeering cliffs of Mingulay towered over them. Only the might of a surging backwash kept them clear. At midnight, the *Annie Jane* took the ground on the sands of the Traigh Shair. The first huge wave took those on deck and drowned the women and children trapped below. By daybreak, she was in three parts. As the tide fell the few folk that lived on Vatersay fashioned a gangway from the wreckage to help off the survivors.

A grave was dug by hand in the dunes and, gently, side by side, mothers and children were laid. No blessing, no Mass, just a fretting wind in the marram grass to honour the last hugs and hopes buried under the sands of Vatersay.

◆

*Rhum* lay over, light on the helm, flinging the chop on to her spray-hood, raking the currents left swirling astern, racing down to Mingulay. With 'ay' suffixed on every name, we drove hard past Sandray of the broad white bay, of homes since Neolithic times, Bronze Age cairn and standing stone. 'Sand Isle' to the Norse, their settlement on the north-west corner at Sheader, a name perhaps corrupted from the old tongue – *setr* meaning 'dwelling place'.

Of more recent date is the fireside yarn of a young Sheader girl who, in the sharing fashion of those days, was crossing the hill to get cow's milk from another island family. She wasn't to see Sandray again – the only trace a broken pail. Years passed and, in a West Indies café, men with the Gaelic tongue met a woman – the girl from Sandray. She'd been snatched as a child and sold into slavery. Similar 'traders' one night in 1739 called at Finsbay, Harris. Over one hundred islanders were loaded for a long 'holiday' in Jamaica. Their fortunate escape in Ireland brought to light the dealings of two esteemed Skye chieftains, MacLeod of Dunvegan and Mac-Donald of Sleat, who saw profit in arranging plantation 'breaks' for disposable clansmen – a travel agency with a line in slavery.

By 1825 the scant payments made to their laird from the takings

of the Sandray fishing boats, *Mary*, *Margaret* and *Flora*, drew forth
another scorcher from General Roderick MacNeil. An Adam's
apple yo-yoed from under a freshly starched collar. Father Angus
MacDonald, a man dedicated to saving souls rather than to
MacNeil's bank account, read it twice:

> You will do well to advise your friends at Sandray, and all the
> Leaders as they are termed, to mind well what they are about, if they
> wish to remain at Barra. They are of little or no importance to me,
> whatever may be their value to you, and if I don't on my arrival find
> them heart and hand engaged in fishing, I pledge you my honour
> they shall tramp, and the land shall this ensuing spring be occupied
> by strangers.

Bombast came naturally to the General – straight from me
medals you understand, no diluting authority by idle consideration.
Menials out, sheep in, plus a few imported shepherds. The last
human inhabitants, the 'land raiders' who abandoned Mingulay in
1908, were now along the way to light bulbs and flushing loos. A
standard Highland story, fallen gables by choice or force turned into
CD sleeves and price-tag paintings for tourist information centres.
Sandray and its ruins fell astern.

*Rhum* romped on to a course for Pabbay, out across the sound,
230 on the bulkhead compass. Ease the mainsheet a fraction and
tighten the jib. I tied a bit of shock-cord to the tiller. Look, no hands
– she sailed herself. Six knots and throwing the odd splash on to the
spray-hood for fun. 'Go on, boatie!' Islets came on transit in the
Pabbay Sound: Fodday, the Norse 'floating isle'; Lingay; Greanamul. I spied at them. Rock outcrops breasting the Atlantic swell,
only approachable in the flattest calm. Green tops. I guessed a
landing of wedders would fatten on the rich geese-dropping grass.
Ropes and a sure foot, boys. But getting them off? A net, maybe a
rifle job? No playground for soft hands. A seascape made of
adventure and danger.

Pabbay abeam, we rounded the grass-moulded peninsula of
Rosinish, a Gaelic corruption of the old Viking words for 'Horse
Headland'. Years later I was to come to Rosinish in my wee
*Mingulay* boat on a July-time when the sea had no movement

and the ephemeral light of the islands lived for that day alone. In the sloc we landed, sheep shears, men and dogs, below an Iron Age dun, and tied our boat side-to-side in the way the longships would lie in days before Dunan Ruadh had its galleried walls eaten by north-east gales. Twenty gimmers or more we gathered against a tall rock face. Three held them behind a sheet of hessian bags tied end for end and Archie, Sandy and I clipped them. Six men and home by the west side in a small boat full of wool, her gunnels low, and Calum at the helm, for he knew best the hidden reefs in the Sound of Sandray. I'd walked a springing turf peopled with orchis and sea thrift and utter peace flowed in the cry of the green plover about me and from amongst the rocks came the soft gurgling which belongs to a tide on the turn. I'd looked on a white bay and the roofless walls above a sandy hillock which held the bones of prehistoric days and knew of a symbol stone found there which, by its markings, joined Pict to Christian. 'Hermit's Isle' in the Norse and then, a thousand years ago, part of the Bishop's Isles of Iona dynasty. And I wanted to buy Pabbay.

Families came and went in the 1800s, not always swayed by holy zeal, more by the enterprise of Glancy, an Irish interloper who busied himself supplying their spiritual needs from his 'premises' beside a little burn which flows on the west side and into a sloc bearing his name. But the end came to this tiny community by the way of the sea. On 1 May 1897, all the Pabbay men fished south of Barra Head, twelve miles from home, by means of sail and oar alone, using the island's only boat. John Gillies from Barra had gone with them, unwillingly, for the prangs of a disaster were on him. A south-west gale sprang from the blackness that enveloped the day. They made back for Pabbay. Violence burst from the Sound which separates Barra Head and Mingulay, its hurricane force filled the air with spume, blotted out their homeward bearing. They fought. Dipping oar, tearing sail. Fury whelmed their boat.

The storm howled over Pabbay. Families in the horrors of apprehension struggled to the high point of the island and, in the face of the gale, watched the sea. Darkness but no sail, no boat fighting the turmoil. The bodies of the breadwinners of Pabbay were washed ashore on the coast of Ireland. Many years before, a Mingulay girl with the 'gift of sight' saw a lone boat hauling long lines south of Barra Head and foretold the hunger of the Cuan a'Bhocain, the 'Sea of the Ghosts'. For an island people stripped of their manpower there was no future save, each year, faithfully said in the Church of Castlebay, is a Mass for the Pabbay fishermen.

The wind tightened over our starboard quarter. Harden the mainsheet, a squint at the sail slot, screw the jib sheet a turn. On her fastest point of sail, a foaming *Rhum* skimmed the point of Pabbay by a cable and there, unveiled by Rosinish, was the island of Mingulay. To the north, a head tilted in the arrogance of rearing cliff and burrowed arch, flinging aside Atlantic's journey with a scorn that broke the back of many a sea. And, eastwards, the rounded hills of Carnan and Hecla sheltered a slope which fell to land that took the plough into simple ways and arms which held a bay, the umbilical of island life. We roved in. I dropped sail, lashing the jib along the for'ard rail and securing slip-knot ties on the main. *Rhum* glided into an unruffled bay. The *Boy James* lay to the south shore. A touch of engine and we made over to her. Anchor hung ready. A wave to the Seal Woman, no word needed. She slipped the gear lever into reverse. Four fathoms on the depth sounder? She nodded yes. Anchor away, a burring of chain, harsh in the silence. Under my feet, the deck came to rest and *Rhum* settled in our destination.

The fresh breeze that sped *Rhum* across the channels faded to a heat engulfed by the island's shelter. I faced east, just one moment. On a sea of imperceptible movement floated the cones of mainland hills, remote traces forgotten by change, hills whose summits had grown the pangs of longing. But here, vast, open, endless, oceanic west, the elation of space in the green of island, the heraldic blue of azure sky. Its blending flowed beyond clear white shallows in a living colour of light which spread over a necklace of ivory sands until it covered the fields and homes of generation upon generation and left the imprint of vibrancy mystic upon each mind. Waters of stunning turquoise shone with the eye of memory. Desirable, dangerous, I saw again the eye of old Paterson's South Seas regret told to a child on a sea chest, his paradise the turquoise sea, the colour of his dream.

My telescope steady on the edge of the spray-hood magnified the activities ashore. Sheep were gathering; men and dogs were moving them towards what appeared to be roofless gables standing on higher ground some distance from tumbled piles of stones. Outboard engines or aluminium paddles are for floppy guts, aluminium paddles for children's play pools. The strength of the day, the scent of land unexplored, I opened shoulders and pulled ten-foot oars. The small inflatable shot towards the beach and left a white yacht dipping in the bay.

A scrunch and we were ashore on Mingulay. Many times I'd answered, 'Bound for Mingulay.' Now cloudless, sunburnt, eye-blinking colour, my feet sank ankle-deep into the fine white sand. Sand, dazzling bright against the hard black rock of sloping ledges. I hauled the dinghy up the beach of a small bay. The sand reflected an intensity of sunlight, cliffs shone with salty dampness, trapped the smell of brine, reeked of astringent cleanness. No marks on the beach – our footprints were its first. Creviced rock above me sheltered clumps of pink ocean flowers. Yellow buttercups with trailing roots lifted wide petalled-faces. They grew profusely beside a burn which trickled into the sand amongst huge rounded stones – purple stones filling the mouth of a tide-worn gully, smoothed by easterly gale. Empty of people but still a homecoming full of welcome and, on the dark rocks, I saw the home of a Seal Woman, auburn-haired against the sea.

◆

Village ruins edged the wide bay north of our landing. Rough stone and rounded end for the oldest homes, semi-dressed and straight gable for the more 'modern'. Of these, an odd doorway lintel remained and the gape of tiny windows. Not a roof left between them and sand-blow filling the empty interiors. A wide hollow of fertile land – the islanders had called it 'the glen' – sloped up from the village towards cliffs second only in height to St Kilda. Behind turf and stone dyke, the fields had yielded corn crops which justified a tiny watermill in the burn behind the village. An island beset by current and storm had small chance of allowing a cutting of seaweed to pack the lazy bed with nutrient, but fish guts and a winter's dung from the small black cattle which lived as family kept fertility to Mingulay's shallow soil.

Though cutting areas were dwindling, the end of May would see rows of four peats leaning together up on the bank to dry but, by the

1890s, for the able young, ready cash beckoned from haymaking and harvest on the mainland. Farm records from the Parish of Petty, east of Inverness, have these entries: 'To wages of the Barra men at a shilling a day'. Young men were off to 'modern' farms and bonnie girls to Aberdeen, following the herring migration as far as Lowestoft to gut the fish familiar from childhood. Old folk and children were left turning the peats, tethering ponies and herding livestock out of the island's hay meadows, the tattie patch and their strips of 'black oat'. For island youth, those years of the Boer War glory were more than 'Goodbye, Dolly Grey' – they sang goodbye fish-oil lamps and good evening Glasgow's gas lighting under the Hielanman's Umbrella. And there would be no Holy Water sprinkled on the first seed corn sown each year under a waxing Easter moon.

Land clearances on Barra actually put families to Mingulay in 1835 and fifty years later the island reached its most populous times with about thirty families in a communal lifestyle. Barring a fill o' the baccy pouch, keeping the sugar dry and a lid on the tea caddy, harvesting the land, the birds and the rock fishing waters supplied most needs. At that time a fully equipped forty-foot Buckie-built fishing boat cost a daunting £400. Financial speculation ever gambled on others' elbow grease and loans were forthcoming via the island's landlord, Lady Gordon Cathcart. To repay them, five-men crews fished the 'great lines' – there were a thousand baited hooks on half a mile of line astern. Hand-over-hand in a running sea. Their catches were sold in Castlebay or as far away as Northern Ireland. Ninety miles south of Barra Head on the full Atlantic with a compass and four days of west wind to see them to 'Derry and back' and a canvas cover and a case of 'Mountain Dew' to separate the crew from the rigours of an open boat.

Intelligent, practical people, the islanders were becoming increasingly aware of what they perceived as a menial lifestyle and certainly lacking in 'the three Rs'. Such schooling as existed on Barra largely confined itself to producing priests. Illiterate grannies thought it high time for the young to 'better themselves'. By the 1850s, chief agitator for a resident teacher was Duncan Sinclair, a Protestant shepherd from Appin in Argyllshire who, by courtesy of General MacNeil of Barra, had become a leading crofter on that most exposed of all the Atlantic islands, Barra Head. To shepherding skills soon would be added seamanship.

The philanthropy of the Highland Ladies Association, erstwhile the Free Church of Scotland Ladies Association, saw free education bearing a torch with which to 'diffuse the gospel light where Popish darkness still prevails'. Motives apart, their benevolence brought schooling to Mingulay for young and old. In 1859 to a village with its total population devout Roman Catholics, came Ross-shire tailor's son from Lochcarron, John Finlayson, a staunch Presbyterian.

Appointee, plus trunk, aiming for Barra Head, sailed from Castlebay to assume his post. A storm forced them to land on Mingulay. Gunnel-clutching, Finlayson decided far enough. Into family lodgings with scant privacy he moved, his school a dripping one-roomed hovel in which eager scholars of all ages were belaboured with Latin grammar and a Gaelic translation of *The Pilgrim's Progress*. The latter, as heavily as he chose to step in a religious minefield, must surely have struck a cord when the leaking roof turned the school in to the Slough of Despond. A delivery of exercise books was much delayed. Roofing slates arrived from a wreck and clay-pipe stalks made pencils for children scratching their three Rs. Navigation lessons were added for the boys, sewing for the girls and a Schools Inspector appeared to check on Finlayson. His Gaelic usage was barely tolerated, lessons were to be in English – no career could hope to advance speaking the native tongue. His evangelical report? None out of ten – no lambs led into the Presbyterian fold. The Ladies Association deemed his results 'not cost-effective'. Children attend Sunday Bible lessons or the school closes. Education had its price. A study of comparative religions was not included.

Poor Finlayson, twenty-two years of his life crammed along with a roll of forty scholars ranging from four to fourteen in an unlined stone bothy. Whilst the 'Ladies' considered their position, in 1881 the nation's education budget stretched to a 'new' school. There were thirty pupils, the official capacity of this modern building, and its cost was just short of £500. Island scholars were catered for at £16 a head, inclusive of 'dry' privies discreetly situated at the end of the playground. Thirteen years later, the Education Authority added a two-up-two-down teacher's house, the envy of the island. No running water, but so what? It had a dry closet below the stair, gable fireplaces and wooden floors – fit for a bride. And soon Finlayson carried a Mingulay girl over the threshold. Through the wall, his wood-lined classroom possessed a stove, children's desks to replace shipwreck planks and slates on the roof. The peace and charm of remote living must have compensated for Finlayson's difficult teaching years.

With shades of the natives of Stroma, an island in the Pentland Firth whose agitations for a jetty saw their flitting as the structure's first cargo, so the taste for a faster treadmill which Finlayson brought to Mingulay helped douse the flicker of an ancient culture. Staunch in his persuasions, their first teacher displayed the intellectual wisdom of leaving others to their own faith. Retirement came but Findlayson couldn't bring himself to leave the island. An erudite man, a self-taught naturalist and lover of the isolation found on Mingulay, he left, as he arrived, by storm. In March 1904, to prevent a burial at sea en route to Barra, his coffin was lashed vertically to the mast. As island yarns go, the storm delayed his arrival in Castlebay and, too late for an interment that day, the remains spent a night on a chitty in the bank's safe deposit.

Finlayson's successor proved to be a man more in the mould of island proclivities. At nineteen, with little more than ample native intellect, John Johnston, a born Mingulay man, took up the chalk and 'must try harder' reports. Owning his own boat and being a keen navigator allowed of not infrequent 'visits' to Castlebay to check on curriculum. Strenuously pulling for Mingulay one night, daylight revealed his navigational skills undermined by a stern rope tied to the jetty. Similar excursions necessitated opening the school on a Saturday, not popular with the crofters' weekend labour requirements. Female teachers came cheaper and Mingulay's last teacher hailed from Glasgow. Mrs MacShane took up duties early in 1904 as marking the register was becoming less of a chore. Any attempt to halt declining school numbers came too late. The second of her children was the last baby born on Mingulay. With nine scholars left, in 1910 the school closed.

Thousand of years' settlement on an island demanding of physical strength and stoical grit retreated towards a lifestyle less in the thrall of harvest dearth, earth floors and bare necessities. From the days when Mingulay tenants paid rent to MacNeil of Kisimul in fat young shearwater or bird feathers at nine pence a pound and received 'call-up papers' for his '45 Jacobite outing, to the 1890s when cash arrears owing to Colonel John Gordon, the exacting Aberdeenshire landlord, amounted to something over a thousand pounds, the islanders bolstered any possible inability to pay with a marked unwillingness. A government inspector checking on poor relief and 'health care' in 1906 pointed to Mingulay School. Not a penny of rates has ever been collected he fumed when considering legal action. Norse two-fingers to authority and Celtic blarney were built into the islanders' survival kit.

Hauling boats on the beach became the killer – manpower was declining and the womenfolk were less inclined to wet their bloomers wading up to the waist when young male muscle was away touring the world with the great Glasgow shipping companies. Cottars from both Castlebay and Mingulay fixed their eye on Vatersay, just one narrow crossing to Barra, the very doorstep of civilisation. This fertile island emptied by evictions in the 1850s had been given to a sole tenant who both farmed profitably and paid his rent timeously – a point noted by the scrupulous owner, Colonel John's widow, Lady Gordon Cathcart, who suspected on past Mingulay experience any additions to Vatersay's population from that direction might be less so inclined.

To her fury, a land raid was launched in July 1906. Forty cottars and three from Mingulay pegged out sites and even knocked up wooden huts. Next January, the Mingulay folk arrived in force and with cattle and ponies. Tattie ground was turned, if not slit trenches dug. Farmer MacDonald was furious and the factor tried pulling rank. Futile. Her Ladyship flagged up the law. An alarmed Victorian government considered this a grievous abuse of the feudal system. It might spread to the shires – a mini Peasants' Revolt. Gunboats? Still up the Yangtze Kiang forcing Britain's Indian opium on China. Westminster dispatched Sheriff John Wilson, a less careful choice of investigator than would have been made by the current administration. Wilson sided with the land raiders.

Meantime, the good widow attempted to cash a belly-up investment by flogging her islands to the government. Standard Whitehall intransigence. She pressed on, financial consideration apart, the law could not be flouted and certainly not by cottars. It was her duty to 'society'. Stand firm. In June 1908, ten Sunday suits lined up before a judge at the Edinburgh Court of Session. Public support for the crofters' case rekindled by memories of eviction and immigration reached far beyond the Highlands. Idle sentiment. One must move on. Guilty. Take these men down, officer. Best clothes were folded and little arrow outfits donned for two months in the 'Calton cooler', but no humiliation. The raiders, now heroes, paraded on Castlebay Pier to the skirl o' the pipes and a suitable libation. The following year, Her Ladyship trousered well over six thousand pounds of taxpayers' cash for Vatersay and a precursor of today's Crofters Commission, the Congested Districts Board, divided the island into fifty-odd crofts. Allocation of a holding was by ballot which the Board fiddled in an attempt to debar the original 'squatters'. It failed.

The cash was pleasant but Lady Cathcart was a thwarted woman. The few remaining families on Pabbay and Mingulay may well have wanted to leave but, behind their backs, she let the islands for grazing to Jonathan MacLean, whose people owned the Craigard House Hotel and a busy village shop. For the islanders, possible eviction and seizure of stock might follow. Mingulay emptied and was given over to the bleat of sheep. In 1912, the last of the migration waded out to boats with what bits and pieces they possessed and pushed off from the beach below the village. They left fields of fertility built by cattle and plough, homes of love, birth and death to await gales to strip the thatch and wooden crosses to rot in a burying ground just an earshot from yesterday, voices by the shore to murmur in the ebb tide of old beliefs.

◆

Well, well, that's the way, but sheep there must always have been and in plenty throughout the Western Isles, for the power of Viking ships lay in woollen sails. Certainly not knit one, purl one and work in a Raven emblem – no knitted sails for the longship boys. Theirs were of strong woollen yarn and they drew the galleys faster upwind and sailed them closer than a modern canvas. Riding night anchor off a hostile coast? Hot-water bottle? Softly, be a man and wrap your feet in the sail. Each ship's sail was a cherished possession, and rightly so – it could require a year's wool from two thousand sheep. Fleeces were plucked by hand from a particularly hardy Norse breed of sheep with long-fibre wool that was lanolin-rich and durable. Drop spindles and looms turned yarn into flexible woollen cloth – the painstaking work of the womenfolk or slaves over many months, perhaps a year, when weaving a sail of eighty or ninety square yards. The Danish fleet of King Canute the Second, setting out to attack William the Bastard, ex-Viking Conqueror whose Hastings arrows traject across the Bayeux Tapestry, was an armada of seventeen hundred ships. Woollen sail power? Shepherds played no small part in Norse success.

Bleating sheep, infectious to an ex-shepherd, prompted a scramble up the gully and, to hide my excitement, a stroll over to the ex-school with its gable and back wall supporting a sheep fank of wooden pens and a concrete dipper. Dykes built some hundred years back to contain playground games now held the island's blackface flock. Gathered from hill and cliff that morning, they milled round in an iron-fenced area once the teacher's vegetable patch. Behind me, a lifetime of cattle and sheep, familiar sounds and smell of a fank, the two-toned chorus – high-pitched from frightened lambs and the deep baa-baa of worried ewes who knew what was coming. The soapy whiff of sweaty wool, the acid cringe of nervous peeing, add woofing dogs and shouting men as batches were drawn for sorting and you'd a magnet to those with stockmanship in their system. Mine, a lifetime's, but never before the wheeling of seabirds nor the distant sound of a turning tide. Remote from security, devoid of complexity, the challenge of island shepherding.

I walked into a busy day. A dot of red marking fluid on the head of ewe lambs meant they were selected for breeding whilst the wedder lambs got a twirl of blue in their fleeces. The last of the clipping, missed from earlier gathering, awaited the shears. Busy heads looked round – he's just another a 'yachty'. Archie of the handshake in the Isle of Barra Hotel nodded. 'You made it!' was all that passed. 'Yes, and see the bonnie day I've brought you.' My eye covered a pen of quality lambs, admiring the clean horn of thriving growth, the wide jaw of vigour. 'Strong lambs, boys.' A vault over the rail and I was beside Archie and Sandy MacLean, fisherman Roddy, Neil Sinclair, his son Calum, John MacLeod, owner of the *Boy James* and his son Donald Beag, in short a version of the team from the Captain's table getting tallow on their hands. Few shepherds arrived at Mingulay by yacht and catching the Gaelic word for sheep in a phrase spoken quietly by Sinclair, I guessed the rest. 'This bugger's been amongst sheep before.' A high recommendation in Neillie's estimation. When I borrowed his shears, that clinched his assessment.

Early evening brought a heaviness. Motionless air radiated the day's warmth from every hollow of bent grass and rashy bog on the slopes of Hecla. Westering beams highlighted a trillion motes cavorting in the yellow spectrum. An erratic trace, mimicking the conundrum of particle physics – a lump-raising menace for those of tender hide. The midges attacked us in battalions. Clamorous bleating rose a full tone. Highly restive ewes, ear-flicking and head-shaking, wanted away to the fresh ridges and a sniff of Atlantic breath. Ewe lambs destined for the flock were freed and began pumping mothers' udders with an impatience which lifted their hind ends off the ground.

That day no clouds patterned the water; its colour followed the light. The last pen of lambs was handled and the fleeces packed. Hecla darkened – the sun had gone – and, on a ripple-free bay, a deep shade of emerald surrounded the two anchored boats.

Ready, boys? Lambs poured from the playground gate, a stream of leaping and skipping – freedom from lessons or fank, lamb or child, the innocent age. A line of us stretched out a long length of sacking to hold the racing drove from heading for their last suck at the back of Hecla. They made down the track towards the tidal ledges. In behind them with the sacking, steady, get them against the steep rock edge. Little by little, gently, boys, keep the sacking tight, knock back any jumpers. A ring of men and dogs coaxed the nervous creatures, shelf by shelf, towards the sloping ledge which provided a jetty. Woolly bodies pressed tight, the edge of the sloc was close. Keep your feet, man and beast. A straight drop. One went fifty feet and thud. Out of sight. The rest we forced on to the ledge and held. Terrified eyes glinted as the sea glistened and tiny rolls of tide lapped their feet. In rowed John

Joe from the *Boy James* in the white dinghy which the island men called the *St Winifred*.

John Joe was no novice but an ex-ship's bosun, an expert at the oars and, moreover, his people were Mingulay folk. Five years of his life passed as a prisoner of war at the hands of the Japanese. In true bosun fashion, he cut men's hair and, for years to come, he was to give me a trim. A prior pint of Guinness steadied his hand and two to follow completed the deal. On one occasion, he unwrapped the clippers as I sat in the rain on a beer keg at the back door of the Craigard House Hotel. 'Come round to the front,' he said, 'it'll be drier.' Poor John Joe, as pleasant a man as I've known, had memories to hide.

Dinghy ropes were held. The lambs stood silent. Calum ran back to the house for a long rope as Sandy and I edged our way up the innards of a sea cavern. Without weed or barnacle, its throat glittered with seams of pink and grey. The fallen lamb lay on a rumble of stones, far in. It staggered with a broken hip. One lunge and the sorry beast was easily caught. Archie dangled the rope to us, I made a double bowline round the lamb's middle and he hauled away. The lamb sailed aloft – a dangerous pull for the man above.

John Joe sculled a little and held the *St Winifred* broadside to the ledge. Sandy jumped aboard, Archie and I keeping our feet on the slime of ten minutes of evacuated bowels. I captured, he threw, hand under neck, a hold of the tail-head and a lamb flew through the air. Sandy, tall and long-armed, caught and packed the boat. Fifteen a fill and room for the bosun to row them alongside the *Boy James*. From a dinghy rocking against the fishing boat's hull, Sandy, without fuss, grabbed each lamb and, standing on the thwart, lifted it over the rail in one heave. Strength, balance and knack.

A dozen runs and a full deck cargo showed their heads and horns above the rail. An extra burst of bleating came from the school and on the darkening face of Hecla white streams hurried uphill. Roddy and Donald Beag had emptied the fank. I went for *Rhum*'s dinghy. Men, dogs and a wool sack made the last load out to John's boat. 'Follow us up,' he said, 'I've an empty mooring, you're welcome to use it.' Hard on their tail with *Rhum* at full revs, we left a purple island, shapely on the rose sea of a Hebridean gloaming.

Skyline printed outlines, black on mauve and the silver ribbon of evening on a flat Atlantic. East of Vatersay, the *Boy James* slowed for us and, tight on her stern, I learned the short cut between islets that saved rounding Muldoanich. In under the lights of Castlebay pier and *Rhum* laid alongside John's boat as I helped flip her cargo over the rail and drive them up the street past bank door and shop to a grass park behind the hotel. John, or Iagan as they sometimes called him, came aboard the yacht and we picked up his mooring. Chain aboard, *Rhum* safe, any further business? 'You'd better come to the office.' I rowed the dinghy smartly to the village slip. Up the street at a good clip and through a swing door. Ah man, here was the team, impregnated with the smell of a fank, busy on cane-back chairs, damping down its memory. 'A hard day, boys,' John the Bar grinned and turned to the optics. Big George, the boss, shook hands. Archie, Sandy, Neillie Mòr and the rest, legs still in leggings, considered the day's happenings in that home of homes, The Castlebay Bar.

Shorn of the mantle of 'yachty', Barra years unfolded. From the window a dim outline rode her mooring under the walls of Kisimul Castle, the very home for *Rhum*.

# 29

# 'You Pair of Bloody Pirates'

Pipes stuffed with dreams often burn low on reality; those thumbed with inaccessible islands tend to go out. For those confined to Mingulay and paying MacNeil of Barra in manpower to attend the Culloden slaughter, plus £12 a year rent for their 'runrig' livelihood, dreams were of escape. By the winter of 1846–47 under Colonel Gordon's ownership, the rental stood at £82 and the previous summer's continuous rain had led to starving islanders eating their seed corn whilst contending with an outbreak of cholera. Discomfort for his widow, Lady Gordon Cathcart, by then owner of Barra Head, Mingulay and Pabbay in 1910, amounted to the unpaid rents of these perverse natives. To offset impressive arrears or hasten evacuation, or both, over the islanders' heads she leased their grazings to Jonathan MacLean, landlord of Castlebay's Craigard House Hotel. In 1912 the outflanked islanders pushed off to raid Vatersay and MacLean became the buyer of properties vacated by families whose only claim to a home after generations of hardship amounted to a sentimental attachment.

Hopes of profit slumped as fast as sheep dropped off cliffs and lamb ferrying had its 'hairy moments' – a dose of reality which prompted MacLean to flog the isles to John Russell, Esq., a dreamer and wild colonial boy whose shepherding days in Australia and

Montana bolstered his fancy for a life in the Hebridean outback. Seven lambings were to curtail Mr Russell's enthusiasm at the very moment dream island syndrome afflicted a Mrs Peggy Greer. Cast like mayflies on the still waters of Flatford Mill, the chequebook of a Suffolk lady farmer, whose connection to the tip of the Long Island appeared about as distant as the mountains of Montana, landed in the islands.

Had the famed taste of Mingulay tatties reached Southend-on-Sea? If not, she hoped it might. A small, hang-on-to-the-handlebars-and-hurry-behind, two-wheeled Trusty Tractor crawled up the landing rocks with instructions to her helpful shepherd, John MacNeil, to plant potatoes. Patches of the old arable were ploughed. After he'd flitted to Scourie in Sutherlandshire, John related what happened to me as we sat at his fireside. 'You see, Thomson, the sheep didn't touch the shaws so we did get something of a crop.' 'What did you do with them?' Eating seemed too obvious. 'Send them to Essex?' 'Ah, well, no. I'll tell you, we stored them upstairs in Mingulay Church and threw some out to the ewes at the lambing. So the sheep got them in the end and a few went here and there of course. What a taste.'

Given the location, a Saint Columba's church on Mingulay would suggest religious fervour backed by cash. Correct. To the saint's memory, in the closing years of the 1800s, £700 built a substantial two-storey place of worship upon a walled cnoc overlooking the thatched hovels of devout villagers. Its erection was the bold concept of Castlebay's Father Chisholm and Barra merchant, Tad Glancy. The latter, it may be recalled, a name featured in times past on Pabbay when also engaged, though less openly, in matters spiritual. Fire water into fire escape? Whatever. Dressed rock and mortar offset by imported sandstone lintel and corner stone supported a steeply pitched roof of Ballachulish slate. Five rooms off a commodious entrance hall provided accommodation for the visiting priest and his housekeeper. Devotions were via an outside stairway opening into a long church room lit by three east-facing dormer windows. The whole effect, when set against rough stone packed with moss, six-foot eaves and fish nets holding down a thatch which drained rain into the wall heads, imparted an air of permanence, if not a touch of grandeur, to this remarkable religious passion.

Noting four chimney pots, I remarked to Sandy, 'They'll burn a fair stack of peats.' Barely ninety years built and we stood outside the church to consider taking a contract for its repair. Although each westerly gale peeled slates from the back roof, ten days' work should see it watertight. 'What's it like inside?' We pushed the door into a sickly sweet smell. Tentacles of wet rot climbed walls of faded blue emulsion. Broken laths stuck out of ribcage ceilings. The steady drip of rain driven under slates made circles of rot on floorboards carpeted with fallen plaster and broken coombing. A decaying carcass in need of gutting. I climbed the stairs to a church room of gaping holes and stained rafters. Its frameless windows looked down on the dotted heaps of homes filling with sand – a culture already gutted.

We spoke quietly, touched nothing, the incense of holiness lingered, perhaps in our minds, for the altar made by John MacKinnon, the last Mingulay joiner, was taken by the leaving people to serve as a side altar in Castlebay Church. An Eriskay priest said the first mass in Mingulay Church. The following day, no less a person than the Bishop of Argyll and the Isles confirmed forty-four children gathered from the three islands. Bare feet, hand-me-down clothes and Sunday shyness, fifty years later, spread on the same floor, a few tatties, gathered from fields of innocence.

Luneberg Heath, May 1945, VE Day, and the demob lads with carnage fresh in their minds wanted semi-detached homes and a welfare state; they more than deserved both. Unlike today, uninhabited islands, peripheral to picture house and chip shop, found no appeal and Mrs Greer was stuck with three. Perhaps the Mingulay fire robbed her of her enthusiasm – it certainly curtailed any profit. A tiring day, gathering and shearing. 'No humphing wool sacks to the landing tonight, boys.' A year's clip packed the schoolroom. MacNeil the shepherd and his helpers rowed out to a waiting boat. One turned. 'What's the smoke, John?' A thick column rose from more than the old school's chimney pot. They hurried back. Leaping flames fired crackling slates high in the air; the nearest water was eighty yards up the burn and they only had pails. Sweat and blackened faces, but luckily the inferno failed to consume the teacher's house. The school roof crashed and with it Mrs Greer's island venture. A 'For Sale' sign hung on the rocks in a buyer's market.

Two MacDonald daughters, Bel and Morag, were to marry Barra crofting friends, Lachlan MacLean of Craigston, a fertile holding on the west side of the island, and Neil Sinclair, a fisherman-crofter from the township of Ledaig just round the tideway from Castlebay. The girls' father, a Protestant miller's son from North Uist, came to a croft in Allasdale just over the ridge from Craigston. Known as Archie Beag, he took to sheep dealing, a trade which goes with being 'a bit of a character'. MacDonald was both and his sons-in-law weren't far behind in the banter stakes. Who'd married the bargain? 'Now, Lach, you got a topper!' A wink to me. 'Well, Neil, you didn't do bad if she'll put up with you!' And the two women would laugh. If hard work and kindness be coupled to consideration and family values, then I'd call it a draw. Softly spoken women, wise and gentle ways, staunch to the last in the old belief, I came a stranger to their table and was welcomed as one of the family. What more to count?

Lach's wife Bel, in the way of the island women, milked the house cow, helped with hay and harvest and brought up four sons and a daughter. Lach had a good pair of hands and could turn them to most jobs. During the war, he built RAF runways down in England, driving heavy machines never seen on Barra – a fair step from the concreting of his byre when sacks of sand and gravel were pushed a mile from the beach slung on the crossbar of his bike. The croft-land at Craigston, though not so extensive as the north end of Barra, lies to the sun, is rich in shell lime and its level acres are easy on a pony's shoulders at the ploughing. Communal hill pastures rise abruptly from the flats in a series of rocky outcrops. Many years later, Sandy and I fenced this hill ground. The hardness of its Lewisian gneiss had the compressor drill 'stotting' and required us to take lunchtime rests at the Isle of Barra Hotel.

Lach MacLean farmed with attention to fencing, drains, tatties, hay and oats and the quality of half-bred lambs his land was fully able to produce. By the time Archie, his farming son, returned from agricultural college in Ayrshire, the crofting lifestyle had parted company from a decent income but the island needed a modern slaughterhouse, and in 1980 the concept of Barra Meats came into being. A huge steel box with doors, empty except for an overhead track-way, arrived at Craigston and, with plenty of laughs and the help of various locals, Archie and I built on the facilities it needed. Ronnie Cramond, my pal from the days of NFU junkets and by then director of the Highlands and Islands Development Board, performed the opening ceremony with gusto and, thanks to a little raiding party down to Rosinish Point, also enjoyed a taste of Pabbay lamb. One of the Board's better projects has since grown to a successful business. That year of its building, the Fergie tractor pulled a horse mower as Archie and I cut the last crop of corn on Craigston. It dried where it fell, in long rows on the 'bout', and we made bales with an ancient hay baler which Sandy coaxed into action. Crofting's manual labour and outmoded crop rotations retreated before B & B at £10 a night. Lach watched us from the window, declining years for him and his lifestyle.

Bel, his wife, had always a three-course supper on the kitchen table at six. Archie likened me to a gannet – we ate so well. I sat on a horsehair couch by the window and, from underneath, Rab the collie pushed his nose to my hand. Lach moved his chair to the Rayburn and lit a cigarette. Our day's work was covered so then came world affairs. The years put a stick at his side but failed to overtake Lach's brain or outlook. As a slim young man, at the Barra Games along on Borve Machair, he could outstrip the best and, sixty years before any thought of a swimming pool coming to Castlebay, the beach had fitted him to be a water-polo player for his regiment. Breeding top lambs for the Oban sales powered his crofting interest and the politics of a thriving industry, as it was after the war, took him on to the Crofters' Panel. Disgust at paper farming overtaking sound practice became a topic between us in the back shed as he cut sticks for the fire in his latter years.

Rheumatic hips confined him before the death of Bel took its toll. He was the older by a little and had wished to go first. Their joining was not long to be. We thought alike, talked the same underpinning sympathies. One hand could count those I have held in such regard. Craigston, the mother church of Barra, a step from his door, a Gaelic service simple as a burial on the machair beside the Atlantic. Sun and warmth graced the void. I held a cord at his grave – a privilege and lasting bond.

Archie Beag's son, 'Non', was rated the most imperturbable man I ever met. He gave up his small slaughterhouse on the east side of

Barra to spend many years as the respected Castlebay pier-master. CalMac skippers came and went. One happened to be Iain Dewar, a friend who, during early sailing trips on *Rhum*, gave me navigation tips needing only pencil, chart and compass. He skippered the Oban–Castlebay run on a day when the yacht sat motionless and fog bound the bay – the two-yard type.

The *Clansman* approached Barra, making good time at full knots and tooting her foghorn. On the end of the pier, waiting to take her ropes, Calum Sinclair, or Calum Neillie as he's known, and Archie, the pier-master's son, stood listening. They looked at each other. 'She's coming at a fair toot.' It was the very verb, taking invisibility into account. On her bridge Captain Dewar studied the radar. 'Hard a'starboard, helmsman.' 'Shouldn't we slow down a little, Captain?' 'No, I've a clear picture.' Fatal words, the screen went blank. Kisimul Castle demolished by a CalMac steamer? No, missed by a coat of paint but not the pier. Ship's bows rose suddenly above the boys' heads. They ran for their lives. Crash. Crumple. Dewar walked down the gang plank to study a buckled bow. Passengers stood in silence and took off their hats. Up to the pier office he strode. Poor Iain – one of CalMac's top skippers was the victim of a gadget. 'I'll get the phone for you, Captain,' 'Non' remarked quietly.

◆

Barra Head is also known as Berneray and its Norse name is Bjorn's Isle, the northern seafarers having made a limited settlement there and left boat graves in the lee of its central ridge. Long prior, on the Atlantic-eaten cliffs, less restless Iberian peoples had built a dun of galleried walls. Watchtower or defensive, it stood in the salt-laden updrafts from pounding breakers atop seven hundred feet of sheer drop. 'Lighthouse' Stevenson spotted the potential, drew plans and engaged a James Smith of Inverness as building contractor. Employees laboured in gales which rolled a forty-ton rock, and on another occasion the blast overturned their horse and flung its cart into the air.

Sturdiness outbid height for the twelve thousand pounds it took to build this light, the second constructed in the Outer Hebrides after Scalpay, Harris. Three classically proportioned cottages surrounding a flagged courtyard lie under the less elegant tubby tower and were connected to the lighthouse balcony by speaking tube. At a little distance from the households, the families' loneliness and remoteness are measured by the graves of keepers and their children recorded on the plaque in a stoutly walled burying ground on the edge of the cliff. Three summers saw the lighthouse built and, in 1833, oil-fired lamps were flashing thirty miles over the Atlantic. Neillie Sinclair, for years a keeper and polisher of the reflecting mirrors, showed me the brass and steel mechanism which had produced their occulting effect. 'One flash every fifteen seconds,' he said, rightly proud.

Thirty years after Stevenson's light became operative, a Captain Otter skippered the *Shamrock* under an Admiralty commission to take soundings off the Barra islands. With him travelled globetrotting writer Isabella Bird, a lady whose memory is recalled on a iron Victorian casting at the pier in Tobermory. Otter anchored off the Barra Head slip and came ashore to a tumultuous welcome from the islanders. Isabella was charmed as she avoided slipping on a fish-oily jetty, to be greeted by Duncan Sinclair, the incomer and sole Protestant. Norse origins, via Normandy and Caithness to Argyllshire before you reach Barra Head? To defy the Catholics, General Roderick MacNeil of Barra brought this Protestant shepherd to Vatersay. Was it to better himself this man took his wife and chattels to a croft on an island with small hint of civilisation beyond a landing slip? Be that as it may, Sinclair proudly escorted Isabella to 'the lightest, cleanest, best appointed Highland hut I ever entered'. Driftwood furniture balanced the luxury of tea and tobacco.

For such a momentous occasion, the women folk wore their homespun striped winceys and crinolines flared by the hoops of shipwreck barrels as wooden bowls of cream were served. During the party, Duncan's ten-year-old boy dived from a rock and swam out to the *Shamrock* returning dripping and ruddy to read aloud a passage from the English Bible his father had traded for a box of dried skate, the island's currency. The lively-minded Berneray folk were healthy and self-reliant. Miss Bird admired their intelligence and learned of a lifestyle that involved pole-catching cliff birds and drying fish, lifting tatties and salting a lamb in October. Isolation? Yes, but hardship, in contrast to Glasgow life for the common man of that era? Bread riots by the industrialised proles of the cotton giants, the Calton Weavers' uprising, which was followed some thirty years later by a strike at the Carron Ironworks that led to the Battle of Bonnymuir and the hanging of Wilson, Hardie and Baird for High Treason. The Gorbals had a battery-cage system for housing factory fodder. Pissing in the sink, squalor without an exit. Hardly so streetwise however, the islanders got their first sighting of a black man – not the devil, as they feared, but the *Shamrock*'s Negro cook. Miss Bird's lingering impression? The generosity of a people who had so little.

Another of Duncan's sons, Padraig Mòr or Big Patrick, remained at his Barra Head home long after other children moved to Mingulay and Barra. As a premature baby of just a few pounds, he was wrapped in plucks of wool that awaited the spinning wheel and given a day to live. In Nordic times, one glance from his father could have labelled such a weakling not worth rearing and exposure out of earshot would conclude the appraisal. Genes thriving or unrefined cod liver oil, milk, mutton, tatties and herring grew a man of exceptional size and strength – a cert for the helm of any longship. True to Norse genes, cattle and seamanship also entwined. Each spring, Padraig ferried his newly calved cows from Barra Head to Castlebay and milked them as the village's mobile dairy. Further afield, a travelling show billed him the 'Barra Giant', and at six foot eight with strength to match it wasn't far wrong. A season or two of strongman curtain calls and he lost a taste for 'rollup, rollup', Cheap John's, proclaiming his bar-bending feats alongside wicker baskets full of pottery rejects. Lifting a heavy anvil above his head to amuse a few locals on Castlebay pier, his strength was to bring about his death. The anvil slipped from his hand and killed him.

Although Barra Head's advantage of a concrete landing slip gave modest access in settled weather and its teeming fish stocks created something of a boom at the turn of the eighteen hundreds, the island lacked two vital commodities – peat banks and schooling. A bed of straw on the floor for children lying under a plaid was out; literacy was in. Barra Head's last boat, *The Three Brothers*, belonged to Peter Sinclair and it was time to make Castlebay the family base. In the spring of 1911, he was the last man to leave Barra Head. A croft at

Ledaig became the Sinclair home, yet it still meant the sea and fishing.

Neillie Mòr's father became coxswain of the Barra lifeboat and, when wartime's SS *Politician*, making for America, steamed up the wrong side of the Long Island and found the bottom of the Eriskay Sound, he was first aboard to save her crew. From the heroics of lifesaving, attention focused on saving her cargo – a specialist operation by its nature, requiring the minimum of illumination of either moon or the authorities, plus a goodly supply of spades. Wads of newly printed dollar notes sloshing about the hold were ignored. George Washington may have frowned but Johnnie Walker had fallen amongst true friends. A wreck deserted by day became a hive of industry by night. An armada of little boats jostled alongside, each pulled away with water lapping at the gunnels and a salute from upturned bottles. On beaches were stacked case upon case to service a distribution system backed by consumption. Sinclair quietly assisted in an exercise ennobling the cause of free trade. The Viking spirit lived on, yet to be dimmed in Barra by the punctilious.

Ledaig saw the rearing of eleven Sinclairs – nine girls and two boys. Morag, resilient as her sister Bel, worked between children and croft in the spells Neil was away at sea. In the same manner of Craigston, I was made at home – a meal on the table when I fenced about their croft. A patient woman who, after putting a last tea and sandwich through to us, would go quietly to bed and leave Neil and me to a dying fire and stories which grow old. By comparison to the MacLean's fields round at Craigston the croft-land at Ledaig was hard and unyielding. No matter – what farming lost, fishing gained. There was a good shingle beach for hauling boats and, of equal importance in latter years, from a comfortable bungalow, the panoramic front window offered coverage of all the bay's activities – each steamer's gangplank contingent; the morose gathering on the Royal Bank's doorstep; or, more significantly, those exercising the swing door of The Castlebay Bar. Entrances and exits, all could be scrutinised. Those who faced the doom of a bank grill or the escaping uplift of 'elevenses', each came under the sharp eye of a man who knew every trick of the sea and most especially the movements of every boat in the bay.

In flat calm, *Rhum* lay to her mooring beside Kisimul Castle when, with some slight twist, the ground chain slipped its shackle and the yacht began to drift imperceptibly towards the rocks. I was away on the mainland. Neillie, on retirement duties, was sitting at the command-post window when his eye caught her drift. His hand made for the telephone. John Allan, the lifeboat coxswain, lifted his phone, looked out and was aboard in minutes to make her safe. The first man aboard a drifting vessel may legally claim her as salvage but pirate days were generations astern. John Allan MacNeil in the lifeboat house above the pier had become a byword in Barra for seamanship, courage and judgement.

The waters off the lighthouse of Skerryvore suddenly become shallow and take the full thrashing of any Atlantic storm. Seventy miles of sea compressed between the Outer Hebrides and Northern Ireland rises in waves of terrifying proportions. A hurricane from the south-west lashed them into frenzy and, at midnight, a 'Mayday, Mayday' was received at the lifeboat house. In minutes, the Barra lifeboat powered out from Kisimul. A ship was floundering, drifting towards Skerryvore. Forty miles, running beam seas, putting her stern to the big ones. 'I looked up at a wall – couldn't see the crest.' John Allan's eyes saw it again.

> She'll never make it. She started to dip her anchor on the shoulder. I knew she was going. We pitch-poled, head over heels. Lights went out, the engine stalled, a rope in the prop. It took a few minutes but the self-righting gear did operate and we turned up and lay abeam, disabled. The Islay lifeboat went over that night, making for the same rescue.

For those who have not been to sea, a film entitled *The Perfect Storm* catches similar effects.

Lifeboat engineer Ruairidh MacLean, home from deep sea and married to one of the Sinclair girls, spoke of the night, 'We took turns freeing her prop, cutting away the rope – a few hours' work and we had her underway on one engine. Nothing we could do then but make for home – we hadn't the power.' 'More than jam on the ceiling, Roddy?' 'Aye, a bit of a mess,' he smiled and went on in unassuming manner to speak of his coxswain 'What a man John

Allan, what a seaman.' Two days later, with the lifeboat back in commission 'Mayday' rang again. Lifeboat away – same crew, same indomitable spirit in the helping of others.

After the war Neillie Mòr continued the fishing, Archie Beag MacDonald pursued his dealing and Lach MacLean was expanding his crofting enterprises at Craigston, when an 'islands for sale' advert in the *Oban Times* announced the cooling of Mrs Greer's infatuation for Mingulay. MacDonald's eye never faulted on a deal. Neil's fell on islands from which his family had migrated. Lach was a sheep-man to the core. Hasty phone calls and a meeting between the dealer, his two sons-in-law and a couple of fishing boat owners, Domhnall William MacLeod and John MacLeod, established the Barra Head Isles Sheepstock Company. Lach and Neil knew sheep, Donald William, John knew the sea and their boats solved the transport problem. Shares were drawn up and fourteen thousand pounds, no small sum in the 1950s to crofter-fishermen rearing families, meant the three isles were triumphantly back in the hands of locals.

To lighten the bill, seven thousand was recouped from the sale of the church house to a Mr Archer who stayed in it a couple of times before the tiring of his investment which hastened the building's collapse. By contrast, enthusiasm for the company project had Lach and Neil shouldering fencing material from the sea-level landing at Skipisdale out to the west side of Mingulay's nine-hundred foot cliff in their attempt to cut down on sheep suicide.

Cliff edges fertilised by bird droppings grew lush grass and encouraged the sheep to hop from one to another without considering an exit strategy. Either by gale or a ledge eaten to bare rock, a cheerio ticket arrived. Headlong into the sea. Equally dangerous was fencing off this death trap, even for two fit young men. Wet grass, sudden updraughts . . . don't speak about it. But there were pleasant evenings in the bothy over a dram. The only detraction was that Neil's snoring rattled the slates more effectively than the Barra Head foghorn and left Lach bleary-eyed each morning.

Overnight stays at sheep handlings or general work turned the schoolhouse into a bothy. Ex-army beds of the cross-wire mesh and solid mattresses variety filled the two attic bedrooms. Army blankets that were hung on door corners between trips to discourage mould rather encouraged the use of sleeping bags. Downstairs, the living room, for whatever reason, exuded a homely, welcome-on-the-mat feeling. Was it the simplicity, the total absence of other contact or perhaps an 'in from the storm effect' – that feel-good survival response affecting all life forms – or did the essence of a happiness enjoyed by the house's early occupants remain? Anyway, I sensed it time and again – even in writing about it, the sensation remains. I'm fonder of the old semi-ruin than any house I've known.

A scrub top table stood behind the wooden door and, on the back wall, a tall dresser, bequeathed by the last teacher in 1908, was stacked with assorted crockery of similar vintage. Intriguingly, its top shelf displayed a large collection of label-less tins – ex-army rations dating from a commando exercise in 1947. Two mantles lit by Calor gas jutted on curved arms from the heirloom's head-piece, their glass bowls long gone. On the gable wall, a massive enamel-fronted gas stove, befitting of any Victorian mansion, grilled our breakfasts and boiled tea water in a two-gallon kettle. A gas cylinder tucked in the corner flanked its one side and a bench and a galvanised pail with water straight from the burn, the other. Washing up? Simple – on the window ledge in an orange plastic basin supplied by the tide. And, for those tending hairstyles, a mirror hung in good light, with the door open.

Lift the hatch to a living room of emulsioned primrose yellow, past its best. Tongue and groove boarding, a faded Indian rug – a gem from a Pakistani salesman – the faint carbolic smell of sheep-dip, a bargain for some persistent agri-rep, and worn wooden boards whose joists hinted at the mustiness of under-floor rot. A distinctive sensation often augmented by the haze of bacon and eggs crackling on the stove. Twixt door and table a grandfather chair, strengthened by wire ties and polished by Neillie over many years, had fallen to me. Archie manipulated the cooker from a second grandfather chair and took the top end of the table when the grub was ready. Sandy, an ace at manipulating cans, took side place. Donald Beag sat by the window whilst the younger gatherers, Calum Neil, sometimes his brother, Donald Archie, the red-haired Donald William, Roddy MacLeod's son, and Sandy's nephew, the sheep-keen Iain Ruairidh, together with various helpers, perched along the benches to catch the stories from old hands. Outside, sunshine drove mists from Hecla and dogs, waiting for a move, put noses on paws as their growls died. Out on a turquoise bay, the *Boy James* lay to the tide. Faint white ripples showed its strength. Iagan would stay aboard to watch her anchor for, if she dragged and no one was on board, we were stuck.

Plans for the gathering required settled weather and a round or two in The Castlebay. A touch of north in the wind, nights without darkness, the raiding days of old. Sometimes it was Roddy's blue-hulled *Spray* that drew away from the pier. Sticks, oilskins, a box of rations. Lively talk and dogs, tails up, running the deck. Islands churned past, colours bright as the June light bounced off our wake. Roddy, one hand on the wheel, laughs and jokes, until close in, on a band of mist above the shore, rested the hills of Mingulay.

I walked out one gathering with John Joe. We made for the ridge by way of the sanded ruins above the Traigh Mhòr. Our step took us over the last of an encircling stone dyke and into the burying ground, a mossy hummock whose marram grass in trailing clumps entwined the pale-leafed silverweed with bird's-foot trefoil and hid the nesting skylark. Village and graves were as one, no distance lay between. Pebble sand and cement, a fish box mould. It made the cross, now half-buried, angled by the gale. John Joe knelt before another, bared a bowing head. His folks belonged to the island, to a village dead of people, alive in murmured prayer.

We climbed to the ridge which ran north from the shoulder of Carnan. On a bright green sward of sedge and moss, sea milkwort scattered in dots of crimson, hiding the most rare of Hebridean plants, the sea holly. Here stone-piled 'cleits' faced the full Atlantic – Iron Age graves, Viking burials or stores for birds caught by noose? Maybe one use became the other – who would know? – but corpses, rotting or curing, heard every note the wind could play. Who knows what the dead may hear? With a suddenness, the turf ends. Nothing prepares for the edge of the great cliff. A cavity in space beneath your feet. A staggering enormity, tempting, pulling, insane with the attraction of vertigo. A hideous black chasm, gnawed from the igneous thrusts of a young earth that blew molten magma, flaming and pouring, to build this dungeon of no return. Unclimbed, no steps, from the pit of a ravenous sea, its tongue flicking white and deliberate. A shepherd's stick, propped to my chest, balanced the tugging draught. Falling, so simple. What thoughts are carried by the crawling seconds which tick us to eternity?

The cliff's name is Biulacraig, the rallying cry of Clan MacNeil, and a hundred years past or more, its surging currents were the nursery flights of the majestic white-tailed eagle. Bird of isolation, aristocrat of sea-born cliff, master of the gale, it was victim of the pathetic 'sportsman'. Ammonia saturated the funnelled air which blew in my face. Beady eyes floated at my feet as I craned over as far as I dared. Wing upon wing spiralled below, smaller and smaller amidst an endless screeching – a fractal pattern upon a restless screen of foam, defying all analyses. A living precipice spattered white with droppings and every sea pink ledge home to egg or chick. Kittiwake and spitting fulmar, the killer blackback that takes the fallen nestling. Worlds within worlds that question our blatant certainty and, beyond their living stench, the Atlantic rolls its blue-black distance and curves the sky to the pureness of a circle.

Ferocious seas lash these cliffs, blasting spray to their tops. No sheep that descended to a ledge will live. Burrowing seas smashed the arch which once held the huge stac of Lianamul to Mingulay. It lay to my north as I waited for Calum and his father's old dog Sweep to move the ewes and lambs which stood watching my young dog Voe, a promising lad if ever there was. I got him a pup from Ali Flaws in Shetland and he lived with me aboard the yacht, canine Mensa and character combined. Once in a westerly gale off the Point of Sleat, I'd run into Mallaig for shelter and hardly alongside when the pier-master cup-handed down, 'Move round to the inner harbour,' and cast us off. I turned *Rhum* about, towing the inflatable. Voe, not a year old, for some reason took a flying leap into it. Moments later a violent gust sent dog and dinghy sailing in the air. Fishing boats powered in. Alone, I needed all my time to handle *Rhum*. Voe was on his own without a life jacket.

I caught the baleful white of his eye as he looked back at me before setting off, his head disappearing in and out of the waves as he swam on a straight course, three hundred yards to the further shore. I saw him climb the bank, shake his coat and trot towards the village. By the time I swung *Rhum* to her berth, to my utter surprise, his paws and a wag of the tail were on the edge of the harbour wall above me. No sign of reproach in his greeting as I took up the ropes. Come evening, he and I made up for a pint. 'Is this your dog?' enquired a chap, patting Voe's head. 'I saw him come down the main street this afternoon, dodging the traffic and trying a bitch some women had on a lead.' I pulled Voe's ear. 'That's my boy.' A year or two later I gave him to Kenny 'the Manager' in Achiltibuie. Near Isle Oronsay pier on the Isle of Skye, a car which Voe didn't dodge killed him. Wise, top dog who'd kept 'the Manager' right and a miss.

The art of gathering on dangerous ground lies in anticipation of the sheep's mind. Man and dog place themselves cannily at the exact point of a circle which heads the animals along a route towards an experience which they strenuously wish to avoid. Equally, sheep read the shepherd's intention and know if he or his dog has left an escape route. It's a three-mind operation. This gathering fully qualified. One eye held the ewes looking down at me, stamping an odd foot and still to budge, my other viewed the unnerving scape of ground that plunged vertical over an abyss at my feet and rose beyond to the bird-hovering sea-stac of Lianamul. It's said the fowlers swung over to this pillar on a horsehair rope. Hundreds and hundreds of birds were taken using a noose on a pole. Razorbill, puffin, guillemot and shearwater went into salted winter rations at the price of death from falling.

I crouched. Buffeting winds sometimes took the ceaseless bird cries away from the unremitting thump of the sea. As middle man in the gathering line, I watched the narrow neck of sheep track which connected, by natural arch, the dun to Mingulay. John MacNeil told me that, in his shepherding days, he rowed through it. Never again, he said – intense gloom and a premonition that one day it would crash and make the dun into a stac. On the west side of this grim bastion, a cave perches above the Atlantic. There a Barra priest, Father Grant, went into hiding after the '45. His betrayal to red-coated Hanoverians prowling the Hebrides was, strange to say, by one of the villagers. Intense guilt and haunting voices drove the informant to America.

At last, time to move. I whistled up to Calum who came into line with a cut of sheep to join my watching bunch. Sheep were now threading off The Dun. Archie's voice shouted to Rab. At one gathering, I'd seen a dog go too hard. A ewe bolted, lost her footing. Eight hundred feet, two bumps into free fall. The angle of the slope I followed was severe; the penalty of a slip, the more so. Sandy, out on the high top, fleet feet in light black shoes, long legs flying, turned ewes and lambs off the shoulder of Carnan for Calum and Sweep to push round. I held the ground above the cliff. Ewes were racing down, I ran below them, relieved as the slope eased off. Archie held the track back on to The Dun. Lines of sheep strung ahead of us, ewes calling lambs, hurrying mums looking back, hearing our whistles and seeing the driving dogs. Round the south side of Mingulay on hoof-beaten tracks, the cliffs are lower and grazing kindly. There Barra Head is stark across a Sound, whose pouring tides are breasted by the islet of Geirum Mòr. Crofters, to their last days before abandoning Barra Head, hoisted wedders to fatten on its guano-green top. Watching a storm in the 1860s, they saw a gigantic wave, a hundred and eighty feet judging by the height of the isle, which smothered the summit and washed away their sheep.

I turned my glass on the islet – sheer sides, a fertile cap and a supposed chapel or hermit cell. Some holy man seeking mortification of his soul through dread of the raw forces that pounded his eyrie? Aesthetics apart, he needed rock-climbing ability. I closed the glass. Sheep lined along winding trails, over the remains of field dyke and stone circle. The freshness of the breeze came off a sea blinding with sunlight. Light in electromagnetic brilliance, hill and shore, wild and primitive, untrammelled by trash. Humps that were homes held the feel of passing seasons and the minds of a people who saw their freedom as space.

As I crossed the burn which flows to Skipisdale, without warning, a huge bird attacked me, hooked beak, wings beating at my head. A dark mottled body and white flashes prominent on its wings, the mate of a nesting great skua. Swooping close, he meant business. I beat him off with my stick and ran across the undulations which were the last dwellings of Skipisdale. They seemed friendly in the way that stones promise shelter when a gale beats with rain, warm when their cattle came in to a milking. The sheep crossed ahead of me and followed the shoulder of Hecla. Archie had the longest round, down by the shore where the bulk of the sheep now milled.

I ran down to help, the keen dog Voe tight to heel. Small groups of ewes and lambs tried to break back. Run, shout and wave, a few still made it. Donald Beag held the shoulder of Hecla. A bleating gathering drew together above the landing. The boat at anchor swung its reflections on the bay. The flock squeezed through the schoolhouse gate. Neillie stood at the door, tea-towel on his arm, 'Well, boys, you made it. What kept you?'

◆

Several years of working on the islands passed. The idea of living on Mingulay for a summer strongly appealed. It would require a smallish boat that I could handle easily – in fact, a second *Mrs Seal*. I bought a similar fourteen-footer from Jim Hogan at Caley Marina in Inverness, named her *Mingulay* and, one autumn, towed her out of Gairloch astern of *Rhum* on twenty fathoms of plaited rope. Roughish conditions hurried us round Rubha Hunish on the north point of Skye and into Loch Dunvegan to anchor west of MacLeod's castle and wait for a break in the weather. A lull came at midnight. Up anchor and I threaded out from the scatter of islets at the head of the loch on flashing lights. The silhouette of Dunvegan Head against breaking stars set my course for South Uist. Once in The Minch, a heavy beam sea was running. Neist Lighthouse is on the most westerly point of Skye and I'd no sight of its flash. Visibility was closing. At intervals, I shone a torch along the tow rope to check that *Mingulay* was still attached. Its woolly beam could just pick out a small craft, a white dolphin leaping over crests, diving out of sight in the troughs. I feared she might roll and go down. A slack of rope during a dip and I took a turn on the port winch to take strain off the stern cleat. Progress was sluggish. A dense sea fog had enveloped The Minch. Gone was any chance of sighting the lighthouse on South Uist for a bearing. Speed and distance – I must be well across? The fog ahead suddenly reflected a yellow glow. In moments, a six-foot pillar flashing a bright yellow was alongside. It vanished astern. Tie the tiller down to the chart table, not on the chart. Tow rope, tide and swell, *Rhum* making a lot of leeway? Too far north? Benbecula? A lee shore? How tight would *Rhum* take the wind? Only the working jib was set. Haul sheet on the starboard winch. She came round ten degrees. Enough? Come on, daylight! It arrived, groggy with lousy visibility. Hills and islands appeared in the nick of time. The heavy swell pushed us amongst skerries. Was that an island?

I swung her nose to wind – a dull flap, flap of sail. Get the tow rope off the port winch. On to stern cleat, quick. Will she come through the wind? We lost way. *Mingulay* slithered alongside. No engine running, at least no tow rope fouling the prop. Gybe her round, wind to tail. *Rhum* slowly pulled over, weathered her way between a small island and a low grey skerry. Safe passage or hidden rocks? I stood on the cockpit locker, foot on the tiller, eyes straining into a thinning fog for any dark lump or hint of broken water.

Out clear, The Minch again, lucky *Rhum*. Chart table. 'Oh, Thomson, boy!' I spoke aloud with relief. Loch Eynort lay to the north and Loch Boisdale, five miles south. We'd been amongst the Stuley skerries, off the South Uist coast, not a place to play. Gloom and the sea fog lifted as I anchored over from the CalMac jetty and sauntered to the Loch Boisdale Hotel. Next day a fresh sou-easter made a spanking sail down to Castlebay in weather that put a curl on the sea and had *Mingulay* jigging astern, frothing through the tops to salutes from an Eriskay fishing boat which hauled past us. Mid Minch at three in the morning, a yellow light? Enquiries in the Castlebay Bar drew a blank.

◆

Ledaig croft needed a cattle grid at its road end. 'Not a problem, Neil – we'll make you a topper, fitted and complete, side fences, the lot, £600.' Contractors, MacLean and Thomson, anywhere, anytime, nothing too tricky, we assured Neillie as he sat on his favourite Saturday night back-to-the-wall pew in our company's business premises. 'On you go, boys.' A glance and twirl of the finger and John the Bar brought a clinching round. Some time later, it could be said much, and the deal well sealed, the swing door closed thoughtfully. 'We'll need to find lengths of steel somewhere, Sandy,' I communicated the obvious as his tall figure aimed towards the lights of a car in which waited his loving wife, Kirsty Peggy. 'Don't worry, Thomson, boy – I have a plan. We'll take *Rhum* and your wee boat next gathering. Have you a decent screwdriver aboard?' I quoted our company maxim, 'Not a problem.' And I steered for pier and dinghy – something more of a problem.

'*Rhum* ahoy!' wakened me. The sun was ablaze and busy making reflections off the sea on the cabin ceiling. I looked out of the cockpit. DP and Iain Beag had created the disturbance. 'Have you a big screwdriver and some sort of penetrating oil?' 'No problem, Donald.' 'Some demand for screwdrivers on an island that makes do with nails,' I muttered, rummaging about before handing over an aerosol can and a hefty red-handled driver as DP brought his dinghy alongside. They headed over to the castle slip and advanced on MacNeil's fortification. Iain knelt before its studded portal. Surely not a saintly invocation? No, he appeared to be fiddling at something. DP put in the boot, I heard the crash and Kisimul's invincible door flew open. Back they came. 'Come aboard, boys! A victory – the first time in history MacNeil's symbol of terror has been stormed by two men, a screwdriver and a squirt of rust remover.'

We sat in the cockpit. The water-lapped pile of a castle would be chilly after the winter. A tourist season loomed – as did a resumption of DP's ferrying duties. 'The castle'll be bit damp for the tourists, Donald?' 'Not as damp as some of them,' he said, implying his trippers tended to be on the wet side. 'Slàinte Mhòr!' Long pause. 'You and Sandy are making brother Neil a cattle grid, they tell me?' 'Probably.' Pause. 'Anyway we're clipping down on Mingulay tomorrow if this weather holds.' 'It will and be sure and make your contraption soundproof,' he advised, looking over at the church clock. Ten to eleven, Captain DP Sinclair, a stickler for punctuality, made the office doorstep on the dot.

A grey even sea awaited dawn. *Rhum* eased through the short cut and past Vatersay Bay in half-light with the wee boat in tow. 'Make for Barra Head,' Sandy instructed. I set the autopilot and fried bacon and egg. Island followed island until Mingulay came abeam. One sound to cross and we anchored off Barra Head slip. 'Take that big screwdriver,' Sandy instructed. Without comment, I rowed *Mingulay* into the landing. A lighthouse equipment shed stood above the slip, padlocked and secure. Not for long. A pile of hinge screws and we were in without even touching the padlock. The value of a screwdriver was revealed – as was a smart red Fergie tractor, the pride of Neillie Sinclair, the last lighthouse keeper. No battery. 'It'll never start, Sandy.' 'Wait you.' He climbed on, I pushed and the pair flew downhill towards the sea. 'I hope he ejects in time.'

A jump start averted immersion and the stunt man reversed up the slipway through a cloud of fumes, only to be followed by the densest, most saturating of morning fogs. It quickly hid *Rhum*, the little *Mingulay* boat and the whole world as we drove up the track to the lighthouse. Mist weaved amongst tumbled stone work. A house was built into the dripping bank. One window ledge remained of the home of Neillie Mòr's shepherding forebear. Box-bed and curtain on the back wall, children ben the room, hardy by necessity, captured in the peace of Barra Head – the price?

My driver stopped under shattering foghorn blasts and we walked down a slope, past the byre in which lighthouse keepers had kept their milk supply and there, in the corner overgrown of a dyke, was a horde of brass fittings and long lengths of beautiful steel tubing, even painted white. 'The very stuff, Sandy – top-quality Stevenson.' 'Well, they didn't want it when the light was being modernised so "somebody" cached it here. Everything has its use – it only needs somebody to bring things together.' We set off for the slip. Fifteen lengths tied behind our 'hired' tractor trailed their ends down the track. With the tractor housed, everything neat and tidy and hinges re-screwed, in no time we had the ends of a fair load of steel poking over the stern of *Mingulay*. No move in the fog. Too early for burn-off, still, it had the promise of a blistering day – handy cover too if the rest of the gathering team aboard *Reul na Maidne* appeared early.

'Head for Skipisdale.' 'Right, boy.' Skipisdale, from Old Norse meaning 'ship valley', was a Viking haven on the south side of Mingulay. Most appropriate. I took distance and bearing on the chart. 'Stand on the bow, Sandy, and shout loud – land's bound to show in ten minutes.' Towing our 'find' with dry ice swirling round Sandy's legs we coasted gingerly over the Sound. 'Whoa, whoa.' Into reverse. Damn smart. Fend off the cargo. Only inches separated a smash, front and back. We lay a-hull, eyes X-raying the fog. A dent indicated some sort of hollow. 'This is it.' Sandy nipped into *Mingulay* and poked her into a tiny cliff-flanked slit. Knobbles of rock on and above its ledges couldn't be better placed. Four lines left the tow boat in the centre, floating clear. Not the first plunder to lie snug. A Viking depot – pity no horsehair ropes. 'OK now, boy?' 'Fine.' Each shout called back, un-choked by the fog. A flat sea gurgled under ledges. Who listened? I touched the nose of *Rhum* towards the protruding lengths of metal. Sandy crouched like a frog. One leap – tricky.

No outlying rocks, we crept away, groping round the south end of Mingulay, just yards off. Grey figures peered down. Cliff pillars in swirling nightshirts, silent and clammy. I watched the depth sounder. A short red flash on the dial – thirty feet under the keel. Track the four-fathom contour. The compass followed round to due west. Quicker than comfort, the bleep indicated two fathoms. Twelve feet below – shallowing fast. Heading for the beach. I swung north. Three fathoms came up. 'This'll do.' Splash and rattle – a good sound, in the right place. The crackle of bacon – even better. On cue, up came the fog-melter and the schoolhouse peeped out, then the Traigh Bheag and, as the circle widened, a fishing boat appeared off the point of Pabbay. We'd finished our second fry-up as the *Reul na Maidne*, Donald Beag's new boat, anchored astern. Dinghy, dogs and gathering men rowed for the landing, 'Are you long here?' shouted Donald. 'Long enough for a decent breakfast.' We set out to the gathering. 'A heavy fog – you did well to get down,' he remarked, just the hint of a question in his eye. 'Yes, you're right, Donald.'

A cracking day – sun off the sea, sheep off the hill and banter and laughs to the clack of shears in the schoolhouse fank. Cheese and cans of lager and, by mid afternoon, Neillie came to the door. 'Tea, boys.' He busied about in the east room, a tea-towel over his arm and mock grumbles of 'A woman's work is never done.' Bread and corned beef vanished and, by evening, a dram finished the day. 'On you go, you lot – we'll tidy up and see you up at the office.' The *Reul* steamed north until the Rosinish Point of Pabbay put her out of sight. Promptly, round to Skipisdale steamed *Rhum*, tow line on a cleat and north on a night of star spangled banner. 'Turn up the CD, give us a Scottische, Thomson, boy.' Dancing feet thumped the cockpit sole with the Wallochmor Ceilidh Band at full pitch playing our national anthem. 'Father John MacMillan of Barra' had Mingulay, boat and island bobbing astern on the crimson cushions of sunset. 'A wee toot, Sandy?' 'Why not?' The peak of Heval took us safe through the Snuasimul passage and close on midnight we were unloading our cargo into Sandy's truck on a mercifully deserted Castlebay slip.

Much hammering and the blinding flicker of a welding arc in the big shed at the back of Sandy's bungalow saw a cattle grid take shape, eight feet long, twelve feet wide and beautiful to behold. Sandy's father, Lach MacLean, stopped cutting sticks to watch progress, 'That's the best of steel you've got there.' Another disguised question. 'Yes, we're a quality company, Lach – do an honest job.' All ready. Next day, pick and shovel dug the pit, concrete side walls, block supports – it called for several visits to the 'office' to finalise plans. 'Early – like, really early, before Neil's up – we'll fix it in place.' 'How about changing the colour?' 'We'll chance it.'

Dawn revealed no boyfriends' cars nose down in the gaping hole we'd left unlit. Ledaig slept. Ropes hauled, fencing punches levered and, with a deafening clang, the grid fell into place. We stood back, panting and proud. 'Man, what a great fit.' This was barely spoken when Neil strode down. 'My Jove, you boys can fairly do it.' His face beamed. Gratitude and pleasure shone as wide as Barra Head light itself. Thence to a closer inspection. He looked down keenly. 'Not one hoof will cross that, Neil.' Sandy was laying it on a bit. I studied the face of our prospective paymaster. Dawn crossed it in a flash of recognition, a sort of sunrise in reverse. I stood back. 'You pair of bloody pirates,' it fumed from behind thunderclouds, 'if you'd have been left down there any longer, you'd have dismantled the whole bloody lighthouse.'

No word of pay packet. That evening up in the 'office' at the back pew, Sinclair's special reserve remained empty. Sandy and I sat with Archie. We half told him the dilemma. Funds were low and heads were shaking over the 'You've done it this time' comment when the swing door announced Neillie. A nod to the counter and he joined us. No mention of his modern access from him and certainly not by us. After the third round of thaw tactics, an envelope passed across to Sandy. 'Now, Neil, there was no hurry.' 'Oh well, boys, I know the kind of girls you are.' A fair chunk of the cattle grid vanished in conviviality before the church clock struck one and transport conveyed us over to Ledaig to reassess our triumph by moonlight. Neil was claiming there was a star spangled banner somewhere and, even later, we parted the best friends ever. 'Well, Sandy, lucky it wasn't too expensive for us or him.' 'Now didn't I tell you, Thomson? There's no such thing as a problem – just a situation.'

# 30

# 'Poor Thomson's Gone'

A dram with Neil,
The hour that stalks the night,
I walked the bends from Ledaig round the sleeping croft,
A bearing on the boat.
No voice nor car, a village prowled by silence,
In the spell of Heval's peak.
Thin, a fingered moon flits beyond the bay,
To light upon the hill.
Seconds flight by speed of light,
Miles, two hundred thousand, more.
Four billion years, a birth in space,
Ten million tides till consciousness bore quest.
Two thousand years, a summer's pulse,
One speck in time, no more.
A humble birth, a statued hill,
The spin of chance, or more?
That night it's light, a tiny glow, shone icy, deathly, still,
Madonna and Her Child yet may die of winter's marble chill.

Late the year of hoist and trim,
Lone mast amidst the local boats, beside a castle wall.

Curves encased in stillness, to each a favoured course,
Till their mistress calls the tide.
My echoed shadows clung, the rock of Peter found,
Our Lady, Star of Fisher Sea.
Moon bright arms sloped from twelve.
'Each gale, the big hand slows,' I often heard them say.
Cold winds of change blow from lava plain,
No distance now her dappled face,
Lunar mountain, footstep trace.
As the sun illuminates her landscape,
So its stealthy beam counts the tick of faith.

Pendants into circles,
Sinuous water dark, the back of autumn seal.
In memory's grasp, so Neillie told,
A cub came crying, lost to Ledaig's shed.
The boy who killed, in little time,
Was taken by the tide.
I drifted on a silver thread that laced the billowed cloud,
The empty isles, a hollow bay,
That spun the steepled hands which hear the mortals pray.
Indigo hush each measured drip,
Intense the ushered change.
Cheek-brushed air, the merest breath,
Did carnal moonflesh wait?
Child in Arms, Seal Woman's night,
Deep the myths which draw man to his fate.

Hand on mast, I stood gauging the morning's weather. An insipid day, chilled by the greenish light of a November sun buried deep in a haze which cloaked the stratosphere. Dull grey clouds smudged a featureless horizon, waiting for some force to harry them to a purpose. Peevish ripples clattered onto MacNeil's stronghold.

An instinct attuned to survival? An uneasiness, nagging and churning, almost a fear. A warning? I hesitated. The bow of *Rhum* swung to the first hint of wind. A week had passed with the *Mingulay* boat tied alongside, ready for sea. All but fresh food remained to stow. A fortnight's fencing awaited me. Gales tomorrow, probably?

Well, today I'd sail, yes, sail whatever – head south, down to Mingulay.

The boat sat low in the water. Fencing wire and my heavy fencing tools together with pulleys, rope and a sizeable Bruce mooring anchor filled the bottom boards – more than ample ballast. Calor gas bottles, tinned food and spare fuel were jammed into the next layer. Under the small open-fronted cabin were stowed all I trusted to remain dry. Sleeping bag, spare clothes, matches and, wrapped in a sail bag, a cassette player with forty tapes. Snuggled inside the sleeping bag, bearing warmth in mind, if not a touch of stress, I'd carefully rolled two bottles of mental emollient.

An hour before a falling tide to help me south, I rowed to the jetty, gathered the milk and oranges from Willie the Butcher and, with neither guidance nor surprise, pushed the swing door of The Castlebay. Donald Patrick waved me to a chair and we sat together over a dram. 'How long are you planning away?' 'About a fortnight, maybe.' 'Take plenty grub,' the voice was half serious, 'there was a Father MacDonald about a hundred years ago went to Mingulay Church to say Mass – it was over seven weeks before he got back here. You're thin enough. Take a rifle – there's plenty rabbits.'

I rose and his eye went to the window. 'Isn't it Friday?' he remarked. 'Watch yourself, Iain. Don't pass Pabbay if there's any sea in it, land behind Rosinish.' The saying, 'Never go to sea on a Friday' turned in my mind as I stowed the rifle.

Out through the Vatersay channel, tight to each headland. Wind over tide, a sea was building. A turmoil in the tide rip off Sandray Point. Waves broke over the gunnel. I steered amongst them, pumped hard, hesitated. Turning a small laden boat is a dangerous trick in broken water. West of the sound, Atlantic rollers burst on the Greanamul skerry. It dipped in and out of sight as each swell passed under us.

I ran on for Pabbay. This wind might force a landing in the sheltered north sloc. Cross seas, water aboard, up the oilskins' sleeves. Steering and pumping again, I put her nose round the Rosinish Point. The bay opened to starboard. I'd no tent. The roofless ruin up from the beach would stand a shelter if I turned and got ashore. Waves beat in.

'Don't pass Pabbay if there's any sea in it,' was DP's warning.

Waves into a small boat. A hungry sea? The epitaph in Hebridean homes: 'Lost at sea.'

'Keep on, Thomson!' Waves coming more on the bow, she's taking them, tossing spray at every plunge. Keep on, steer for Hecla – 'hill of the hooded shroud' as the Old Norse had it. Mingulay's ahead. Here's to those hardy men of the sea.

By way of a booster, I sang to the wind, 'Heel ya ho, boys, let her go, boys, pull her head round, now all together. Heel ya ho, boys, let her go, boys, sailing homeward to Mingulay.'

Island on the bow, winter grey. Seas hammered the cliffs below Macphee's Hill, climbed the slocs. Into the bay we rode, broadside now, roll her over the crests. What a fine wee sea boat. Towards the beach. I stood. Greenbacks thumped the sands, spread froth and filled the air with the tang of wildness. A deserted island, yes. A refuge, no. A home to petty lines I'd written – 'through every pounding thrust is born a child of beauty'. The energy of wildness, the revelation of beauty is granted only to those alone in its presence.

A flat between waves. I swung her sharply, bow to sea, outboard pushing slowly ahead, judging depth and distance, intent on grappling the seabed. I trusted she would swing to the anchor and lie stern-on to the sand without grounding. It would be over the side, into the swell, wade ashore, kit and supplies, Swiss Family Robinson style.

Over the kit, on to the foredeck, no fiddling knots, anchor loosed in seconds. I stood up, ready, watching. A green surge burst under the forefoot, her bow leapt sharply. Now! I hurled out the anchor. The bow dipped, almost pitched me overboard. I clutched behind, dropped to my knees. Chain raced out, staccato through the stem-head. Into a trough, the boat paused, chain slowed, I checked it with a foot, slipped a turn on the cleat. Braced, pay out, hand over hand.

The sou-easter, onshore and freshening, snatched orange oil-skins. Emerald seas hurried down on man and boat. A horizon of heaving shoulders. Low November sunlight broke from clearing clouds. Wave crests hung over turquoise curves, translucent, fragile moments before cascades of crystal. Sun, wind and sea, into reality.

Lifting her nose to breaking rollers the boat fought her chain. Slack, taut, slack. Would the anchor bite? I glanced astern. White fans spread on the sand. The beach was close. Swiftly I bent, took the tension, hauled, it came.

'God, it's not holding,' I shouted at the elements. The thud and hiss of tumbling waves took my words. We were close in. I looked fearfully at the shore. Would the anchor grip?

The black-backed gulls wheeled from their station on the dunes, hovered on tilted wing, jeering cries. I faced the sea. A heavy wave rose ahead, steep, slow to break. Up *Mingulay* climbed. I lay back on the chain, braced, balancing.

The stern struck, a shudder raked the boat, the first blow of shipwreck. The bow reared skyward. I poised to leap, frightened she would flip. Her nose broke the peak, foam swept to my waist. She swung broadside, rolling violently. I was flung under a towering curl of water.

Terrified of being trapped below the boat, I clawed away from the lunging hull and fell choking into soft moving sand. Sucking water dragged me out into a gritty mass of receding foam. In panic I caught the chain and clung in desperation, knowing I'd be buried under the next swell if caught under the boat, drowned.

It came, white, roaring, measured, deliberate, swinging the boat's bow on to the beach and washing me under its lee. In the hull, I scrambled clear, coughing water and spitting sand. Dragging the chain on to firmer beach, I was ashore.

None to know. Neither means nor contact with another soul. Ashore, alone and alive, on the Traigh Mhor, the Big Beach of Mingulay.

I stood dripping and panting. The island welcomed me – I knew it, felt it, clear as though she spoke. Mingulay, in all its wild remoteness, welcomed me. The mantle of a spirit world that holds the island in its power enfolded me. I was elated, gloriously happy – happy as a homecoming to the land of some long ancestral memory. Free from the outside world, free from the trap of civilisation, space and freedom.

◆

The boat lay broadside as waves poured into her. Save the kit and grub, empty the hull. Items already floated, oars, the rubber inflatable. A dozen oranges, yellow blobs in the foam.

Action. Strip. Bare feet, chest and backside, I waded waist deep into a surprisingly warm sea, hauling and carrying. Outboard, rifle, fencing tools, food and rucksack – a one-man relay on to the nearest safe rocks. Heavy work, I hurried. The boat was filling with silt, filling fast, amazingly fast. The tide turned, she lay over, half full of sand, rolling and sloshing, burying herself in the soft beach, truly stranded. I lamented – not for my dilemma, for a troubled friend.

Spade, bucket, no picnic, I dug and baled, dug and baled, waves still slopping sand. An hour of heaving and cursing. Down to the bottom boards, dragged them out, up the beach. Empty at last, light as I could make her. Come on, boy! Using rope, anchor and pulley blocks, I strove to haul her round, clear of the next rising tide. Hopeless – sand too soft and I hadn't half the puff.

◆

I tugged on a jersey and sat. The sun, long behind Barra Head, turned the day into half light. The sea shone, refusing to die into darkness. It remained pale and living, luminescent as the loveliest flesh might be on some clandestine night of passion.

The rocks spoke in their blackness. The ruined village whispered behind me, drifted and deserted to whirls of sand in the wind. Lost to the mortals whose remains lay but yards from their homes in a simple burying ground of broken crosses. Lost? The quick and the dead? Who shall divide the soul of incarnation from the spirit ascending, from the divine embrace of procreation? Love, the energy of the universe?

Black rocks beside me, I stared out. Farthest hill, sky and water were swallowed into night. I shivered. What to do to save the boat? Still I sat, staring at her, a dim white spectre on the crunching sand, a phantom of skeleton wrecks and struggling souls dragged by the whirlpool of despair on a voyage to the long horizon.

Gently a golden edge came to hills, old as old to exultant youth. Slowly, shy as a bride's undressing, the lustrous moon crept over their jagged wrinkles and lay on the bay below me. And away by the black rocks, the incarnation of her beauty sparkled in a thousand moon-kissed shells, in the breath of the island, in the longing, sweet and entwining, of yielding flesh, of auburn tresses, tumbling free, over the curves of a man's desire.

◆

The tide had fallen and the boat lay clear on a wide rim of sand. I hurried down and, with an oar and much grunting, levered her bow round to face the sea. 'You'll hold this time.' I dragged the anchor to the end of its chain and stamped it out of sight at the edge of a turning tide.

The moon at her zenith gave me light to make ready an 'endless hauler' of rope and pulleys. My intention was to row *Mingulay* across to the more sheltered south side of the bay, drop the heavy spare anchor and let her drift in on the 'endless' to the rocks at the Traigh Bheag. Then, rope in hand, I'd leap on a ledge and pull her back out before she struck.

The tide swirled in around the boat and I scrambled aboard as she floated. In the running tide, she rode with an easy motion to a holding anchor. Our distance from the beach lengthened. I waited for the top of the tide. Had I the strength to pull away? A second grounding or, worse, a grinding on to the rocks, might finish me and, for sure, the boat.

Breaking waves in white flashes signalled some idea of distance. We seemed well out. Stiff and cold, surely the tide's full? Oars ready, I hauled the boat up on her chain. A rise of the bow wrenched the anchor clear. Quick stow, we're drifting fast. Oars out, pull.

I dug in, lay back, full weight. Watch now – a broken oar means the rocks. Angle across, row hard between the waves. I pulled until the gaunt schoolhouse stood out above the steep rocks of the Traigh Bheag. That's my bearing. Ship oars, shackle the heavy anchor, over the bow with it.

The boat drifted astern, held with a jerk. Good. The endless rope ran out. Steady it. Keep her nose to the sea. The cliff loomed, cut the moonlight. Sudden gloom, I peered for the ledge needed to make a landing. Damn! The end of the loop and I was still twenty yards out. I rowed back, weary arms, lifted the anchor and let her drift in closer.

Second run. I stood at the stern, rope in one hand, paying out. Five yards, three, hold her. Waves swept in, sucked back. I flung the oars, clatter up the rocks. Rowlocks, rope in hand. Wet, slippery rocks, one slip? Next wave. Leap.

Bare feet gripped cold clean rock. Lucky boy. The boat pitched from under me down a retreating trough. I heaved on the 'endless'.

She rose to the next breaker. Haul like hell or she'll be smashed on the ledge. Her nose turned, one touch of her keel. Close. Dip by dip, fainter and fainter, I pulled her to the end of the anchor chain until she became a tiny bobbing gull, hardly so buoyant by her angle to the flow of the waves.

I felt about for a jutting rock, found a crevice, high up, tied ropes to a rock and jammed them tight. The oars, essential in the ultimate predicament, I carried up the jumbled cliff and headed for the kit. Trousers on, bare feet into wellies, rucksack and food box and a tired walk along the village track to the door of the schoolhouse.

Padlock and a wired-up door presented a challenge in daylight. Much fiddling and muttering. At last, the familiar waft of dusty wooden floor, sheep dip and over-used tea towels. Fortunately I knew my way about the room blindfold. Storm shutters covering the windows produced the same limitation.

Now for a body-warmer – into the soaking sleeping bag and out with one of its circulation stimulants. Highland Park, no less. Bottle to mouth – wow, an absent-minded fire-eater sucking instead of blowing would recognise the effect. A hunk of cheese, another enlivening swig, shirt and jersey over a chair and into the sleeping bag to heat it up. Another gulp. *Uisge beatha*, water of life? What an understatement.

Silence filled the house, hissing in my ear. I stopped breathing, lay motionless, listening. Not a living soul on the island, surely? I thought of the dead. The house had been locked, the way we left it, two months back. I lifted my head, stared. Could I make out the old cupboard? The room felt different. There was a presence. I was not alone.

A slight movement? I listened intently. Was that breathing? A rustle, a faint timid rustle, down on the floor near my head. I stared. The cheese paper stirred. A guest at this hour? A laugh of relief. 'Well, well, mousey, it's mature cheddar – help yourself.' Would I offer a drop in the bottle top? On, on reflection, er, er, no. 'I've met tipsy mice before – f . . . fighting cats, yeesss, big cats, an . . . and . . . n . . . I'm . . . no . . . I'm . . . no . . . ch . . . chanc . . . ing . . . it.'

◆

A crack of light sprang through the shutters. A crisp, fresh day, sunshine poured on the island. I raced out to greet it, goose pimples and all, down to the edge of the cliff. Turquoise waves, white tops, sparkling crests, the bay was alive. *Mingulay* pranced around her mooring. The Minch, a quivering green, chased the hills of Rhum into cloudless blue. Sea, islands, hills, cliffs, the cry of birds, the scent of salt, of moorland, everything vibrant, vital, I breathed it, drank it, romped the circles of a puppy.

Matches dried in the warmth of sun on the window and, water in a pail from the burn, I fired up the old Calor gas cooker. Soon the smell of bacon and eggs outdid the dip. Tea and a rescued orange. Famished? I ate with the relish of a starving glutton. A lively morning of carrying and sorting. Sleeping bag and clothes to the fence, food on to the high shelves of the unique dresser. I eyed label-less tins stacked on a lower shelf. They became a morose feature of another expedition. The box of music tapes dripped water. One made feeble voices on the squeaky cassette player. Lucky the accordion stayed with the yacht. I lashed the inflatable dinghy under a sheltered rock high above the landing ledges and shoul-dered the bottom-boards of the boat up to the house. By afternoon I was at the fence, digging in strainers and stretching new wire, working my way over the shoulder of the hill until the turning light of Barra Head on ochre skies outshone the evening's glow. East-wards, against drumbeat clouds, hurried white staccato wings. Wailing gulls, shrill voices above the steady pound of sea, a warning in their cry. Will tomorrow understand? I headed towards the outline of the schoolhouse and my rationed tot of Oh Be Joyful.

That night, above the hiss of tilley mantles, the wind throbbed, the sea rumbled. The boom of breakers rolling on to the rocks of the Traigh Bheag quivered through the stonework of the gable. A storm built as wise gulls huddled in their dunes. I wakened in the first dim light to the rattle of slates, the tremble of a gable. Head down into a sou-easter I made for the cliff. *Mingulay* wallowed, half submerged, in heavy, sweeping seas. To reach her and bale would be madness. I turned back and made breakfast. I worked the day in sight of her struggle. As the loom of Barra Head outlined the crest of Hecla, she went down.

Donald Beag, the fisherman son of John MacLeod and owner of the *Reul na Maidne*, true to her name (*Reul na Maidne* translates as 'Star of the Morning'), left Castlebay early with Archie MacLean and food on board. Ten days since my leaving, Donald headed her south to shoot nets for a trawl off Barra Head. In darkness, they edged into Mingulay Bay and swept it with the spotlight. No boat. 'Perhaps he pulled into Pabbay – the run down would've been rough enough.' Donald turned out, heading north to search. Archie stood at the bow. Misgivings began to gnaw. Light grew slowly. They steamed into the Bagh Ban on the south-east side of Pabbay.

The spotlight flickered over sand and rock, steadied on roofless gables. No boat hauled on the beach, no life at the ruin. Winter greyness, the Hermit Isle empty as the day its people left. 'Ah well,' a quiet comment. Looks and thoughts. A drowning man will tear off his oilskins, kick off boots. The eyes of a drowned body are open, there is none to close their choking terror. The sea will do strange things to a body. Hide it, bloat it, chew flesh to bone. Few fishermen are strangers to this.

They turned south for Mingulay in a gentle swell. Archie stayed at the bow, lifted his eye from sea to Macphee's Hill. He'd known these islands since boyhood, since the days when their purchase was the talk of Barra. That morning his mind turned to the fate of the boy who gave his name to the hill and almost his life.

No boat was coming from Mingulay to pay the rent and MacNeil of Barra wondered at this and, by and by, sent down a boat and men of his own to investigate. The youngest of the crew, a boy of seventeen who had escaped from the island of Eigg in the arms of his father, Kenneth Macphee, when the Macleods of Skye burnt alive the people of that island in their church-cave. Well, the older men of the crew put him ashore to search the houses of Mingulay village for no one had appeared to welcome their arrival.

The boy ran from house to house and then back to the shore waving and shouting, 'Oh God, they're all dead.'

The boat stood off as one of the older men called over to the boy, 'If it's the plague that killed them then you've got a bellyful already – you'd better stay where you are.' And they hoisted sail for Barra. The boy ran to the headland pleading and crying till the boat vanished behind Pabbay.

Many, many weeks passed, six anyway, and him alone and the corpses stinking in every house, until the boy's father forced the truth out of MacNeil and another boat ventured down to see if the lad was alive. Well, well, he was and the laird told Macphee to take men with him to the island and it would be theirs rent free as long as any of his generations lived.

And the boy told that each day he would climb this lookout hill to see if there was any sign of a boat coming and that's over seven hundred years ago and still we call it Macphee's Hill even today.

On an eastern horizon the mist was thinning. Gulls hung in half-light, hoping for fish guts or the leavings of breakfast. Archie studied the sea. Gales, no fishing boats down for a week. His mind said, 'The worst has happened.'

The first rays of sun caught it. Off the starboard quarter. Something yellow. Floating. A body? Donald swung the helm, followed the pointing arm. They gathered at the rail to stare down on drifting oilskins.

'Ah, Dia, poor Thomson's gone.'

Archie sat, turned his back on Mingulay, and lit a cigarette. They steamed on into the bay without more being said. The thoughts of men of the sea need no words.

◆

Was that a fog horn? Again, a long toot. Close. I opened an eye, the skylight. Yes. There, rocking in the bay, a fishing boat and a fine morning, what a splendid combination. Ten days had flown in hard satisfying work, never a moment's loneliness, nor care for jostling commuters or traffic jams, but food was low. I sped from bed to dinghy and was soon greeting faces grinning down on me over the gunnel of the *Reul na Maidne* – splendid name for a rescue.

'Well, boys, you've made it.' I laughed up. 'We've made it! Damn you, Thomson, you nearly gave me a heart attack,' was Archie Lach's opening blast. 'Where's your boat?' I pointed to the seabed. 'Aye, aye,' Donald nodded and lit his pipe as I clambered aboard for breakfast. No need of his anchor on a clear still morning when lines of creamy fleck marked currents on The Minch. The *Reul* barely dipped and drifted slowly. The sea was flat. Donald leant on the rail, smoking quietly as he looked into translucent water. 'Here's your boat!' His call interrupted bacon and egg. *Mingulay* lay on her side, thirty feet below us, her white hull and red anti-fouling creating a wavering corpse. A grapple caught her chain and the fishing hauler brought her water-pouring hull to the surface. Aboard in a jump, I bailed and considered. Put her back to Castlebay on the deck of the *Reul?* Take a chance. She would take us home if the weather behaved. I secured *Mingulay* back on the 'endless', a jaunty and pleased little boat.

Only ripples ran onto the Traigh Bheag. Archie sat in the stern of the inflatable, stores in the bow. Any attempt to trim the dinghy with a visitor of considerable power and proportions to match was pointless. I rowed ashore with the nose cocked in the air and Archie's backside lapping in the water. Donald Beag turned south to his day's fishing, gave a toot clearing the headland and left a promise to be back in a week or so, weather permitting.

We fenced by daylight, spruced and painted the kitchen by gaslight, learned Irish songs from the repetitious tape and rationed ourselves to a dram a night. By our second day, November gales lifted tops off the sea, hurled them east and blotted any horizon.

The boat went down again but this time she lay just below the surface. One morning she was gone. 'Dinghy or nothing now, boy.' Row for Castlebay? Hoch, not a care. The world about us ours, so long as the grub held out. What the hell, we could always kill a sheep. Macphee managed.

Evening drew on. We had the fence finished, the last staple hammered home. Donald Beag's promised return tomorrow? Archie made to the house. Supper would need his skill with food a diminishing feature of our existence. To collect an unused fencing strainer, I skirted the shoulder of Hecla and zigzagged the slope to Skipisdale. Its landing was no more than a gash in the cliff where softer rock had worn down and left the ledges smooth. Steady heads would climb and carry for the face had natural steps.

A gentle tide swirled fronds of seaweed as I looked down. Skipisdale – a name to thrill the tongue, bygone times flowed in its syllables. About me, on the south-facing slopes, were the hummocks of prehistory, circles of stone, burying grounds beside. Iron Age? Who cares the detail? I saw the people toiling at tiny fields, summer days herding, fishing, gathering eggs and Mingulay village over the hill their civilisation. And the sky piled cloud upon cloud beyond Barra Head in the coming of Atlantic storms and they crouched in huts and combed the tousle-haired children. And Viking galleys chaffed the rocks below.

Skipisdale on Mingulay. My words that day, theirs a thousand years past – *skipis*, 'a ship', *dale*, their 'valley'. Did they know I would be speaking to the twilight of a setting sun over a sea they loved and ravaged? They climbed the cliff, bare armed, tunics leather over wool. They shouldered casks, cursed and swore; hammered on the antechambers of a mind in whose vision their existence lurked. How to live beyond?

The tide now ran strongly in the Sound at my feet, pressed around the islet of Geirum in its midst. Who had built the chapel? Asceticism or masochism – a thin divide. What devotion would drag a man to this turret of isolation? What wisdom in its utter desolation? The cravings of introspection, a worship of the unknowable, the hope of securing life beyond the sunset of his evening prayer?

I watched the ending of a sun's journey, saw the children, just a hundred years past, forebears of those I knew. A day in Mingulay school, back to crofting homes on Barra Head. Sail or shoulders bent to row, arms and oars on the edge of the Atlantic. Children, small faces above the gunnel. An open boat, a pitiless Sound. Young minds on a journey. The sunrise of comprehension, or the sunset of destruction?

Orange light tinged the hillside. The tide below me had watched the pageant of the planets, swirled about the islet of a holy man's yearning to belong, to give himself to some power beyond. Would the tide he watched, perhaps in fear, flow beyond our childlike faith and into eternity or would it bow before man's unravelling of its simple beauty?

The sea faded into streaks of crimson. Wave tops beat on Barra Head. I carried the strainer down to the old schoolhouse on my back.

◆

Through a dawn of unmitigated greyness we spotted the *Reul* heading south to trawl off Barra Head. She pounded a fair swell, spray flying, red keel showing. A big sea ran into the bay. Getting off the island would be risky – very. By afternoon, we prepared to leave. A cup of tea, goodbye ex-army tins, glad we didn't identify your contents.

In the last of the day, we clambered down to the landing ledge at the south side of the bay and waited. No chance of taking any kit home – ourselves would be load enough. Along the rocks east of us, for a short spell in the late 1800s, a derrick arm hung over the sea from an iron tripod on a concrete platform. Baskets swung out for human cargo, canvas slings for cattle; a well-meaning effort to help the island survive, it was long eaten by wave action, washed away, and useless anyway. They'd salvaged the hefty iron ladder and plonked it by the pathway. Sandy and I often cast an eye over it. Heavy, but it could have a use if a contract came the way. For Mingulay villagers, a low-geared winch and cable above the Traigh Mhor, which they suggested, might have sufficed and no dangling in space.

Idle speculation. Wave backs undulated along the rocks, lumbering past our feet to burst on the sands of the Traigh Bheag with ominous booms and much disconcerting foam. Small wonder the old folk called them seahorses. Between each black lunge we looked down a roller-coaster drop with little thought of fairgrounds.

Buffets of wind had gulls hunched one-legged on the sands of the Traigh Mhor. The sky reflected raw November melancholy. I watched the leaning showers, lines of chilling whiteness, driven ranks that faded the outlines of Pabbay, and I fell to an unspoken sadness. Not known a moment lonely, I was leaving a place whose intimacy grew with isolation, where affinity to a bygone people dwelt in its desolation. The heart beats slow in the security of belonging.

A navigation light, red and cheery, appeared round the headland and the *Reul* steamed into the bay and lay well out, rolling broadside – too dangerous to come close. Nothing they could do but watch whatever befell us.

'Keep the rope, Archie, until I'm clear.' I waited for the next wave-top. It came, deliberate and nonchalant – a dark round back, white-edged, licking along the rocks. It drew level. One sharp move, I launched the inflatable, stepped in, oars to rowlocks, and waited for the rush.

Down she swooped. Archie threw the rope into the bow. 'Look out. For God's sake don't get trapped under the ledge.' I pulled hard, kept her off. Over my shoulder, the next peak. I pulled in. The ledge came level. 'Right, MacLean, now.'

One step, into the stern, bow shot in the air. 'Keep your weight fo'ard.' Down the back of a pouring wave we tipped, sliding, oars digging. The ledge rose above us. Black water, a roaring gurgle, sucking us under the overhang. If trapped, we'd swill back and fore, drowning flotsam. As bad, the next crest could flip us. Swim for the beach? No chance.

Another curling top bore in. Don't break an oar against the rocks. Nothing in the bow, Archie's weight astern, could flip us. This is it. 'Kneel fo'ard, keep a hold of the dinghy whatever – she might flip.' He grabbed the side-ropes. Over my shoulder watched the rising crest.

'Pull, now, pull for your life, Thomson boy, mine as well. If we go we'll go together.' I rowed without goading or instruction, angling across the run of the waves, meeting each peak with a left-arm pull. It seemed familiar. Donald approached the landing, edging close as he dared.

The side of the *Reul* never looked smarter. I flicked a coil of rope, poked up the oars. Donald Beag, steady and unperturbed, took a hand. The gunnel lurched and made our step easier. 'Lucky I noticed you,' he remarked in his idle sort of manner, 'standing there like a pair of bloody cormorants planning a dive. Thought you'd be inside on a day like this trying out the old army tins.' 'To hell with those tins, Donald. Get us to Castlebay and we'll chance another kind.'

Two hours later, it need not astound you, there we were, without a care, fencing forgotten, adjusting our horizons to that glorious pitfall of civilisation, The Castlebay Bar.

# 31

# 'I Want a Castle as Long as my Yacht'

One Hebridean spring of unruffled days I spent wandering the Isle of Rum, my floating home anchored in Loch Scresort. May is the month for taking long legs to the hill. Barometer steady at thirty-one inches and cloud-free horizons, it revitalises the western seaboard, not to mention man and beast. An open-neck shirt, air by the lungful, I strode the ridge and peak of Rum. Sou-west, Minch met Atlantic at the Oigh Sgeir Lighthouse without a ripple. Canna's delicate profile, a stone's throw to the west, Coll and Tiree, their beaches white and empty. At my back was a procession of mainland tops to keep Munro-baggers on the hop. Swing the glass, a grace of landform, an acuteness of detail, toss in a blaze of colour contrast – Kodak would boast they'd made it.

The bald dome of Ben More dominated Mull's vivid greenness. A sweep of twenty degrees and the lens of my old Ross telescope, still crystal sharp after a hundred years, picked up Beinn Resipol. Its broad base guards the remoteness of Moidart and under its shadow is a secretive anchorage in the lee of wooded Eilean Shona. A week before, in contrast to the heights of Rum, I'd tramped its island pathways. No sky and dripping with claustrophobia, a jungle lushness home to wild cat and pine-marten and also the gifted writer Mike Tomkins who'd exchanged London journalism to live in its seclusion and study the less exotic life forms about his door.

*Rhum* lay in a sheltered pool beside the decaying MacDonald stronghold of Castle Tioram. Tidal shingle connects its site on Eilean Tioram to the mainland and a well lies within the massive walls. Though Tioram means dry, it's unlikely the name referred to any lack of strong drink. Barring a fifteenth-century attack by the Campbells, isolation kept Tioram safe. A premonition of death brought its end. Allan Mor MacDonald set out in 1715 to raise the Jacobite standard on the Braes of Marr. The Catholic cause of the Old Chevalier. 'Moidard no more, I will not return alive.' In keeping with Macdonald's melancholy frame of mind were instructions to burn the stronghold. With his instructions carried out, the smoke of torch and flame trailed his departing step. Less popular was a previous chief, Donald the Cruel, who hanged his cook due to her addiction to snuff. It was a harsh penalty for a harmless habit. Her addiction to snuff had prompted the gross oversight of stealing the laird's snuff box. In turn, the horrors of various excesses, unconnected with the island's name, led Donald to be haunted by the image of a huge toad with its flicking tongue dragging him before Satan.

Beyond Tioram, in winding Loch Shiel, the ruined chapel on Eilean Fhianain is named after Saint Finan, a contemporary of Columba. In a burying ground of ancient stones the remains of John of Moidart lie below a stone upon which Celtic design twists about his claymore. Nearby, on a small cross the face of Christ is carved. No other area of the Highlands, in oak wood and mist, can better conjure the times when age-old superstitions mingled with religious belief. Little surprise the men of Moidart marched to Glen Finnan with Charles Edward Stewart and took their medicine on the Moor of Drumossie.

Lacking the freshness of a sun-driven breeze on the heights of Rum, Moidart was not for me. I sat with the glass and picked out hill after hill. Furthest north, Beinn Sgriol raised its cone over a peninsula that the Norse called Sleat, meaning 'the level land'. I swivelled across the Sound of Rum. The dominant Skye's Cuillin range lifted no higher than my eye. Bared of cloud, they were possessed of a startling clarity. I steadied my glass against a shepherd's stick. Crag and pillar, handholds that challenged the climbers of tweed jacket and shepherd boots, I felt the tension of an anxious step, yet their image looked kindly, stretching on to waters without a tremor, for the Sea of the Hebrides enjoyed a remarkable placidity. I swung the glass again – the Atlantic rested from winter's gales and, on the curve of its rim, soft and appealing, the far line of islands seemed like creatures of the sea and, across the diver-crying lochans of Benbecula, I thought I spied St Kilda.

Orval's Viking heights slope westwards to the sands of tiny reef-locked Guirdil Bay. Stout oars, only three miles over the Sound to the green Isle of Canna, a stepping-stone on a Minch idle in the intensity of its blueness. The shielings that clustered about me spoke of a feast of scenery, the flush of youth and the glimpse of a girl's white thigh in the perfume of the heather. Easily forgotten were the days as a ghillie spent crouched amongst the moss-stone remains of the shielings of Strathfarrar, midge and driving rain and the pony with his head slumped. I walked the broken edge of cliffs that kept south-west gales from the shielings to a place where the Neolithic settlers of Rum quarried the island's violent beginnings.

Aeons beyond counting, a young Earth's axis wobbles. Its equator crosses Scotland with steam and swamp. Emerging continental masses redistribute. Centrifugal spin against the grip of gravity. Crash and grind, the planet shakes, great leaves of land collide. With immense weight and pressure they drift over the planet's face. The Atlantic widens, ocean waters drown Atlantis. Rock-melting temperatures find weakness. Magma bursts skywards. Day darkens to nights of swirling green sunlight. Searing heat and foul sulphurous fumes. Molten rivers coagulate, tempered by the sea. Rum is born. The spasm passes, an interlude. Life returns to another scene in the cosmic play.

Veins criss-cross the island's face with the pattern of an alcoholic's nose, and on these weathered cliffs of Sgurr Mhor a crystalline silica can be found. Sometimes purple, though its predominant colour is green, often it is flecked with red – hence the name bloodstone. Similar in properties to flint, when cracked it takes a razor-edge fit to gralloch and skin. At a base beside Loch Scresort leather-clothed knappers chipped away, shaping flakes of bloodstone into arrowheads. Transparent and highly polished, these exquisitely beautiful items seem like works of art to us but were works of necessity to them.

Each slender conical peak boasts a Norse pedigree, horizon markers for their run down The Minch. Eastwards I climbed by the north shoulder of Barkeval and across the deep bealach to Hallival where the shearwater burrow their nests in soils washed from its summit. Around the foot of Askival and on to the summit of Trollval. Hills of trolls, thought the Viking. Nocturnal voices whispered from holes in the ground – eerie on a night's air, the talking of nesting birds. These graceful hills surround a bowled corrie, south-west facing and of perfect form. An icecap had thickened to half a mile of land-crushing weight until, slowly, the sun had returned north and now the glacial scoopings on the heels of volcanic flow fall in gentle contours towards the sea. Vegetation is lush and varied, reflecting the trace elements spewed from the Earth's core and the human tillage of a glen where islanders told the weather by light and shade on the distant peaks of Barra and South Uist and turned their lazy beds into lifestyle. Unknowing, their native glen, Harris, gave its name to a crystalline rock so far unique to Rum. The Apollo moon missions brought back samples to which it relates. Astrophysicists named it Harrisite. What scenes await in the cosmic wings? Where leads the script that wrote solar power into comprehension?

◆

Clanranald held sway over Rum in historic times until, come the fifteenth century, they misjudged a deal. The 'great galley' of MacLean of Coll, Rolls-Royce prestige symbol of the times, appeared a fair swap for an island had not her timbers been rotten. No island and a braw boat with a slight tendency to sink. As elsewhere throughout the nineteenth-century Highlands, under MacLean's ownership, sheep did for Rum's natives. It cost MacLean's descendant something over a fiver a head in 1820 to export three hundred of the indigenous folk of Rum to Cape Breton aboard the *Highland Laddie* and the *Dove of Harmony*. Eight thousand blackface ewes and an enhanced rental took their place. Left behind was a cattle-dung fertility which, for the shooting toffs, soon to pop up, could put a stag over the scales at twenty stone. More unattractive for sporting socialites was a colony of midges which rendered wearing the kilt little short of a variation on the Highland fling.

Notwithstanding undignified scratching, this mode of dress was inflicted upon his Highland workforce by Sir George Bullough, a man at the apogee of nouveau riche ostentation. The Bulloughs of Accrington made their brass from the Lancashire cotton boom of the 1800s. Bales of plantation cotton were horse-drawn from Liverpool dockland to red-brick factories where the racket of the cotton gin separated fibre from seed. A man with a long pole, the 'knocker-up', tapped bedroom windows, at five in the morning, of row upon row of back-to-back terraced housing. Off to work at six, clogs on cobbles. Children of eleven spent half a day at school and half a day up t'mill amongst the deafening clatter of lines of the Hargreaves' spinning jenny.

Flat caps and waistcoats; Albert and chain, if you were a foreman; smock dresses and petticoats for the women, their hair in a bun to keep it out of the machines. Day of rest, meat and two veg after church, children packed off to Sunday School, Grandma asleep in her chair and an hour's sex in the tiny back bedroom. Holidays ran to a day on Blackpool sands. In 1914, posters on every wall pointed Kitchener's finger, 'Your country needs you'. Young men rushed into SD tunics, more to escape the grind of mill-town life than by way of patriotism. When Messrs Joffre and Haig organised the Somme and lost six hundred thousand men to a twenty-mile advance, the East Lancashire Regiment was amongst those 'going over the top'. Twenty thousand fell on the first day and over five hundred were from Bullough country.

Sir George's father, already the owner of Meggernie, most notable of Perthshire estates, had bought the Isle of Rum for a rumoured £35,000. Georgie boy inherited the island and chuffed into the bay aboard *Rhouma*, his clipper-style steam-engine schooner. What a splendid prospect. 'I want a castle as long as my yacht.' At a hundred tons of coal a day, his steamboat had the coolies sweating. His monument to pomposity proved equally consuming. Industrial Accrington's joiners and masons were imported, measured for the kilt and set to work building Kinloch Castle. Bullough, favouring the MacKenzie tartan, paced the lawns checking their kilt length. Sadly the castle's site was cramped between two burns. On it arose a ludicrous pile of pink porous sandstone bearing no proportion to the dignity of its surrounding landscape but amplifying the heights to which human ego can be carried on the back of clattering cotton machines, a twelve-hour working day and a workforce imbued with the sentiments of '[a]ll things bright and beautiful'. Sir George found this hymn much to his liking, especially its verse: 'The rich man in his castle, the poor man at his gate, God made each high or lowly and ordered their estate.' – a divine arrangement, most comforting. Other than shedding a wealth which filtered through the pockets of the workers, in meaningful terms, his lifestyle was a mere puff of idle smoke.

My yacht's well-used engine developed a 'won't start' feature. To keep her in trim I'd run a charter venture, going pub to pub round the Hebrides, St Kilda, Ireland – wherever time and money took the fancy of nautically-minded punters. After five seasons every nook and corner of island and coastline had felt her anchor. One evening we lay on the east side of Mull in Loch Spelve. Three London lads aboard needed to be at Oban station next morning. A raven flew over the boat as I anchored. 'That's death to this damned engine, boys.' Foolish comment. Daylight and no wind. Brrr, brrr. No engine. I begged a tow out of the narrow gut at the mouth of the loch and we found enough breeze to catch the Saturday train. Oban's lifeboat engineer sniffed the twin cylinders of *Rhum*'s Volvo Penta and applied a massive boost of electricity. It fired up. Overnight under the flash of Ardnamurchan Lighthouse, Sunday morning had *Rhum* on a mooring at Ardvasar in Skye on the Sound of Sleat but, more importantly, the business base of John Mannel, friend, sailing expert and fellow yacht charterer. I pulled the engine stop.

'John,' I said over a dram in the Ardvasar Hotel, 'I've a filming date on the Isle of Rum on Wednesday, a sort of *Rhum* calls at Rum idea, interview by BBC's ace presenter, Jimmie MacGregor and then sail into the distance type of feature, the usual stuff and, John, I've stopped the engine.' 'So?' All day Monday, cawing away and charging batteries – no joy and over the side a flat calm. Tuesday, I said to John, 'We used to put a shovel of red coals below the sump of tractors that wouldn't start.' Last trick, engine oil into a pan on the stove. Black, smoking oil, full batteries, recant the oil, and bzzz, it started. Thanks, John. Still flat calm but, by afternoon, with a trail of engine fumes astern, I pulled up below Kinloch Castle ready for a dinner appointment with Dennis Dick, the film director, and the loquacious MacGregor. More vital than a bow tie, I left the engine running.

The outside of Sir George's scenic infliction did not prepare me for its innards. The Lancashire knight himself lolls from a balcony which surrounds the Great Hall. All six foot eight of Guards officer, trimmed tash, tweed kilt, the lot – a larger than life-size painting matched by the flattering oil of Her Ladyship who warms herself above the hall's log-devouring fireplace. Twee landscapes of the island on a good day guided quests round the gallery. Delighted moths inspect a row of stags' heads which were accompanied by the obligatory mementoes of tribal processions to the hill – stalker, toff, rifleman-ghillie and ponyman. Downstairs, what Geordie's pedigree lacked he padded out with a contentious display of objets d'art, leaving the viewer in no doubt his cash had plundered oriental bazaars and the hunting grounds of the Dark Continent. Stained glass gives a puritanical atmosphere. Lions and tigers lay spreadeagled on parquet floors. Glass eyes think of happier days, their jungle home none the better for the room's extensive hardwood panelling. Elaborate bronzes in every corner gave dusting maids nightmares. The two vast seven-foot maroon vases surely accommodated genies.

Standing in for Accrington's Salvation Army brass band is a German-built, outsized pianola. Deep inside its chambers a blast of wind is forced through holes in paper rolls and, from a bewildering array of trumpet-shaped pipes, it plays anything from 'God Save the King' to Beethoven's *Moonlight Sonata*. More to my liking, beside this musical windbag there gleams a Steinway concert grand. I was forbidden to strum the ivories, though a Mozart piano sonata lay open on its music stand. Genius and cash are rare bedfellows – poor Wolfie lies in an unmarked pauper's grave in Salzburg. Not so the Bulloughs. Georgie's dad, the money-maker, was interred in a mausoleum quarried on the slopes of Glen Harris with the family coat of arms and various other motifs in mosaic tile plastering its walls. When a guest, influenced by Bullough hospitality, likened the burial place to a tube-train urinal, Sir George at once spotted the connection and, thoughtfully removing Dad, had it blown up. Something more tasteful in the form of a Greek temple stands over the furrows of the islanders' lazy beds and in this distinguished sarcophagus rest Sir George and Lady Bullough. Who says making money isn't clever? Spending it, even cleverer?

Dinner was served. Dennis, the film director, led the way to the dining room – not by a secret door which represented Sir George at his most whimsical but past more dour reproduction oil paintings of Scottish kings, designed to conjure some vague connection to our lamentable aristocracy. Evening light shone on Loch Scresort. I glanced through immense French windows which featured *Rhum* lying at anchor in flat calm. Smoke trickled from her stern. The engine was still ticking away. Good. The dining room's suite of solid mahogany came from the state room of his steam yacht, *Rhouma*. A fine depiction of her hung above us and she was flying a commodore's flag, I observed.

As we were served chicken soup, I was told that specially heated ponds in the grounds had contained both alligators and turtles. Tiring of the latter when one of them ate a diamond ring which George carelessly dropped in their pool, they were found alternative accommodation in cooler waters off the Isle of Canna. Stories rattled on, each more bizarre: forty of a staff, many of whom worked in the garden; horse-drawn carriages; heated greenhouses by the hundred yard; two Albion cars; shooting lodges built at Harris Glen and Papidal. I'd walked to Papidal years before. A mysterious place, its lodge is in ruins beside a bonnie lochan just up from the shore but hidden. Mull and its green hills were in the distance and I thought my glass could pick out the holy island of Iona. The Norse name has Papidal as a place of priests and perhaps they did look out to the isle of their saint. Whatever may have been, the haunted feeling of Papidal, as I sat that day watching the trout make ripples where the birch come to the water's edge, left Kinloch Castle empty.

No film crew relaxes without encouragement and, in that frame of mind, I was shown the castle's crowning glory. Glasgow lays claim to the fame of putting the most bottoms on lavatory seats the world over since Thomas Crapper invented the flushing loo. 'Shanks o' Barrheed' had done the Bullough bathroom in a big way. Two enormous baths – the Health and Safety Executive would have insisted upon lifebelts – were fitted with canopied hoods over their ends. Thence to the problem, which knob to turn? Each one squirted a jet of water and there were many from which to choose. Pick the wrong one and a geyser would blast you under the kilt. Switch on the lot and you were in a car wash. Behind the scenes, plumbing mimicked lead spaghetti. More delights awaited, in spite of Lady Bullough's bedchamber being robbed of a four-poster reputed to have been the playground of Marie-Antoinette. In the ballroom the cut-glass chandelier ideal for swinging on, deep sofas, even a minstrel's gallery, but the sprung dance floor – I did a whirl or two. Why didn't I take the accordion ashore? Who could take this lot seriously? Aladdin, Ali Baba? Poor George – symptoms of insecurity manifest by ostentation, the pickings of a magpie with money.

Dennis thought it was time to go. I rowed back to *Rhum* to find the engine still running. 'Sailing By' heralded the midnight shipping forecast and issued a dire warning: Malin, Hebrides and Rockall – west, gale eight, backing and increasing later to force eleven. I slept soundly. The engine pounded the night away. Filming in the morning.

In fairness to the Bulloughs, they expended a fortune on an unproductive and obscure island which obviously held their affections. The spin-off from extravagance can be far reaching. Few remained on Rum who could claim to be local, but imported workers, tradesmen, suppliers, a wide range of people benefited considerably from this entrepreneurial family during a period which saw the nine-day General Strike of 1926 and PM Stanley Baldwin using troops to maintain the nation's food supply. Lodges and connecting roads, tree planting and the layout of castle grounds were all schemes where hand labours scored. Interest in stag breeding and deer management also benefited the Rum strain of Highland pony: strong, compact animals, sometimes chestnut coloured with silver tails that touch the ground and the fullest mane to match. Bonny beasts with a dash of Norse blood judging by their likeness to breeds in Norway today. The Vikings maybe dropped off a stallion, breeding men or beasts was in their line of business.

The impact of Hitler reached Rum in the shape of Donald Cameron. He was young, lean and son of the auctioneering shareholder of Fort William Mart. Sir George had done his bit in the Great War by lending his steamboat and cash to the government. Indeed, during the Boer War she had served as a hospital ship in South Africa and eventually brought home wounded soldiers to convalesce in his new castle. The Second World War however obliged widowed Lady Bullough to stock her island as part of the nation's attempt to feed itself. On stage Cameron. For a £50 rent he began to pile on sheep and cattle. A top-up to £100 and Donald, with the shyness natural to most Highlanders, became reluctant to talk numbers. At a possible seven thousand, along with cattle and deer, they were pushing the grazing. Donald packed it in and handed over the tenancy to Walter Mundell, a Ross-shire boy. Tall, burly and rugby-playing with the good Black Isle farm of Tarradale Mains at his back, he journeyed to Rum with more than supplies of midge repellent. Clippings took on a carnival atmosphere. I knew them both – great lads and nothing much stood in their way.

Walter got the heave when widow Bullough sold Rum to the Nature Conservancy Council, a back-to-nature quango, £23,000 of taxpayer funds with the castle thrown in as a luckpenny. Mr Mundell, versed in the Highland tradition of numerical under-statement, removed his stock quietly and boffins descended on Rum. One legacy of Sir George, the vainglorious dreamer and mini-Lord Leverhulme, traces, via Accrington, to the activities of two Lincolnshire-born brothers, Charles and John Wesley. This pair played no small part in turning a Victorian workforce to an acceptance of the industrial sweatshops of northern England. Their speciality was a nonconformist religion which preached strict adherence to an ordered and coherent lifestyle. Charles composed six and half thousand hymns whilst his brother, as a young man home from Uncle Sam, experienced a visionary 'conversion' and took to itinerant preaching. For fifty years he travelled country roads on horseback delivering the torrid outdoor sermons which were to become a central doctrine of Wesleyan Methodism. Top of John's list of don'ts was drink.

Licensing laws, such as they existed up to the early 1900s, virtually allowed a landlord to serve booze as long as it suited him and his customers remained standing. A 'Go and fetch your father from the pub' scenario. Ale, the English tipple, passed through many bodies by the gallon, again making fortunes, not least for a family who came to the Inverness area – the Baillies of Burton-on-Trent. The Wesleyan total abstinence dictum formed Sunday School children into the 'Band of Hope'. Dressed in white, they held street parades with banners proclaiming 'Feed my Lambs' and similar insights on the side-effect of alcohol consumption. Grown-ups joined 'The White Ribboners' and dedicated themselves to saving spineless blue-collars from the DTs. With the zest of 'I know what's best for you', victims and children alike were inveigled into 'Signing the Pledge' – strong drink shall never pass my lips. In Lancashire these well-intentioned movements had every reason to be a notable force. To own something called Rum, oh dear, an Accrington family with social responsibilities must avoid censure from the pulpit.

To the island's ancient spelling an 'h' was added. Sir George, a feudal industrialist gilding the petty emotion of snobbery with trimmings of calculated philanthropy, bequeathed to a spectacular Hebridean island a monumental symbol to the aping of Victorian gentility. He certainly made their ranks, lavishing his brass on underlining the point to those who cared and brow-beating those whom he'd obliged to wear the kilt.

It took the NCC years and many insect jars to learn what any switched-on hill man could have told them over a dram. Sheep, goats and deer are grazing rapists while cattle are fertility builders and biodiversity enhancers. A fold of Highland cattle was introduced but the symbiotic relationship which existed between the old organic crofting agriculture and the natural environment would be turning the clock back to an attitude and lifestyle thankfully abandoned when the thatch blew off. There were less contentious schemes and, to the credit of the NCC and, more especially, Inverness naturalist John Love, the re-establishment of the white-tailed sea eagle brought over from Norway in the 1970s proved a remarkable success. I watched their six-foot wing span in loping flight when sailing under the cliffs of Papidal. A fine bird to emphasise the wildness of the Hebrides. Which proud sportsman shot them to extinction?

◆

No welcomes were extended to visitors on the north end of Rum and the ruined clachan of Kilmory was out of bounds. A local authority act had allowed the erection of a substantial anti-trespass fence which, hung with intimidating signs and the banner of Cambridge University, allowed the genetics of red deer to be investigated by Tim Clutton-Brock and Fiona Guinness, in the strictest privacy. To interview Miss Guinness on their progress, I was allowed through the barricade and, along with BBC producer Chris Lowell, took the track to a cottage which had the lap of the tide on the shallows of Kilmory bay for company. Our welcome was most effusive and, aware of the connection between Miss Guinness and the delights of Dublin, I cast an eye over her wine rack. It boasted the finest. Did she recognise me? I saw no reason to jog her powers of recall.

Some years previously I anchored quietly in the bay, well out, for it shallows. At the tide's edge, September migrants lifted their wings and for moments held them arched and stretching. Whimbrel and godwit, their subdued calling carried over the water, they were anxious at a disturbance I was loath to make. There was no voice to detract from their syllabic notes. Hinds grazed about humps of ground that had been homes in the times when a church had honoured the Virgin Mary and had given their clachan its name. A burn carves through sandbanks as it enters the bay. There is no hurry in its flow – the glen that holds a meandering water rises only gently to the bealach. On green banks, clear of winter's flood, little more than a few steps from the life that had peopled these scant acres, is the mound of their burying.

I rowed ashore. From the remaining well-appointed cottage, a lady marched down the beach. An English accent, with the imperious tone of an Oscar Wilde dowager, shouted, 'There is no landing permitted here by law. Please leave.' I countered with a nod and a smile and walked to the scatter of burial stones. One read:

Erected by Murdo Matheson in memory of his beloved children, Rebecca who died September 1873, aged 17 years. John, who died September 1873, aged 12 years. Christina Ann who died September 1873, aged 8 years. Murdo, who died September 1873, aged 6 years. William John, who died September 1873, aged 4 years. All of which died of diphtheria between the 7th and 9th of September 1873. Archibald Duncan, who died April 1871, aged 7 months. Suffer little children to come unto me and forbid them not for such is the Kingdom of Heaven.

A ship put seamen ashore to collect fresh water and brought the plague to the croft of Kilmory. The Mathesons sailed for Australia where they had two more children. The Rum of values past left with them a vacancy which money didn't fill. My sister, Hilda, died of the same illness, aged six. I discounted Miss Guinness and her studies in the scheme of things important.

◆

Nine sharp and a morning that was brighter than several heads had the filming team trooping behind Dennis to the jetty. Still flat calm and a ticking engine. The shipping forecast from Oban coastguard was a frightener. I rowed to the pier intending to beat it up to Ullapool the moment this filming lark was finished. Cameras were buzzing, MacGregor stood at the edge of the stonework, not too close. I threw up the painter. 'Can you catch a rope, boy?' He didn't. A retake. He caught the rope but couldn't tie a knot. Our conversation turned brief – very. Dennis waved me away. 'We'll be filming as you sail out – want to catch the boat's name as you turn. Don't forget to wave.' 'If you want out of here, leave in the next hour,' I shouted up to the line of faces.

Back aboard I hauled up sail, then anchor. Now engine throttle. An enormous billow of dense blue fumes enveloped me, the boat, her name, any sight of the jetty. Wave to them? I was gasping for breath. Sad for Dennis, Loch Scresort vanished under a smoke screen. It was the last time I heard from him.

Rounding the Point of Sleat, an October gale lifted spindrift and drove us up the Sound of Kylerhea narrows. Force eight blasts and belching black engine smoke shot *Rhum* through its whirlpools. At

Kyle I set the storm jib and called Stornoway coastguard – gusts to force eleven by midnight. Off Applecross the autohelm failed. Darkness thickened. We tore on, a howler under the stern quarter. Rona light abeam and huge seas – no Ullapool tonight. I swung into Gairloch Bay. Waves beating the headlands identified Sheildaig. Getting stopped at seven knots? I swung round her mooring buoy. Nose to the gale. Loose the sheet. Rifle cracks from a flogging jib. Up the deck. In a second, we drifted alongside the buoy. I hooked the floating line, dragged the heavy strop on to the Samson post. *Rhum* jerked round and pranced the night away. I sat at the chart table and pulled a cork and then the engine stopped. Never another wisp did it make. Two days later *Rhum* lay alongside Willie MacIntosh's fishing boat at Gairloch pier and, good friend, he slung the smoking film star ashore by his derrick. The gale ensured it was three days before Dennis with his unique film clip landed back from Bullough's island dream.

◆

*Rhum* took me over The Minch many times, sometimes rough. I left Castlebay early on one occasion heading for an Edinburgh committee meeting. CalMac's *Claymore* had been storm-bound overnight in South Uist following a westerly gale. Wind was down, the sea up. Ten miles off Canna the *Claymore* passed ahead of my course, disappearing in the troughs, except for her twin funnels. Seven miles off the island, the seabed rises quickly. That morning, so did the sea. Three waves took us. The second fell on the boat and tore off the dinghy which I had lashed on the stern. As it passed and number three reared astern, I looked ahead into streaked water, over the top of a thirty-foot mast. Good sea boat she was, *Rhum* kept her tail to them and her nose out of the hollow. To the south, the sky made a masterly painting – every shade but mainly purple and yellow. I pulled into Loch Scresort, on the east side of Rum, and, with no means of reaching the telephone, called Oban coastguard. Please phone and tender my apologies. Kindly they did – against rules. Next morning I breakfasted complacently off the Point of Sleat. The tail of the gale hit a cross-current. *Rhum* broached and put her boom in the water. Egg, beans and plate flew over the side. 'Pay attention, Thomson,' I said aloud. Crossings were best following the sun's direction.

Heading westwards, I sailed from a night's dancing to Bobby MacLeod in Tobermory. His folks hailed from Laide in Wester Ross and it meant 'a news' when the accordion stopped. Smooth sailing, all canvas drawing before the lightest south-easterly air. The low-lying Isle of Muck to port, fields to shore and well farmed. The Isle of Eigg to starboard, Viking burial mounds and a black basalt ridge of toppled larval columns below the landmark Sgurr. Keep centre channel to dodge the Godag skerries. Just the lightest helm and noiseless sailing closed the southern cliffs of Rum. Papidal is hidden from the sea. Great Viking peaks press down. The Glen Harris, wide and deep in grass, curves away to their foot with the open arms of somewhere to live with seclusion on the doorstep. I swept the place with my glass. A burn divides the pastures, entering the sea through a glimpse of yellow beach. Ruddy-brown Highland cattle munched away, heads waggling, horns flashing in the sunlight. A bull chased one round Bullough's Grecian temple. It takes an honours degree in pomposity to deface a classic scene with monumental graffiti.

Dolphins were leaping far to starboard as the channel for Canna opened. Further astern, a little one surfaced. I set the tiller and hurried fo'ard to lean over the bow and whistle. A couple of minutes' wait and, below the surface under the forefoot, diving side to side, was eight feet of sleek glossy dark skin, a stream of silver bubbles at fin and tail, a trickle from the vent on the top of his head. The second one, smaller, cut in. I laughed and whistled. Without warning, just a yard off, a burst of speed and the big fellow leapt clear, his beautiful white underside emerged from a shower of water – arching body, strength in beauty, glistening, level with the deck. For a second, our eyes met. Sscur-ploosh and a cascade thumped back on the sea. No animal fits nature with a bonnier shape. Harmless, knowing creatures, surely they played with me, cavorting about the bow. The wee one hadn't showed and without warning they disappeared, perhaps at the noise of the anchor chain which I unflaked as we neared Canna harbour. A family having a day out, I shared their fun.

*Rhum* drifted quietly as I stowed sail and a childhood tale came to me – one of many told with colour and description by Father when he came home from sea. Rock and current abound in the Sound between the North and South Islands of New Zealand and, for twenty years or more, each incoming ship would be met by an albino dolphin and the sailors called him Pelorus Jack. Leaping and dancing well ahead, the helmsman would follow him and be navigated unfailingly through the dangers. Once the ship reached safety, the men threw him fish and, with a whistle, Jack would turn and head back for the open waters. A strange vessel entered the Sound, running before a storm, and Jack appeared, sure and faithful. The crew thought it an omen of shipwreck – a white sea-monster luring them on to rocks. To steady his terrified crew, the captain took a rifle and shot Pelorus Jack.

Canna's profile resembles these shapely mammals, suggesting the name has a Gaelic derivation. However, Norse names are common throughout the island and their old language translates Canna as 'tankard', a description its speakers would have preferred. Late afternoon sun was warm on my back as I rowed to the tidal islet of Sanday. Low in gentle undulations, the Bronze Age people found easy digging and, whatever they believed, there, under rounded mounds, are their graves. Up from the shore is a small church and amidst dust and disuse the scent of incense remained. Religion divided Catholic Canna from Protestant Rum more effectively than the short sea crossing. The MacLeans of Coll, as lairds, forced their tenants on Rum to abandon Rome but Canna clung to the old faith, honouring the times of a Columban nunnery on cliffs above the south-facing Tarbert Bay they gave name to its memory – *Sgnor nam Ban Naomh*, 'The Scree of the Holy Women'.

A footbridge beyond the empty school put me over to the main island and I climbed a knoll which looked down to scarred bays, lustrous and green, but without shelter. Crossing the island was an easy stride and I came on a group of dwellings sunken into the ground, perhaps Bronze Age, but not the Viking connection I sought. The edge of the north cliff guided me – the turf had such a spring, I ran. Insects and flowers in bewilderment, some I knew, milkwort and creeping willow and one which dotted the slope I followed with its tiny white starred shape and then, as the cliff relented, the land led me down to where it jutted into the sea. The Norsemen farmed Canna – their house sites remain – and here, in raw openness on the small Langanes Peninsula, they are buried.

Not the tame dunes of Sanday favoured by the southern folk where friendly puffin nest the rabbit holes but here, under a pagan sky, where the north wind rides the crests of The Minch and the spindrift blows. It's told there lies a King of Norway beneath the gathered stones which shape his boat. No spray covered his resting place as it would in times of gale. My day, in its gentleness, let the pimpernel bloom by the shore, and in a hollow amongst the boulders, I slept. The air made eddies of warmth, curing the hay for the people filling their barns with the fragrance of meadow grass and the tiny flowers that yield their scent to a drying sun. On evening's stillness were the voices of the girls, calling, calling, and the cattle came from the slopes of wild fescue, slowly on their chosen path, and brown arms bent and golden hair tumbled against a mossy flank and the milk tasted of hills untouched. And laughing eyes, blue as the sea, turned their gaze.

Time lingered, lingered as the note that waits, poised on the fingers of a melody that guides the pain of beauty into trance. Ocean bird life wheeled, their cry above the hiss of unfolding ripples. The canvas filled, a raven soared above the making tide, a dragon prow nodded to the swell, to a sun alone above the Uist hills. Northwards trailed the Isles. Their skyline pointed homewards and took living eyes to a land they saw in sleep. Over a sea they sailed by day, to a sea they hoped to cross in the trance of death.

At the time of my walk, only one local family remained on Canna – the MacKinnons. By evening, round at their house beside the phone box, we talked livestock. The island is a grassy gem and in 1820, debt-riddled MacDonald of Clanranald sold it, complete with crofters, to Hector MacNeill. Kelp prices crashed, rent arrears spiralled and a couple of hundred crofters were turned off the island to make room for his cattle-farming enterprise. By 1881, MacNeill was losing money and a Glasgow ship-owning family bought him out. The Thoms' reign, as benign as MacNeill's was ruthless, lasted over fifty years and saw them build a pier and the substantial Tighard House. The anchorage has good shelter, allowing crews to pass a storm daubing the rocks above its jetty with their fishing boat names and those east-coast fishermen of Presbyterian faith to walk the little distance from the pier to the quaint memorial church built by Alan Thom in his father's memory.

The thirties' depression rafted ships into batches side by side and left them to rust. Men with Master's tickets queued in the labour pools of the nation's seaports hoping for a berth. The crash whittled away the Thoms' fortune and in 1938 Canna was bought by a leading entomologist, John Lorne Campbell. Who better to recognise the connection between farming and the world of insects? Campbell's American wife, Margaret Fay Shaw, took an objective view of the changing Hebridean lifestyle and by photos and recordings illustrated the decline of a culture based on crofting. The couple lacked an heir and, in his lifetime, Campbell generously gifted Canna to the National Trust for Scotland, expressing the wish that they might continue his theme of woodland establishment allied to an agriculture which would enhance integration between soil microbes and the variety of insect and plant species which the island supports in profusion.

◆

More pressing work on Mingulay awaited MacLeod and Thomson, contractors and experienced chancers. It meant an early start, out by a broad-topped stac upon which are the remains of a fort known as 'The Prison'. Legend has it some ageing laird of Canna had installed a young wife and to offset his bouts of jealousy there she remained until her death. A magnetic hill on the corner is supposed to throw the compass. I didn't notice and, rounding Canna's northern shore, we picked up the first of a sou-east breeze. I trimmed sheets. She'd sail herself – a morning to recline on the cockpit locker. Islands thought so too and spread themselves round the horizon. White-striped razorbills flew from a round-topped sea stac tucked under the north cliffs. From an oily green sea it stood erect and proud, so appropriate a symbol to the island's fertility and its western margins of flower-covered pastures where the buxom Norse women would be tending their cattle and watching the sea.

Face to the sun and an eye on the compass, five hours at six knots on 270, I'd hit Barra if I fell asleep. *Rhum* sailed west to the slow breathing of The Minch having a long lie. We cut through a huge raft of Manx shearwaters, I lifted an elbow to the gunnel and

watched their sickle-winged flight. Dark, powerful bodies, close to
the water, they would sit the tides until dusk and then hey-ho for the
high peaks of Rum and chicks in nest holes making the mewing of
hunger. Over the port gunnel, five miles due south, the column of
Oigh Sgeir Lighthouse poked above the knobs of low-lying islands.
Coll and Tiree, producer of fine cattle and stopping point of
Atlantic rollers which bring the world's surfers to help salvage
the crofting economy. Cocktails, sunbeds and seafront chalets?
Beauty is an elastic commodity, best savoured in comfort – it snaps
easily with rain down the neck.

Over the spray-hood I picked out the Bo Vich Chuan, the
fairway buoy that leads to a 'Never-Never Land' where everything
will do tomorrow. Barra on the bow but a noisy dot was approaching fast. Rifle on board, yes, no guided missiles. Short of winging his
rotors, I was reduced to shaking a fist. An outrage was being
perpetrated off Muldoanich, in home waters, and Castlebay round
the corner. I was being buzzed. Sails fanned faster than the blades of
the overhead extractor in my favourite bar, on a ceilidh night. The
chopper banked not fifty feet above the mast, Royal Navy clear
along its side, a supercilious grin from its cockpit. Naval type, pity
Gigs was away with his commodore's flag. Several minutes' surveillance and, quick as a dung fly to a midden, the contraption
whizzed off to vanish amongst grey radar antennae protruding
incongruously above the Vatersay skyline. Were the natives revolting? Fact or opinion, send a gunboat or merely agree? It would take
more than kid-glove treatment if DD Campbell and The Vatersay
Boys were warming up for a session.

*Rhum* gathered way. The Dubh Skeir pillar came abeam. Hold
course, a couple of cables, open the bay, not cutting corners. With a
nautical swagger, I put up the helm, controlled the boom and over-
cracked the mainsail canvas. Tiller against my thigh, I heaved taut
the Genoa sheet. Winches burred and we heeled hard – a full press.
It was slick stuff. A proud bow wave headed towards Kisimul castle,
a sighting to the windows of The Castlebay. Cronies could be
watching – John the Bar noted every yacht that entered the bay.
Nelson and Trafalgar – 'England this day expects every man to do
his duty'. How true. If I'd known the flags, I'd have signalled 'Set
'em up.'

Kisimul abeam. Some of DP's clients focused cameras from the battlements. I aimed for the slipway, in behind the pier. Sail down with a rattle, we coasted in. The slip seemed busy. A Hymac digger, A & M MacLean on its boom, sat well back. Men waved frantically. What a welcome! I spotted Sandy with both arms flailing. Midges or pinta time? The latter always flexible. He bent, picked up a long white cylinder and began waving it round his head, running on to the pier at the same time. Michael on the digger dodged back in his cab. My God, a stick of 'gelly'. Hard over helm. No tin hat. Whoosh. Bang, thunderous and echoing. Water shot in the air accompanied by rock. *Rhum* took direct hits.

Smoke poured up the village as raucous singing drifted down. I let *Rhum* settle. What in the world? A swaying bunch of uniforms sang their way on to the pier, carrying a body. More racket. A chopper zoomed from behind Vatersay, scattered the vocalists, collected the prone form and vanished in an easterly direction. All this as a smart blue launch with a perky flag on the bow cut across the bay at ten knots to halt with a roar of reverse alongside the pier. Revellers helped each other aboard and, with more arm-waving and singing, the 'liberty boat' vanished with equal velocity, leaving the strains of a rather lewd version of 'Rule Britannia' floating in its wake. Investigation was required. I moored gingerly on the far side of the pier and, collecting the demolition expert in passing, strode to The Castlebay.

John the Bar was mopping the lino. I could see his forehead required similar attention. 'Oh, boy.' No word of serving customers, he sank on to one the chain chairs. 'The till's choked – I couldn't pump the optics fast enough.' I glanced across. Only dregs remained in a line of bottles. 'They took more in half an hour than you lot can stow on Saturday night when the Vatersay Boys are playing. Thirty sailors at least and look at the pool table – they burst in before I could get it covered.' John was clearly upset – more so than Big George the boss would be when he checked the bulging takings.

A year previous, almost to the day, the Royal Yacht *Britannia* anchored in Vatersay Bay. 'By all means allow the crew a little shore leave. Let them visit the village of Castlebay – it's so pleasant.' 'Yes, Ma'am.' The Queen herself had, many years before, stepped ashore on the landing slip and to quite a welcome. Indeed the enthusiasm for our monarchy which existed in the hearts of several of the villages had that day led them to pre-empt the celebrations in The Castlebay, and on the suggestion of the constable they viewed the proceedings from the window of the local cell. Best forgotten. A little shore leave was ordered and in steamed the royal launch loaded with sailors availing themselves of Her Majesty's generosity. Ah, the allure of Castlebay. They were to misconstrue her gesture. More than the launch steamed back to *Britannia*. A proportion of the crew were confined to the scuppers. The Royal Yacht's schedule had to be put on hold. Knock, knock, 'Come in. This must not happen again, Captain.' 'Yes, Ma'am.'

Twelve months had passed and the attractions of Castlebay had not dimmed, neither in the minds of sailors, nor in those elevated by luck of birth. 'Let the crew stretch their legs, a short walk on the sands of Vatersay.' 'Yes Ma'am.' Iain Allan, between being the lifeboat coxswain and generally helping anyone with a seafaring problem, ran the Castlebay to Vatersay ferry. His small work-boat plied the channel several times a day – ten folk aboard made a crowd. The two o-clock run, Iain Allan pulled away from Vatersay. 'Hold it, hold on, stop the bus!' A horde of arm-waving matelots appeared on the skyline running pell-mell towards him. Before he knew it they had his boat well below her plimsoll line. A determined stride up Castlebay High Street left their destination not in doubt nor, as Sandy and I entered, was there any doubt as to the cause of John the Bar wiping his brow with a dish cloth.

John made it back round the counter and poured the dynamite enthusiast and me the remains of a Famous Grouse. 'The buggers went wild – stuffed the juke box. That was OK but then they started dancing on the tables – crazy. One bloke leapt across on to the snooker table. Two or three of them doing a hornpipe on the good baize, another couple fencing with the cues, me trying to keep up with the rest bawling and thumping the counter for more drink. I'll tell you, lucky that bugger fell off the table and broke his leg or they'd have wrecked the place.' 'So what, John boy, supplier of booze to the *Britannia* and the honour of holding up the royal tour – a moment to be proud of.'

Late next day, from the windows of The Castlebay, the Royal Yacht *Britannia* and her naval escort were spotted heading out of Vatersay Bay. Doubtless Phil whistling 'What shall we do with a drunken sailor?' and Brenda 'not amused'. Maybe the captain was in chains.

## 32

# 'I'm from Guadalupe'

Too late, damn it, spotted, cover blown. 'Coo-eee! Coo-eee!' floated from the window of the cocktail lounge of The Castlebay. Jean Balfour, past chairwoman of the Countryside Commission and Morton Boyd, boss of the Nature Conservancy Council, waved me in. 'How wonderful to meet you here.' And, presently, viewing the bay, they ask, 'So that's your yacht?' 'Er, yes.' I was always a slow thinker. 'We're *so* keen to get to Mingulay – you're not going that way by any chance?' 'Well, I . . . I . . .' 'Tomorrow – shall we say nine?' It required a circuit of the working man's bar to regain my equilibrium.

An imperative tap on the side of *Rhum.* 'It's half past nine, Iain.' A day was unfolding without due consideration to the night before. The lifeboat coxswain's ten-year-old son, good with oars and a dinghy, had been press-ganged. 'Here we are.' I pulled them aboard and, to a whistling kettle, headed south. The sea behaved impeccably, mirror-calm. I heaved the couple ashore on Mingulay and they hastened towards the high cliffs, equally impeccably, I observed, not hand in hand.

The evening glowed as we powered towards Castlebay Pier and so did they. 'Such a wonderful day – thank you *so* much, Iain.' Concrete piles, fifty yards ahead, reduce revs, reverse hard. The confounded engine wouldn't come out of gear. Yank, yank on the lever – no result. Pull engine stop, smartly. We shot alongside, just avoiding more than scraping the paint. A wave and more profuse thanks and away the delighted couple trotted, unaware they could have been leaving a sinking ship. Long arms, stout oars and I towed *Rhum* out to her mooring by the castle. Next haul was to the captains' table where the conversation was most reassuring after talk of tagging kittiwakes.

Ten in the morning is no time to take on the malfunction of a yacht's engine. I stretched full length beside *Rhum*'s malfunctioning one in a space no bigger than a rabbit hutch. Had the gearbox any oil? Maybe stripped a tooth? Iron filings inside the casing should tell me. I unscrewed the plug and gently inserted the middle finger of my right hand – a most useful finger but the little one would have been wiser. No filings inside the hole, quite a relief, but get out the finger. In past the knuckle. I poured oil down it, pulled, screwed, full strength both arms – it might tear off. It didn't. Stuck fast to my engine, on my side, nobody to come near me. This could spell amputation with a hacksaw. No more accordion. I'd learn the fiddle – if I didn't bleed to death. You've done it this time, Thomson boy.

Close to dislocating a shoulder, I twisted round and reached the ship-to-shore, VHF. 'Castlebay pier, this is yacht *Rhum*.' Silence. The boys had knocked off – no steamer until tomorrow. *Rhum* wasn't sinking and I wasn't drowning so I let an hour pass. Nobody missed me at opening time – strange. Last shot. 'Mayday! Mayday!' I didn't elaborate on the predicament. Another dose of silence.

Time passes slowly with one's finger attached to an engine. A certain amount had passed when bump alongside and three faces, avoiding laughter, peered into my cubbyhole, Iain Allan, the coxswain, Roddy a'Bhuidheach, the lifeboat engineer, and Dr Bickel, the Castlebay quack. 'Try doing circles,' the doctor suggested, 'the finger might screw out. I did that once under a car.' I admired his humorous touch but this situation was more confined. Did I need morphine? Amputation was under consideration. The coxswain took charge. Within three hours, he and Roddy had the engine reduced to spare parts and filling two fish boxes on the cabin floor. I emerged from the hutch carrying the gearbox below my left oxter and with a finger still vanished into its oil hole.

Up the slipway I went in the same pose. A crowd had gathered. Even for Castlebay, a village not unaccustomed to the unusual, was it commonplace for a man to be attached his yacht's gearbox? Did I need a coat over my head? To the lifeboat shed we filed. Now to release the trap. Shinning cogs dropped out. The last one stuck on the shaft. No budging. Held by an Allen key and needing real power to unscrew. News of my dilemma, unusual even by Barra standards, had circled the island and Archie Lach looked in, much concerned. The very man, the only chap on the island with enough grip. Even his face coloured with the strain. Bingo. Gearing freed, the empty case remained. We looked inside. A finger waggled back, easily mistaken for a plump sausage.

Iain Allan fitted a new hacksaw blade. 'Hang on – I'll take a dram if that's your plan.' 'Don't worry, you'll either get your finger back or there'll be a ring on it.' And he made two precise cuts in the casing. 'Now put it on the anvil.' One deft swipe with cold chisel and hammer – wallop. No ring! I held aloft a triumphant finger, cut to the bone but in one piece. Deserving a cheer but, instead, I went up to the lifeboat house and ran it under the tap. Could have been in the frying pan.

A surprised Dr Bickel applied a bandage with the warning, 'Don't do anything for a month.' Gratitude is something else and a week later across on Iain Allan's Vatersay croft I clipped his sheep – foolish shepherd, wise doctor. A few days later, I was on his doorstep as a red mark progressed up my arm. He looked serious and scribbled a note. 'Get to Glasgow, pronto.' Archie raced me to the daily plane. They held it, ticking over on the cockle strand. Splashing through the incoming tide, we zoomed away. I didn't fancy my chances in Glasgow so I jumped on a train to Aberdeen with my throbbing arm, unaware of a football derby – Dundee versus the Dons.

The thrill of the match showed clearly as I entered Casualty. It was full. The least injured held cut heads and there was much blood and groaning. I sat gingerly on the end of a bench bravely reading *The Financial Times*. A nurse took particulars. 'Name?' Simple. 'Address?' More difficult. 'Er, it varies, according to wind and tide,' I added, by way of explanation. 'Religion?' – an enquiry of a more philosophic nature. 'Well, to be honest, I've thought of setting

up one of mine own – most seem to make money.' She eyed me with
suspicion and wrote 'Nil'. Was this patient attending the right clinic?
'Occupation?' At that point, in an attempt to stop a seriously
haemorrhaging bank account, I'd taken to dabbling in long-shot,
make-your-fortune Australian mining shares. 'Stockbroker,' I re-
plied instantly – it had a more elevated ring than gambler. She
scribbled without comment and hurried into a cubicle.

Moments later her head popped round the door. 'Mr Thomson.'
Was I queue-jumping or merely considered dangerous? I fancied
my growling companions would be as capable of inflicting an injury
as receiving one so it was not a time to dally and into the consulting
room I shot, thumped my newspaper on the desk and sat down. A
white back remained turned to me, considering both the letter from
Castlebay, which doubtless described the cause of my enfeeblement,
and the nurse's notes. Some time elapsed, in silence, as though he
was debating which to examine first – head or hand. The consultant
swung round. His eye flicked from bandage to newspaper. The
nurse exposed my wound. He eyed my hand, then back to *The
Financial Times* and, with a curt nod to the kindly nurse, remarked as
he swept out, 'It's a long time since your hands shuffled bits of
paper, Mr Thomson.' I've discovered many times that a rolled copy
of *The Financial Times* below your oxter eases one's passage through
life.

◆

Few cement mixers are subjected to a dip in the seas off the
Hebrides. This one, in danger of filling its barrel from their waters,
hung over the Traigh Bheag on a sagging rope. I'd rigged up an
'endless' twin-pulley and rope system to stretch between a rusting
iron spike driven into the Mingulay landing rock and a fencing
post, hammered home and stayed at the top of the cliff. Archie
Lach provided our motive power, fuelled from a box of Bell's
Afore Ye Go which we'd thoughtfully stacked beside him. Sandy
and I busied ourselves on the rocks below attaching things to the
transporter – window frames, corrugated-iron sheets, bags of
cement, various items of two building tradesmen's requirements.
Perched on the cliff top with foot against the fencing post to avoid
ejection, Archie pulled on the rope and, from time to time, as

pressures increased, on the fuel cell installed by his elbow. Consignments swayed merrily to the cliff top with little more effort than a sweating Archie.

The mixer left the landing more doubtfully. Under considerable weight the rope stretched. Our contraption plunged towards the tide. There it hung, dabbling its wheels in the tide in a carefree manner. At cliff top our engine had stalled, indeed was in some danger of being catapulted towards us. I raced to the top of the cliff. Archie lent back at seventy degrees, his muscles bulging – a one-man tug-o'-war team about to head skywards. Not a position for refuelling. I grabbed the rope-end and lashed to it the bottom of the post. Archie sank to the ground. 'You bugger, Thomson, you'll be the death of me yet,' all he could gasp. 'Have a little Afore Ye Go, Archie – ye nearly went.'

The fishing boat vanished behind Rosinish, taking any possible contact with civilisation, baring a fortnight's supplies left clear of the tide. Sandy, me and the Seal Woman, beautifully settled weather, The Minch, blue as a retired colonel, and the old schoolhouse to re-roof, re-window, concrete a floor and repair holes in stairs and landing which, to the thrill of going to bed by a shaft of moonlight through the tiny attic window, was added the prospect of breaking a leg.

Improvisation, always the watchword of Messrs MacLean and Thomson, had slates rumbling down the roof to land unbroken on Neillie Mòr's flock mattress, a clever trick considering the snores of its user had done much to slacken their hold over the years. Driftwood became scaffolding. We'd brought nails and a ladder. Concrete sand came from the beach, loaded on my back. In ten days, we were boxing the gable skews and had the corrugated iron looking truly smart. On calm evenings, the midges swarmed and got into ears and eyes. We had the sense not to wear the kilt but tried mud packs on sunburnt faces. No use and, given that washing was limited to a pail from the burn, not pleasant. We retired inside for a can and a 'wee toot'.

Such enchanting weather couldn't last. Supplies were getting low and there were still repairs to finish. One morning our Vatersay friend Hector and his fishing boat, *Lady of the Wave*, lay in the bay, rolling to a swell. I rowed out to him in *Rhum*'s rubber dinghy and exchanged the Seal Woman and nights by a moonlit tide for three boxes of rations. Sandy waited on the rock landing.

As Hector and his passenger pulled away north, I pulled back towards the ledge – although dangerous, this was our only possible point of leaving or landing. We were alone again – left to consider Mingulay's attractions and its problems as a hefty swell of creamy tops arched along the rocks.

I laid the dinghy off at a comfortable distance and watched the waves rear on to the shelving ledge, pause with menacing effect and then sluice down again, leaving slippery rocks and an unpleasant undertow. The dingy was rising and falling eight feet. Roping up the first box crossways, I pulled in close to the ledge, just close enough. A swift heave of the line and it was caught by the waiting Sandy. To avoid being swept out to join me, he was obliged to bob up and down in time with each swoosh. I too went up and down, judging each surge. A smaller wave came. Now, pull hard. I spun the dinghy and swept it under the ledge. A measured move, it allowed Sandy to hoist aloft our vital links to the Castlebay grocer. Bow away, I laid to the oars, keeping the dinghy's nose to the swell so that it would be safe from capsizing and a grinding on the rocks for it and me. The second box also made it ashore without any problem but, come the third box, the surge took me virtually under the ledge. Sandy hoisted but the dangling box caught the overhang. I dug the oars trying to fight clear, fully aware that, being so close in, the next wave could flip the dinghy and I might be sucked beneath it.

Sandy appeared less concerned. As I struggled with the sea, he stood with the corner of a box to his mouth, gulping the fluid which trickled out. I lay clear, watching for the next high surge. It came – a broad back rolling from rock to rock. At the exact moment, a swift pull on to the crest and it lifted the inflatable well up the ledge. Sandy grabbed the rope and hauled and I stepped ashore. To her credit, the Seal Woman had embarked by the same exhilarating method but her downhill water-slide version was more frightening.

We carried our lifeline well up the rocks. I looked at the soggy boxes. 'To hell, Sandy, did you leave any?' 'Deeprivaashun is a turrible thing,' as Para Handy would say. I ripped open the last box. 'Ah, man, look at that!' A broken half bottle. We bemoaned the tragedy of some proportion which was only diminished by the discovery in the first box of a huge bowl of Sandy's wife's delicious but deadly Mingulay trifle. Topped with cream, each nightly helping filled the old schoolhouse with alcoholic fumes and lifted our spirits no end as the weather worsened.

I'd brought the .22 rifle and, to vary our diet, Sandy stalked and shot a cormorant. Into the oven with it, an onion stuck in its gullet to offset the taste of fish. We feasted for a day before rabbits took over the menu. I'd shot several where hollows above the Traigh Mhor once wintered island boats when, dash it, I slipped and the rifle clattered on a stone. Nights later the torch beam picked out the red eyes of nibbling larder replenishments. Bang, bang, they munched on, we returned empty handed, the rifle's foresight had been knocked. Only the greaseproof paper of our last Mother's Pride remained. The forty-year-old ex-army tins, minus labels, lined up on the dresser cast their spell.

We opened the first one for breakfast. Processed cheese. Mmmmm. We cut the yellowing dollop down the middle. Equal shares, for the moment. Those as yet to dine on hunks of ageing rubber will be unfamiliar with the difficulties presented by its mastication. Three days, three times a day and we were still to discover any tins without cheese. Excitement wore thin. The effect on moral and bowels, never mind the empty trifle bowl staring at us after an evening's chewing, was far from conducive to our well-being. On the third night, I had half a tin to myself. Trap a sheep or row a rubber dinghy to Castlebay – neither an easy option.

Sandy dodged breakfast and spent the morning sitting on the school dyke gazing at the horizon. I worried about him – the last lager tin had been used for target practice a week previously. 'The sea's down,' and after a pause, 'surely today.' We packed up in case. I avoided lunch and wandered to the beach. Young herring gulls in smutty plumage fought over a scrap – perhaps the dead puffin chick of a late brood from the slopes of Macphee's Hill. In a rowdy trail, they followed the arc of a bay so often under watching eyes in times of hardship. It reflected the weakness of today's dependent masses if the environment turns to cheese. We still had tea bags. I blew up the dinghy.

'That's an engine,' Sandy called down from the house. I walked up for my towel and sleeping bag. Leaving Mingulay should be a pipe tune, a lament, it was never a joy to lock the house and turn the back. Fishing boat ahoy. 'Skit', one of our 'down the counter' friends, manhandled the dinghy into the well of his work boat, 'You might have shaved, boys! Which of you's Man Friday?' 'We ate him, have you any bread?' The wheelhouse locker contained a loaf. 'Skit' cut it into slices, about four. Ravenous. 'The Staff of Life' took on new meaning, in both hands. The threat of army tins faded and a pot of strawberry jam vanished too.

◆

Admiration for a watertight schoolhouse, rather than our escape from cheese poisoning, saw Pabbay needing a new sheep fank and dipper the following year. One island nearer to Castlebay, a fortnight's work and a camping job. Specialists in privation and reduced rations, weren't we just the boys? Landing on Pabbay is a mite easier than Mingulay but still double handling a dinghy, rock and jump ashore affair. Donald Beag, with Archie, Calum and 'Coppertop' to help unload the materials, ran us down from Castlebay in the *Reul*. To my delight, a lust for castaway islands brought the Seal Woman.

On level ground, a little way from the conical burial mound which is such a remarkable landmark on the island, we were erecting an equally surprising feature. Hardly prehistoric, yet not lacking a certain hint of bygone times when Britain's Empire held sway, a brown bell tent arose. Sandy flailed about inside, holding its single pole as I pegged down guy ropes. 'This is some tent, where did you get it?' I didn't imagine for a moment he'd deviated from company policy and made a purchase. 'On the Castlebay tip.' 'A good find, boy.' 'Yes,' the pride in his voice muffled by folds of mouldering brown canvas whose aroma betrayed its recent fall upon hard days. Indeed, some of the guy ropes exhibited a frailty one might associate with veterans from the Relief of Mafeking. OK, the sides drooped here and there but, once set up, it took cement bags, all our precious rations and the one-man camp bed which, given my favoured circumstances, I was pleased to pass over to Sandy.

Under Archie's guiding hand, supported by the attentive hand of John the Bar, we'd devoted many precious hours to planning the fank's layout. It took shape as I dug prehistoric stones from a ruin and wheelbarrowed them across a plank to the dipper site. Vandalism, spelt as recycling, the vanguard of progress. Morning air, clear as the sound of the surf that tumbled in the bay, also carried with it a blue haze from the open flap of our company tent – Sandy had the frying pan sizzling. The ridge of my small green hiking tent peeped from a hollow on the hillside; the Seal Woman slept. Arcadia and bacon and eggs. Then the first droplets hit my tomato ketchup.

The tornado struck with swirling fury. No warning, wham, bham, it threw corkscrewing rain at the sky, at us and, more alarmingly, at the bell tent. Wind and stinging hail tore round its cone, dancing with the devil. Guy ropes went pinging. Sandy raced inside, closed the flap and grabbed the pole. In moments, he was enveloped. Brown canvas cavorted round him, billowing like an Egyptian belly dancer, agitated by a wasp. The last rope pinged, tent skirts lifted and twirled skywards, revealing all our supplies and Sandy clutching the pole as he swayed in tempo. Lightning smoked into the hill behind. I beat whipping canvas. A deafening crash of thunder cut his piteous bawling, 'Save the sugar, save the sugar!' Sandy had a sweet tooth.

Rain lashed. We threw stones on the squirming remains of the tent and fled for shelter, of a kind, behind the gables of the roofless house up from our camp, the only cover between us and Castlebay barring my two-man tent – a thought which crossed my mind as the drenched Seal Woman ran to find us. An equally rapid clearance to shirt drying sunshine and grinning clouds is the way of the west. We looked down to a brown heap which steamed uninvitingly. Homeless – not a problem. The galvanised dipper had yet to be sunk in place, there was driftwood and the remains of our tent. Two hours installed Sandy in a new home. We selected a rock face with the most comfortable lean. Half a sheet of beachcombed plywood, posts, rails, folds of tent for the roof, produced a semi-watertight shanty fit to carry the company name. On its front wall I painted, MacLean and Thomson, contractors – somebody might call in passing. The dipper, turned on its side, stored the company sugar.

A 'wee toot' each evening, an aperitif to corned beef and beans that allowed us to relax. Not a soul to intrude from Pabbay to

Castlebay. I reclined on the camp bed outside Sandy's abode. Progress was good. A day of concrete mixing and laying it by hand – enjoyable work in surroundings which made tube train stress appear insanity. A week since we started and nobody to break the seclusion. The ground about us once grew hay, now it was home to pied wagtails, flicking their tails and catching flies, quite unafraid. Sandy carved the corned beef. My line of vision, over a glass, took in the prehistoric burial mound. A man was bent, digging into its slope. 'Sandy, some devil's across on the gravesite. He's got a spade, he's digging away. There must be a yacht in the bay.'

Sandy looked up, furious – after all, he part-owned Pabbay, 'I'll soon stop that.' 'No, no, Sandy, keep still – he thinks the island's deserted. Watch this.' I rose silently and shouldered the rifle. Crack. The first shot split the air over his head. The man leapt in terror. A second kicked a spurt of sand three yards above him. 'Watch you don't hit him.' Little chance, the intruder dropped his spade, accelerated down the dune, curls of dust rose from heels. 'I won't even wing him at that speed.' Blood was up, the third round whined off a rock.

We waited and then peeped over the ridge which hid us from the bay. A yacht lay anchored. Dinghy oars were smacking the water like the wheels of a paddle-steamer about to blow its boiler. I aimed, 'Will I let the wind out of his tyres?' 'Go easy, Thomson – he might have a rifle on board.' 'Don't worry, Sandy boy. We will fight him on the beaches, in the streets, in the hills, we will never surrender.' 'There's no streets here,' Sandy remarked dryly. To his mind, Churchill's rhetoric was of a lesser consequence than jottings in the notebook of the Castlebay bobby.

The evening settled round us. Gulls returned to the shelter of the dunes and puffed out their feathers. The light dimmed away to that glow which is ever off a resting sea which awaits the touch of the first stars. We lit a driftwood fire and lay back, warming our feet – the undisputed Kings of Pabbay. It called for another 'wee toot'. 'Our man seemed in a hurry.' 'Aye, you're right, Sandy.' Flames danced down the amber trickle filling my glass. 'Slainte. At least we hadn't the bother of burying him. Mind you, it's quite a handy spade.'

◆

*Rhum* turned eastwards up the Caledonian Canal, my hand on her tiller for the last time. Hills lost the profile that leads the eye, fresh water, the scent that drives the urge to sail, life the tempo it takes from a dipping bow. The uncanny bond which exists between a human being and their boat is a hard one to break, harder to explain. All the attributes of a stalwart companion are encapsulated in some inanimate object. Step aboard, she comes alive. Let her pick your way through a storm and you have a true friend. Born in the forests, fashioned to fit the sea, she carries you through the peaks and troughs of emotion at the elements' command. Parting is a wrench, deep and real. *Isolation Shepherd* had been on bookshelves for several years when it came to the attention of film director Edwin Mickleburgh and scriptwriter Brian Walsh. Camera skill and sympathetic interviews together made *An Element of Regret*, a subtle and elegant film following the changing pattern of life in the glens of Affric and Strathfarrar. Writing talent and years in Antarctica produced *Beyond the Frozen Sea*, a thoughtful tribute to the South Polar explorers, which won a McVitie prize for Edwin. A Hebridean film next? Perhaps the Mingulay story? Edwin bought *Rhum* but our idea failed to find a backer and together we brought her round from Gairloch to Inverness. My two young sons, Robbie and Alasdair, came aboard at Fort Augustus and *Rhum* was back on the pontoon from which she'd sailed ten years previously. Time for feet on dry land.

Lord Seafield's estates once stretched from Cullen on the Banffshire coast to the Cairngorm hills. I took the tenancy of one of their small Boat of Garten farms which look across the Spey to busy ski tows. Around that time, impending financial problems obliged Lord Lovat's Beauly estates to displenish their herd of sucker cows at MacDonald Fraser's Inverness Mart. Back I went to a familiar sale ring and beside me was Aberdeenshire pal, Harold Murray, a self-made man and expert on all farming affairs where the canny approach pays. Repeated glances at the auctioneer resulted in a hundred and forty head of cows with calves being knocked down to the account of Strathglass Farms, a spur-of-the-moment name in reply to mart manager George Tait's query, 'What'll you call your outfit?' *Rhum* and a lot more capital besides landed on four legs – a dream involving hard work and interesting prospects.

Glen Affric hills and Caledonian pine forests are the backdrop to the alluvial lands of Strathglass. These spacious flats on the south side of a strath had, ninety years previously, given a living to six family farms. It became an organic ranch to which the Lovat cows returned for eighteen thousand a year rent. Weeks after the enterprise began, BSE struck the UK cattle industry and the Strathglass herd's value fell 40 per cent. Returns for most cattle units slumped to a level at which government subsidy formed by far the major proportion of income – lean years when some called it a day. During this period, the simple and genuine mistake of being a week late handing in a form to the Department of Agriculture office lost Strathglass Farms a whole year's subsidy payment – well-fed, petty, paper officialdom, still in the business of cutting the throat that feeds them. We hung on, pouring in more capital. Foot-and-mouth disease followed BSE. End prices remained depressed. Touch and go – the wrong time to be back on dry land.

Tragic deaths overtook the Lovat family. Beaufort Castle and most of their remaining land went into a sale brochure. A farming empire crumbled and much else with it. A family, who'd given paternalistic stability and kinship to a community for five hundred years, fell in five. For three million, the castle went to Mrs Gloag, part-owner of the phenomenal Stagecoach bus and rail company. Crofters routinely bought their land and sold sites. Ridiculous energy-hungry houses swallowed fields. Pony jumps and stables, and a torrent of new faces pouring into Inverness to work; economic and cultural upheaval hit the Highlands. Clever money went into housing speculation. I purchased six hundred acres of Strathglass and continued farming. No route to a quick buck but healthy.

Pedigree Aberdeen Angus cattle now number in the ranks at Strathglass, mostly bought from John Moore's North Moss farm of my schoolboy paper round. Manager and partner in this famous herd is Angus Baillie, one-time shepherd at Cape Wrath across the Kyle of Durness. I crossed the Kyle once on a visit to the lighthouse. It was easy to see Viking longships beached on its wide sands awaiting weather to round the Cape, snug in the safety below today's farm of Balnakeil. Angus's late father, John, made that farm famous by the hardy tups which he bred and I used to buy – Highland connections. I knew John well and interviewed him in his energetic eighties for a BBC series. John was the last to drove flocks and sleep the night in the heather on the three-day trek from the Cape to the noted Lairg lamb sales. He came near to making a hundred healthy years. Shepherding the old style – it's good for mind, heart and bellows.

◆

A West Highland skiff sat on the beach a little way from the Badachro Inn. Eighteen feet on the waterline and eight of beam, double-ended and a wee cuddy at the bow, an ideal 'boatie' to sail the Viking way from the Butt of Lewis to Barra Head. It belonged to namesake, Iain Thomson. At his HQ, we topped off a Guinness. 'May I borrow your boat for a month, Iain?' 'Certainly, she's called *Spiragh* and Skye-built with a lug sail and she's easy to handle.' Good – BBC next. Inverness boss Maggie Cunningham, with Scalpay connections, and Glasgow producer, Elaine MacLean, with a North Uist father, both approved the idea. I rigged a tarpaulin for sleeping aboard and producer John Fergusson from BBC Orkney turned our journey into four programmes. Down the Outer Hebrides *Spiragh* sailed, a delight to handle. Iain forgot to mention she leaked on the port tack.

Admiral Gigs resurfaced, the justly proud owner of *Paleyma*, a centre cockpit Nicholson 38 ketch of classic design. The Caribbean beckoned, palm trees and grass skirts and lying below them. Was I interested? Maybe. We sailed Inverness to Ardvasar via a night in Tobermory. The accordion of Bobby MacLeod's son brought daylight and my shoulder being shaken. A policeman's face looked concerned. 'Are you alive?' I lifted my head from the dinghy; twenty yards separated me from an incoming tide. 'A lady out early reported that her dog found a body on the beach.' 'Good of her to notice. I broke an oar and drifted in here – I'm just resting.' Farewell Tobermory, round to the Sound of Sleat for a week of adjusting some of *Paleyma*'s gadgets and taking on supplies. John became impatient. 'Are you coming or not?' he called up. Decision time. I stood on the jetty with the Seal Woman and our two small boys. 'OK.' Kit bag, passport and shaving gear and a pier-head jump. The mainsail rattled aloft and filled. Three figures, getting smaller and smaller, waved and waved.

Away west by the cliffs of Rum and the low profile of Canna, over the Stanton shallows which break the back of the Atlantic, Skerryvore lighthouse to port, getting thinner and shorter, a sea-bound minaret. The cliffs of Barra Head stood clear and sunlit fifteen miles to starboard and the compass swung round 230. Tory Island and the tip of Northern Ireland lay forty miles south. We dipped along before a north-east breeze in back-tanning weather on a thoroughbred yacht of proven lines. Old-fashioned perhaps, but with an ancestry claiming trading schooner and tea clipper, *Paleyma* sat the sea with the pride of a dowager. Home waters fell to our wake. The trust that comes of familiarity with bay and headland was replaced by elation and a twinge of unease. The flash of Barra Head circled the last evening clouds. By midnight it had vanished and out of glittering heavens Venus shone bright and friendly.

We headed sou-west for the Rockall Deep. Get off soundings were the instructions to John from Inverness ex-dentist friend and solo Atlantic circumnavigator Mike Allan. He'd given us indistinct photocopies of his voyage which Gigs studied with a view to making the Canary Islands our first stop. Lacking detailed charts, anywhere else in between could be more difficult. Sixteen degrees W. Mike advised – the desired longitude seemed long out. We turned south and ran thirty miles off the coast of Ireland. 'You have good night vision, Iain, it'll be better if you stand watch from say, eleven until dawn.' An agreeable routine fell into place. John cooked, navigated and lay listening to 'traffic' on our powerful two-way radio whilst I steered, trimmed sail and washed up, the latter on the side deck in a canvas pail of seawater.

The nor-easterly wind kept up a steady blast. White tops and sun by day, a black treacle sea raced down the port side at night, crest yellow and leaping as far as the horizon under the light of an enormous moon. Skipper's orders, 'Keep our speed below five knots during overnight.' Ramming whales or a half-submerged container played on his waking thoughts. Once the snores erupting from the companionway matched the swish of the hull I let her go. John would call to the cockpit, if he wakened, 'Everything OK?' 'Fine!' I was a light sleeper. We roared down towards Fastnet and, as he sat at the chart table with his morning coffee plotting our run, Gigs would be amazed at our overnight progress. This tactic during the trip improved our tally no end though the Admiral would sometimes flash a torch from his bunk on the speedo and say, 'You're over five knots, Iain.'

I slept in a for'ard bunk from six in the morning until nine, and sometimes in the evening – a difficult change of sleep pattern. Three days out, fully awake, I sat in the cabin looking out to a sun-bright cockpit. John, at the wheel, was not in my sight. Totally clear and real, on the starboard locker, against the bilge pump, sat a young man. Blue jersey, fresh face, a half beard and dark curly hair, he was obviously a sailor. We had a third person aboard. He concentrated on doing some sort of knotting with two pieces of thin rope. I watched, keen to see what he was making. It seemed a long time before the chap glanced up from his work. Questioning eyes looked intently into mine. Straight blue eyes, sharp as salt air. My father? No, his eyes were brown. In that moment's consideration the sailor vanished. Yet I knew the eyes. They were the eyes of Captain Paterson but not the eyes of the old man in bed firing a child's imagination. I'd met the man, young in his love of the sea, keen as the windjammer trades. Without the least alarm, I called to John, 'I've just seen a man in the cockpit.' He looked a little shocked. 'You take the helm, Iain.' And, rummaging in his bunk-top library, he turned up a page headed 'Hallucinations'.

Where the Atlantic hits Europe's continental shelf, it's rough. It was, and it coincided with my nightly vigil. We ploughed through darkness, running under the furling headsail, powered by an unceasing nor-east half gale. I winched in a few turns to ease the motion and put an eye round the horizon, preparatory to a wee illicit snooze. A row of lights stretched right across our course. Were we approaching a lee shore? Impossible – the nearest land was two hundred miles away at least. Then it dawned – line abreast fishing boats and they were bearing down on us, fast. Each ship steaming in a circle of bright green sea with the wave tops ablaze from rows of halogen lights strung to either side on fifty-yard booms. We were headed about fleet centre. I shouted below, 'Armada ahead.'

John bounded into the cockpit. 'Where? Where? I can't see!' And he immediately flicked on our radar set whose manual he'd been studying most of the day. A row of buttons flanked its screen. Gigs proceeded to play them with the ease of an accomplished accordionist. A beam circled the dial, dots flashed and distances zoomed in and out. It looked exciting, though not as exciting as my view through the cockpit window. The red port light of an oncoming vessel was fine on our port bow, very fine, fine enough for a collision.

'Hard to port,' he ordered. 'John, there's a ship hard on our port bow.' 'No, it's to starboard, I have it on the screen, less than half a mile.' 'John, I'm looking at her now, right now. She's close – we'll hit her.' I swung *Paleyma* hard a'starboard. A boom full of blinding lights swept past our mast. Let's hope her nets don't get us. I spun back on course to miss her neighbour's boom – a close one. Gigs agreed, watching the fleet vanishing astern on the screen. His fingers rattled over the buttons for some time before he concluded the machine had a fault and switched it off. Could have been a bum note – most accordionists play them. John turned in with a warning, 'Keep a sharp eye astern in case they steam back.'

They did, in the raw light of dawn, with their booms folded away but not, however, their gutting knifes. A huge trawler steamed alongside us. Swarthy, evil-looking faces lined her rail. They glared down, shouting, gesticulating, fists waving and, more unpleasantly, making throat-slitting signs with rather long knives. John bobbed in and out of the cockpit. 'I want them to think there's more than two of us.' The Spaniards had us at their mercy. Ram us? The bearded fellow leering out of the wheelhouse window looked capable – a straight lift from Goya's *Saturn Devouring One of His Sons*. I could only hope his vessel's name, *Santa Maria*, indicated a modicum of restraint. Her props suddenly boiled the sea. She sheered across our bow, yards to spare. 'You know, Iain, yachts are looted, then just vanish.' I was inclined to believe him. To a list of aversions I added dago and tinned tuna.

Five hundred miles west of Biscay and five days becalmed hardly makes a seafaring yarn. We sunbathed under a cloudless ozone hole, and between times fitted up a 'goose-winging' arrangement to run *Paleyma* down wind, should it blow that way. Everything that moved or creaked we tied down. The sound effects, not to mention the motion, were of a long slow roll of yacht and spars on an unbroken sea, night and day, and it was ten days since we'd seen a ship or any human sign. Even my watch was suspended. Our masthead light circled the same group of stars that I counted once every four minutes. By day, we lay on a great dish, the centre of a flat, sun-bronzed ocean, too bright for the eyes. Time lolled under us and each roll awaited the next with the momentum of a stupefying pendulum. The same gang of jellyfish had basked beside us for days, too lazy to squirt themselves elsewhere. Maybe weed was creeping up the hull.

More than Coleridge's imagination might be afflicted. The roar of our engine wakened me. Dawn had still to waken France.

'To hell, we'll motor out of this.' The angle of *Paleyma*'s wake quickly widened. I took the helm. John prepared breakfast. A mug of tea and a bowl of muesli popped up to the cockpit. I'd noticed daily rations falling off a little. Between mouthfuls, a cloud appeared on the southern horizon and under it, yes, amazingly, a sail. Smallish, red and reaching, she'd angle across well ahead of our course. 'Sail'o!' John focused the binoculars. 'Port 30 – we'll close him, Iain.' Hornblower style, he rammed the throttle to full revs. *Paleyma* heeled under the burst – she'd a great turn of speed.

Whoever watched us in return altered course immediately. 'They're running off, Iain.' Now we were into wind. 'Clap on sail, boy.' I scampered to mast, up full main. John let rip the jib. At eight knots, touching nine, we bore down on the red sail, closing fast. Gigs whooped and whooped. 'We've got her.' By John's demonic look I expected to hear, 'Grapples ready. Prepare to board.' I threw out a fender and stood at the bow instead.

An elderly man sat on her coachroof as we took his wind and drew alongside. White beard and tanned as a prune, he was doubling for the ancient mariner but more worried. 'Good morning,' John called over – a bit tame given the chase, 'Do you need any food?' That we had any spare was not obvious to me. 'Perhaps, ze, I, er, ze please, cooking oil.' John dug out a bottle, tore off the label reading 'Best before December 1992' and winged it across on a line. We chatted. 'Dutchman, thirteen years at sea. Now I go home – Amsterdam. My last voyage.' I thought of the cooking oil – he could be right. 'Are you single-handed?' He seemed not to understand. 'Alone?' The cabin door opened at that point and out stepped the most delicious black girl. Long legs fitted with ebony curves all the way up. She looked surprised and rubbed her eyes. So did we – it was clear she slept in very few clothes.

Conversation changed tack. The old boy looked peeved. She'd hitched a lift. 'My Dutch friend is kind. I want to start my career in Holland – I'm a dancer.' That we could well believe. 'Where do you come from?' 'I'm from Guadalupe.' If she were a sample, we were heading the wrong way. 'How would you like to come to the Canary Islands?' 'Maybe, yes.' The old boy jumped to his feet and without so much as goodbye, put up helm and turned nor-east. We filled sail and eased away. 'Damn it, Iain, we should have boarded him – she'd have come with us.' 'You're right, John, she would've done and saved you giving him the cooking oil.'

Some mornings later the swish of a soda siphon interrupted breakfast. I looked up. At a hundred miles off Madeira, a soda siphon seemed an unlikely explanation. We'd been motor sailing and a startled Gigs dived out to the cockpit and switched off the engine. I joined him in the cockpit. A huge fountain jetted twenty feet into the air and soaked the deck. 'Don't move, Iain, this is dangerous,' he whispered hoarsely, 'if he rubs us, even a flick of his tail and the boats in pieces.' I sensed John was not of the calibre of Captain Ahab and he had a point. 'Don't speak,' he growled dramatically.

We peeped cautiously over. The brute lay alongside, its back almost gunnel level. Twice the length of *Paleyma*, it was a long grey submarine with a slowly undulating tail. I could've stepped on to a broad hump of shining blubber, yards wide. We awaited its pleasure – a poke with the boat hook was not on. It seemed to be breathing – we did, a shade faster. I'd ample time to consider Jonah predicting the destruction of Nineveh. It bought him a three-day trip in roomy-looking accommodation. Our tense inspection continued until, with a mighty plughole swirl, the leviathan subsided into the deep. 'If he rubs his barnacles against the keel we're done for.' I waited for *Paleyma* to eject. Half a mile ahead, the whale blew again. Gigs emitted a similar sound. 'Yachts vanish without trace every year – that was really dangerous.' I believed him, though how dangerous only became apparent on dry land when John checked our life-raft. It didn't inflate. Incidentally, some whales suffer from halitosis.

We didn't keep a ship's log, and though John marked progress south on the photocopy chart, I'd lost track of days. One night, a month, maybe more since, Barra Head dipped astern, a lighthouse beam appeared ahead. I roused Gigs. 'Well navigated, John, where is it?' He spread the chart and announced, 'Porto Santo – we'll turn in here instead of Madeira.' Easier said than done. A walloping swell ran under our tail and turning beam on to head in had John worried that we'd be swept into a narrow channel with no exit. Four hours plunging and rolling put us into a large marina. I hoisted the bunting and John donned his smart going-ashore dress. A large black African sat at the Customs desk. He studied a piece of paper.

Five minutes passed, ten minutes, no move or sign that we existed. John paced up and down, coughed and rustled the ship's papers. Twenty minutes and the chap looked up, took our passports. 'Come back tomorrow.' Gigs fumed. A nice official touch, I thought, given the white man's colonial record.

Anabatic winds rip off the cliffs of Tenerife. Four days later, keeping out of their blast, we coasted close in, waving to nudists on secluded beaches of black volcanic sand. Round the island and in behind the breakwater of Mogan Marina, we pulled up, weather-beaten and hungry. Though John's cooking ability was not in question, our supplies had reduced to a carrot. He halved it for supper on our last night at sea. Plenty of laughs in John's good company and never a cross word, but I flew home a stone lighter.

My first taste of Atlantic voyaging with no land in sight for weeks, it hadn't seemed strange or alarming and was far from boring. Casting an eye round the yacht or out to the horizon brought continual interest – schools of striped Rizzo's dolphins, storm petrels, changing cloud-scapes and the succession of colours they impart to the sea and, above all, the uncanny effect of space. In the depth of a night's watch as the wind falls light and an ink-black sea is peopled with stars, the ability of space to feed the brain with imagination is stunning. When the search for ripples of gravity succeeds, then will begin our quest to discover the wavelengths of imagination that drive an evolving cosmos, the Holy Grail of Understanding.

# 33

# 'Hell's Teeth – We've Lost the Life Raft'

Few bars of my acquaintance tend to be festooned with bras and skimpy knickers, and nor in general do their walls exhibit a profusion of scrawls, which indicate, by their libidinous wit, such attractions as may inspire the competent graffiti writer. Gentle reader, let not a name misguide you – one such paradise of spontaneous humour and nubile virtuosity is to be found on the east side of the British Virgin Islands.

Driftwood built its counter,
Wreck and plank its walls,
Fish nets hold the palm leaves which thatch a snuggled roof,
And each day the tide-white sand is spread upon its floor.
This shanty has no garden need,
The surf that brings Sahara's heat,
Is doorstep, brush and bell,
And Marley throbs the fire-fly night,
And wits compose by candle light.
But eyes entwine and saucy smiles fall on turquoise scrolls,
Wild dreams are stirred, sly fingers stray,
And then the fun begins.

For who would put a measure on a tot of rum?
It fuels an evening's jig, elixir by the swig,
And once the crowd's Nirvana bound, shy females can't be found.
Beware, oh bashful reader, avert capricious eye,
For now's the hour a carefree moon,
Leads maidens to its path.
And pants and bras are wall-peg hung,
And laughing nymphs with ivory bums,
Are luscious shapes which hand in hand,
Scamper down the starlit sand,
For who would clothe young Nature's ploy?
Not sailor lads like me.

They plunge and frolic, laugh and squeal,
The music beats, lazy man, my how it seeps.
And nipple proud the dimpled sea,
Lets wicked little moon drops fall, upon each secret curl
'Til wave tossed, dripping, out they come,
And smiling teeth in brown faced gleam,
Hand a naughty T-shirt's cling,
To each enchanting form.
Ah me, this wanton beat, my dear,
Fair lifts your dancing feet,
I fear your T-shirt treat, my love,
Is just a trifle neat.

Who invented things that sway,
Eyes that flash the night away?
What sailor lad would think to sleep?
For youth and beauty seldom keep
A lock on Paradise door.
And those who lift its latch and peep,
May sail the endless deep.

I stepped off a BA flight to the smell of coconut and sun-burnt forests. Gigs drove me through a playground of vista villas to *Paleyma*'s berth. She'd cruised the Caribbean for several years and lay awaiting her homeward passage at Road Town Marina in the topical heat of Tortola, largest of the Virgin Islands. A floating city towered above her at a neighbouring wharf. Tourists under panama hats disgorged, ambling uptown with shouldered ciné bags and sweaty armpits. Palm trees greeted them. Wherever nature grabbed a space, they poked their ribbed trunks into a glaring sky. Heat rose from pavements in a hugging warmth. Speeding BMWs and rotting pick-up trucks raised a dust bath for hens loitering outside the mammoth glass doors of a Chase Manhattan Bank. I tried to let a couple in. A scowling commissionaire foiled the attempt. His financial emporium enjoyed the coolest of air-conditioning. I sat on an elephantine leather couch. Briefcases and smartly pressed 'ducks' murmured discreetly, if not furtively – an offshore haven with taxation on its mind.

John knew his way about the Virgin Islands and waiting for a skipper and crew gave us ample time to sail amongst the green tree-topped islands. Breezes were fresh by day and calm by evening. Almond-scented bays, fringes of white coral sand, and palms beyond, were the image of a Stevenson adventure – 'tipping the black spot', Spanish doubloons and Ben Gunn's cave. A ninety-foot West Indian trading schooner lay to anchor in a remote bay. Black-hulled, three-masted and tarred rigging, she could be the pride of any pirate's heart. We sailed gently in. Here, for leisured days, we anchored. The water was clear as Vatersay Bay, but warm, and it was easy rowing distance from this stately example of an age when brown-skinned native boys holding a knife between their teeth would dive for sponges and octopus tentacles would lash at their legs. Parrots called amongst the palm tops breaking the silence. *Paleyma* lay in a pool of sunlight and rocked while we swam.

The skull-and-crossbones image lay over from us, untrammelled and deserted. Apparently two Scots lads owned her. Not poring over a crumpled map and digging round a single palm tree types, but treasure hunters nonetheless, for, when jungle bird life whistled goodnights from the shore, heavy rock struck up. A floating night-club swamped the bay with light and sound. Boats appeared from nowhere and stacked up alongside her. Thirty knot, hair streaming, hundred horsepower darts screamed in. Gin palaces roared up – the luxury accommodation of the Ritz afloat. Men in white suits, dark glasses and bodyguards in jackets that bulged. Girls with curves that defied gravity, bandannas reeking of musky scent. The aft deck broke into musical pandemonium. The beat sent ripples to the beach. Glasses lined the gunnel, smoke of combined ingredients circled the glint of fast-emptying bottles and, I might say, of lightly clad dancers. Meat Loaf? All raved up and nowhere to go? Don't you believe it, baby. Some Yankee babe wrapped herself round me and swayed into dancing mode.

Boy, the dancing. The deck slopped slightly, more so as decibels beat night air into submission. And phew – what heat! I hit the planks with this American honey but she bounced up smiling with wicked, let's-go eyes. You bet. Boy, the beat, the heat – soon girls were diving off the flight deck, leaving clothes behind to keep them dry. Some stretched their length on the bar to be anointed with full-cream waterproofing. Boy, boy, the beauties, dripping their way up the ladder, back on deck, under the swinging lanterns, shaking their hair, cool, refreshed and dying for more rock'n'roll. No point in getting one's own shirt wet either.

The gloom of our sail back to Road Town three days later lifted when Rob Adam flew in. A Badachro boy from Wester Ross, I'd warned his father years before, 'Don't let your son take up farming.' He hadn't. Even better, Rob had crossed the Atlantic several times, worked in Florida, married an American girl and, more interestingly, he knew the backwoods of the Virgin Islands like a native. That evening's flight brought Anne Pilcher-Gough, our Aussie shipmate. Custom officials studied her outlandish passport. It merited a night behind bars. Could it be the hyphen? We soon found this social impediment of little consequence. A topper of a girl, she'd sailed halfway round the world and rubbed shoulders with it too.

Caribbean harbour rot could be setting in and Gigs, who'd hired us to sail his yacht back to Scotland, was keen for us to leave – but we were keener to stay as long as the cash held out. Rob had friends and soon so had we – more nights amongst the dusky maidens. Lovely, carefree folks just oozing rhythm. John preferred his Rotarian chums and, chief amongst them, was a most sophisticated gentleman. Gigs introduced him, 'This is my friend David Jones.' His connection with lockers gave a twinge of concern. Still, Mr Jones had access to American military weather forecasts and such secret information enabled him to talk yachts across to the Azores by daily radio contact. A hundred quid would see us guided eighteen hundred miles in safety by his plummy voice. Huge antennae slowly revolved on the roof of his premises. Isobars on screens altered their shape with the ease of amoebae on a laboratory slide. The latest in predicting wave heights could induce seasickness. John, a technology buff, signed him up. 'Don't trouble to call us our first day out,' Rob told 'Davie'.

Gigs stood on the pontoon torn between waving us off and gazing glumly at stacks of old yachting magazines and rotting Calor gas containers which had made locker space for several trolley loads of grub. Rob's instructions to Mr Jones turned into our last exotic night. No sooner did John become a worried speck on Road Town quay than we nipped into a yacht-choked marina on the far end of the island. Many boats with swimming platform sterns awaited pale-faced charter crews who after ten days would head home with all-over tans. Tycoon toys, eighty feet long and alarmingly tall, had real sailors, white suits and peaked caps with braid. A shade humbled, we rowed ashore, keeping an eye on the road which led town-wards. From a peak in Darien, stout Cortes, destroyer of the Aztec Empire, had scanned the Pacific and *Paleyma*'s owner might also want a parting glimpse of his valuable yacht bracing herself for the Atlantic. Meantime, more bracing entertainment was at hand.

Each roller's beat is tempo and tune to the Caribbean. Islands of indelible colour and sound, yet how could ten fifty-gallon diesel drums, albeit painted red, dish out such laid-back music that's bum-note free? Between dancing with Anne and our comely dark waitress, I quizzed the steel-band lads. 'Each drum has a dished top?' 'Sure, man, we weld themselves ourselves.' 'How do you know where to hit that hollow to get the right note?' 'Just let yourself go, man – flow, man, flow. Just hit the easy beat, man.' Their loose-limbed style made von Karajan look stiff as a board. The waitress flowed in similar manner. She smelt of ripe plums or maybe some sort of leaf? It dawned – a lotus leaf. The ancient Greeks hit on the idea. Alfie Tennyson sexed-up the formula. Take a basket of lotus fruit. Pick a sea-view palm tree. Lean back. Bread, wine and dancing girls sway one towards happy oblivion. You'll never leave the glorious Caribbean. That could read 'never survive'.

◆

Morning light slid over a mellow sea steadily gaining intensity, mixing colours and stirring the ocean as though it were a vast tub of dye. Grey to mauve, mauve to the shade of sea pink, herald of a red swath that flared our path. The mainsail's white took on a rosy glow, tingeing the deck. For a moment, an eye was safe to watch the tiny cuticle of sun emerge. Dark specks pocked its surface. To the ancients, the curve of this rising segment indicated its smaller radius compared to the vastly wider curve of the Earth's circumference. Common sense said that each day the sun circled a flat earth. Three thousand years ago the Phoenicians chanced it. They ventured west between the Pillars of Hecules expecting to fall into Hades, that cavern beneath the earth – the abode of the spirits of the dead guarded by Cerberus, the three-headed dog. Hugging the coast, they turned south, kept the terror of an empty horizon to starboard and probably circumnavigated Africa. Sunrise on the empty sea, ember red into blinding glare, the magnificence of colour and scale brought awareness of the power of ideas to construe, to challenge or subvert, to overawe, and this would be all the more so if your beliefs included the possibility of sailing off the edge of the world on a dark night. We laugh at their innocence but who will smile at ours? I turned. The first of the day's warmth on my shirt would soon turn to blistering heat.

Copernicus also dodged the flames. His treatise, *On the Revolutions of the Celestial Spheres*, wasn't publicised until the year of his death. Holy processions lost of one of their best theorists. Perhaps creating fresh ideas is our surest concept. Islands astern slowly merged. Black-green palm leaves on spindle trunks, unruly tufts that fringe barefoot beaches of squeaking sand became matchstick Lowrys. Then a haze, then a smudge, then nothing – all swallowed by the translucent arc of blue upon blue. Hedonism, that blissful philosophy, was stranded under a cartwheeling Caribbean sun.

Rob organised watches. Two hours through the day, three through the night. Turns at cooking and, sharp at six each night, a sundowner. Anne handed out the glasses, timed to a second. I knew my way round the boat having sailed her south with John. The skipper worked his way through *Paleyma*'s intricate wiring system which Gigs had forbidden me to touch. Certain fuses and switches remained a mystery. Morale fell low for us boys – we'd left the island lovelies for six weeks at sea. OK, we'd had a stop at the Azores but who could put up with Davie's crackle on the radio at ten each morning? Anne spent her off-watch hours on the sundeck and then the ocean view ahead improved immeasurably. Keeping an eye on the compass became less demanding and our course more erratic – miles were added but, you see, the girl might burn. But not Anne – she turned to a film-star shade and the boys' morale shot off the scale.

A setting sun has much to tell. Day after day the massive orb lowered itself gently into the sea until sometimes a last orange tip shone through the horizon's waves in a flash of vivid green. It gave us settled weather and a breeze to drive us east, a deck warm to lie on and watch the tiny Portuguese men-of-war voyaging chartless under their pink filament sail. Without warning, dolphins would be leaping round us, beside us, often twisting their bodies in midair. Clouds played shadows with the sea, lightest blue to darkest marine, and sometimes, for no reason, they became a deep, deep green and there was only the swish-swish of our bow, dipping and dipping. All day the mast made a sundial on the deck, until the last angled rays lit the helm and faintly, out of waves that jostled away to a smooth red horizon, appeared the first of the evening's stars. As the sea grew to purple, so Venus shone with a brilliance which drew a pencil line of light on a fast darkening surface. These were not the twilight latitudes of home but the shutters of the tropics. For that brief space the skies are hers. Goddess of love, she kindles the lust of the sun and, from a night of privacy in the halls below the Earth, there comes a swelling moon.

We dismiss such beliefs as haverings of the ancients, an ignorance of the facts, even of the 'truth'. The insights of our modern world are the latest myths on a road whose milestones were carved by yesterday's thinkers. Venus helped shape our present culture. She was Ishtar to the Babylonians, Astarte to seafaring Phoenicians, Aphrodite of the Greeks and Romans. Known to Jason and his Argonauts when they stole the Golden Fleece, watched by Odysseus in his wanderings after the fall of Troy, her lineage is given to us by Homer. The daughter of Zeus, God of Gods, Father and ruler of all mankind, the dispenser of good and evil whose shield is the thundercloud and weapon the thunderbolt. Aphrodite, we are told, 'sprung from the foam of the sea'. Milestones of belief that mark a journey. Those who create the facts of today chip out the myths we leave at the foot of tomorrow's climb.

Venus, the star of evening, passes closest to earth of all the planets. A short flight of twenty-four million miles brings you to her hills which rise to thirty-five thousand feet in the Highlands of Aphrodite Terra. In March 1966, a Soviet space probe crash-landed on the planet. She is in our sights. Is her future in human hands or perhaps of new life forms we have currently under development? To three sailors with uncluttered time and all the space of the old mid Atlantic, she had yet to lose her mysterious power to beguile.

A fitful wind all day sometimes backed the sails and heat – the deck would burn your bum. Davie of the locker potential had delivered his 10 a.m. Atlantic-sailing assessment with no hint of anything untoward. Indeed, to confirm the squiggles on his screen, he generally asked Rob, 'What's your weather like?' 'Hot and sultry' was that day's replay. Yet, by the late afternoon watch, although the barometer held steady, the air that ruffled wavelets into smacking our hull took on an unusual chill. Astern, the north-west horizon loomed intensely black. Great rolls of cloud puffed into weaving shapes. Shafts of orange and red moved as searchlights, probing the upper sky, flickering across the thin band of white which divided an ultramarine sea from a trapped sun.

We gazed aft. 'Wasn't it dawn rather than evening that came up like thunder?' Kipling's 'Mandalay'. This looked more serious. Wind gusted the sails into life. Rob ordered, 'Get the main down.' Anne was braced at the halyards, shirt flapping. Full darkness closed, with a snap. 'Half the jenny now.' I hauled on ropes in the cockpit.

Astern, forked barbs tore from the underbelly of great ponderous clouds, cracks splintering a black glass. Flashes, one, two, three, lull, then again, illuminating the vast western seascape, each showing a yellow mass of racing wave tops; 30,000 amps and 50,000 degrees sent Rob down below, pulling out fuses, cursing the system. The wind hit us. The jenny took the blast, once, twice. Too much sail, 'Winch, winch, don't let the headsail blow,' he shouted up. You bet Anne and I winched.

Black billows over us now. Crazy zigzag caught us. White, sizzling charges hitting the water, lunging into the sea – great spears of the gods. All round us. What distance now? Thunder crashes cut voices. Count the seconds. Nil. Crash, deadly plummet, simultaneous. Splintering crackles, bright as a thousand welding arcs. The thunder cracks pressured eardrums. The air bristled – smelt, cordite, acrid. We were dead centre of a violent electric storm.

We must be struck. Lightning hits the highest point. Our mast? Least damage, electrics burnt out, engine blown, a fire. Worse, a holed hull – 'locker' prospects. A cyclonic gale tore at us. Rob fought the helm, arms rippling straight. The storm had us, forcing us along its path. Forked stabs smacked into the sea; every blinding flash showed us racing on a foaming pond. Nothing but watch, hold on. Hours passed – a night with the three of us counting flashes, waiting, counting on luck.

Slowly the storm pulled away south-east. A few grumbling rolls, then silence. Dawn came – bleakish, heavy and grey, but dawn. The wind fell light as quickly as it had risen. The sea flattened – our friend again. We sat in the cockpit over tea and a breather. Not for long – a noise astern. Anne looked up. 'Oh help!' Out of the haze, a white line approached, beating the sea's surface to the frenzy of a herring shoal. A waterspout following the storm? We waited. No writhing coil vanished skywards, instead, torrential rain, pouring vertical, drumming the deck. Soon it was drumming brown bodies in a luxurious shower. Soap and warm fresh water washed off all the salt and along with it went the night's concern.

The skipper fiddled amongst a maze of electrical connections which hung above the chart table. Their hasty dismantling left some wires without an obvious function. By a series of careful experiments, the pride of John's control panel, our expensive two-way radio, broke into life. Ten sharp, Rob had Davie the locker's voice plumbed in. 'Did, by any chance, an electrical storm pass through last night?' it enquired. 'Yeah.' 'Sorry about that – seemed to build out of nothing. I couldn't raise you.' 'Yeah, lucky you raised us now.' 'Oh, really. Well, today's course . . . Now let me see . . .'

◆

Anne's voice wakened me. 'Your watch now, Iain.' With a quiet call at
ten to midnight or some nights ten to three, I climbed from a warm
bunk into the cockpit with a cup of tea and my share of a Mars bar.
With comments on her watch – 'The wind's shifted more west; no ships
tonight; we're running about seventy' and the like – Anne filled a hot
water bottle and hopped into her bunk. I checked the radar for blips on
the screen. Our navigation lights had cut out, obliging us to sail by
stealth. The masthead whirligig measured speed only when its wires
made sporadic contact – another feature which didn't worry us
unduly. Our fourth crew member, however, was much more important. This tubular self-steering device mounted on the stern did
much of the steering with enviable skill. Its plywood wind vane
feathered to each breeze and, if set to the desired angle, an ingenious
counterbalancing weight controlled the auxiliary rudder. Steel wires,
running through pulleys, stretched from its paddle effect into the
cockpit and were locked to a drum on the helm. As the wires yawed
back and forth, our wheel turned by unseen hand. Ten degrees either
way, it kept us heading for the Azores. Stars for the picking, and to save
peering at the compass, I chose a bright one which lined our bow
roughly with the course. *Paleyma* ran on – no lights and a ghostly helm.

Middle of the night, alone and alert, I leaned on the companionway
doors, watching a helm that moved by the will of the wind. Every creak
became louder, the ocean closer, its thrumming on a listening ear. The
compass light, a dull red glow, was diffused by the outlines above me.
Nothing to dim the stars dodging in and out of the rigging as the wind
shifted our course a degree or two. The Plough wheeled around the
North Star, and each night the tiniest of the heaven's eighty-eight
constellations fell lower on the horizon. The Southern Cross appeared
tilted as the arm that hurried a fiery cross about the Highlands. A tape
played in my headphones. The fiddle of Duncan Chisholm – 'Red-
point', 'Leaving Storr', 'The Lady of Ardross', tunes by an expressive
bow, sounds of home and the generations that made it so. Sometimes a
ship crossed our course – just a pinprick on the horizon. Or the blaze of
a liner, bound for some unreal world, far beyond the steady drumming
of sea passing under *Paleyma*, could be seen.

One moonless night, the traces of plane after plane headed east.
Fourteen tail lights glowed amongst the stars, all on exactly the same
track, no distance apart. Smart bombs, Middle East bound? Blast

apart a civilisation whose Babylonian calculations set us on the road to modern astronomy?

The route for intelligence or the dead end of stupidity? On the scale we sailed, detachment infects a mind surrounded by magnitude. The Milky Way clustered over the masthead, not as a blur but as million upon million bright pinpricks — their light of such intensity that it fell in a broad band on the dark sea. Will the spiral arms of our galaxy uncoil like a spring or would the energy hole at its centre find power enough to rewind the coil? Could its concentrated information and the flow of intelligence pass through the eye of a singularity into another universe? Different dimension, emergent realities? A sea of slow undulations was a curved mirror, distorting the reflection of starlit heavens and, under its mesmerism, thoughts wandered without limit and theories grew.

Sometimes the dolphins played beside us, attracted by nights when a breeze toppled the wave crests into small white flurries. Black shapes leapt amongst the brightness, first at a distance, next round the hull, their capers ending in salvos of phosphorescence. Just for a second a little dark eye would scan us. Unlike a vacant fishy stare, their glance was the eye contact of intelligence and I thought of the thousand drowned each year in the nets to ensure a tuna salad.

By day, the sea became a lighter green — we were approaching land. But, a few nights before sighting the Azores, the dolphins appeared early. Smooth sailing gave little heel and we ate a supper of pasta and tinned mince in the cockpit. Events in the sky being our vital hourly weather forecast, we stood watching a wide orange moon edge over a sharp coolish horizon. Barely was she half clear than leaping dolphin silhouettes, far out, criss-crossed against her rising. A circle of churning water sparkled out of the semi-darkness — an aquatic circus ring with the moon as a hoop. Perhaps its light drew a shoal and the dolphins were feeding. We laughed with pleasure and friendly feeling. I did a shepherd whistle but they vanished without coming over to the yacht and we didn't have their curiously reassuring visits again.

Two mornings later, a heavy following sea drove us between breakwaters into Horta, the main harbour in the Azores. Nine islands of volcanic origin are the tail end of the mid-Atlantic ridge, an underwater chain of mountains made famous in a yarn put about by Plato on the hearsay of some Egyptian priests. It concerned the fabulous land of Atlantis, sadly no longer above the waves, where, he averred, delights existed not dissimilar to those presently to be found in the BVI. That apart, mountain greenery and terraced hillsides dotted with airy-fronted houses descend to a waterfront where the Moorish arches of a white Catholic church leave the six hundred years of Portuguese ownership in no doubt. The Moors of North Africa occupied much of Spain and Portugal between the eighth and fourteenth centuries and, had the Christians not eventually driven them back across the Straits of Gibraltar, then Muslim influence might well have extended beyond the island's architecture.

◆

Anne's Aussie passport concerned the Azores Customs. Birth in wallaby land did not gain one instant entry to civilisation and it confined our shipmate to *Paleyma*, pending further investigation. Rob and I hastened along the waterfront to the confinement of Peter's Bar. A good Scots tongue beats passport formality. Some time elapsed taking in the cosmopolitan atmosphere of this great crossroad of the oceans – i.e. Peter's and the smell of curried tuna and thick black twist. Tattooed seamen quaffed pints of rum amongst a selection of yellow wellies struggling to regain their land legs. A pointless effort as the afternoon wore on. We chatted, elbowed amongst their jolly ranks, no fresher than the rest. Bold Atlantic voyagers all, they included a morose Welsh doctor who, between gulps of whisky, confided to us that he hurried away from an ugly divorce. It became by no means clear that his wife had survived the proceedings. His crew mate, an agile little Barbadian, seemed more at ease. He sat cleaning his finger nails with a seven-inch stiletto.

Spanish galleons and noteworthy yachts sailed the walls amongst a collection of ships' bells and vicious fleshing knifes from the nostalgia of whaling days. Peter, a large gentleman of Scandinavian extraction, possibly the leftover from a harpooning crew, sat at a kiosk beside the bar plugging in phone calls to anywhere from Venice to Vladivostok. Currency exchanges as disparate as the yen and the Deutschmark? But a mental calculation. He switched languages according to client and their cash with equal dexterity.

A one-man bank and telecom service who obviously admired Clydesdale Bank notes, for he held each of mine up to the light, and, yes, he'd heard of Robbie Burns. Extra funds arrived and departed. Sailors home from the sea, or was it the hill? How did the poem go?

Foliage on a mountain top which overlooks the harbour split the evening sunshine that was guiding us back to *Paleyma*. Our conversation ranged from boomerangs to Botany Bay. Rob held the bunch of flowers behind his back. 'Anne, ahoy!' No Anne. The convict either sprung or more effectively detained? Our new friend, Peter, an oversized bouncer, was the most likely man to help. The flowers lay on the edge of the quay. A wreath? We retraced our steps. Left turn at the top of the pier, into the gents showers and toilets. I paused. Much steam and a dreamy rendering of 'Waltzing Matilda' floated across the cubicles. We ran round and hammered on a door, 'Anne, Anne, are you safe?' What relief, our shipmate, wet-haired, fragrant and desirable. Flinging her towel over the cubicle door and taking an arm apiece we set off. Show her to Peter. He was overjoyed to see us again, admired our steaming Anne and took more than a passing fancy to her Visa card.

Shipboard artists of varying talent painted the evidence of their stopover in Horta. Yacht names and emblems in the brightest colours filled the breakwater quay to which we were moored. They afforded an interesting study each morning as we wandered up to Peter's for thick sweet coffee. It seemed many's the ship sailed with an artist aboard including, to my approval, Greenpeace's *Rainbow Warrior*. Our ship's artist, Anne, did *Paleyma* a distinctive shield. A kangaroo, which could have been be a dolphin couchant, lay between two bandy-legged sailors on a blue field – a bold device worthy of any pavement artist's cap. John would approve. To add interest for future passers-by, I suggested a faded motif along the lines of '*Santa Maria*, 1542, China bound. Up your kilt Marco Polo, signed Chris'.

Rob and Anne were itching to sail. Our Friday morning wending took in the local Met Office. A printout of Atlantic weather showed tightly packed isobars of a deep low which would cross our homeward route in the next few days. An equally deep low filled the pit of my stomach. I'd experienced the same warning sensation twice before, and on both occasions the next day I was in a car crash. The second smash, with the car on its side, involved spilling petrol. It'd been a close squeak. 'Never go to sea on a Friday, wait until Monday,' I argued the case, but neither Rob nor Anne felt pangs of concern and, after a brief discussion, with marked reluctance on my part, I agreed. The caution of age or idle superstition? 'The edge of the low will swing us north,' claimed the skipper. Of that I had no doubt.

At midday, we took on diesel. I phoned Jane who was waiting for me back at home. 'This is a bad idea but they're both great sailors and we're a happy crew so we're off.' Other yachts were leaving too – going west. Just one headed north. A racing machine, she hoisted sail ahead of us. We didn't see her again. Drizzle and a cooler wind puffed down from volcanic peaks. I wasn't sorry to leave. Not quite a town of carefree abandon. Nightfall had the wind gusting five to six and the lights of the last towns were dipping in a heavy quartering swell. By middle watch, the Azores were passing into memory. Less frolics than banana-land – lucky the lads putting longitude behind them. But it was good to be back at sea. Activity cured misgivings and I had the next sundowner's joke to remember.

◆

Night watches became colder, the air less relaxing and sleeping bags not so welcoming as body heat was our only means of drying them. Anne needed a hot water bottle. If we ran short of water, our tea would be cycled through rubber. Three nights out, on my nine to twelve watch, we ran through frequent showers. Perhaps I speak of the moon too often but I tell you, reader, in isolation's grip, on land or sea, you watch her. That night she rode high and mean, cocked on her back, racing through rags of dark calico, bright as cold steel. 'There's tempest in yon horned moon, and lightning in yon cloud; but hark the music, mariners, the wind is piping loud.' My father's voice reciting, existing, imprinted, sixty years after his death.

Stars flickered only in spaces of sky. Winds of the upper atmosphere were in violent circulation. I smelt weather and watched sea and cloud. One moment, each brush stroke quivering on their restless surfaces was lucid, fresh as wet varnish; next, shadows advanced over a scintillating ocean, the darkness of annihilation.

I sailed a fathomless expanse without point of reference, in the grip of an unwilling circulation. A sun-dragged ocean, the might of its inertia hauled around the planet by heat and spin, its low-pitched grumble loud in my ear. Suddenly, out of a jagged opening shone the arch of a moonbow. Clear and sharp-edged, it curved from a deep recess in the clouds and down the grey face of an approaching shower. Seven colours, the complete spectrum, a gigantic halo plunging into wave tops. It hurried ahead, throwing colours on the sea, casting apprehension from the prism of its raindrops. Abruptly, all went dark. The clouds had closed.

The day passed. A grey sea built under our port quarter. The helm needed watching. So far, the self-steering kept our course. Would it react fast enough to avoid a broaching if the conditions grew heavier? At the chart table, we each wrote up the log before cooking or sleeping. A tap on the barometer saw its needle jump points at a time, falling unpleasantly hastily towards the word 'stormy'. A low spiralled towards us in the tight contours of an impending gale. Our masthead ananometer sent irregular signals, its digits leapt from twenty to forty knots of wind. Better not to knowing. The weight of a coming gale pressed eardrums. The rigging began to tremble and whistle. *Paleyma* surged north-east. Latitude 42 12', longitude 24 31', a thousand miles of sea room, in all directions. Noise built. At watch-change, from under dripping oilskin hoods, we smiled and shouted. Our sundowner dram needed balance.

Towering rollers gathered as dusk fell; their height brought the horizon close. Tops began to spill down oncoming faces with a deep throaty rumble. An enraged sunset, saw purple shot with streaks of green – violence twinned with garish colour. We looked down to purple wave bases, up to steep breasted fronts of oily green. Foaming crests, a moment's yellow spray, before the roar that poured towards a cavernous night without starlight or glint of exit. The yacht was coping. Running under a token jib and reefed mizzen. The self-steering vane bent willowy on the height of a crest yet held through troughs whose depth shielded us from a blast now stripping foam from wave tops. Breakers on the port side. *Paleyma*, rolling deeply, sloshed solid chunks of water into the cockpit. Stay tied on, watch helm, pump, pump.

Only starboard bunks were now tenable. The stern cabin, claustrophobic and wet, was taking water through the deck. The main cabin bunk allowed rest in the angle against the hull. Thuds and crashes beside your ear. The yacht rode off tops, smashing into downsides. No horizon, couldn't see, spray lashing us. Up *Paleyma* heaved. The white cascade of a monster burst out of blackness, careered towards the bow. A lull, the next and the next. Sounds, deafening, disorientating, a tearing note became a high-pitched whistle, rising, reaching a crescendo, then falling an octave. Summits passed under us, howled into oblivion. The night rode us. Turmoil threw us. *Paleyma* shook, water slouched down her decks. She was an old boat – a fine sea boat, but was she sound?

Her engine lay directly below the cockpit floor. No self-draining cockpit scuppers. Water had one route, down below, over the electrics. We pumped. Counted. Wait for the sucking. Fifty strokes. Bilge empty. Back to the helm. Snap your safety harness to the bulkhead bolt. The tally of pumping strokes increased. Shuttle between helm and pump, a throw across the cockpit could fling you over the side, bye-bye. The masthead whirligig sprang to life, signalled forty knots and then died again. A mid-Atlantic storm opened the throttle.

Dawn brought just an easing of darkness, no easing of the fury. I came on watch at six. Anne was tired after three hours' pumping. The cockpit floor was slippery with difficulty we transferred her bedding to the aft cabin. The sea had risen all night. I looked out to vast crumbling mountains of water. *Paleyma*'s stern rose. Wind howled at fever pitch. Wave tops sprayed into smoke before they broke. Boiling foam raced down the decks. A broach in this could roll her. A white oblong canister lashed on the aft cabin roof was our life raft. We'd left Road Town knowing one of its two bearers wasn't bolted to the cabin top. I looked through the cockpit's rear plastic window. No canister. 'Hell's teeth – we've lost the life raft.'

Rob wasn't sleeping. 'Need to check out the life raft, skipper.' He joined me in seconds. I hung out of the cockpit. Thank somebody, it had only shifted. 'It's still aboard, Rob – could be taken by the next whopper to fall on us.' Rob stayed next to the helm, in case. Anne roused, emerged from her bunk, more of a trap. I looked out bits of rope, waited for a moment of level deck and moved astern to lie beside the raft. It dangled from the one sound bearer. The roar of the ocean doubled. The bottom of wave, looking over the side, a long way down, next, on to the stern, water up the oilskins. Only a spare hand, the other clung on. Safety harness attached. Washed overboard in this lot? Towed to a horrible drowning? I fiddled with ropes. They had to be secured in such a way that a knife cut instantly freed the canister. Three hours of careful lashing and Anne helped me into the cockpit. 'Have to chance it – what else?'

We tried the engine, knowing that, when the wind dropped, the sea wouldn't. Motor power could help steerage. It started. 'That's something anyway.' It coughed to a halt. Not good. The storm tore on. A trip to the heads, a serious manoeuvre. Crashes flung you about the cabin. Worse, I spotted the yacht's main bulkhead flexing. A horrible two-inch see-saw threatened the foc'sle cabin door with splitting. Shouldn't happen in a fibreglass boat. Would the hull split? The gale raged on. Drove us through another night, slithering across the cockpit. Pump, torch on the life raft, mast top must be doing eighty degrees from one side to the other. Darland, the Flying Dutchman, condemned to sail the gales and, worse still – that night Annie's hot water bottle burst.

Mid morning of the third day. A sun, its first flicker lifted the heart. The clouds were whitening, taking on more definite shapes. The shrieking in the rigging dropped to a whine. The wind eased, shifted more northerly, still taking tops before it. Strong light revealed the sea in horrifying power. Crests broke from peaked centres, spreading wider and wider, bowling over and over, un-curling in a long line until they fell with a resounding thunderous boom. Their collapse flattened acres and acres into bright green. *Paleyma* came to a halt, even-keeled on these great flattenings. Ahead a broad shoulder of sea lumbered away, grey and streaked like an old sailor's beard. Slowly her stern rose. We gathered to a formidable speed. From the cockpit, the view downhill was into a deepening wave trough at an alarming angle. We were in the big stuff – the stuff of head-over-heels pitch-poling.

By afternoon, though, the wind dropped away and the sea state increased. The gale no longer blew wave-top spray horizontal, levelling their surface a fraction. Instead the waves joined forces and grew. The sun shone on an Emil Nolde painting. *Paleyma* sometimes sailed along a ridge. Over her side, I looked into deep pits of black water, hidden from sunlight by the mountain that followed. The sea had holes, huge holes. At a little distance, a towering peak flopped on its head and surged away, trailing long streaks of foam down its back. To be under that one . . . A yawning hole to oblivion.

The shelter of each trough cut off an already failing wind and left our self-steering vane waggling and useless. Steerage was imperative – an understatement. Lying a-hull amongst these giants, we might be de-masted, rolled. We tried the engine. Go, you, you. It fired. Thank the Lord. Into gear, please don't stop this time. *Paleyma* moved slowly ahead, keeping pace with the breakers. It gave us a night at the helm keeping her tail square on to the up, pause and down the other side motion. Early morning and the stars brought friendly heavens. Daylight greeted us with a quiet sunrise.

Anne made breakfast for three weary sailors. Any reflection on the storm went unspoken. At their fiercest, the elements had us by the bilges. Little did we realise the engine's exhaust elbow was about to fail. Had it done so at the height of the 'greybeards', a gusher of water would have filled old *Paleyma* quicker than we could have pumped.

◆

The sturdy fulmar is a true bird of the sea. She visits land but once a year to nest any cliff from Muckle Flugga to Mingulay. A group of them lifted off the slight swell and flew eastwards. We'd left Road Town in March, now it was May – nesting time for birds and our skipper. No longer that intense ultramarine of an Atlantic too deep for a blip on our depth sounder, its shade had quickly lightened to almost olive green at times. Digits came up – thirty fathoms. Slender white kittiwakes headed towards a smudgy horizon. Follow the birds – they smell land. So did the radar. At latitude 55 North, longitude 9 West, give a few minutes, sniff, sniff – thar she blows. A whale? No, no, land ahoy! Paddy's Isle, blest with afternoon sunlight – Ireland, emerald green, begorra! Doubles all round.

Aran Isles first, then weather-beaten Tory island. By midnight watch, Malin Head and the sweeping light on the rocks of Inishtrahull. I'd wanted to come by Castlebay, put an eye over Mingulay. A ninety-mile detour? No. Pity. Rob was in a hurry. Anne so excited she'd climbed the mast at daybreak and reported hills – or a mirage – to the north. 'Did you stand on the masthead?' Sunrise exposed the Paps of Jura – our first sight of Scotland. Late evening, tied up at Ardfern and Rob's wife had us round the table for supper at their Argyllshire home.

Three hours later we were at sea again, catching the tide up the Sound of Jura, powering north under engine. A cracker of a night, frosty stars and hills with outlines you'd travel the world to see. Banavie and the Caledonian Canal – the lock gates opened. Gigs, who'd flown back; Jane and her old blind spaniel, Katie, all waving. Jane hoisted bunting and balloons on our rigging. John preferred a blue ensign but seemed relieved to have *Paleyma* home in one piece and thanked us.

Such a welcome! Jane raced for beer and old Katie, in her ninetieth doggy year, celebrated our safe return with a swim in the canal. Rob caught a bus home and, best of all, three days later his wife produced a baby boy. Jane took her dog for a walk. Gigs and I sat down below. The stillness of *Paleyma* seemed unnatural. I rocked side to side, acutely aware of the bonding of a boat, the elements and the shipmates who'd sailed her back to Scotland.

After a silence John enquired about the cargo, 'Are my bottles safe, Iain? You didn't touch them, did you?' He well knew the calibre of the crew and, who knows, his 'booty' might now be empties lying on the bottom of the Atlantic.

# Epilogue
# Pathways to Paradise

Since brushwood flames first cast shadows on painted cave walls, science, religion and the environment have driven civilisation – three evolving entities with science in the van, religion dragging its heels and the environment subject to pressures global, galactic and species-induced. Today's astronomical calculations and the manipulations of a modern electronic computer began as the geometric theorems of Thales of Miletus and his student Pythagoras. In that same Grecian era, Mount Parnassus hosted the consummately powerful Delphic Oracle. From a site, deemed to be the centre of the Earth, a sepulchral voice deep inside the Temple of Sun God Apollo turned out to be the priestesses Pythia who, for a fee, issued sagacious guidance to the civilised Greeks. Throaty utterances had their profundity enhanced by spring water primed with the hallucinatory effects of ethylene. By about AD 390, however, the Romans rumbled the girl's con and the oracle was shut down amidst great lamentation. An influential Pythagorean brotherhood who preached immortality via the transmigration of souls met a similar fate – nothing should detract from the promotion of Christianity. So on and so forth – science and religion, ever-unhappy partners bouncing on the springs of a cosy environmental bed.

Colonisation of the planet by the human form of life, particularly over the past twelve thousand years, has enjoyed relatively stable environmental conditions. Science and religion have both evolved and flourished. Comparative rates of development in these two forces and their impact on the behaviour of our species shows, for the moment, the pace of scientific advance to be far exceeding that of religion. Science probes the relationship between matter and energy from colliding galaxies on the edge of space to the limits of measurements within a framework of the velocity of fundamental particles. A femtosecond laser beam can now examine the neurochemical functions of a single cell without destroying it; nanotechnology can etch the entire twenty-eight volumes of the *Encyclopaedia Britannica* on the head of a pin – the same pin over which early Christian theologians argued as to the number of angels able to dance on its head. Current Western and Middle Eastern religions appear to have stalled on a reluctance to venture beyond the concept of monotheism. Meantime, the third force acting on our behaviour – that of the environment – would appear to have developed a rate of change whose acceleration is set to challenge that of science and certainly outstrip that of present religious inertia.

Applied imagination, catalyst of change, is the power behind two of these systems which drive our species to dominate this planet and beyond. The influence of science has radically modified the images portrayed by theology, reducing many aspects of belief to harmless totemic symbolism. Has science also undermined the central tenet of most religions, a faith in omnipotence? Is science's own search for a unified theory of forces just another faith evolving on the wings of sophisticated imagination? Could these two unsympathetic paths have a meeting point?

Death, afterlife, an eternity in paradise – are they concepts of our current type of reality hooked on its own immortality beliefs? Eternity? Current techniques for fixing the duration of a second are accurate to one part in thirty million years. They are set to improve dramatically as the caesium clock gives way to a strontium timepiece. Measuring our way towards infinity? We might be on a track to cracking the problem of eternity. Perhaps eternity is not the constant we like to believe it to be, but a frequency of change. The fond image of swanning with a large malt at your elbow, blissful ever-more on a beach in paradise, is under pressure.

A prototype brain which functions, as do our own, by the interchange of chemical ions, sits in a dish of reactants in a Bristol laboratory awaiting a small flexible robotic form. Using artificial eyes and a blend of synthetic hormones, it's hoped to create movement and emotions. A sentient being opening the door to hybrid silicon-chemical logic gates – a cross between electronic hardware and neural chemistry. From universes to planetary species, none is immune from evolution's pressure. Human cloning is only one pathway which will feel the push. Geneticists and electrophysicists will link. The faculty of imagination will evolve as we design hybrid brains which are super-intelligent, more powerful in processing information, self-repairing and ultimately able to replicate. Reality will alter its perspective and our current gods may then be seen as a historic figment of the human species' imagination. Who, then, is God? On a cosmic scale, demise of our species in present form is imminent – obsolete as a Neanderthal, dead as the dodo whose flightless trust allowed us to eat it out of existence. Can we preserve information as a continuum and with it our gift of imagination? Or is this the hubris of a present science?

We convert all sensory inputs, from the photons of light which pass through our eyes to the touch of our fingertips, into a version of reality which, by an electrochemical process called cognition, provides us with imagination. Science is the knack of converting imagination into a tangible reality we can put to use. Natural selection, as it applies to evolution on this planet – hitherto the result of pressures largely outwith the control of most species – is now on the bandwagon of one species with the ability to effect its own evolutionary pathway by expanding its imagination. Clever stuff. The chemical precursors of life are widespread in the cosmos – even simple life forms, amino acids, made a good start. High energy particle plasma, galaxy formation, solar systems growing planets – we don't yet know inter-planetary seeding rates or the speed of galactic colonisation but they're subjects to fertilise the imagination.

Bye-bye, Big Bang. Were you the handiwork of some mysterious creator? Perhaps you were a gigantean implosion, an accretion of black holes, twisting and crushing and distorting space, before a mega, mega explosion, resembling a billion supernovae, accelerates us into our current four-dimensional universe? Or were you a collision between the fundamental building blocks of matter which vibrate as strings in ten-dimensional space and are the postulate of the brane theory as it ponders the recent discovery of the split image of two apparently identical galaxies.

Goodnight, Einstein. Differentials in the speed of light and the driving force of solar wind will allow our emergent species to explore the galaxy. Antimatter is at hand in CERN's particle accelerator – the production of mini black holes going beyond theory. We already have a toehold in our solar system. Can we harness quantum entanglement to safeguard and disseminate information? The danger for this theory lies at the heart of an all-consuming black hole. Death to information? Hawkins says it can escape, but if he's wrong this type of universe may be a one-off and we must rely on religious belief for our next dimension.

◆

Meanwhile an acceleration in rate of change of the Earth's eco-system is proven. Science is grasping the enormous complexity and dynamic of species relationships. We are one of an estimated five to thirty million life forms of which about one and a half million have so far been identified. Creatures great or small, the impact on organic life of temperature change, shifting climate patterns, rising sea levels and less salty oceans will be far reaching. Global warming may be part of a natural cycle but human activity is stepping on the gas. We are informed that the point of no return for this radical shake-up of the planet is within the average life span of those presently retiring. Today's babies will experience the early results from icecap melt before they die. A completion of melt in several hundred years could alter weight distributions on the planet's surface, affect tectonic stress and possibly the Earth's axis of tilt. Are we having our pants frightened off by the vested interest of science? Probably not.

Leading scientists from ninety-five countries produced a detailed assessment of global ecosystems. The report was rated the fourth news item behind the starving to death of an American paraplegic, a football story and the court case of a bizarre Yankee pop idol. Levels of atmospheric $CO_2$ are up a third – 60 per cent coming in the last forty years. Planetary fresh-water systems are under pressure and a quarter of the Earth's land surface is now under cultivation. Since nitrogenous fertiliser was invented over half of the umpteen million tons globally applied has been spread these last twenty years. The leaching of nitrates into drinking water, acid rain, forests completely gone from twenty-five countries and 90 per cent from another thirty, fire and floods quadrupling during the past half century in the northern hemisphere, rising sea levels and salinity set to affect major areas of population, degrading of soil structure, species decline, a shift in the range and mutation of pathogens . . .

A wide variety of global pollutants ignore political boundaries – one nation's pleasure is another nation's plight. Population growth, viral pandemics, political and religious unrest. Preventive military strike, smart bombs, depleted uranium and gun-barrel democracy spreading the self-centre prodigality of the American Dream as politics drift towards oligarchic dictatorships. Widening wealth gaps – 20 per cent in the US during the last thirty years – will increase population subjection via the interrelation of capital and technology. Within the kernel of global change lie the seeds of anarchy and mass destruction.

Are there solutions before the planet puts our backs to the wall? An international body, similar to that which currently struggles to take measures on global warming, must be set up to address the loss of biodiversity. Immediate priorities are: a dramatic slowing in the rates of carbon emission and species extinction; halting soil erosion; energy and water conservation; and solving the storage of nuclear waste before embarking on further expansion of this method of energy production. Secret consideration given to incinerating waste with the consequent radioactive release illustrates the follies of which vested interests are capable; add a terrorist potential and you go off the stupidity scale. Had the same volume of research and finance applied to nuclear energy production been directed at solar powered initiatives, then households could be self-sufficient in energy requirement and many industries likewise.

International effort in these major areas is hindered by politico-economic self-interest. Meantime, scientists are planning climate control – everything from sun shields in space to burying carbon below the Earth's crust. Households wait until the Western World extravagance and Far Eastern developments hike oil beyond $100 a barrel. Solar panels and photovoltaic tiles will appear on roofs, mini wind turbines on ridges, geothermal bore holes in the lawn and bicycles on the driveways until we can afford that solar-electric car. The wartime slogan 'Is your journey really necessary?' will apply to air travel as damage to our upper atmosphere intensifies. Tourism, one of our most destructive luxuries, will be back to a day at Blackpool.

Farming should be done without any damaging chemical input. Harness sunshine and heat by the polytunnel effect. Large livestock units will turn methane into their power source. Basic foods could be grown at local level, cutting transport costs. As the public decide their health and what they eat go together, organic farming will no longer be a shot of comfort for those hoping to avoid cancer. Those lucky enough to have a garden should swap their lawn-mower for a spade. Our problems are not unsolvable – the snag is that much global control lies in the hands of planners and politicians whose understanding of food production doesn't go past a plate. It's a product which just appears and they believe will continue to do so, ad infinitum.

Twenty-first-century farming in the UK faces six interlocking challenges: maintaining food supplies in the face of climate change; designing eco-sustainable agricultural systems which have public support; coping with the introduction of cloned livestock; finding a workforce; shaking off subsidies and the stranglehold of pen pushers; and raising the price of food in the shopping bag. Scotland could show a lead. A parliament building constructed to energy efficient and eco-friendly standards instead of vanity would have been a good start. Sadly, plenty of cunning politicians are on show but intelligent ones are harder to spot. Don't depend on planners or hot-air politicians – public fear and the pending environmental wobble will dictate. The resulting scramble will not be pleasant. Farmers and the countryside will be under pressure to sustain those left in the city trap and cope with escapes. Steady, Thomson, do we really need this doom and gloom curbing the lifestyles? Mass ennui – shouldn't we just let it rip?

◆

Towards the end of Hitler's war my father commanded an American Liberty ship, the *President Warfield*. In 1946, she was bought by the US Zionist movement. On the strength of the 1917 Balfour Declaration and universal sympathy after the Holocaust, this ship was used to convey many American Jews returning to the Promised Land. Indigenous Palestinian Arabs were confined to camps, Israel became a nuclear power and America, with its oil reserves sucking at the bottom of the barrel, replaced the UK as the overriding influence in the Middle East. Shock and awe placed Iraq on the road to Hollywood, to the vexation of Muslim hardliners. America, currently in the grip of a Christian Evangelical revival, has burgeoning debt on tick to the Chinese. India and China, now making friendly noises to each other, are the world's next economic powerhouses. Politicians strut on a big stage these days, with egos to match. The fewer the hands into which power is concentrated, the more dangerous it becomes. Will the US dump the UN and rattle the sabre of new weapon designs? They have the Non-Proliferation Treaty heading for the rocks and it's still a struggle to get environmental issues to light the front burner.

Whither now a democracy championed by the Mother of Parliaments? Whatever the rights and wrongs of invading Iraq, failure to impeach a Prime Minister considered by most to have misled, if not deliberately lied to Parliament, is a savage blow to honest and open government. A precedent has been set. Election rigging is the next tactic. What credibility has a gerrymandering UK government got in the eyes of decent people? What right to criticise other regimes guilty of similar behaviour? Does it matter? In the race to control the planet with superior weaponry allied to corporate strength, autocratically inclined politicians are ripping up democracy behind the back of somnambulant nations.

As terrorism gains expertise, where now freedom, that lauded cry of democratic politicians? The UK variety turns the screw – trial without jury and evidence in secret, sometimes obtained by secondhand torture. Been stopped by the police lately, swept in along with citizens innocent of any crime, just happen to be in the vicinity of an accident? DNA testing all round – volunteers and suspects alike. The National DNA Database retains the samples – currently 8 per cent of all adult white males and 32 per cent of adult black males. More insidiously, the samples from which the DNA is profiled are retained. The Database board can decide what research is to be carried out on this material. With the current advances in genetic coding and the unravelling of which genes account for various characteristics, telling the colour of hair and skin from a given sample is easy. Thinking patterns and disposition are next. The ability to read your mind from a distance via its magno-electric field is just round the corner. So far much of the legal delving into who you are and how you might tick only applies to England and Wales. Wake up, Scotland! It's not the first time you've fought for individual freedom.

◆

Back to earth, portentous events unfold. The Jews return to Palestine and Evangelicals look knowing, the Day of Rapture approaches. For Muslims, a martyr in their cause is on the path to Paradise. For Christians, it's the sanguineous route of communion, not to be confused with the symbolic cannibalism of ancient beliefs. Buddhists, without any specific god, head for the eradication of all desires by dissociation from the body and the absorption of self within some infinite force. Many varying claims, generally coupled to a belief in some universal power tweaking the cosmos, have led our species to a multiplicity of organised religions which are generally in conflict. Is one belief valid beyond others? Would it stand a better chance in some emergent condition? If one idea proved accurate in some state beyond the grave, will its believers and others be expected to shake hands and bury their differences? If religions adjust to the evolution being wrought by science, as they have in times past, will our current God be in for a re-vamp or just fade away to an outdated judgemental immanence? A case can be made for ditching present religions and hitching faith on to a form of enlightenment which takes cognisance of the latest cosmic revelations. But, then again, are we the chosen species, on a preordained path, or are these questions simply rhetorical nonsense?

Worldwide reaction on the death of Pope John Paul II underlines the eminence and influence still welded by religion. His reactionary stance on matters of sexual morality and the unborn child, whilst deifying the path which science now treads, is logical within the frame of a belief in the sanctity of all human life. His support for an ecumenical movement together with a war on poverty was second to none amongst church leaderships. The tears shed in Rome and round the world, by many more than just the faithful, demonstrate a hunger for enlightened humane guidance, not the hypocrisy of dissembling politicians with dead and limbless children laid at their door. What made John Paul an example to mankind was not his assertion that angels exist but his stand against the slaughter of Iraq and, above all, the face-to-face forgiveness and blessing of his would-be assassin.

The tide of emotion which the Pope's death generated suggests that an inner flame still burns – the need of expression still exists. Will the latest UK survey figures concerning matters of belief startle major churches into action? Thirty years has witnessed believers in God falling from 77 per cent to 44 per cent with young people showing the greatest swing.

Only a third now believe in heaven, hell or the devil and less than half count immortality as a option. Worse still, of those claiming to believe in God, only a small percentage bother to dodge cutting the grass by going to church. A surge in American Hot Gospellers lights a fire around Darwin's feet. Is religion in the UK also in need a revolution if it wishes to stay in business or should we sit back and enjoy local churches becoming art galleries?

Not all scientists are misanthropists or atheists. Many may be agnostic but so be it. Should not church leadership attempt to bridge the gap between science and religion before the gulf becomes too wide? Most professionals and an increasing number of the public are deeply concerned over the pathways which social morality and our environment now tread. Could not pulpits show an equal concern for both? The death of John Paul II provides an opening for one of the world's leading independent religions. Will Catholicism rally to another crusade or are the ocean currents, cloud cover and climate change the responsibility of somebody whose purpose we must not question?

Maybe so, but why not attack mendacious, warmongering politicians and utterly condemn arms' sales and the scramble to produce new-style atomic weapons. Support the United Nations, the World Health Organisation and the World Bank in their efforts to improve general health and sustainable living standards in the developing world. Shame the developed countries into parting with a higher percentage of their GDPs. Make pressure for action in attempting to slow the effects of the approaching rearrangement of the Earth's major systems both an individual and a corporate responsibility. The pending environmental shake-up will hit the poor before the rich.

Drop reactionary religious thinking. Outmoded dogma could be quietly put to one side in the greater good of ecumenical interests. Integrate religion with a knowledge of our planet's ecosystem. Foster an understanding of the place of our species in a universal system, rather than continue the self-interested mouthing of syco-phantic worship. Turn Holy into Holistic – even if that sounds pagan, all life-forms deserve equal concern, not least the future of the children of today and the generations as yet unborn. Match spiritual morality with environmental morality. Plead its dualism from pulpit to ballot box – there's nothing to lose except influence and congregation. Failure to synchronise the rate of change of mankind's three driving forces and all the world's religions may not be worth a puff of smoke. Don't spin the coin of fate – take action.

◆

Many years ago the *Mairi Dhonn* left Mallaig. Making for home in Castlebay were a husband, his son, a nephew, a father of seven, and the stillest of August days, The Minch as bonnie as the boat's name – 'Mary of the brown hair'. Some at a beach on the west side of Barra told of a tempest that afternoon which spiralled off an unbroken Atlantic, lashing the waters of their bay to a fury beyond even the witness of the very old. Terrified children were flung by its path. The face of the sea twisted in reckless cruelty. The cyclone howled over sand and rock, over croft-land and hill and, in moments, out across The Minch. The *Mairi Dhonn* was taken. Three weeks passed, and on the shores of Eriskay, father and son were found together.

We stood by the rail of Castlebay pier, Archie, Sandy, DP and me. The ropes of island fishing boats filled the bollards across from us, the flags and bunting, strung between deckhouse and mast, hung without tremor. A day without motion. No hint or sound of tide on the shingle at our back, no stirring in the sun-drenched air that drew beads of sweat to weather-hardened faces. Over the heads of an island people, young and old, push-chair and stick, who crammed the pier, we looked to a canvas-covered lorry. I stood amongst a thoughtful unified crowd, many with reason to pause. Social cohesion, a comfort through sorrow and adversity. Slowly and quietly, melody and voice rose together as though in memories drawn from the element by which so many islanders had perished. The gathering began a Gaelic psalm, '*As an Doimhneachd*', 'Out of the depths I cry to Thee, Oh Lord, Oh Lord hear my prayer.' With the hills about us and the castle across the water, centuries as yesterday, the old language and the old faith came together as one. I shaded my eyes and looked away south. Empty islands tipped the horizon in silent understanding.

Five priests turned the lorry platform into an altar. A Mass was said – the Fisherman's Mass. Respect to the sea, thanks for its bounty, loving care, Eternal Father for those who place their lives at its mercy. Father Callum, an Eriskay man, walked slowly along the pier. Above each boat he paused. In quiet words, he spoke a blessing. Few are those who put to sea without faith.

Whistles blew and fog horns hooted, children ran about the decks, laughing sunburnt faces. Boat engines revved and ropes were cast off for a race round the bay and back. A wellie-hurling competition, children clambering over hatches, shouting and waving, mothers waving and calling warnings and all to the blue smoke and smell of frying herring. Fresh from The Minch that morning, they were caught and cooked by Dol William. The island laughed and chatted and then the band struck up. No altar now – the old lorry springs bounced to the thump of the Vatersay Boys, accordions blasted out 'Father John MacMillan of Barra', the crowd stamped feet and I was happy to play along until the sun dropped behind Ben Tangaval.

◆

Nothing had changed inside the old Mingulay schoolhouse. Same table, chairs, old dresser and cooker, same smell. Nothing had changed since Sandy and I had spent our summer on its roof, years before. Outside, the sheep fank seemed a shade more dilapidated – winter gales don't change. On hillside and field, the island's greenness was silent. Sheep had gone. The island was empty of livestock for the first time in thousands of years – sheep out, tourists in.

We sat about the kitchen. I was in Neillie's chair, Archie and his son Aonghais beside the dresser, Dolald Beag at the corner by the window and three other men uneasily on the bench. Archie poured a dram. It had meaning. Mingulay, Barra Head and Pabbay belonged to the National Trust for Scotland.

Late that night I called round at Ledaig. Neillie seemed an old man. He talked of Lach, his lifelong friend, their work on Mingulay, the islands they bought, the sheep stock they built. Ambition and struggle, crofting and fishing had risen to a challenge. Through our quiet conversation, I glimpsed the depth of his feeling for the islands. In partnership with his friends, he came to own the isles upon which his forebears had lived in little better than a hovel. He stared long into the fire – fencing again with Lach above the great cliff, gathering and clipping, landing once more on Mingulay and there, that night, he felt his bones should rest. Little more than a year passed and I sat with Archie and Sandy at his funeral Mass.

◆

Mingulay held in her grip those who knew best each changing mood, each track the sheep would take, who shared a purpose, who shared of her history and perhaps of her holiness. It's a grip which does not slacken. More than charm, more than can be told by book, more than can be felt by those who pass as migrants. Not in words at the fank, they were of the land, and sheep, and of the sea, but in eyes that glowed with fondness as an anchor rattled down and, on the shore of Traigh Bheag, the swell was gentle.

Compress the timescale of human existence on this earth to an hour and our present flights of fancy span but half a second. The birth of Mingulay brought together the wholeness of the elements that made us and added her dimension, the imprint of our past, the unease of our present and our hope of a future.

For those who trod its empty fields, looked westward from its cliffs and heard the voice of the Atlantic in caverns at their feet, the Mingulay days of peace and beauty are an unspoken call. For me, the nights by its shore, when moonlight turned to flesh, are the dream of an endless tide.

### Moonflesh

Down to the evening's blushing tide
Which croons the shore,
The soulful shore that knew a flesh
White in the light
Of a thousand shells
That sparkled the sand,
Soft in the touch of a moonflesh night.

Down to the night of a raging tide
Where you lay on the rocks,
Black thoughtful rocks,
Thinking of white flesh
Against their callused claim
Of knowing a passion
Strong in the stealth of a moon split bay.

Down to the morning's tideful day
That sweeps the shore,
The rock bound shore,
Which knows the flesh of a thousand deaths,
Black on the white of a flesh.
Lost to the beauty of love,
On the swirl of an ebbing tide.

In printed time, our planet dies,
Held in the arms of a bay,
Whose mingled flesh still marks the void,
Where emotions hide, in spirit free,
Beside a turquoise sea.

And planets play 'til night is day,
'Til seas will surge, and flow, and urge,
And entwining life shall dream once more,
On the shores of an Endless Tide.